AF745485

APPLICATION OF MACHINE LEARNING

Edited by
YAGANG ZHANG

Application of Machine Learning
Edited by Yagang Zhang

Republished by InTech
Janeza Trdine 9, 51000 Rijeka, Croatia

Copyright © 2010 InTech
Abstracting and non-profit use of the material is permitted with credit to the source. Statements and opinions expressed in the chapters are these of the individual contributors and not necessarily those of the editors or publisher. No responsibility is accepted for the accuracy of information contained in the published articles. Publisher assumes no responsibility liability for any damage or injury to persons or property arising out of the use of any materials, instructions, methods or ideas contained inside. After this work has been published by the Intech, authors have the right to republish it, in whole or part, in any publication of which they are an author or editor, and the make other personal use of the work.

Technical Editor Sonja Mujacic

Cover Designer Dino Smrekar

Additional hard copies can be obtained from orders@intechopen.com

Application of Machine Learning,
Edited by Yagang Zhang
p. cm.
ISBN 978-953-307-035-3

We are IntechOpen, the world's leading publisher of Open Access books

Built by scientists, for scientists

4,200+
Open access books available

116,000+
International authors and editors

125M+
Downloads

151
Countries delivered to

Our authors are among the
Top 1%
most cited scientists

12.2%
Contributors from top 500 universities

WEB OF SCIENCE™

Selection of our books indexed in the Book Citation Index
in Web of Science™ Core Collection (BKCI)

Interested in publishing with us?
Contact book.department@intechopen.com

Numbers displayed above are based on latest data collected.
For more information visit www.intechopen.com

For EU product safety concerns:
IN TECH d.o.o., Prolaz Marije Krucifikse Kozulić 3, 51000 Rijeka, Croatia,
info@intechopen.com or visit our website at intechopen.com.

Meet the editor

Yagang Zhang received his Ph.D. in Electrical Engineering from the North China Electric Power University (NCEPU). He is currently working at State Key Laboratory of Alternate Electrical Power System with Renewable Energy Sources, North China Electric Power University, China. His research includes relay protection of power system, wind power and nonlinear complex system theory.

Preface

In recent years many successful machine learning applications have been developed, ranging from data mining programs that learn to detect fraudulent credit card transactions, to information filtering systems that learn user's reading preferences, to autonomous vehicles that learn to drive on public highways. At the same time, machine learning techniques such as rule induction, neural networks, genetic learning, case-based reasoning, and analytic learning have been widely applied to real-world problems. Machine Learning employs learning methods which explore relationships in sample data to learn and infer solutions. Learning from data is a hard problem. It is the process of constructing a model from data. In the problem of pattern analysis, learning methods are used to find patterns in data. In the classification, one seeks to predict the value of a special feature in the data as a function of the remaining ones. A good model is one that can effectively be used to gain insights and make predictions within a given domain.

General speaking, the machine learning techniques that we adopt should have certain properties for it to be efficient, for example, computational efficiency, robustness and statistical stability. Computational efficiency restricts the class of algorithms to those which can scale with the size of the input. As the size of the input increases, the computational resources required by the algorithm and the time it takes to provide an output should scale in polynomial proportion. In most cases, the data that is presented to the learning algorithm may contain noise. So the pattern may not be exact, but statistical. A robust algorithm is able to tolerate some level of noise and not affect its output too much. Statistical stability is a quality of algorithms that capture true relations of the source and not just some peculiarities of the training data. Statistically stable algorithms will correctly find patterns in unseen data from the same source, and we can also measure the accuracy of corresponding predictions.

The goal of this book is to present the latest applications of machine learning, mainly include: speech recognition, traffic and fault classification, surface quality prediction in laser machining, network security and bioinformatics, enterprise credit risk evaluation, and so on.

This book will be of interest to industrial engineers and scientists as well as academics who wish to pursue machine learning. The book is intended for both graduate and postgraduate students in fields such as computer science, cybernetics, system sciences, engineering, statistics, and social sciences, and as a reference for software professionals and practitioners. The wide scope of the book provides them with a good introduction to many application researches of machine learning, and it is also the source of useful bibliographical information.

Editor:

Yagang Zhang

Contents

1

MACHINE LEARNING METHODS IN THE APPLICATION OF SPEECH EMOTION RECOGNITION

Ling Cen[1], Minghui Dong[1], Haizhou Li[1]
Zhu Liang Yu[2] and Paul Chan[1]
[1]*Institute for Infocomm Research*
Singapore
[2]*College of Automation Science and Engineering,*
South China University of Technology,
Guangzhou, China

1. Introduction

Machine Learning concerns the development of algorithms, which allows machine to learn via inductive inference based on observation data that represent incomplete information about statistical phenomenon. Classification, also referred to as pattern recognition, is an important task in Machine Learning, by which machines "learn" to automatically recognize complex patterns, to distinguish between exemplars based on their different patterns, and to make intelligent decisions. A pattern classification task generally consists of three modules, i.e. data representation (feature extraction) module, feature selection or reduction module, and classification module. The first module aims to find invariant features that are able to best describe the differences in classes. The second module of feature selection and feature reduction is to reduce the dimensionality of the feature vectors for classification. The classification module finds the actual mapping between patterns and labels based on features. The objective of this chapter is to investigate the machine learning methods in the application of automatic recognition of emotional states from human speech.

It is well-known that human speech not only conveys linguistic information but also the paralinguistic information referring to the implicit messages such as emotional states of the speaker. Human emotions are the mental and physiological states associated with the feelings, thoughts, and behaviors of humans. The emotional states conveyed in speech play an important role in human-human communication as they provide important information about the speakers or their responses to the outside world. Sometimes, the same sentences expressed in different emotions have different meanings. It is, thus, clearly important for a computer to be capable of identifying the emotional state expressed by a human subject in order for personalized responses to be delivered accordingly.

Speech emotion recognition aims to automatically identify the emotional or physical state of a human being from his or her voice. With the rapid development of human-computer interaction technology, it has found increasing applications in security, learning, medicine, entertainment, etc. Abnormal emotion (e.g. stress and nervousness) detection in audio surveillance can help detect a lie or identify a suspicious person. Web-based E-learning has prompted more interactive functions between computers and human users. With the ability to recognize emotions from users' speech, computers can interactively adjust the content of teaching and speed of delivery depending on the users' response. The same idea can be used in commercial applications, where machines are able to recognize emotions expressed by the customers and adjust their responses accordingly. The automatic recognition of emotions in speech can also be useful in clinical studies, psychosis monitoring and diagnosis. Entertainment is another possible application for emotion recognition. With the help of emotion detection, interactive games can be made more natural and interesting. Motivated by the demand for human-like machines and the increasing applications, research on speech based emotion recognition has been investigated for over two decades (Amir, 2001; Clavel et al., 2004; Cowie & Douglas-Cowie, 1996; Cowie et al., 2001; Dellaert et al., 1996; Lee & Narayanan, 2005; Morrison et al., 2007; Nguyen & Bass, 2005; Nicholson et al., 1999; Petrushin, 1999; Petrushin, 2000; Scherer, 2000; Ser et al., 2008; Ververidis & Kotropoulos, 2006; Yu et al., 2001; Zhou et al., 2006).

Speech feature extraction is of critical importance in speech emotion recognition. The basic acoustic features extracted directly from the original speech signals, e.g. pitch, energy, rate of speech, are widely used in speech emotion recognition (Ververidis & Kotropoulos, 2006; Lee & Narayanan, 2005; Dellaert et al., 1996; Petrushin, 2000; Amir, 2001). The pitch of speech is the main acoustic correlate of tone and intonation. It depends on the number of vibrations per second produced by the vocal cords, and represents the highness or lowness of a tone as perceived by the ear. Since the pitch is related to the tension of the vocal folds and subglottal air pressure, it can provide information about the emotions expressed in speech (Ververidis & Kotropoulos, 2006). In the study on the behavior of the acoustic features in different emotions (Davitz, 1964; Huttar, 1968; Fonagy, 1978; Moravek, 1979; Van Bezooijen, 1984; McGilloway et al., 1995, Ververidis & Kotropoulos, 2006), it has been found that the pitch level in anger and fear is higher while a lower mean pitch level is measured in disgust and sadness. A downward slope in the pitch contour can be observed in speech expressed with fear and sadness, while the speech with joy shows a rising slope. The energy related features are also commonly used in emotion recognition. Higher energy is measured with anger and fear. Disgust and sadness are associated with a lower intensity level. The rate of speech also varies with different emotions and aids in the identification of a person's emotional state (Ververidis & Kotropoulos, 2006; Lee & Narayanan, 2005). Some features derived from mathematical transformation of basic acoustic features, e.g. Mel-Frequency Cepstral Coefficients (MFCC) (Specht, 1988; Reynolds et al., 2000) and Linear Prediction-based Cepstral Coefficients (LPCC) (Specht, 1988), are also employed in some studies. As speech is assumed as a short-time stationary signal, acoustic features are generally calculated on a frame basis, in order to capture long range characteristics of the speech signal, feature statistics are usually used, such as mean, median, range, standard deviation, maximum, minimum, and linear regression coefficient (Lee & Narayanan, 2005). Even though many studies have been carried out to find which acoustic features are suitable for emotion recognition, however, there is still no conclusive evidence to show which set of features can provide the best recognition accuracy (Zhou, 2006).

Most machine learning and data mining techniques may not work effectively with high-dimensional feature vectors and limited data. Feature selection or feature reduction is usually conducted to reduce the dimensionality of the feature space. To work with a small, well-selected feature set, irrelevant information in the original feature set can be removed. The complexity of calculation is also reduced with a decreased dimensionality. Lee & Narayanan (2005) used the forward selection (FS) method for feature selection. FS first initialized to contain the single best feature with respect to a chosen criterion from the whole feature set, in which the classification accuracy criterion by *nearest neighborhood* rule is used and the accuracy rate is estimated by *leave-one-out* method. The subsequent features were then added from the remaining features which maximized the classification accuracy until the number of features added reached a pre-specified number. Principal Component Analysis (PCA) was applied to further reduce the dimension of the features selected using the FS method. An automatic feature selector based on a RF2TREE algorithm and the traditional C4.5 algorithm was developed by Rong et al. (2007). The ensemble learning method was applied to enlarge the original data set by building a bagged random forest to generate many virtual examples. After which, the new data set was used to train a single decision tree, which selected the most efficient features to represent the speech signals for emotion recognition. The genetic algorithm was applied to select an optimal feature set for emotion recognition (Oudeyer, 2003).

After the acoustic features are extracted and processed, they are sent to emotion classification module. Dellaert et al. (1996) used K-nearest neighbor (*k*-NN) classifier and majority voting of subspace specialists for the recognition of sadness, anger, happiness and fear and the maximum accuracy achieved was 79.5%. Neural network (NN) was employed to recognize eight emotions, i.e. happiness, teasing, fear, sadness, disgust, anger, surprise and neutral and an accuracy of 50% was achieved (Nicholson et al. 1999). The linear discrimination, *k*-NN classifiers, and SVM were used to distinguish negative and non-negative emotions and a maximum accuracy of 75% was achieved (Lee & Narayanan, 2005). Petrushin (1999) developed a real-time emotion recognizer using Neural Networks for call center applications, and achieved 77% classification accuracy in recognizing agitation and calm emotions using eight features chosen by a feature selection algorithm. Yu et al. (2001) used SVMs to detect anger, happiness, sadness, and neutral with an average accuracy of 73%. Scherer (2000) explored the existence of a universal psychobiological mechanism of emotions in speech by studying the recognition of fear, joy, sadness, anger and disgust in nine languages, obtaining 66% of overall accuracy. Two hybrid classification schemes, stacked generalization and the un-weighted vote, were proposed and accuracies of 72.18% and 70.54% were achieved respectively, when they were used to recognize anger, disgust, fear, happiness, sadness and surprise (Morrison, 2007). Hybrid classification methods that combined the Support Vector Machines and the Decision Tree were proposed (Nguyen & Bass, 2005). The best accuracies for classifying neutral, anger, lombard and loud was 72.4%.

In this chapter, we will discuss the application of machine learning methods in speech emotion recognition, where feature extraction, feature reduction and classification will be covered. The comparison results in speech emotion recognition using several popular classification methods have been given (Cen et al. 2009). In this chapter, we focus on feature processing, where the related experiment results in the classification of 15 emotional states for the samples extracted from the LDC database are presented. The remaining part of this chapter is organized as follows. The acoustic feature extraction process and methods are detailed in Section 2, where the feature normalization, utterance segmentation and feature dimensionality reduction are covered. In the following section, the Support Vector Machine (SVM) for emotion classification is presented. Numerical results and performance comparison are shown in Section 4. Finally, the concluding remarks are made in Section 5.

2. Acoustic Features

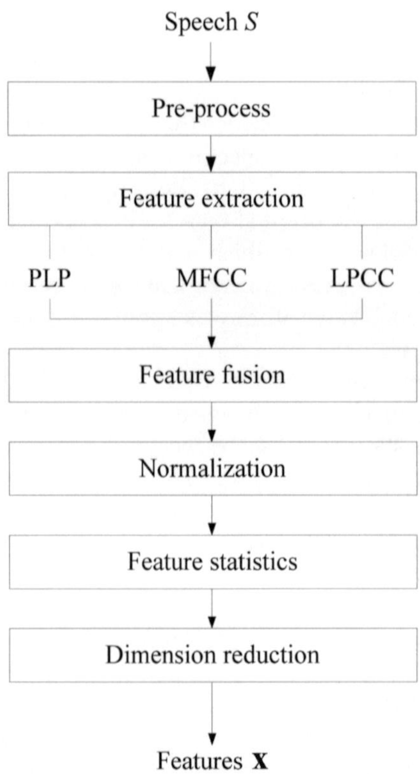

Fig. 1. Basic block diagram for feature calculation.

Speech feature extraction aims to find the acoustic correlates of emotions in human speech. Fig. 1 shows the block diagram for acoustic feature calculation, where S represents a speech sample (an utterance) and $\mathbf{x}$ denotes its acoustic features. Before the raw features are extracted, the speech signal is first pre-processed by pre-emphasis, framing and windowing processes. In our work, three short time cepstral features are extracted, which are Linear Prediction-based Cepstral Coefficients (LPCC), Perceptual Linear Prediction (PLP) Cepstral Coefficients, and Mel-Frequency Cepstral Coefficients (MFCC). These features are fused to achieve a feature matrix, $\mathbf{x} \in R^{F \times M}$ for each sentence S, where F is the number of frames in the utterance, and M is the number of features extracted from each frame. Feature normalization is carried out on the speaker level and the sentence level. As the features are extracted on a frame basis, the statistics of the features are calculated for every window of a specified number of frames. These include the mean, median, range, standard deviation, maximum, and minimum. Finally, PCA is employed to reduce the feature dimensionality. These will be elaborated in subsections below.

2.1 Signal Pre-processing: Pre-emphasis, Framing, Windowing

In order to emphasize important frequency component in the signal, a pre-emphasis process is carried out on the speech signal using a Finite Impulse Response (FIR) filter called pre-emphasis filter, given by

$$H_{pre}(z) = 1 + a_{pre} z^{-1}. \tag{1}$$

The coefficient a_{pre} can be chosen typically from [-1.0, 0.4] (Picone, 1993). In our implementation, it is set to be $a_{pre} = -(1 - \frac{1}{16}) = -0.9375$, so that it can be efficiently implemented in fixed point hardware.

The filtered speech signal is then divided into frames. It is based on the assumption that the signal within a frame is stationary or quasi-stationary. Frame shift is the time difference between the start points of successive frames, and the frame length is the time duration of each frame. We extract the signal frames of length 25 msec from the filtered signal at every interval of 10 msec. A Hamming window is then applied to each signal frame to reduce signal discontinuity in order to avoid spectral leakage.

2.2 Feature Extraction

Three short time cepstral features, i.e. Linear Prediction-based Cepstral Coefficients (LPCC), Perceptual Linear Prediction (PLP) Cepstral Coefficients, and Mel-Frequency Cepstral Coefficients (MFCC), are extracted as acoustic features for speech emotion recognition.

A. LPCC

Linear Prediction (LP) analysis is one of the most important speech analysis technologies. It is based on the source-filter model, where the vocal tract transfer function is modeled by an all-pole filter with a transfer function given by

$$H(z) = \frac{1}{1 - \sum_{i=1}^{p} a_i z^{-i}}, \tag{2}$$

where a_i is the filter coefficients. The speech signal, S_t assumed to be stationary over the analysis frame is approximated as a linear combination of the past p samples, given as

$$\hat{S}_t = \sum_{i=1}^{p} a_i S_{t-i}. \tag{3}$$

In (3) a_i can be found by minimizing the mean square filter prediction error between $\hat{S}_t$ and S_t. The cepstral coefficents is considered to be more reliable and robust than the LP filter coefficents. It can be computed directly from the LP filter coefficients using the recursion given as

$$\hat{c}_k = a_k + \sum_{i=1}^{k-1}\left(\frac{i}{k}\right)c_i a_{k-i}, \qquad 0<k \leq p, \tag{4}$$

where c_k represents the cepstral coefficients.

B. PLP Cepstral Coefficients

PLP is first proposed by Hermansky (1990), which combines the Discrete Fourier Transform (DFT) and LP technique. In PLP analysis, the speech signal is processed based on hearing perceptual properties before LP analysis is carried out, in which the spectrum is analyzed on a warped frequency scale. The calculation of PLP cepstral coefficients involves 6 steps as shown in Fig. 2.

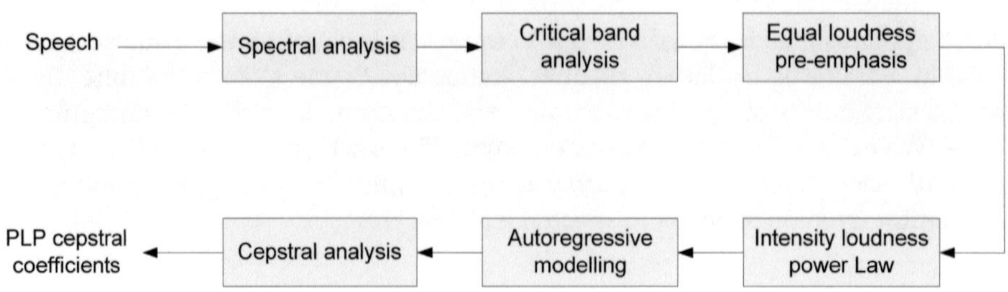

Fig. 2. Calculation of PLP cepstral coefficients.

Step 1 Spectral analysis

- The short-time power spectrum is achieved for each speech frame.

Step 2 Critical-band Spectral resolution

- The power spectrum is warped onto a Bark scale and convolved with the power spectral of the critical band filter, in order to simulate the frequency resolution of the ear which is approximately constant on the Bark scale.

Step 3 Equal-loudness pre-emphasis

- An equal-loudness curve is used to compensate for the non-equal perception of loudness at different frequencies.

Step 4 Intensity loudness power law

- Perceived loudness is approximately the cube root of the intensity.

Step 5 Autoregressive modeling

- Inverse Discrete Fourier Transform (IDFT) is carried out to obtain the autoregressive coefficients and all-pole modeling is then performed.

Step 6 Cepstral analysis

- PLP cepstral coefficients are calculated from the AR coefficients as the process in LPCC calculation.

C. MFCC

The MFCC proposed by Davis and Mermelstein (1980) has become the most popular features used in speech recognition. The calculation of MFCC involves computing the cosine transform of the real logarithm of the short-time power spectrum on a Mel warped frequency scale. The process consists of the following process as shown in Fig. 3.

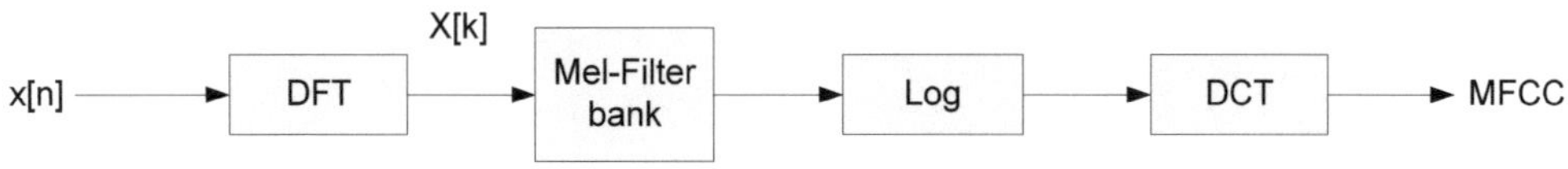

Fig. 3. Calculation of MFCC.

1) DFT is applied in each speech frame given as

$$X[k]=\sum_{n=0}^{N-1} x[n]e^{-j2\pi 2\pi/N},\ \ 0 \le k \le N-1. \tag{5}$$

2) Mel-scale filter bank
The Fourier spectrum is non-uniformly quantized to conduct Mel filter bank analysis. The window functions that are first uniformly spaced on the Mel-scale and then transformed back to the Hertz-scale are multiplied with the Fourier power spectrum and accumulated to achieve the Mel spectrum filter-bank coefficients. A Mel filter bank has filters linearly spaced at low frequencies and approximately logarithmically spaced at high frequencies, which can capture the phonetically important characteristics of the speech signal while suppressing insignificant spectral variation in the higher frequency bands (Davis and Mermelstein, 1980).

3) The Mel spectrum filter-bank coefficients is calculated as

$$F[m]=\log\left(\sum_{k=0}^{N-1}|X[k]|^2 H_m[k]\right),\ \ 0 \le m \le M. \tag{6}$$

4) The Discrete Cosine Transform (DCT) of the log filter bank energies is calculated to find the MFCC given as

$$c[n]=\sum_{m=0}^{M} F[m]\cos(\pi n(m-1)/2\mathrm{M}),\ \ 0 \le n \le M, \tag{7}$$

where $c[n]$ is the nth coefficient.

D. Delta and Acceleration Coefficients

After the three short time cepstral features, LPCC, PLP Cepstral Coefficients, and MFCC, are extracted, they are fused to form a feature vector for each of the speech frames. In the vector, besides the LPCC, PLP cepstral coefficients and MFCC, Delta and Acceleration (Delta Delta) of the raw features are also included, given as

Delta Δx_i :

$$\Delta x_i = \frac{1}{2}(x_{i+1} - x_{i-1}), \tag{8}$$

Acceleration (Delta Delta) $\Delta\Delta x_i$:

$$\Delta\Delta x_i = \frac{1}{2}(\Delta x_{i+1} - \Delta x_{i-1}), \tag{9}$$

where x_i is the ith value in the feature vector.

E. Feature List

In conclusion, the list below shows the full feature set used in speech emotion recognition presented in this chapter. The feature vector has a dimension of R^M , where $M = 132$ is the total number of the features calculated for each frame.

1) PLP - 54 features

- 18 PLP cepstral coefficients
- 18 Delta PLP cepstral coefficients
- 18 Delta Delta PLP cepstral coefficients.

2) MFCC - 39 features

- 12 MFCC features
- 12 delta MFCC features
- 12 Delta Delta MFCC features
- 1 (log) frame energy
- 1 Delta (log) frame energy
- 1 Delta Delta (log) frame energy

3) LPCC – 39 features

- 13 LPCC features
- 13 delta LPCC features
- 13 Delta Delta LPCC features

2.3 Feature Normalization

As acoustic variation in different speakers and different utterances can be found in phonologically identical utterances, speaker- and utterance-level normalization are usually performed to reduce these variations, and hence to increase recognition accuracy.

In our work, the normalization is achieved by subtracting the mean and dividing by the standard deviation of the features given as

$$x_i = \frac{(x_i - \mu_{ui})/\sigma_{ui} - \mu_{si}}{\sigma_{si}}, \tag{10}$$

where x_i is the ith coefficient in the feature vector, μ_{ui} and σ_{ui} are the mean and standard deviation of x_i within an utterance, and μ_{si} and σ_{si} are the mean and standard deviation of x_i within the utterances spoken by the same speaker. In this way, the variation across speakers and utterances can be reduced.

2.4 Utterance Segmentation

As we have discussed, the three short time cepstral features are extracted for each speech frames. The information in the individual frames is not sufficient for capturing the longer time characteristics of the speech signal. To address the problem, we arrange the frames within an utterance into several segments as shown in Fig. 4. In this figure, f_i represents a frame and s_i denotes a segment. Each segment consists of a fixed number of frames. The sf represents the segment size, i.e. the number of frames in one segment, and Δ is the overlap size, i.e. the number of frames overlapped in two consecutive segments.

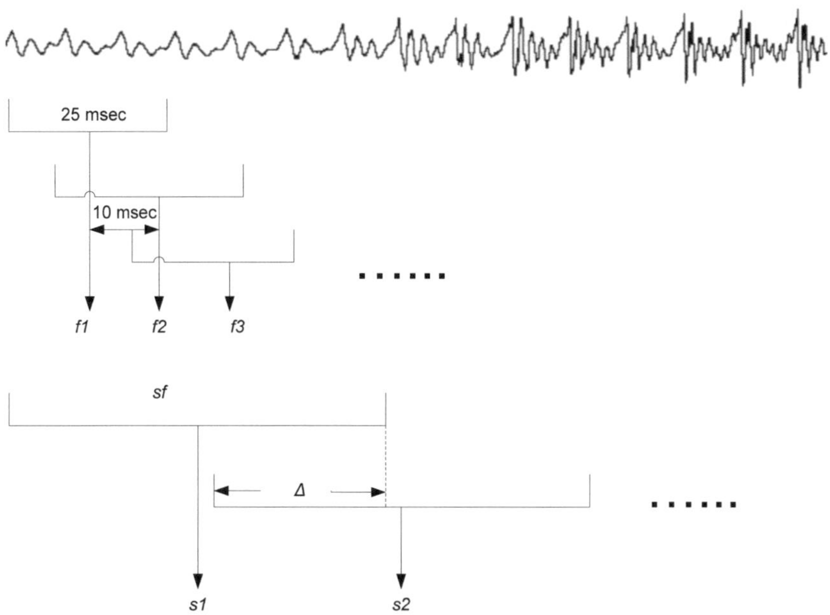

Fig. 4. Utterance partition with frames and segments.

Here, the trade-off between computational complexity and recognition accuracy is considered in utterance segmentation. Generally speaking, finer partition and larger overlap between two consecutive segments potentially result in better classification performance at the cost of higher computational complexity. The statistics of the 132 features given in the previous sub-section is calculated for each segment, which is used in emotion classification instead of the original 132 features in each frame. This includes median, mean, standard deviation, maximum, minimum, and range (max-min). In total, the number of statistic parameters in a feature vector for each speech segment is $132 \times 6 = 792$.

2.5 Feature Dimensionality Reduction

Most machine learning and data mining techniques may not work effectively if the dimensionality of the data is high. Feature selection or feature reduction is usually carried out to reduce the dimensionality of the feature vectors. A short feature set can also improve computational efficiency involved in classification and avoids the problem of overfitting. Feature reduction aims to map the original high-dimensional data onto a lower-dimensional space, in which all of the original features are used. In feature selection, however, only a subset of the original features is chosen.

In our work, Principal Component Analysis (PCA) is employed to reduce the feature dimensionality. Assume the feature matrix, $X^T \in R^{N_S \times M}$, with zero empirical mean, in which each row is a feature vector of a data sample, and N_S is the number of data samples. The PCA transformation is given as

$$Y^T = X^T W = V\Sigma, \tag{11}$$

where $V\Sigma\Sigma^T$ is the Singular Value Decomposition (SVD) of X^T. PCA mathematically transforms a number of potentially correlated variables into a smaller number of uncorrelated variables called Principal Components (PC). The first PC (the eigenvector with the largest eigenvalue) accounts for the greatest variance in the data, the second PC accounts for the second variance, and each succeeding PCs accounts for the remaining variability in order. Although PCA requires a higher computational cost compared to the other methods, for example, the Discrete Cosine Transform, it is an optimal linear transformation for keeping the subspace with the largest variance.

3. Support Vector Machines (SVMs) for Emotion Classification

SVMs that developed by Vapnik (1995) and his colleagues at AT&T Bell Labs in the mid 90's, have become of increasing interest in classification (Steinwart and Christmann, 2008). It has shown to have better generalization performance than traditional techniques in solving classification problems. In contrast to traditional techniques for pattern recognition that are based on the minimization of empirical risk learned from training datasets, it aims to minimize the structural risk to achieve optimum performance.

It is based on the concept of decision planes that separate the objects belonging to different categories. In the SVMs, the input data are separated as two sets using a separating hyperplane that maximizes the margin between the two data sets. Assuming the training data samples are in the form of

$$\{\mathbf{x}_i, c_i\},\ i = 1, \ldots, N,\ \mathbf{x}_i \in \mathbf{R}^M, c_i \in \{-1, 1\} \tag{12}$$

Where $\mathbf{x}_i$ is the M-dimension feature vector of the ith sample, N is the number of samples, and c_i is the category to which $\mathbf{x}_i$ belongs. Suppose there is a hyperplane that separates the feature vectors $\phi(\mathbf{x}_i)$ in the positive category from those in the negative one. Here $\phi(\bullet)$ is a nonlinear mapping of the input space into a higher dimensional feature space. The set of points $\phi(\mathbf{x})$ that lie on the hyperplane is expressed as

$$\mathbf{w}\cdot\phi(\mathbf{x})+b=0, \tag{13}$$

where $\mathbf{w}$ and b are the two parameters. For the training data that are linearly separable, two hyperplanes are selected to yield maximum margin. Suppose $\mathbf{x}_i$ satisfies

$$\begin{aligned}&\phi(\mathbf{x}_i)\cdot\mathbf{w}+b\geq 1,\ \text{for } c_i=1,\\&\phi(\mathbf{x}_i)\cdot\mathbf{w}+b\leq 1,\ \text{for } c_i=-1.\end{aligned} \tag{14}$$

It can be re-written as

$$c_i\left(\phi(\mathbf{x}_i)\cdot\mathbf{w}+b\right)-1\geq 0,\ \forall i=1,2,\ldots,N. \tag{15}$$

Searching a pair of hyperplanes that gives the maximum margin can be achieved by solving the following optimization problem

$$\begin{aligned}&\text{Minimize } \|\mathbf{w}\|^2\\&\text{subject } c_i\left(\phi(\mathbf{x}_i)\cdot\mathbf{w}+b\right)\geq 1,\forall i=1,2,\ldots,N.\end{aligned} \tag{16}$$

In (16), $\|\mathbf{w}\|$ represents the Euclidean norm of $\mathbf{w}$. This can be formulated as a quadratic programming optimization problem and be solved by standard quadratic programming techniques.

Using the Lagrangian methodology, the dual problem of (16) is given as

$$\begin{aligned}&\text{Minimize } W(\alpha)=\sum_{i=1}^{N}\alpha_i-\frac{1}{2}\sum_{i,j=1}^{N}c_i c_j\alpha_i\alpha_j\phi(\mathbf{x}_i)^T\phi(\mathbf{x}_j),\\&\text{subject } \sum_{i=1}^{N}c_i\alpha_i=0,\ \alpha_i\geq 0,\ \forall i=1,2,\ldots,N.\end{aligned} \tag{17}$$

Here α_i is the Lagrangian variable.

The simplest case is that $\phi(\mathbf{x})$ is a linear function. If the data cannot be separated in a linear way, non-linear mappings are performed from the original space to a feature space via kernels. This aims to construct a linear classifier in the transformed space, which is the so-called "kernel trick". It can be seen from (17) that the training points appear as their inner products in the dual formulation. According to Mercer's theorem, any symmetric positive semi-definite function $k(\mathbf{x}_i,\mathbf{x}_j)$ implicitly defines a mapping into a feature space

$$\phi:\mathbf{x}\rightarrow\phi(\mathbf{x}) \tag{18}$$

such that the function is an inner product in the feature space given as

$$k(\mathbf{x}_i,\mathbf{x}_j)=\phi(\mathbf{x}_i)\cdot\phi(\mathbf{x}_j) \tag{19}$$

The function $k(\mathbf{x}_i, \mathbf{x}_j)$ is called kernels. The dual problem in the kernel form is then given as

$$\text{Minimize } W(\alpha) = \sum_{i=1}^{N} \alpha_i - \frac{1}{2} \sum_{i,j=1}^{N} c_i c_j \alpha_i \alpha_j k(\mathbf{x}_i, \mathbf{x}_j),$$
$$\text{subject } \sum_{i=1}^{N} c_i \alpha_i = 0,\ \alpha_i \geq 0,\ \forall i = 1, 2, ..., N. \tag{20}$$

By replacing the inner product in (17) with a kernel and solving for α, a maximal margin separating hyperplane can be obtained in the feature space defined by a kernel. Choosing suitable non-linear kernels, therefore, classifiers that are non-linear in the original space can become linear in the feature space. Some common kernel functions are shown below:

1) Polynomial (homogeneous) kernel: $k(\mathbf{x}, \mathbf{x}') = (\mathbf{x} \cdot \mathbf{x}')^d$,
2) Polynomial (inhomogeneous) kernel: $k(\mathbf{x}, \mathbf{x}') = (\mathbf{x} \cdot \mathbf{x}' + 1)^d$,
3) Radial basis kernel: $k(\mathbf{x}, \mathbf{x}') = \exp\left(-\gamma \|\mathbf{x} - \mathbf{x}'\|^2\right)$, for $\gamma > 0$,
4) Gaussian radial basis kernel: $k(\mathbf{x}, \mathbf{x}') = \exp\left(-\frac{\|\mathbf{x} - \mathbf{x}'\|^2}{2\sigma^2}\right)$.

A single SVM itself is a classification method for 2-category data. In speech emotion recognition, there are usually multiple emotion categories. Two common methods used to solve the problem are called one-versus-all and one-versus-one (Fradkin and Muchnik, 2006). In the former, one SVM is built for each emotion, which distinguishes this emotion from the rest. In the latter, one SVM is built to distinguish between every pair of categories. The final classification decision is made according to the results from all the SVMs with the majority rule. In the one-versus-all method, the emotion category of an utterance is determined by the classifier with the highest output based on the winner-takes-all strategy. In the one-versus-one method, every classifier assigns the utterance to one of the two emotion categories, then the vote for the assigned category is increased by one vote, and the emotion class is the one with most votes based on a max-wins voting strategy.

4. Experiments

The speech emotion database used in this study is extracted from the Linguistic Data Consortium (LDC) Emotional Prosody Speech corpus (catalog number LDC2002S28), which was recorded by the Department of Neurology, University of Pennsylvania Medical School. It comprises expressions spoken by 3 male and 4 female actors. The speech contents are neutral phrases like dates and numbers, e.g. "September fourth" or "eight hundred one", which are expressed in 14 emotional states (including anxiety, boredom, cold anger, hot anger, contempt, despair, disgust, elation, happiness, interest, panic, pride, sadness, and shame) as well as neutral state.

The number of utterances is approximately 2300. The histogram distribution of these samples for the emotions, speakers, and genders are shown in Fig. 5, where Fig. 5-a shows the number of samples expressed in each of 15 emotional states; 5-b illustrates the number of samples spoken by each of 7 professional actors (1st, 2nd, and 5th speakers are male; the others are female); Fig. 5-c gives the number of samples divided into gender group (1-male; 2-female).

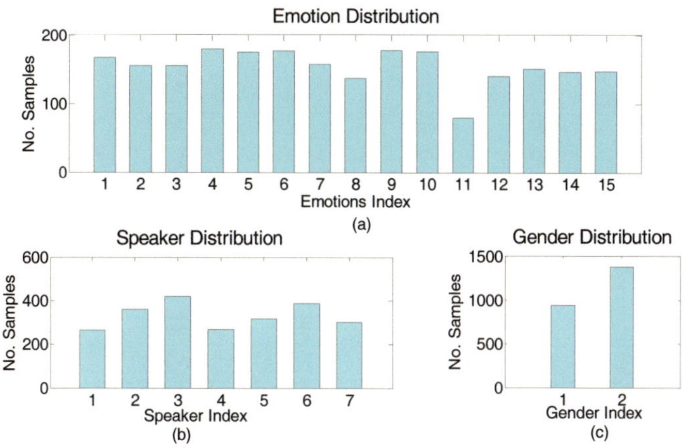

Fig. 5. Histogram distribution of the number of utterances for the emotions, speakers, and genders.

The SVM classification method introduced in Section 3 is used to recognize the emotional states expressed in the speech samples extracted from the above database. The speech data are trained in speaker dependent training mode, in which the different characteristics of speech among the speakers are considered and an individual training process is hence carried out for each speaker. The database is divided into two parts, i.e. the training dataset and the testing dataset. Half of the data are employed to train the classifiers and the remainder are used for testing purpose.

4.1 Comparisons among different segmentation forms

It is reasonable that finer partition and larger overlap size tend to improve recognition accuracy. Computational complexity, however, should be considered in practical applications. In this experiment, we test the system with different segmentation forms, i.e. different segment sizes sf and different overlap sizes Δ.

The segment size is first changed from 30 to 60 frames with a fixed overlap size of 20 frames. The numerical results are shown in Table 1, where the recognition accuracy in each emotion as well as the average accuracy is given. A trend of decreasing average accuracy is observed as the segment size is increased, which is illustrated in Fig. 6.

sf / Emotions	30	35	40	45	50	55	60
Anxiety	87	86	84	84	88	87	81
Boredom	82	78	82	77	74	76	79
Cold Anger	62	69	65	62	59	63	59
Contempt	72	66	72	60	63	66	58
Despair	68	68	68	53	61	55	60
Disgust	81	78	81	72	78	78	73
Elation	78	71	71	67	67	67	70
Hot Anger	79	79	76	82	79	75	69
Happiness	62	58	56	62	48	47	45
Interest	55	50	53	50	52	43	38
Neutral	92	82	82	71	69	82	72
Panic	70	65	62	61	61	61	58
Pride	28	33	28	26	28	22	24
Sadness	71	68	61	63	63	64	61
Shame	53	53	44	45	43	45	36
Average	69.33	66.93	65.67	62.33	62.20	62.07	58.87

Table 1. Recognition accuracies (%) achieved with different segment sizes (the overlap size is fixed to be 20)

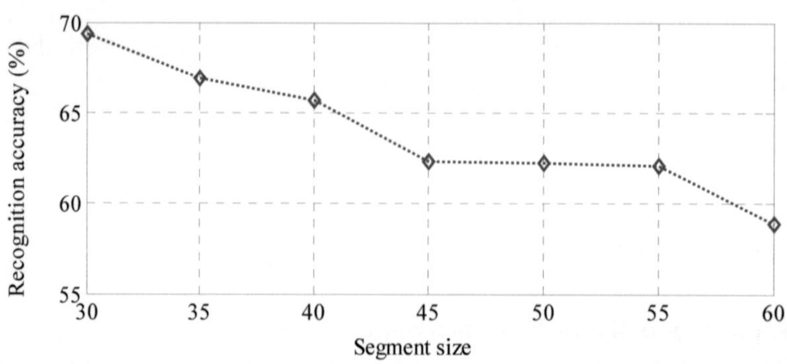

Fig. 6. Comparison of the average accuracies achieved with different segment sizes (ranging from 30 to 60) and a fixed overlap size of 20.

Secondly, the segment size is fixed to 40 and different overlap sizes ranging from 5 to 30 are used in the experiment. The recognition accuracies for all emotions are listed in Table 2. The trend of average accuracy with the increase of the overlap size is shown in Fig. 7, where we can see an increase trend when the overlap size becomes larger.

Emotions \ Δ	5	10	15	20	25	30
Anxiety	81	84	83	84	84	84
Boredom	73	73	77	82	82	79
Cold Anger	68	56	62	65	65	67
Contempt	63	64	71	72	74	76
Despair	60	59	63	68	59	69
Disgust	71	71	72	81	74	76
Elation	72	71	75	71	71	76
Hot Anger	75	76	81	76	78	81
Happiness	48	47	60	56	64	63
Interest	45	44	45	53	58	52
Neutral	69	72	77	82	87	82
Panic	61	63	63	62	63	70
Pride	28	24	29	28	32	36
Sadness	57	60	63	61	61	68
Shame	41	41	43	44	52	57
Average	60.80	60.33	64.27	65.67	66.93	69.07

Table 2. Recognition accuracies (%) achieved with different overlap sizes (the segment size is fixed to be 40)

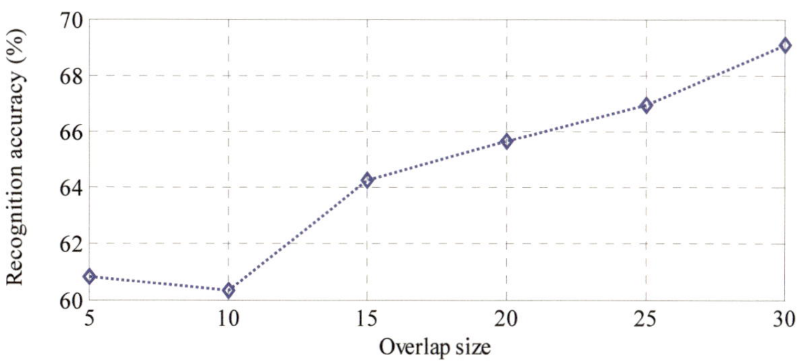

Fig. 7. Comparison of the average accuracies achieved with different overlap sizes (ranging from 5 to 30) and a fixed segment size of 40.

4.2 Comparisons among different feature sizes

This experiment aims to find the optimal dimensionality of the feature set. The segment size for calculating feature statistics is fixed with $sf = 40$ and $\Delta = 20$. The full feature set for each segment is a 792-dimensional vector as discussed in Section 2. The PCA is adopted to reduce feature dimensionality. The recognition accuracies achieved with different dimensionalities ranging from 300 to 20, as well as the full feature set with 792 features, are shown in Table 3. The average accuracies are illustrated in Fig. 8.

Feature size / Emotions	Full	300	250	200	150	100	50	20
Anxiety	84	86	88	86	86	81	71	53
Boredom	82	83	78	77	78	76	60	41
Cold Anger	65	68	64	62	63	64	53	32
Contempt	72	71	71	70	66	56	35	29
Despair	68	64	64	64	57	61	44	33
Disgust	81	80	79	75	79	66	60	48
Elation	71	72	72	76	75	70	49	41
Hot Anger	76	78	78	75	78	76	69	59
Happiness	56	58	56	49	53	40	36	19
Interest	53	55	51	50	53	47	36	26
Neutral	82	82	87	79	82	74	41	23
Panic	62	62	66	62	59	56	49	44
Pride	28	29	30	30	30	28	16	09
Sadness	61	64	64	56	60	51	29	28
Shame	44	44	44	40	45	37	23	16
Average	65.67	66.40	66.13	63.40	64.27	58.87	44.73	33.40

Table 3. Recognition accuracies (%) achieved with different feature sizes

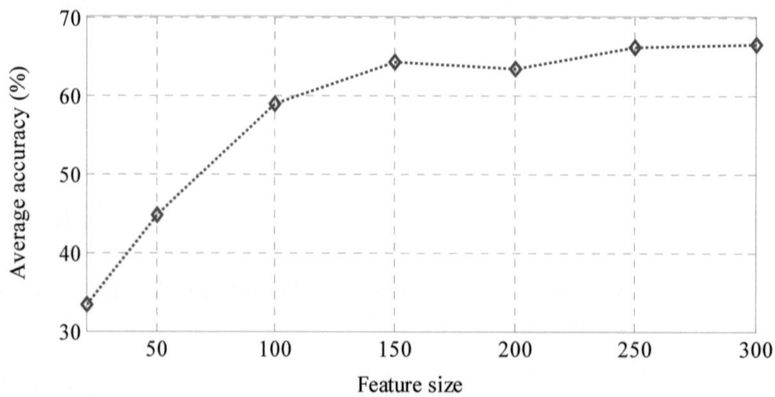

Fig. 8. Comparison of the average accuracies achieved with different feature sizes.

It can be seen from the figure that the average accuracy is not reduced even when the dimensionality of the feature vector is decreased from 792 to 250. The average accuracy is only decreased by 1.40% when the feature size is reduced to 150. This is only 18.94% of the size of the original full feature set. The recognition performance, however, is largely reduced when the feature size is lower than 150. The average accuracy is as low as 33.40% when there are only 20 parameters in a feature vector. It indicates that the classification performance is not deteriorated when the dimensionality of the feature vectors is reduced to a suitable value. The calculation complexity is also reduced with a decreased dimensionality.

5. Conclusion

The automatic recognition of emotional states from human speech has found a broad range of applications, and as such has drawn considerable attention and interest over the recent decade. Speech emotion recognition can be formulated as a standard pattern recognition problem and solved using machine learning technology. Specifically, feature extraction, processing and dimensionality reduction as well as pattern recognition have been discussed in this chapter. Three short time cepstral features, Linear Prediction-based Cepstral Coefficients (LPCC), Perceptual Linear Prediction (PLP) Cepstral Coefficients, and Mel-Frequency Cepstral Coefficients (MFCC), are used in our work to recognize speech emotions. Feature statistics are extracted based on speech segmentation for capturing longer time characteristics of speech signal. In order to reduce computational cost in classification, Principal Component Analysis (PCA) is employed for reducing feature dimensionality. The Support Vector Machine (SVM) is adopted as a classifier in emotion recognition system. The experiment in the classification of 15 emotional states for the samples extracted from the LDC database has been carried out. The recognition accuracies achieved with different segmentation forms and different feature set sizes are compared for speaker dependent training mode.

6. References

Amir, N. (2001), Classifying emotions in speech: A comparison of methods, *Eurospeech*, 2001.

Cen, L., Ser, W. & Yu., Z.L. (2009), Automatic recognition of emotional states from human speeches, *to be published in the book of Pattern Recognition.*

Clavel, C., Vasilescu, I., Devillers, L. & Ehrette, T. (2004), Fiction database for emotion detection in abnormal situations, *Proceedings of International Conference on Spoken Language Process*, pp. 2277–2280, 2004, Korea.

Cowie, R. & Douglas-Cowie, E. (1996), Automatic statistical analysis of the signal and prosodic signs of emotion in speech, *Proceedings of International Conference on Spoken Language Processing (ICSLP '96)*, Vol. 3, pp. 1989–1992, 1996.

Cowie, R., Douglas-Cowie, E., Tsapatsoulis, N., Votsis, G., Kollias, S., Fellenz, W., et al (2001), Emotion recognition in human-computer interaction, *IEEE Signal Processing Magazine*, Vol. 18, No. 1, (Jan. 2001) pp. 32-80.

Davis, S.B. & Mermelstein, P. (1980), Comparison of parametric representations for monosyllabic word recognition in continuously spoken sentences, *IEEE Transactions on Acoustics, Speech and Signal Processing*, Vol. 28, No. 4, (1980) pp. 357-365.

Davitz, J.R. (Ed.) (1964), *The Communication of Emotional Meaning*, McGraw-Hill, New York.

Dellaert, F., Polzin, T. & Waibel, A. (1996), Recognizing emotion in speech, *Fourth International Conference on Spoken Language Processing*, Vol. 3, pp. 1970-1973, Oct. 1996.

Fonagy, I. (1978), A new method of investigating the perception of prosodic features. *Language and Speech*, Vol. 21, (1978) pp. 34–49.

Fradkin, D. & Muchnik, I. (2006), Support Vector Machines for Classification, in Abello, J. and Carmode, G. (Eds), Discrete Methods in Epidemiology, DIMACS Series in Discrete Mathematics and Theoretical Computer Science, Vol. 70, (2006) pp. 13–20.

Havrdova, Z. & Moravek, M. (1979), Changes of the voice expression during suggestively influenced states of experiencing, *Activitas Nervosa Superior*, Vol. 21, (1979) pp. 33–35.

Hermansky, H. (1990), Perceptual linear predictive (PLP) analysis of speech, *The Journal of the Acoustical Society of America*, Vol. 87, No. 4, (1990) pp. 1738-1752.

Huttar, G.L. (1968), Relations between prosodic variables and emotions in normal American English utterances, *Journal of Speech Hearing Res.*, Vol. 11, (1968) pp. 481–487.

Lee, C. & Narayanan, S. (2005), Toward detecting emotions in spoken dialogs, *IEEE Transactions on Speech and Audio Processing*, Vol. 13, No. 2, (March 2005) pp. 293-303.

McGilloway, S., Cowie, R. & Douglas-Cowie, E. (1995), Prosodic signs of emotion in speech: preliminary results from a new technique for automatic statistical analysis, *Proceedings of Int. Congr. Phonetic Sciences*, Vol. 1, pp. 250–253, 1995, Stockholm, Sweden.

Morrison, D., Wang, R. & Liyanage C. De Silva (2007), Ensemble methods for spoken emotion recognition in call-centres, *Speech Communication*, Vol. 49, No. 2, (Feb. 2007) pp. 98-112.

Nguyen, T. & Bass, I. (2005), Investigation of combining SVM and Decision Tree for emotion classification, *Proceedings of 7th IEEE International Symposium on Multimedia*, pp. 540-544, Dec. 2005.

Nicholson, J., Takahashi, K. & Nakatsu, R. (1999), Emotion recognition in speech using neural networks, *6th International Conference on Neural Information Processing*, Vol. 2, pp. 495–501, 1999.

Oudeyer, P.Y. (2003), The production and recognition of emotions in speech: features and algorithms, *International Jounal of Human-Computer Studies*, Vol. 59, (2003) pp. 157-183.

Picone, J.W. (1993), Signal modeling techniques in speech recognition, *Proceedings of the IEEE*, Vol. 81, No. 9, (1993) pp. 1215-1245.

Petrushin, V.A. (1999), Emotion in speech: recognition and application to call centers, *Proceedings of Artificial Neural Networks in Engineering*, (Nov. 1999) pp. 7-10.

Petrushin, V.A. (2000), Emotion recognition in speech signal: experimental study, development, and application, *Proceedings of the 6th International Conference on Spoken Language Processing*, 2000, Beijing, China.

Psutka, J. Muller, L., & Psutka. J.V. (2001), Comparison of MFCC and PLP parameterizations in the speaker independent continuous speech recognition task, *Eurospeech*, 2001.

Reynolds, D.A., Quatieri, T.F. & Dunn, R.B. (2000), Speaker verification using adapted Gaussian mixture model, *Digital Signal Processing*, Vol. 10, No. 1, (Jan. 2000) pp. 19-41.

Rong J., Chen, Y-P. P., Chowdhury, M. & Li, G. (2007), Acoustic features extraction for emotion recognition, *IEEE/ACIS International Conference on Computer and Information Science*, Vol. 11, No. 13, pp. 419-424, Jul. 2007.

Scherer, K, A. (2000), Cross-cultural investigation of emotion inferences from voice and speech: Implications for speech technology, *Proceedings of ICSLP*, pp. 379-382, Oct. 2000, Beijing, China.

Ser, W., Cen, L. & Yu. Z.L. (2008), A hybrid PNN-GMM classification scheme for speech emotion recognition, *Proceedings of the 19th International Conference on Pattern Recognition (ICPR)*, December, 2008, Florida, USA.

Specht, D. F. (1988), Probabilistic neural networks for classification, mapping or associative memory, *Proceedings of IEEE International Conference on Neural Network*, Vol. 1, pp. 525-532, Jun. 1988.

Steinwart, I. & Christmann, A. (2008), *Support Vector Machines*, Springer-Verlag, New York, 2008, ISBN 978-0-387-77241-7.

Van Bezooijen, R. (1984), *Characteristics and recognizability of vocal expressions of emotions*, Foris, Dordrecht, The Netherlands, 1984.

Vapnik, V. (1995), *The nature of statistical learning theory*, Springer-Verlag, 1995, ISBN 0-387-98780-0.

Ververidis, D. & Kotropoulos, C. (2006), Emotional speech recognition: resources, features, and methods, *Speech Communication*, Vol. 48, No.9, (Sep. 2006) pp. 1163-1181.

Yu, F., Chang, E., Xu, Y.Q. & Shum, H.Y. (2001), Emotion detection from speech to enrich multimedia content, *Proceedings of Second IEEE Pacific-Rim Conference on Multimedia*, October, 2001, Beijing, China.

Zhou, J., Wang, G.Y., Yang,Y. & Chen, P.J. (2006), Speech emotion recognition based on rough set and SVM, *Proceedings of 5th IEEE International Conference on Cognitive Informatics*, Vol. 1, pp. 53-61, Jul. 2006, Beijing, China.

2

Automatic Internet Traffic Classification for Early Application Identification

Giacomo Verticale
Dipartimento di Elettronica e Informazione
Politecnico di Milano
Italy

1. Introduction

The classification of Internet packet traffic aims at associating a sequence of packets (a *flow*) to the application that generated it. The identification of applications is useful for many purposes, such as the usage analysis of network links, the management of Quality of Service, and for blocking malicious traffic. The techniques commonly used to recognize the Internet applications are based on the inspection of the packet payload or on the usage of well-known transport protocol port numbers. However, the constant growth of new Internet applications and protocols that use random or non-standard port numbers or applications that use packet encryption requires much smarter techniques. For this reason several new studies are considering the use of the statistical features to assist the identification and classification process, performed through the implementation of machine learning techniques. This operation can be done offline or online. When performed online, it is often a requirement that it is performed early, i.e. by looking only at the first packets in a flow.

In the context of real-time and early traffic classification, we need a classifier working with as few packets as possible so as to introduce a small delay between the beginning of the packet flow and the availability of the classification result. On the other hand, the classification performance grows as the number of observed packets grows. Therefore, a trade-off between classification delay and classification performance must be found.

In this work, the features we consider for the classification of traffic flows are the sizes of the first n packets in the client-server direction, with n a given number. With these features, good results can be obtained by looking at as few as 5 packets in the flow. We also show that the C4.5 decision tree algorithm generally yields the best results, outperforming Support Vector Machines and clustering algorithms such as the Simple K-Means algorithm.

As a novel result, we also present a new set of features obtained by considering a packet flow in the context of the activity of the Internet host that generated them. When classifying a flow, we take into account some features obtained by collecting statistics on the connection generation process. This is to exploit the well-known result that different Internet applications show different degrees of burstiness and time correlation. For example, the email generation process is compatible to a Poisson process, whereas the request of web pages is not Poisson but, rather, has a power-law spectrum.

By considering these features, we greatly enhance the classification performance when very few packets in the flow are observed. In particular, we show that the classification perfor-

mance obtained with only $n = 3$ packets and the statistics on the connection generation process is similar to the performance obtained with $n = 5$ packets and no information on the connection process, therefore achieving a much shorter classification delay.
Section 2 gives a resume of the most significant work in the field and describe the various facets of the problem. In that section we also introduce the Modified Allan Variance, which is the mathematical tool that we use to measure the power-law exponent in the connection generation process. In Section 3 we describe the classification procedure and the traffic traces used for performance evaluation.
Section 4 discusses the experimental data and shows the evidence of power-law behavior of the traffic sources. In Section 5 we compare some machine learning algorithms proposed in the literature in order to select the most appropriate for the traffic classification problem. Specifically, we compare the C4.5 decision tree, the Support Vector Machines, and the Simple K-Means clustering algorithm.
In Section 6 we introduce the novel classification algorithms that exploit the per-source features and evaluate their performance in Section 7. Some conclusions are left for the final section.

2. Background Material

2.1 Related Work

Nguyen & Armitage (2008) identify three basic traffic classification approaches based on machine learning:

- clustering, based on unsupervised learning;
- classification, based on supervised learning;
- hybrid approaches, combining the best of both supervised and unsupervised techniques.

Roughan et al. (2004) propose the Nearest Neighbors (NN), Linear Discriminant Analysis (LDA) and the Quadratic Discriminant Analysis (QDA) algorithms to identify the QoS class of different applications. The authors identify a list of possible features calculated over the entire flow duration. In the reported results, the authors obtain a classification error value in the range of 2.5% to 12.6%, depending on whether three or seven QoS classes are used.
Moore & Zuev (2005) propose the application of Bayesian techniques to traffic classification. In particular they used the Naive Bayes technique with Kernel Estimation (NBKE) and the Fast Correlation-Based Filter (FCBF) methods with a set of 248 full-flow features, including the flow duration, packet inter-arrival time statistics, payload size statistics, and the Fourier transform of the packet inter-arrival time process. The reported results show an accuracy of approximately 98% for web-browsing traffic, 90% for bulk data transfer, 44% for service traffic, and 55% for P2P traffic.
Auld et al. (2007) extend the previous work by using a Bayesian neural network. The classification accuracy of this technique reaches 99%, when the training data and the test data are collected on the same day, and reaches 95% accuracy when the test data are collected eight months later than the training data.
Nguyen & Armitage (2006a;b) propose a new classification method that considers only the most recent n packets of the flow. The collected features are packet length statistics and packet inter-arrival time statistics. The obtained accuracy is about 98%, but the performance is poor if the classifier misses the beginning of a traffic flow. This work is further extended by proposing

the training of the classifier by using statistical features calculated over multiple short sub-flows extracted from the full flow. The approach does not result in significant improvements to the classifier performance.
Park et al. (2006a;b) use a Genetic Algorithm (GA) to select the best features. The authors compare three classifiers: the Naive Bayes with Kernel Estimation (NBKE), the C4.5 decision tree, and Reduced Error Pruning Tree (REPTree). The best classification results are obtained using the C4.5 classifier and calculating the features on the first 10 packets of the flow.
Crotti et al. (2007) propose a technique, called Protocol Fingerprinting, based on the packet lengths, inter-arrival times, and packet arrival order. By classifying three applications (HTTP, SMTP and POP3), the authors obtain a classification accuracy of more than 91%.
Verticale & Giacomazzi (2008) use the C4.5 decision tree algorithm to classify WAN traffic. The considered features are the lengths of the first 5 packets in both directions, and their inter-arrival times. The results show an accuracy between 92% and 99%.
We also review some fundamental results on the relation between different Internet applications and power-law spectra.
Leland et al. (1993) were among the first in studying the power-law spectrum in LAN packet traffic and concluded that its cause was the nature of the data transfer applications.
Paxson & Floyd (1995) identified power-law spectra at the packet level also in WAN traffic and also conducted some investigation on the connection level concluding that Telnet and FTP control connections were well-modeled as Poisson processes, while FTP data connections, NNTP, and SMTP were not.
Crovella & Bestavros (1997) measured web-browsing traffic by studying the sequence of file requests performed during each session, where a session is one execution of the web-browsing application, finding that the reason of power law lies in the long-tailed distributions of the requested files and of the users' "think-times".
Nuzman et al. (2002) analyzed the web-browsing-user activity at the connection level and at the session level, where a session is a group of connections from a given IP address. The authors conclude that sessions arrivals are Poisson, while power-law behavior is present at the connection level.
Verticale (2009) shows that evidence of power-law behavior in the connection generation process of web-browing users can be found even when the source activity is low or the observation window is short.

2.2 The Modified Allan Variance

The MAVAR (Modified Allan Variance) was originally conceived for frequency stability characterization of precision oscillators in the time domain (Allan & Barnes, 1981) and was originally conceived with the goal of discriminating noise types with power-law spectrum of kind $f^{-\alpha}$, recognized very commonly in frequency sources. Recently, Bregni & Jmoda (2008) proposed MAVAR as an analysis tool for Internet traffic. It has been demonstrated to feature superior accuracy in the estimation of the power-law exponent, α, coupled with good robustness against non stationarity in the data. Bregni & Jmoda (2008) and Bregni et al. (2008) successfully applied MAVAR to real internet traffic analysis, identifying fractional noise in experimental results, and to GSM telephone traffic proving its consistency to the Poisson model. We briefly recall some basic concepts.

Given an infinite sequence $\{x_k\}$ of samples of an input signal $x(t)$, evenly spaced in time with sampling period τ_0, MAVAR is defined as:

$$\text{Mod}\sigma_y^2(\tau) = \frac{1}{2n^2\tau_0^2}\left\langle\left[\frac{1}{n}\sum_{j=1}^{n}\left(x_{j+2n} - 2x_{j+n} + x_j\right)\right]^2\right\rangle \tag{1}$$

where $\tau = n\tau_0$ is the observation interval and the operator $\langle\cdot\rangle$ denotes infinite-time averaging. In practice, given a finite set of N samples over a measurement interval $T = (N-1)\tau_0$, the MAVAR can be computed using the ITU-T standard estimator (Bregni, 2002):

$$\text{Mod}\sigma_y^2(n\tau_0) = \frac{\sum_{j=1}^{N-3n+1}\left[\sum_{i=j}^{n+j-1}(x_{i+2n} - 2x_{i+n} + x_i)\right]^2}{2n^4\tau_0^2(N-3n+1)} \tag{2}$$

with $n = 1, 2, \cdots, \lfloor N/3 \rfloor$.
We consider the random processes $x(t)$ with one-sided Power Spectral Density (PSD) modeled as:

$$S_x(f) = hf^{-\alpha}, \tag{3}$$

where α and h are the model parameters. Such random processes are commonly referred to as *power-law* processes. For these processes, the infinite-time average in (1) converges for $\alpha < 5$. The MAVAR obeys a simple power law of the observation interval τ (ideally asymptotically for $n \to \infty$, keeping constant $n\tau_0 = \tau$, in practice for $n > 4$):

$$\text{Mod}\sigma_y^2(\tau) \simeq A_\mu \tau^\mu \tag{4}$$

where $\mu = \alpha - 3$ and A_μ is a constant.
Therefore, if $x(t)$ obeys (3), a log-log plot of the MAVAR ideally looks as a straight line, whose slope μ gives the exponent estimate $\alpha = \mu + 3$ of the power-law component. Bregni & Jmoda (2008) show these estimates to be accurate, therefore we choose this tool to analyze power laws in traffic traces.

3. Classification Procedure

Figure 1 shows the general architecture for traffic capture. Packets coming from a LAN to the Internet and vice versa are all copied to a PC, generally equipped with specialized hardware, which can either perform real-time classification or simply write to a disk a traffic trace, which is a copy of all the captured packets. In case the traffic trace is later made public, all the packets are anonymized by substituting their IP source and destination addresses and stripping the application payload.
In order to have repeatable experiments, in our research work we have used publicly available packet traces. The first trace, which we will refer to as *Naples*, contains traffic related to TCP port 80 generated and received by clients inside the network of University of Napoli "Federico II" reaching the outside world (*Network Tools and Traffic Traces*, 2004). The traces named *Auckland*, *Leipzig*, and *NZIX* contain a mixture of all traffic types and are available at the *NLANR PMA: Special Traces Archive* (2009) and the *WITS: Waikato Internet Traffic Storage* (2009). Table 1 contains the main parameters of the used traces.
Figure 2 shows the block diagram of the traffic classification procedure.

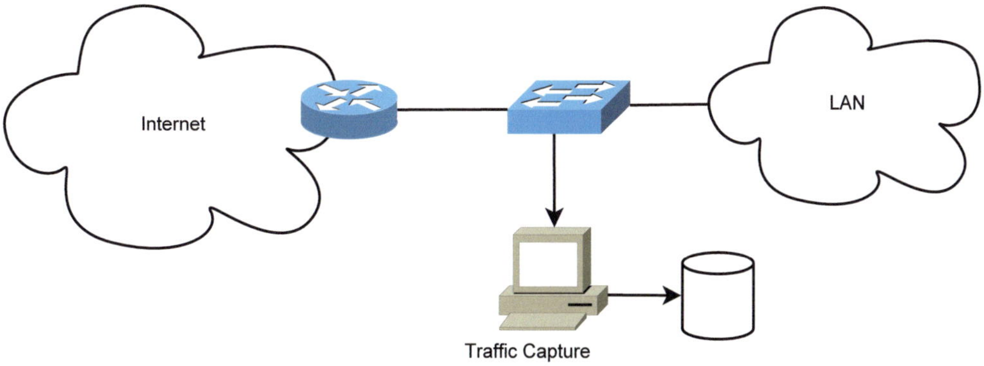

Fig. 1. Architecture of the Traffic Capture Environment.

Name	Length (hh:mm)	Date	Start Time (hh:mm)
Auckland (a)	24:00	June 11th, 2001	00:00
Auckland (b)	24:00	June 12th, 2001	00:00
Leipzig (a)	4:23	Feb. 21st, 2003	12:14
Leipzig (b)	4:24	Feb. 21st, 2003	16:37
Naples	1:00	June 14th, 2004	11:00
NZIX (a)	24:00	July 6th, 2000	00:00
NZIX (b)	24:00	July 7th, 2000	00:00

Table 1. Parameters of the Analyzed Traffic Traces

Given a packet trace, we use the *NetMate Meter* (2006) and *netAI, Network Traffic based Application Identification* (2006) tools to group packets in traffic flows and to elaborate the per-flow metrics. In case TCP is the transport protocol, a flow is defined as the set of packets belonging to a single TCP connection. In case UDP is used, a flow is defined as the set of packets with the same IP addresses and UDP port numbers. A UDP flow is considered finished when no packets have arrived for 600 s. If a packet with the same IP addresses and UDP port numbers arrives when the flow is considered finished, it is considered the first packet in a new flow between the same couple of hosts.

For each flow, we measure the lengths of the first n packets in the flow in the client-server direction. These data are the per-flow metrics that will be used in the following for classifying the traffic flows. We also collect the timestamp of the first packet in the flow, which we use as an indicator of the time of the connection request.

For the purpose of training the classifier, we also collect the destination port number for each flow. This number will be used as the data label for the purpose of validating the proposed classification technique. Of course, this approach is sub-optimal in the sense that the usage of well-known ports cannot be fully trusted. A better approach would be performing deep packet inspection in order to identify application signatures in the packet payload. However, this is not possible with public traces, which have been anonymized by stripping the payload. In the rest of the paper we will made the assumption that, in the considered traffic traces, well-known ports are a truthful indicator of the application that generated the packet flow.

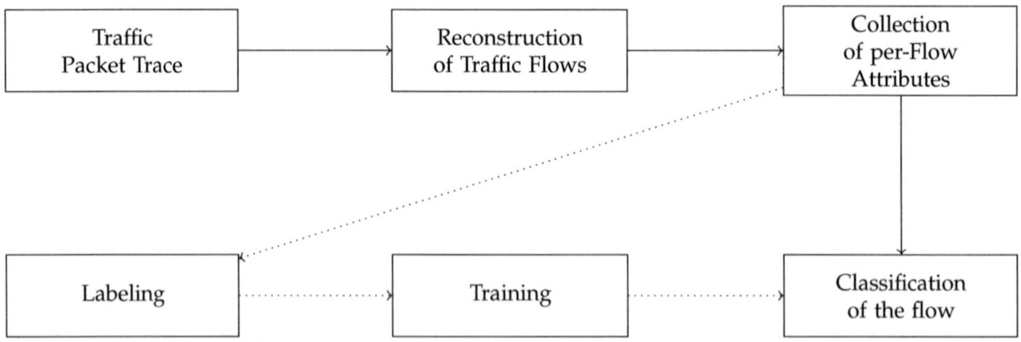

Fig. 2. Block diagram of classification procedure.

The collected data are then passed to the *R* software (R Development Core Team, 2008) to collect the per-source metrics, to train the classifier, and to perform the cross-validation tests. In particular we used the *Weka* (Witten & Frank, 2000) and the *libsvm* (Chang & Lin, 2001) libraries. From the timestamps of the first packets in each flow, we obtain the discrete sequence $x_i^p(k)$, which counts the connection requests from the i-th client, associated to the p-th transport port, in the k-th time interval. Each interval is long $\tau_0 = 1$ s. Each time a new connection request arrives, the sequence $x_i^p(k)$ is updated and we compute the metrics in Table 2.

Metric	Definition
Coefficient of Variation	the ratio between the standard deviation of $x_i^p(k)$ and its mean
Skewness	the standardized third moment of $x_i^p(k)$
Kurtosis	the standardized fourth moment of $x_i^p(k)$
Power-law exponent	the exponent α of the power-law component in the Power Spectral Density of $x_i^p(k)$

Table 2. Per-source metrics.

4. The Power-law Exponent

In this section, we present some results on the power-law behavior of the connection request process by commenting the measurements on the Naples traffic trace, which contains only web-browsing traffic, and the Auckland(a) traffic trace, which contains a mix a different traffic types.

Figure 3 shows the three sequences $x_1^{80}(k)$, $x_2^{80}(k)$, and $x^{80}(k)$. The first sequence is obtained by considering only connections from a single IP address, which we call *Client 1*. Similarly, the second sequence is obtained considering connections from *Client 2*. Finally, the third sequence is obtained considering all the connections in the trace. The total traffic trace is one-hour long and the two clients considered are active for all the duration of the measurement. Neither the aggregated connection arrival process nor the single clients show evident non stationarity.

As discussed in Section 2.2, the slope of Modσ^2 vs τ in the log-log plot can be used as a measure of the power-law exponent. In order to avoid border effects and poor confidence

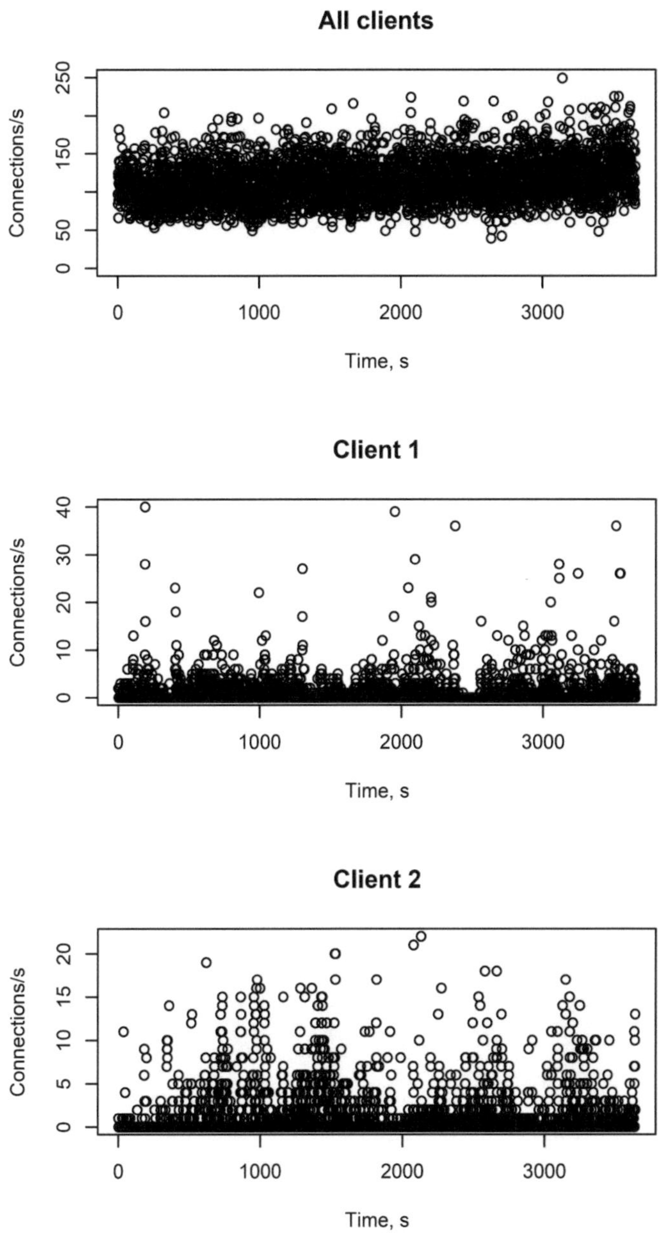

Fig. 3. Connection requests per second in the Naples traffic trace.

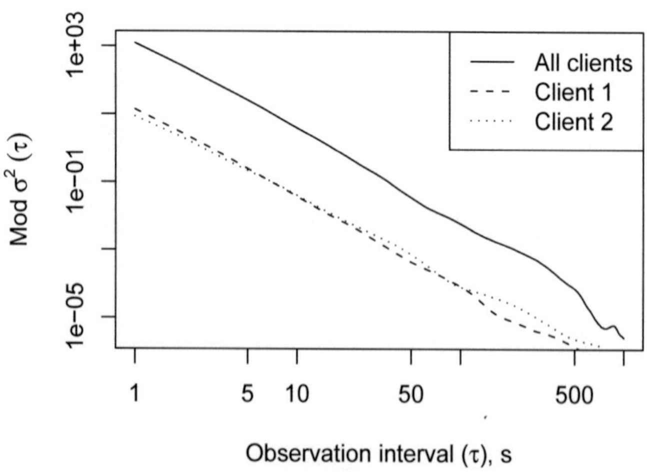

Fig. 4. MAVAR computed on the sequence of connection requests from two random clients and from all the clients in the Naples traffic trace.

in the values of Modσ^2, we calculate α by considering only the range $4\tau_0 \leq \tau < 0.3 \max k\tau_0$, as suggested in (Bregni & Jmoda, 2008). Figure 4 shows the MAVAR calculated on the three sequences. In the considered range of τ, the three curves in Figure 4 have a similar slope, corresponding to the values of $\alpha_1 = 0.28$ and $\alpha_2 = 0.35$ for clients 1 and 2 respectively, and $\alpha = 0.24$ for the aggregated process. These data confirm our expectations that the sum of sequences showing power-law behavior also shows power-law behavior.

We have considered so far only TCP connection requests to servers listening on port number 80, which is the well-known port for HTTP data traffic. We expect that traffic using different application protocols shows a different time-correlation behavior. With reference to the *Auckland* traffic trace, we have extracted the per-client connection request sequence $x_i^p(k)$ considering only requests for servers listening on the TCP ports 25, 80, 110, and 443, which are the well-known ports for SMTP, HTTP, POP3, and HTTPS. We have also considered requests for servers listening on either TCP or UDP port 53, which is the well-known port for DNS requests.

Figure 5 shows the estimate m_α for the various destination ports, obtained by averaging the value of α measured for the clients with at least 50 connection requests in the observation window. The figure also shows 95% confidence intervals for the mean. From the observation of Figure 5, we also notice that the confidence intervals for the estimate of the power-law exponent of the email application traffic includes $\alpha = 0$ both for port 25 and 110, therefore showing no evidence of power-law behavior. Instead, the estimates for web requests, both on insecure (port 80) and on secure connections (port 443) have overlapping confidence intervals not including $\alpha = 0$. Then we conclude that these processes come from similar populations and show evidence of power-law behavior. Finally, the confidence interval for DNS requests does not include $\alpha = 0$ and does not overlap with web traffic, allowing us to conclude that,

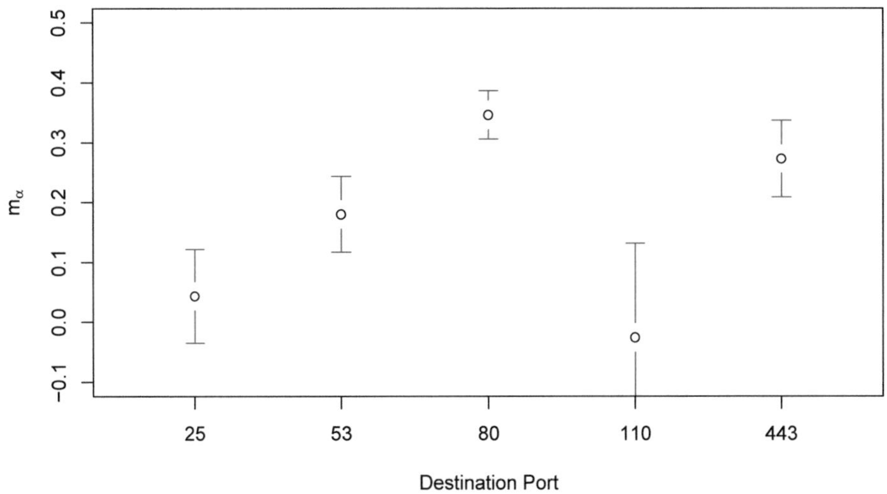

Fig. 5. Estimated power-law exponent of the connection requests process for different destination port numbers in the Auckland traffic trace. Estimations are averaged over all the clients and 95% confidence intervals are shown.

from the point of view of time-correlation, the DNS request process shows evidence of power-law behavior and comes from a different population than web traffic.

5. Comparison of Learning Algorithms

In this section, we compare three algorithms proposed for the classification of traffic flows. In order to choose the classification algorithm to be used in the hybrid schemes discussed later, we performed a set of experiments by training the classifiers using the Auckland(a), NZIX(a), and Leipzig(a) traffic traces and testing the performance by classifying the Auckland(b), NZIX(b), and Leipzig(b) traffic traces, respectively.

To ease a comparison, we performed our assessment by using the same 5 applications as in (Williams et al., 2006), i.e. FTP-data, Telnet, SMTP, DNS (both over UDP and over TCP), and HTTP. In all the experiments, traffic flows are classified by considering only the first 5 packets in the client server direction. The performance metric we consider is the error rate, calculated as the ratio between the misclassified instances to the total instances in the data set. We consider two supervised learning algorithms namely the C4.5 Decision Tree and the Support Vector Machines (SVM), and an unsupervised technique, namely the Simple K-means.

For the SVM, we considered the polynomial kernel with degrees $d = 2$ and $d = 3$ and the RBF kernel. In the polynomial case we normalized attributes in the range $[0,1]$, while in the RBF case we normalized attributes in the range $[-1,1]$, as suggested in (Abe, 2005).

To choose the cost parameter we performed a 10-fold cross validation on the Auckland(a) traffic trace and obtained the best results with the following configurations: polynomial kernel with degree $d = 2$ and cost $C = 10^6$; RBF kernel with exponent $\gamma = 4$ and cost $C = 10^3$.

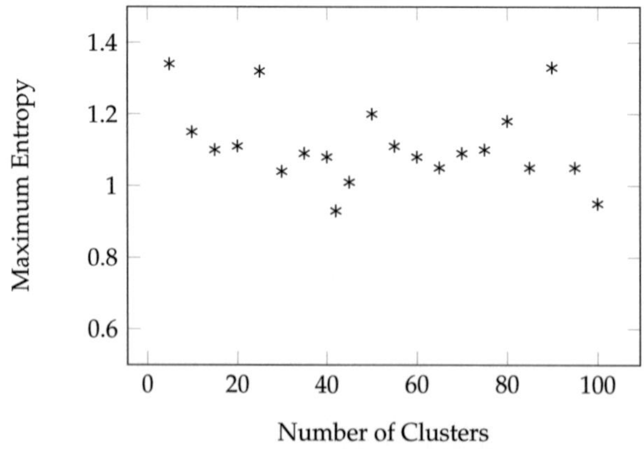

Fig. 6. Maximum entropy of clusters in the simple k-means clustering.

	C4.5	SVM (Polynomial)	SVM (RBF)	Simple K-means
Auckland	0.8%	7.8%	4.3%	11%
Leipzig	0.6%	3.6%	4.3%	12%
NZIX	0.5%	1.9%	0.2%	7%

Table 3. Error rate for three traffic traces with the different classification techniques.

For the Simple K-Means, we tried different values for the number of clusters. Since the algorithm could not perfectly separate the labeled instances, we labeled each cluster with the most common label. To choose the number of clusters, we performed a 10-fold cross validation on the Auckland(a) traffic trace. For several possible choices for the number of clusters, we computed the entropy of each cluster. In Figure 6 we plot the entropy of the cluster that has the maximum entropy versus the number of clusters. The figure does not show a clear dependency of the maximum entropy on the number of clusters, so we decided to use 42 clusters, because, in the figure, it corresponds to a minimum.
Table 3 reports the measured error rate for the selected classifiers in the three experiments. Comparing the experiments we do not see a clear winner. With the Auckland and Leipzig traces, C4.5 performs better, while SVM with RBF kernel yields the best results with the NZIX trace. In the Leipzig case, however, the SVM with RBF kernel perform worse than the SVM with polynomial kernel. The Simple K-means technique always shows the highest error rate. Since the C4.5 classifier seems to give the best results overall, in the following we will consider this classifier as the basis for the hybrid technique.

6. The Hybrid Classification Technique

As discussed in Section 4, the statistical indexes computed on the connection-generation process depend on the application that generated the packet flow. Therefore, we introduce a new classifier capable of exploiting those indexes. The block diagram of this new classifier, which we will refer to as the *hybrid classifier*, is shown in Figure 7.

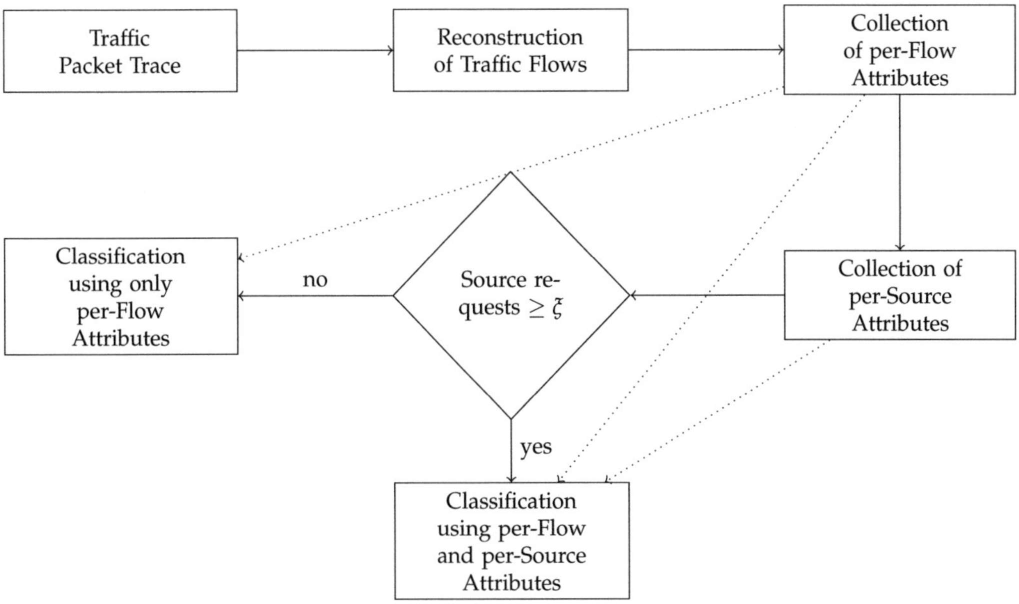

Fig. 7. Block diagram of the hybrid classifier.

As usual, we capture the packets from the communication link and reconstruct the TCP connections. We also collect the per-flow features, which comprise the length of the first n packets in the flow. In addition, we maintain running statistics on the connection generation process. For each pair (IP source, destination port number), we calculate the per-source attributes discussed in Section 3 and listed in Table 2. It is worth noting that all these attributes do not require to keep in memory the whole list of the connection request arrival times, because they can be updated with a recurrence formula each time a new connection request arrives. As discussed in Section 4, when a given IP source has generated only a few requests, the statistical indexes have a large error, so we do not consider them for the purpose of traffic classification. Instead, when the IP source has generated many connection requests, the statistical indexes show better confidence, so we use them for classification. In order to choose whether the indexes are significant or not, we compare the total number of connections that the source has generated to a given threshold, ξ, which is a system parameter. If the source has generated fewer than ξ connections, we perform classification of the traffic flow by using only the flow attributes (i.e. the sizes of the first packets). Otherwise, if the source has generated more than ξ connections, we perform classification by using both the flow attributes and the source attributes (i.e. the statistical indexes). The same rule applies to training data. Labeled flows generated by IP sources that, up to that flow, have generated fewer requests than ξ, are used to train the classifier using only flow attributes. On the other hand, the labeled flows generated by IP sources that have generated more than ξ requests are used to train the classifier using both the per-flow and the per-source attributes. In both cases, the used classifier is a C4.5 decision tree.

The number of the packets to consider for classification is a critical parameter. The more packets are considered, the less the classification error. However, collecting the required number of packets requires time, during which the flow remains unclassified. It would be better to perform classification as soon as possible. In this work, we consider the scenario in which only the packets from the client to the server are available. In this scenario, we have observed that the hit ratio does not grow significantly if more than 5 packets are considered. This is consistent to results in (Bernaille et al., 2006). However, we will show that the average time needed to collect 5 packets is usually in the order of the hundreds of ms, depending on the network configuration. On the other hand, if classification were performed considering only the first 3 packets per flow, the time required would drop significantly. Classification performance, however, would be much worse.

In this work, we propose a hybrid classification technique that aims at achieving good classification performance but requiring as few packets as possible. In order to evaluate the performance of the hybrid classifier, we consider the following configurations.

The first two configurations, which we will refer to as *non-hybrid* perform classification by using only the packets sizes. For each flow, the first n packets are collected and then their sizes are fed to the classifier. The time required to collect the required data corresponds to the time required to collect exactly n packets. If the flow contains fewer packets, then classification can be performed only when the flow is over. We consider the cases where either $n = 3$ or $n = 5$ packets.

The third configuration, which we will refer to as *basic hybrid classifier* splits the incoming flows in two sets, depending on the IP source activity, as explained above. Then, the first n packets are collected and classification is performed by using the packet sizes and, possibly, the source statistical indexes. Since the source indexes are available at the flow beginning, exploitation of these features introduces no delay. Therefore the basic hybrid classifier is appealing because it yields a better hit ratio than the non-hybrid classifier using the same number of packets, n. In this chapter, we consider the case where $n = 3$.

Finally, we consider the *enhanced hybrid classifier*. Similarly to the basic configuration, this classifier splits the incoming flows in two sets depending on the IP source activity. However, the number of packets collected for each flow depends on the set. For the flows coming from low activity sources, the classifier waits for n_1 packets, whereas, for the flows coming from high activity sources, the classifier waits for n_2 packets. Since this second classifier already has valuable information for performing classification, it needs fewer packets, therefore $n_1 > n_2$. This way, the result of classification is obtained more quickly for those flows coming from high activity sources and for which other data are available. We consider the case where $n_1 = 5$ and $n_2 = 3$. Since the decision of which set each flow belongs to depends on the threshold ξ, if the threshold is low, then the classification is quicker, but the hit ratio is lower because the statistical indexes are less reliable. On the other hand, if the threshold is higher, then classification is slower, but more precise. At the extrema, if $\xi = 0$, the performance converges to that of the basic hybrid classifier; as ξ goes to infinity, performance converges to that of the non-hybrid classifier with $n = n_1$.

7. Numerical Results

In this Section, we evaluate the performance of the proposed traffic classification techniques. The first set of experiments is a validation using the *NZIX* traffic traces. The classifier is trained using the NZIX(a) trace and the tests are performed using the NZIX(b) trace. Figure 8(a) shows the error rate obtained with the different techniques. The best results are obtained with the non-hybrid classification considering the first $n = 5$ packets in the flow, which results in a percentage of misclassified flows of about 1.8%. The non-hybrid classifier does not use any

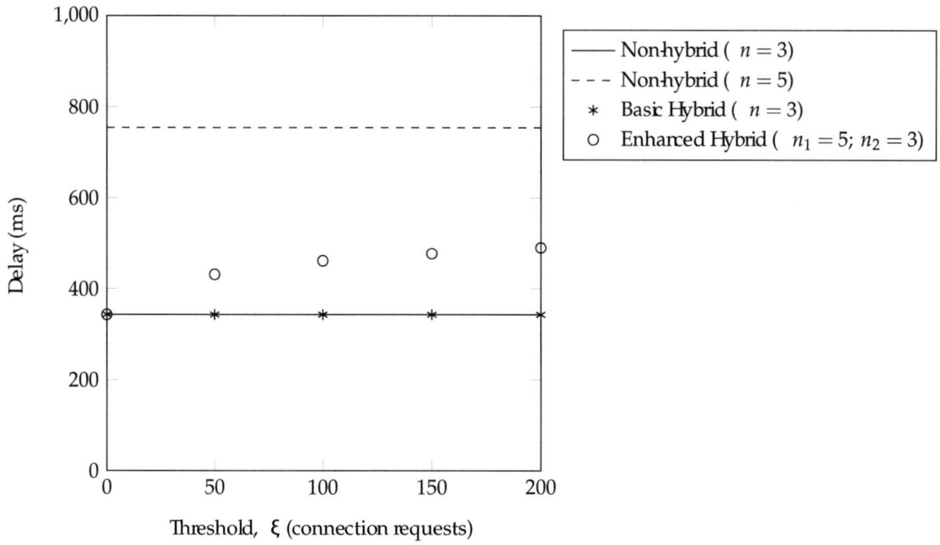

[Error-rate.]

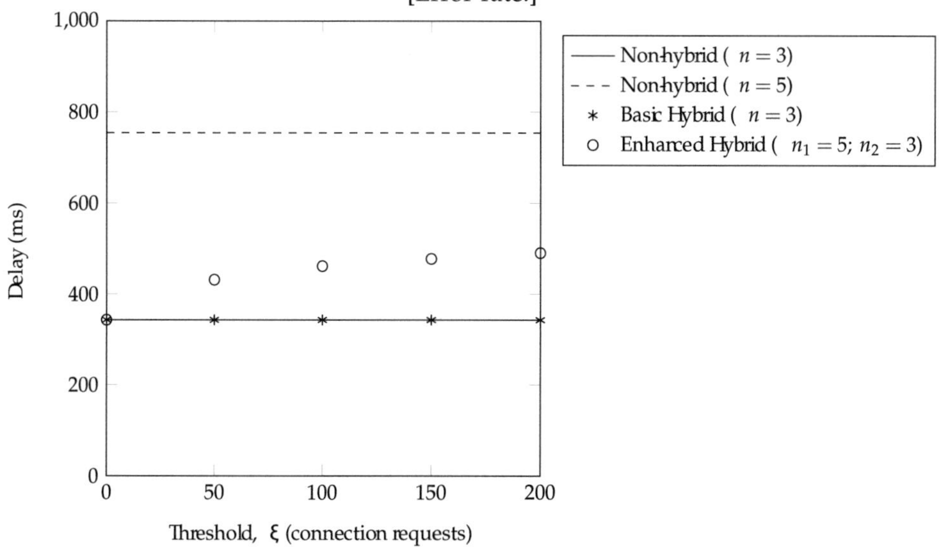

[Feature collection delay.]

Fig. 8. Classification performance. Training with the NZIX(a) traffic trace and tests with the NZIX(b) traffic trace.

per-source attribute, so the results are independent of the threshold ξ and Figure 8(a) shows this result as an horizontal line. On the other hand, the worst results are obtained with the non-hybrid classifier using the first $n = 3$ packets in the flow. This classifier results in an error rate of about 8%. We discuss these results by comparing the achieved classification performance to the delay between the beginning of the flow and the time to obtain the classifier output. In Figure 8(b), we show the average time necessary to collect the number of packets required by the classification algorithm. The non-hybrid algorithm with $n = 5$, which shows the best classification performance, gives an answer after, on average, 750 ms. Conversely, the non-hybrid classification technique with $n = 3$ only requires half of that time, giving its output after only 350 ms.

The hybrid techniques try to achieve good classification performance, while requiring fewer packets. The Basic Hybrid technique only requires $n = 3$ packets, so it yields the same delay as the non-hybrid technique with $n = 3$, the classification error, however, is much lower, ranging from 5.2% to about 6.3% depending on the threshold ξ. The threshold controls the minimum number of connection requests necessary to have confidence in the per-source attributes and use them in classifying the flows coming from that source. Therefore, the Basic Hybrid technique reduces the classification error by 2% yielding no increase in the classification delay. The classification performance is influenced by the threshold, but not to a great extent.

The Enhanced Hybrid technique tries to strike a balance between the error rate and the delay. In Figure 8(a), we plot the classification error rate versus the threshold. When the threshold is 0, most of the flows are classified considering $n_2 = 3$ packets plus the per-source attributes, so the classification performance converges to the classification performance of the Basic Hybrid technique. Independently of the threshold, some flows cannot take advantage of the per-source attributes because these attributes cannot be computed, for example because the source must have been active for at least some time interval in order to compute the power law exponent α; therefore, the results for the Basic and the Enhanced techniques do not coincide. As the threshold grows, fewer flows take advantage of the per-source attributes and are classified using the non hybrid scheme with $n_1 = 5$ packets. On the other hand, the per-source attributes are more reliable and the classification performance is better. Figure 8(a) shows that the error rate drops to as low as 2.5% when $\xi = 200$ connection requests.

The drawback is that, as the threshold increases, more and more flows are classified using more packets and the delay increases. Figure 8(b) shows that, when $\xi = 200$, the classification delay is about 500 ms. This delay is about 150 ms more than the delay obtained with the Basic scheme, which has a much worse classification performance, and is 250 ms less than the delay of the non hybrid scheme with $n = 5$, which only yields slightly better results.

Figure 9 shows a similar experiment with the *Auckland* data set. The classifier is trained with the Auckland(a) traffic trace and the tests are performed on the Auckland(b) traffic trace. In Figure 9(a) we plot the error rate versus the threshold, ξ. With this data set, the non hybrid technique with $n = 3$ packets performs poorly, with an error rate of about 30%. Instead, if $n = 5$ packets are considered, the error rate drops to about 2.5%, which is similar to the error rate obtained with the *NZIX* data set. Figure 9(b) shows that the average delay required to collect $n = 3$ and $n = 5$ packets is similar, being 200 ms and 235 ms, respectively. In this scenario the hybrid techniques are less appealing, because the delay difference is limited. However, these techniques yield some advantage also in this scenario. In Figure 9(a) we observe that, as the threshold increases, both the Basic and the Enhanced schemes show better classification performance. The Basic Hybrid Classifier settles at an error rate of about 15% when the threshold is larger or equal to 100 connection requests. Larger values do not seem to give better results.

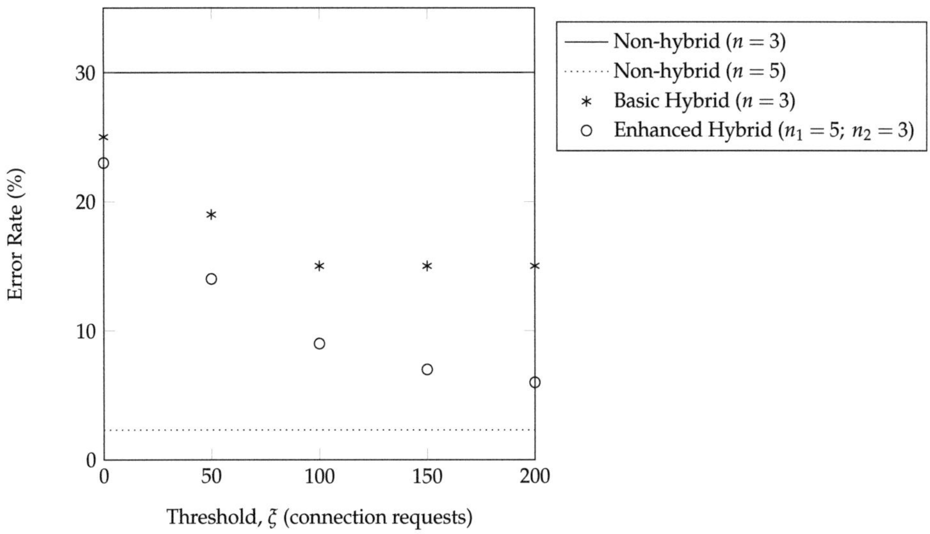

[Error-rate.]

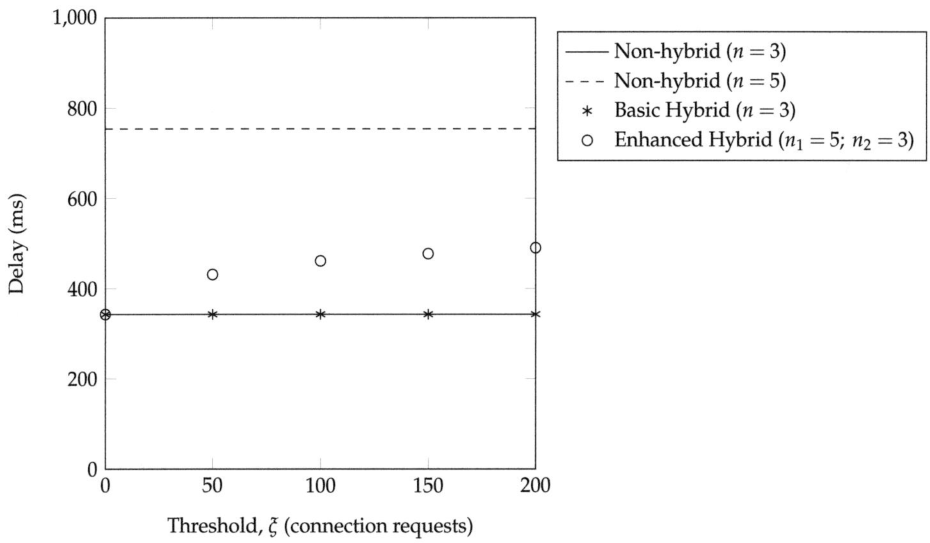

[Feature collection delay.]

Fig. 9. Classification performance. Training with the Auckland(a) traffic trace and tests with the Auckland(b) traffic trace.

Therefore the Basic scheme halves the error rate without increasing the delay. The Enhanced scheme shows even better results: with $\xi = 100$, the Enhanced Hybrid Classifier has an error rate of 9%, which drops to 6% when $\xi = 200$. From 9(b) we observe that the Enhanced classifier shows a delay of about 215 ms for $\xi = 100$ and only slightly more for $\xi = 200$. This delay is halfway between the delay of the non hybrid classifier with $n = 3$ and with $n = 5$.

8. Conclusions

In this work, we report experimental results about the classification of Internet traffic by examining the packet flow in the client-server direction. We focus on the problem of early application identification, which requires to find a balance between the classification accuracy and the number of packets required by the classifier.
The contribution of this work is twofold. First, we compare the performance of some well-known supervised and unsupervised classification techniques, namely the C4.5 decision tree, the Support Vector Machines, and the Simple K-Means. We performed validation tests on three traffic traces containing a mix of traffic from different applications and concluded that the C4.5 decision tree algorithm has the best performance overall, even if the SVMs follow closely. The unsupervised technique always yields the worst performance.
Second, we introduce a new classification scheme based on the observation that the connection generation process from a given traffic source is influenced by the application generating the requests. In particular, we show that, in experimental data, the Power Spectral Density of such processes often shows a power-law behavior. Therefore, we propose to use the measured power-law exponent of the traffic source as an additional feature in the classification of a traffic flow. This new feature comes at no additional delay, because its computation is based on the timestamps of the initial packets of past flows.
By using this feature we were able to significantly reduce the classification error rate in all the considered scenarios. Further, we also propose an enhanced scheme in which we perform classification using the first 5 packets in a flow for low-activity sources and the first 3 packets in flow for high-activity sources. By using this scheme, we obtain a low error rate and, at the same time, we have low average classification delay.
There are some possible future directions for this research. In this work, we did not consider the problem of training a classifier on a data set collected on a given link and used on a different link. We expect that the classification error rate increases, but that the per-flow features still yield an increased accuracy, because the connection request process mainly depends on the application and is weakly dependent on the specific network context. In order to study the portability of a classifier it is necessary to use traces captured at different sites but in the same day and at the same hour. This is because traffic patterns evolve over time. Another possible future work is the study of the temporal evolution of the connection generation process.

Acknowledgements

This work has been partially funded by the Italian Research Ministry (MIUR) PRIN 2006 project RECIPE.

9. References

Abe, S. (2005). *Support Vector Machines for Pattern Classification (Advances in Pattern Recognition)*, Springer-Verlag New York, Inc., Secaucus, NJ, USA.

Allan, D. & Barnes, J. (1981). A modified Allan variance with increased oscillator characterization ability, *Thirty Fifth Annual Frequency Control Symposium. 1981* pp. 470–475.

Auld, T., Moore, A. & Gull, S. (2007). Bayesian neural networks for internet traffic classification, *Neural Networks, IEEE Transactions on* **18**(1): 223–239.

Bernaille, L., Teixeira, R. & Salamatian, K. (2006). Early application identification, *The 2nd ADETTI/ISCTE CoNEXT Conference.*

Bregni, S. (2002). *Time and Frequency Measurement Techniques in Telecommunications*, Wiley, pp. 305–375.

Bregni, S., Cioffi, R. & Decina, M. (2008). An empirical study on time-correlation of GSM telephone traffic, *Wireless Communications, IEEE Transactions on* **7**(9): 3428–3435.

Bregni, S. & Jmoda, L. (2008). Accurate estimation of the Hurst parameter of long-range dependent traffic using modified Allan and Hadamard variances, *Communications, IEEE Transactions on* **56**(11): 1900–1906.

Chang, C.-C. & Lin, C.-J. (2001). *LIBSVM: a library for support vector machines.*
URL: *http://www.csie.ntu.edu.tw/ cjlin/libsvm*

Crotti, M., Dusi, M., Gringoli, F. & Salgarelli, L. (2007). Traffic classification through simple statistical fingerprinting, *SIGCOMM Comput. Commun. Rev.* **37**(1): 5–16.

Crovella, M. & Bestavros, A. (1997). Self-similarity in World Wide Web traffic: evidence and possible causes, *Networking, IEEE/ACM Transactions on* **5**(6): 835–846.

Leland, W. E., Taqq, M. S., Willinger, W. & Wilson, D. V. (1993). On the self-similar nature of Ethernet traffic, *in* D. P. Sidhu (ed.), *ACM SIGCOMM*, San Francisco, California, pp. 183–193.

Moore, A. W. & Zuev, D. (2005). Internet traffic classification using bayesian analysis techniques, *SIGMETRICS '05: Proceedings of the 2005 ACM SIGMETRICS international conference on Measurement and modeling of computer systems*, ACM, New York, NY, USA, pp. 50–60.

netAI, Network Traffic based Application Identification (2006).
URL: *http://caia.swin.edu.au/urp/dstc/netai/*

NetMate Meter (2006).
URL: *http://sourceforge.net/projects/netmate-meter/*

Network Tools and Traffic Traces (2004).
URL: *http://www.grid.unina.it/Traffic/Traces/ttraces.php*

Nguyen, T. & Armitage, G. (2006a). Synthetic sub-flow pairs for timely and stable IP traffic identification, *Proc. Australian Telecommunication Networks and Application Conference.*

Nguyen, T. & Armitage, G. (2006b). Training on multiple sub-flows to optimise the use of machine learning classifiers in real-world IP networks, *Local Computer Networks, Proceedings 2006 31st IEEE Conference on*, pp. 369–376.

Nguyen, T. & Armitage, G. (2008). A survey of techniques for internet traffic classification using machine learning, *Communications Surveys & Tutorials, IEEE* **10**(4): 56–76.

NLANR PMA: Special Traces Archive (2009).
URL: *http://www.nlanr.net/*

Nuzman, C., Saniee, I., Sweldens, W. & Weiss, A. (2002). A compound model for TCP connection arrivals for LAN and WAN applications, *Elsevier Science Computer Networks* **40**(3): 319–337.

Park, J., Tyan, H.-R. & Kuo, C.-C. (2006a). Internet traffic classification for scalable QOS provision, *Multimedia and Expo, 2006 IEEE International Conference on*, pp. 1221–1224.

Park, J., Tyan, H.-R. & Kuo, C.-C. J. (2006b). GA-based internet traffic classification technique for QoS provisioning, *Intelligent Information Hiding and Multimedia Signal Processing, International Conference on* **0**: 251–254.

Paxson, V. & Floyd, S. (1995). Wide area traffic: the failure of Poisson modeling, *IEEE/ACM Trans. Netw.* **3**: 226–244.

R Development Core Team (2008). *R: A Language and Environment for Statistical Computing*, R Foundation for Statistical Computing, Vienna, Austria. ISBN 3-900051-07-0.
URL: *http://www.R-project.org*

Roughan, M., Sen, S., Spatscheck, O. & Duffield, N. (2004). Class-of-service mapping for QoS: a statistical signature-based approach to IP traffic classification, *IMC '04: Proceedings of the 4th ACM SIGCOMM conference on Internet measurement*, ACM, New York, NY, USA, pp. 135–148.

Verticale, G. (2009). An empirical study of self-similarity in the per-user-connection arrival process, *Telecommunications, 2009. AICT '09. Fifth Advanced International Conference on*, pp. 101–106.

Verticale, G. & Giacomazzi, P. (2008). Performance evaluation of a machine learning algorithm for early application identification, *Computer Science and Information Technology, 2008. IMCSIT 2008. International Multiconference on*, pp. 845–849.

Williams, N., Zander, S. & Armitage, G. (2006). A preliminary performance comparison of five machine learning algorithms for practical IP traffic flow classification, *SIGCOMM Comput. Commun. Rev.* **36**(5): 5–16.

WITS: Waikato Internet Traffic Storage (2009).
URL: *http://www.wand.net.nz/wits/*

Witten, I. H. & Frank, E. (2000). *Data mining: practical machine learning tools and techniques with Java implementations*, Morgan Kaufmann Publishers Inc., San Francisco, CA, USA.

3

A Greedy Approach for Building Classification Cascades

Sherif Abdelazeem†
shazeem@aucegypt.edu
Electronics Engineering Dept., The American University in Cairo

Classification cascade is a well-known technique to reduce classification complexity (recognition time) while attaining high classification accuracy. Cascades are usually built using ad-hoc procedures. The mission of this chapter is to introduce a principled way of building cascades using a greedy approach. Given a large pool of classifiers, the proposed approach sequentially builds a near-optimal cascade. Given a set of N classifiers and one powerful classifier with satisfactory classification accuracy, the proposed algorithm automatically generates classification cascades with complexity $O(N^2)$ which means it is fast and scalable to large values of N. Experiments show that the proposed algorithm is efficient and builds classification cascades that substantially reduce the overall system complexity while preserving the accuracy.

1. Introduction

Suppose we have a classification task on which we have already found a complex classification technique that achieves a satisfactory accuracy. Suppose also while such classification technique is very powerful, its time complexity is unacceptably high. This scenario happens frequently in real life as many powerful but very time-consuming techniques have been devised in recent years (e.g. SVM and multi-classifier systems). Our goal would be to build a system that preserves the accuracy of that complex classifier while having much better timing performance.

The high complexity of powerful classifiers might give the impression that high accuracy could not be achieved without sacrificing recognition time. In fact, this is not true. The high average recognition time of a classifier in most cases is due to improper resource allocation. Weak classification techniques while not achieving satisfactory accuracy, they do a good job. They are capable of correctly classifying considerable number of cases. Actually, most of patterns in many problems are 'regular' patterns; that is, they could be classified using a simple classifications technique. So why should we use a very complicated time-consuming classification technique for just few extreme cases? This observation led to the development of cascade systems [Kanyank & Alpaydin, 1997] which is the main concern of this chapter. In such a system, all the patterns to be classified first go through a first stage; those patterns that are classified with confidence score higher than a certain threshold leave the system with the labels given to them by the first stage. The patterns that are classified with confidence scores lower than the threshold are rejected to the second stage. In the same manner, the patterns pass through different stages until they reach the powerful last stage that does not reject any patterns. Figure 1 illustrates this idea.

The idea of classification cascades has been well-known for long time but has not attracted much attention in spite of its practical importance [kuncheva , 2004]. Recently, and since the prominent work of Viola and Jones [Viola & Jones, 2001], the idea of cascade has been attracting considerable attention in the context of object detection which is a rare-event classification problem. To avoid any confusion, we will call the cascades used in the context of object detection "detection cascades" while we will call the cascades used in regular classification problems "classification cascades" in which we are interested in this chapter.

There are many works in the literature that try to build a cascade using some heuristics and ad-hoc procedures [Kanyank & Alpaydin, 1997, Pudil et al. 1992, Giusti et al., 1999, Gorgevik & Cakmakov, 2004, Ferri et al., 2004]. Some automatic approaches of building classification cascades consider the problem as an optimization problem and might be attacked using various optimization techniques (e.g. particle swarm [Oliveira et al., 2005], and simulated annealing [Chellapilla et al., 2006a]). The most elegant automatic approach was that of Chellapilla et al. [Chellapilla et al., 2006b] using Depth-First search. However, the algorithm is of complexity $O(Q^N)$, where Q is a variable suggested to be 32 by [Chellapilla et al., 2006b]. This means that the algorithm is very slow and not scalable to large values of N.

In this chapter, we present an algorithm to automatically generate classification cascades given a set of N classifiers and a powerful classifier with satisfactory accuracy. The algorithm is of complexity $O(N^2)$ which means it is fast and scalable to large values of N.

The remaining of this chapter is organized as follows. Section 2 formulates and states our problem. In section 3, we describe our proposed algorithm. Section 4 presents an experimental validation of our proposed algorithm. And in section 5 we conclude.

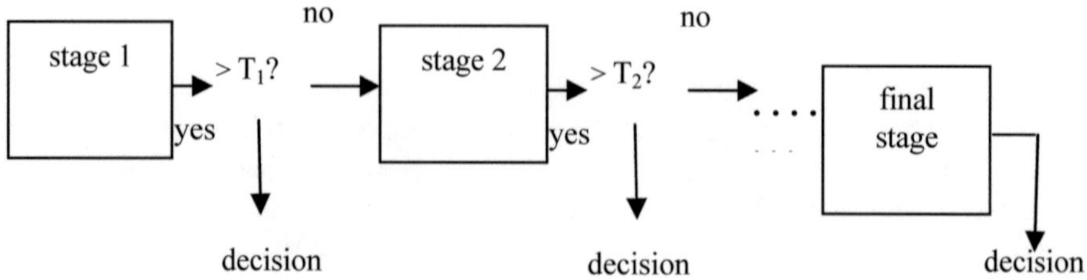

Fig. 1. Typical classification cascade system.

2. Problem statement

We first assume that we have a pool of classifiers of different complexities and accuracies to be candidate members of the cascade. Note that we cannot use all the classifiers of the pool in the cascade. This is because not all cascades are efficient. You may find a cascade that is more complex than the powerful classifier; using a cascade like this is worthless. Also, one subset of classifiers could be better than other subsets. Furthermore, certain ordering of the classifiers in a cascade could be more efficient than other orderings. Hence, we are in need of an algorithm that selects the most efficient *ordered* subset of classifiers.

Our problem could then be formulated as follows. Given a classifier that is powerful and complex and given a pool of classifiers of different complexities and accuracies, we need to select the optimal (or near optimal) ordered subset that if put in a cascade structure gives an accuracy not less than that of the optimal case with the lowest complexity possible.
Now we are going to present some notations that will help presenting our algorithms formally. We denote an unordered set by boldface character surrounded by curly braces, and its elements by the same character but in italics and subscripted by numbers (e.g. $A_2, A_1, A_5, ... \in \{\mathbf{A}\}$). An ordered set (or an array) is denoted by just a boldface character, and is elements by the same character but in italics and subscripted by numbers (e.g. $\mathbf{A} = [A_3\ A_1\ ...]$). Note that the subscripts of an ordered or unordered set are arbitrary and hold no ordering significance. We enumerate the elements of an unordered set {**A**} as follows $\{\mathbf{A}\} = \{A_3, A_1, ...\}$ and the elements of the ordered set **A** as follows $\mathbf{A} = [A_4\ A_2\ ...]$. **C**=[**A B**] means that the ordered set **C** is a concatenation of the two ordered sets **A** and **B**. {**B**}={**A**}-A_i that the unordered set **B** contains all the elements of the unordered set **B** except the element A_i; and if $A_i \notin \mathbf{A}$, then {**B**}={**A**}. In this chapter we will represent a cascade by an ordered set whose elements are the classification stages ordered in the set from left to right. The function *complexity*(**A**) returns the complexity of the cascade represented by array **A** which is estimated using a validation set.

3. A greedy algorithm

We start with partitioning the dataset available for training and testing the system into 3 parts: training set, validation set, and test set. The training set is used for training the available classifier in the pool. The validation set is used by the algorithm that is going to be described in this section to build the cascade. The test set is used to test the performance of the overall system.
We first assume that the powerful classifier we use has accuracy more than any classifier in the pool of classifiers we generated. Then to build a cascade that has accuracy not less than that of the powerful classifier, we should put the powerful classifier as the final stage; hence, we will denote it S_F. The algorithm we propose then has now two jobs: To select an ordered subset of classifiers from the pool to serve as stages of the cascade before S_F and to set the thresholds of the stages. Our algorithm, hence, has two steps presented below.

3.1 Step 1: Set the Thresholds

In our problem formulation, we stated that we do not want to get accuracy less than that of S_F. In a classification cascade, the only source of additional errors to that of S_F is that of the classifiers in the cascade other than S_F. To avoid such source of error, we might adjust the thresholds of all the candidate classifiers in the pool to have almost zero errors. This makes any cascade built using the pool have also zero additional errors to that of S_F. While this procedure will lead to no additional errors to be committed by the cascade, it would make us use too tough thresholds. Tough thresholds make the classifiers reject most of the patterns to the next more complex stages, hence, to lose good opportunities of complexity reduction. Adjusting the errors to give zero errors for different cascade stages is actually unnecessarily too tough a procedure. We actually can let different classifiers commit some errors without losing any overall accuracy. This is because there are some very elusive patterns that get falsely classified by weak classifiers with high confidence scores. If we put in mind not to commit any errors by any classifier in the pool, such illusive patterns will lead us to choose very high thresholds. Fortunately, most of these patterns could be ignored (not accounted as being errors) as they are most likely falsely classified by S_F too; and, hence, will not lead to any additional errors.

Our procedure for finding thresholds of pool classifiers will then be as follows. Using every classifier in the pool, classify the patterns of the validations set and order them according to the confidence scores they are given. Traverse these ordered patterns form the one that has been classified by the highest confidence score to the lowest. While traversing the patterns, monitor whether the patterns are correctly or falsely classified. Once you hit a pattern that is falsely classified, check whether this same pattern is falsely classified by S_F or not. If yes, then this pattern would not contribute to errors of the overall system and can be safely ignored, and we can continue traversing the patterns. We stop when we hit a pattern that is falsely classified by the classifier under consideration but correctly classified by S_F. Then set the threshold of the classifier under consideration to be the confidence score of the pattern we stopped at. We do the same for all the classifiers in the pool to form the corresponding set of thresholds. This procedure is illustrated in Figure 2.

3.2 Step 2: Select from the Pool

Now we have a pool of classifiers (whose thresholds are set) and the final stage S_F. The most direct and optimal way to build the cascade is to try all the possible combinations of the classifiers in the pool (different number of stages with different order of stages), then selecting the one of the lowest complexity. Note that the complexity of the cascade is calculated using the validation set. While this procedure guarantees selecting the optimal cascade, it has a complexity of $O(\sum_{i=1}^{N} \frac{N!}{(N-i)!})$, where N is the number of classifiers in the pool. This makes the procedure not scalable for large values of N. Here we suggest a sequential greedy approach that selects a near-to-optimal cascade that has a complexity of $O(N^2)$.

We start with the powerful classifier S_F. This is the best *single-stage* system that achieves our constraint of having accuracy not less than S_F. Now we search for the best two-stage classifier. This is done simply by trying all the nodes in the pool as a first stage (the last stage will be S_F), and then selecting the one that results in least complex cascade. Now we pick this classifier out of the pool and put it as the first stage in the cascade.

After finding the best two-stage system, we search for the best three-stage system. We assume that the best three-stage system will have the same first stage as in the best two-stage system calculated in the previous iteration. Now we try every classifier in the pool (except the one picked out as a first stage) as a second stage in a three stage system. We pick the one resulting in the least complex three-stage cascade. If this least complex three-stage cascade is more complex than the previously selected two-stage cascade, then the selected two-stage cascade is declared to be the best cascade and the algorithm stops. Suppose that we found a three-stage system that is better than the two-stage system we previously selected, we then proceed to find the best four-stage cascade. We assume that the best four-stage cascade will have the first two stages of the previously selected three-stage cascade as first and second stages. Now we want to select the third stage from the pool (the fourth stage will be S_F). We select the classifier that results in the least complex cascade as described above. And the process continues until the pool is empty or until we select a cascade that is more complex than a previously selected one. Figure 3 shows this procedure through an example. Algorithm 1 presents it formally.

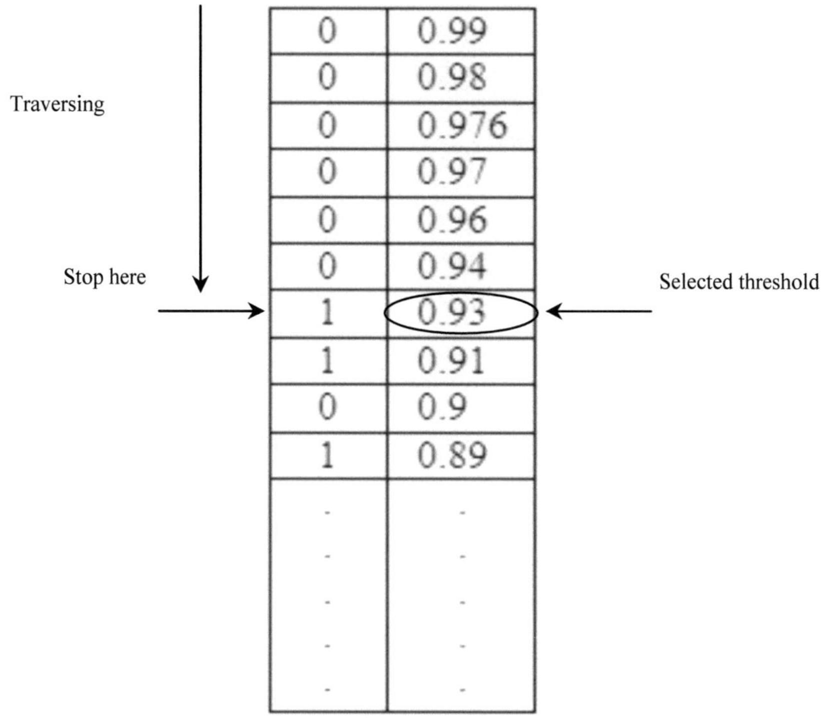

Fig. 2. A hypothetical example illustrating threshold selection process. Each row represents a different pattern of the validation set. The left entry of each record is labeled '1' if a classification error is committed while the pattern is correctly classified by the most powerful classifier S_F. The right entry of each record is the top decision score of the corresponding pattern. The patterns are ordered according to the decision score. This process is done for every classifier in the pool to get the corresponding set of thresholds.

Algorithm 1

```
// we will denote the pool of classifiers by the
//unordered set {S_p},
// and the final stage by S_F.
// the classifiers of {S_p} have arbitrary numbering
// S_c denotes the cascade selected so far
```

Inputs
A pool of classifiers $\{\mathbf{S}_p\}$ and a powerful classifier S_F
Outputs
A cascade S_c.
Initialize
best_complexity = *complexity*([S_F]).
Sc=[]. //an empty array
Begin
while (there are classifiers left in $\{\mathbf{S}_p\}$)
{

$$k = \arg\min_{i \forall S_i \in \{\mathbf{S}_P\}} \{complexity([\mathbf{S}_c \quad S_i \quad S_F])\}$$

$$new\_complexity =$$
$$complexity([\mathbf{S}_c \quad S_k \quad S_F]).$$

if(*new_complexity* ≥ *best_complexity*)
{
$\mathbf{S}_c = [\mathbf{S}_c\ S_F]$.
Terminate.
}
else
{
$\mathbf{S}_c = [\mathbf{S}_c\ S_k\ S_F]$.
$\{\mathbf{S}_p\} = \{\mathbf{S}_p\} - S_k$.
best_complexity = *new_complexity*.
}
}
$\mathbf{S}_c = [\mathbf{S}_c\ S_F]$.
Terminate.

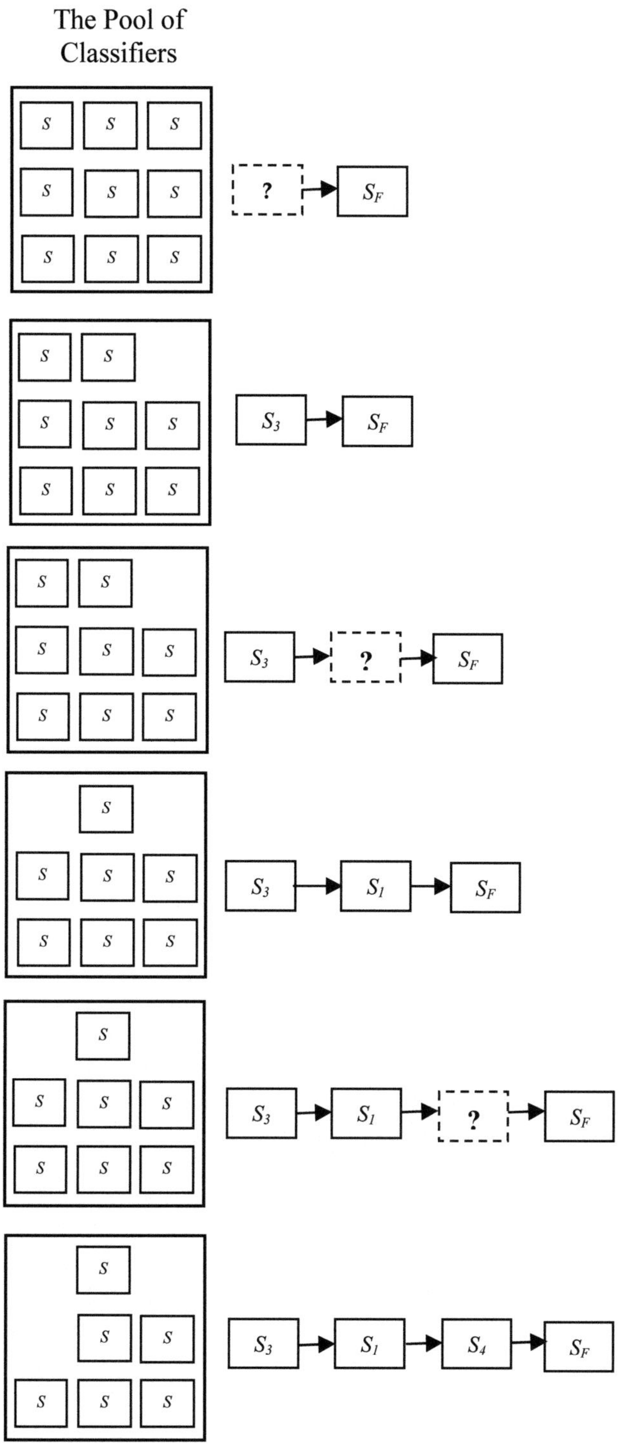

Fig. 3. An example of the process of selecting classifiers from the pool to form the cascade.

4. Experiments

The dataset we used in our experiments is the MNIST [LeCun et al, 1998]. The MNIST has a total of 70,000 digits which we partitioned into 3 parts: i) a training set, which is composed of 50,000 digits and used for training the classifiers, ii) a validation set, which is composed of 10,000 digits used for optimizing the cascade system, and iii) a test set, which is used for final testing of the cascade. We then transformed each digit image of all sets into 200-element feature vector using gradient feature extraction technique [Liu et al. 2003].

We trained 48 different classifiers with different complexities and accuracies on the training set. The strongest of those 48 classifiers has been chosen to be S_F and the remaining 47 classifiers now represent the pool of classifiers (N = 47). Three different types of classifiers are used: one-layer neural network (1-NN or linear classifier), two-layer neural network (2-NN), and SVM. For each classifier type, we generated a number of classifiers of different structures. First we ranked all 200 gradient feature elements according to their importance using ReliefF feature ranking technique [Kononenko, 1994]. Then, for 1-NN network, we generated a classifier that has as the most important 25 feature elements as input, and then another one with the most important 50 feature elements, then 75, an so on, till we finally generated a classifier with all the 200 feature elements. Hence, we have 8 different 1-NN classifiers. The same was done for SVM; hence, we have additional 8 different classifiers. This also was done for 2-NN, but for each number of inputs, we generated a classifier with different number of hidden units: 50, 100 150, and 200. Hence, we have 8 1-NN classifiers, 8 SVMs, and 8×4 2-NN classifier; so, we have a total of 48 classifiers of different structure and accuracies. We chose the most powerful classifier S_F to be the SVM classifier with 200 features as it gained the highest accuracy on the validation set. We measured the complexity of a certain classifier as the number of floating point operations (flops) [Ridder, 2002] it needs to classify one pattern divided by the number of flops the least complex classifier we have generated (that is, the 1-NN with 25 inputs) needs to classify one pattern. That is the complexity of 1-NN of 25 inputs is 1; and it was found that S_F has a complexity 5638.

We applied our greedy algorithm on the generated classifiers. Table 1 shows complexities and errors of S_F and complexities and errors of the cascade built using our greedy algorithm. It is obvious that the complexity is reduced considerably while not sacrificing the accuracy. We would like to note here that not all the 47 classifiers of the pool are selected to be members of the cascade. As shown in Figure 4, the cascade built using our algorithm has only 9 stages (including S_F). The advantage of using a large pool of classifiers is then to give a large room of possible cascades for the algorithm to choose from.

Now to show that our algorithm is near optimal, we compare it with the optimal case which is the exhaustive search we discussed in section 3.2. The exhaustive search has an exponential complexity in N (number of classifier in the pool, which is 47 in our case). Hence, we cannot apply the exhaustive search algorithm on all the 47 classifiers of the pool. We then selected 5 classifiers randomly and applied both the exhaustive and the greedy algorithms on them. We repeated this 15 times and calculated the average of the resulting errors and complexities (see Table 2). Table 2 shows that our algorithm achieves a reduction in complexity that is near to the optimal case. Furthermore, comparing Table 1 and Table 2 shows that applying the algorithm on whole the 47 classifiers has superior results than the case of using 5 classifiers. This shows that using more classifiers in the pool gives more opportunity for reducing the complexity. This fact favors algorithms that are scalable for large values of N like the one represented in this chapter.

5. Conclusion

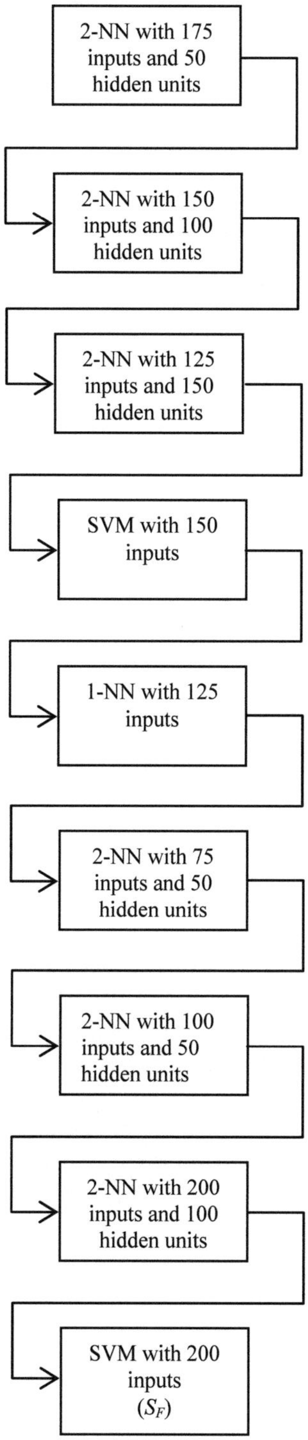

Fig. 4. The build cascade using the proposed algorithm.

In this chapter, we have proposed an algorithm to automatically generate classification cascades. The algorithm is fast and scalable. Experiments showed that our algorithm is efficient and builds classification cascades that substantially reduce the overall system complexity while preserving the accuracy.

	Complexity	Error	# of stages
S_F only	5638	66	1
Cascade built using our greedy algorithm	239.9	67	9

Table 1. The performance of our algorithm when given all the generated classifiers as compared to using S_F only in terms of errors and complexity (both are calculated using the test set)

	Avgerage Complexity	Avgerage Error	Average # of stages
SF only	5638	66	1
Cascade built using our greedy algorithm	480.9	66.9	5.2
Cascade built using exhaustive search	440.7	67.3	5.4

Table 2. The performance of our algorithm when given pools of randomly selected 5 classifiers (plus S_F) as compared to using S_F only and using the optimal procedure (exhaustive search) in terms of average errors and average complexity (calculated using the test set).

6. References

Chellapilla, K., M. Shilman, P. Simard, (2006a) "Combining Multiple Classifiers for Faster Optical Character Recognition", DAS, pp. 358-367.

Chellapilla, K.; Shilman, M. , Simard, P., (2006b), "Optimally Combining a Cascade of Classifiers", SPIE Document Recognition and Retrieval (DRR).

Ferri, C.; Flach, P. ,and Hernandez-Orallo, J., (2004) "Delegating classifiers," Proceedings of 21st International Conference on Machine Learning, pp. 37.

Giusti, N.; Masulli, F. and Sperduti, A. (2002), "Theoretical and experimental analysis of a two-stage system for classification," IEEE TPAMI, vol. 24, no. 7, pp. 893-904.

Gorgevik, D.& Cakmakov, D. (2004), "An efficient three-stage classifier for handwritten digit recognition", ICPR'04, pp. 1051-4651.

Kononenko, I. (1994) "Estimating attributes: analysis and extensions of Relief," ECML-94, pp. 171–182.

Kaynak, C. & Alpaydin, E. (1997), "Multistage classification by cascaded classifiers," Proceedings of 1997 IEEE international symposium on Intelligent Control, pp. 95-100.

Kuncheva, L., (2004), *Combining Pattern Classifiers*, Wiley-Interscience.

LeCun, Y.; Bottou, L. Bengio, Y. and Haffner, P. (1998), "Gradient-Based Learning Applied to Document Recognition", Proceedings of the IEEE, vol. 86 no. 11, pp. 2278-2324.

Liu, C.; Nakashima, K. Sako, Fujisawa, H. H., (2003), "Handwritten digit recognition: benchmarking of state-of-the-art techniques," Pattern Recognition, vol. 36, pp. 2271 - 2285.

Oliveira, L.; Britto, A., Sabourin, R. (2005), "Optimizing class-related thresholds with particle swarm optimization", IJCNN, vol. 3, pp. 1511- 1516.

Pudil, P.; Novovicova, J. , Blaha, S., Kittler, J., (1992), "Multistage pattern recognition with reject option," 11th IAPR, pp. 92-95.

Rahman, A. & Fairhurst, M,. (1999), "Serial combination of multiple experts: a unified evaluation," Pattern Analysis and Applications, vol. 2, no. 4, pp. 292-311.

Ridder, D.; Pekalska, E., Duin, R. (2002), "The economics of classification: error vs. complexity", The 16th International Conference on Pattern Recognition, pp. 244-247.

Viola, P. & M. Jones, (2001), "Rapid object detection using a boosted cascade of simple features", ICPR, vol 1., pp. 511-518.

Neural Network Multi Layer Perceptron Modeling For Surface Quality Prediction in Laser Machining

Sivarao[1], Peter Brevern[2], N.S.M. El-Tayeb[2] and V.C.Vengkatesh[2]
[1]Universiti Teknikal Malaysia Melaka, [2]Multimedia University
Malaysia

1. Abstract

Uncertainty is inevitable in problem solving and decision making. One way to reduce it is by seeking the advice of an expert in related field. On the other hand, when we use computers to reduce uncertainty, the computer itself can become an expert in a specific field through a variety of methods. One such method is machine learning, which involves using a computer algorithm to capture hidden knowledge from data. The researchers conducted the prediction of laser machining quality, namely surface roughness with seven significant parameters to obtain singleton output using machine learning techniques based on Quick Back Propagation Algorithm. In this research, we investigated a problem solving scenario for a metal cutting industry which faces some problems in determining the end product quality of Manganese Molybdenum (Mn-Mo) pressure vessel plates. We considered several real life machining scenarios with some expert knowledge input and machine technology features. The input variables are the design parameters which have been selected after a critical parametric investigation of 14 process parameters available on the machine. The elimination of non-significant parameters out of 14 total parameters were carried out by single factor and interaction factor investigation through design of experiment (DOE) analysis. Total number of 128 experiments was conducted based on 2k factorial design. This large search space poses a challenge for both human experts and machine learning algorithms in achieving the objectives of the industry to reduce the cost of manufacturing by enabling the off hand prediction of laser cut quality and further increase the production rate and quality.

2. Introduction

Reliability and predictability of quality is most important in the choice of precision manufacturing, particularly with the ever increasing move towards "unmanned" machining operations due to the rapid automation of manufacturing industry. The ability to predict, both accurately and effectively, the surface quality during a machining operation will ultimately improve the machining of engineering components, thus reducing significantly the huge machining cost, which can sometimes be as high as 70% of the overall manufacturing cost due to the rework activities (Ezugwu et al., 1995). Recent research activities in artificial neural network (ANN) have shown that ANN has powerful pattern classification and pattern recognition capabilities. ANNs are well suited for problems whose solutions require knowledge that is difficult to specify but for which there are enough data or observations. They learn from examples (training data) and capture subtle functional relationships among the data even if the underlying relationships are unknown or hard to describe. ANN is universal functional approximator (Kuo, 1998). It has been proven that properly designed network can approximate any continuous function to any desired accuracy by many researchers. One has presented wear prediction of polymer-matrix composites, where the ANN was used to calculate the experimental database for short fiber reinforced polymide 4.6 composites, the specific wear rate, frictional coefficient and also some other mechanical properties (Jiang, 2007) . Wilkinson, P. et al. represented an application of an artificial neural network to classify tool wear states in face milling. The input features were derived from measurements of acoustic emission during machining and topography of the machined surfaces. Five input features were applied to the back-propagating neural network to predict a wear state of light, medium or heavy wear (Wilkinson et al., 1999). Neural network capability in developing a reliable method to predict flank wear during a turning process with the input numeric of tool geometry, depth of cut, cutting speed, federate, workpiece properties, cutting fluid (Lee et al., 1996). The cutting force model for self-propelled rotary tool (SPRT) cutting force prediction using artificial neural networks (ANN) has been described in detail. The inputs to the model consist of cutting velocity, feed rate, depth of cut and tool inclination angle, while the outputs are composed of thrust force F_x, radial force F_y and main cutting force, F_z (Hao et al., 2006). The presentation of how to develop a robust approach for prediction of residual stress profile in hard turning for different combinations of material properties, cutting tool geometries and cutting conditions has been carried out (Umbrello et al., 2007). An optoelectronic sensor system has been used in conjunction with a multilayered neural network to predict the flank wear of the cutting tool without interrupting the machining process (Choudhury et al., 1999). Comparison between several architectures of the multi-layer feed-forward neural network with a back propagation training algorithm for tool condition monitoring (TCM) of twist drill wear has also been carried out (Abu-Mahfouz, 2003). Modelling of overcut with neural network analysis for electrochemical surface grinding (ECG) processes. 72 tests were carried out and a back-propagation neural network was trained using the first replicate of the experimental data set. Then, the trained network was tested to be well behaved (Ilhan & Akbay, 1994). A trained multi-layer perceptron to predict spot-weld quality from electrical process data has been presented. This work has centred on the spot-welding and weld-welding of aluminium alloys. Electrical data was sampled in real-time during the spot welding process and the data was processed off-line to extract up to 270 features from each weld. In this case, a multi-layer perceptron, MLP was used to predict output for unseen inputs (Osman et al., 1994).

3. Artificial Neural Network

In this research, the ANN model design follows a stepwise method, progressively adding and comparing possible inputs to output to develop the model. A neural network model

was selected for this work over other techniques because of its ability to model non-linear system, robustness to noisy data, and generic modeling capability. The ANN models in this research were developed, trained, and tested with the Intelligent Neural System to an optimized and satisfactory level of correlation and R-square values before selecting the network for final prediction. Inputs to the neural networks were the numeric of significant parameters which affects the quality of the machining surface. To make the process more accurate and consistent, modeling & simulation is the powerful tool besides experimental exploration of; gas pressure, cutting speed, focal distance (FD), stand of distance (SOD), laser power, frequency and duty cycle. In this prediction modeling, the observed numerical of extreme empirical investigations was used. Since the prediction of the cut quality is our primary aim, the ANN models were initially optimized based on training and testing over all the observed data sets. This methodology was adopted in large scale to ensure the results are met to the satisfactory level of the sponsored industry.
The complete experimental data of 128 sets has been used to train the network. The learning process was stopped after 500 iterations. The number of neurons and layers are calculated automatically based on the network training error based on QBPA algorithm with 7-13-1 architecture. The first step of the calculation is to normalize all the raw input data to values between 3 and 40 as shown in the equation (1).

$$x_i = \frac{40}{d_{\max} - d_{\min}}(d_i - d_{\min}) + 3 \tag{1}$$

The d_{max} and d_{min} are the maximum and minimum inputs and d_i is i^{th} input. Input of ith neuron on hidden layer I_{yi}, calculated by,

$$I_{yi} = \sum_{i=1}^{M} w_{xy} x_i \tag{2}$$

M is number of neurons in input layer and w_{xy} is numerical weight value of the connection between the two neurons. x_i is i^{th} normalized output from the input layer. The output of the ith neuron on hidden layer y_i is to be calculated by applying an activation function to the summed input of that neuron. The output of ith neuron on hidden layer then appear as,

$$y_i = f(I_{yi}) = \frac{1}{1 + e^{-s(I_{yi})}} \tag{3}$$

The s is the slope of the sigmoid function and the values received by the output layer I_z are outputs of the hidden and input layers.

$$Izi = \sum_{i=1}^{M} w_{xz} x_i + \sum_{i=1}^{N} w_{yz} y_i \tag{4}$$

M and N are the numbers of neurons in the input and hidden layers. w_{xz} and w_{yz} are corresponding weights from the input to the output layer and from hidden layer to output layer. The actual output in the output layer is calculated by applying the same sigmoid function as applied for hidden layer.

$$z_i = f(I_{zi}) \tag{5}$$

Error between the desired and actual output in the output layer is given by

$$\delta_{zi} = f^{'}(I_{zi})(T_i - Z_i) \tag{6}$$

Where, T_i is the ith training input to the neuron and $f^{'}$ is the derivative of the sigmoid function. For each neuron on the hidden layer, the error, δ_{yi} is

$$\delta_{yi} = f(I_{yi})\sum_{i=1}^{L}\delta_{zi}w_{yz} \tag{7}$$

Where, the L is number of neurons in the output layer.

4. Methodology

Critical consideration has been taken in designing the methodology of the entire research work. After a detail discussion and investigation with machining experts of the industry together with statistical consideration, the seven most-significant parameters were considered as design parameters in developing the model. The critical methodology of the entire research is shown in figure 1.

5. Laser Machining

Laser beams are used extensively for a variety of material-removal applications because they provide highly concentrated energy sources that can be easily transmitted and manipulated. Micro-mechanical structures are becoming more common with the ever increasing demand for new micro-fabrication tools. As feature sizes become smaller and smaller, i.e. typically below 100 µm, conventional mechanical approaches to cutting, drilling and shaping materials may be replaced with photon or particle beam techniques that enable geometric features as small as laser wavelengths (smaller than a micrometer) to be created with a high degree of precision and repeatability. In addition, laser fabrication processes are non-contact, dry, and clean operations that enable ease of automation (Jimin et al., 2007). The nonlinear behavior of the laser-material interactions plays a significant role in forming the final surface profile and the resultant geometry of the machined micro-features. The need to precisely control a large number of parameters, often with random components, makes the task of improving the process performance very difficult (Basem et al., 2002).

Moreover, modeling all these factors using conventional, analytical and numerical methods poses a substantial challenge. In practice, the operator has to perform a number of experiments to set the appropriate process control parameters related to the laser apparatus, motion control system, and workpiece material. This trial-and-error approach is costly and time consuming especially for a small batch production or prototyping, and does not ensure near optimality with a given set of process conditions and manufacturing objectives. Laser cutting is used in precision industries as it has the ability to cut complex profiles featuring extra ordinary shapes, corners, slots, and holes with high degree of repeatability and small region of heat affected zone (HAZ).

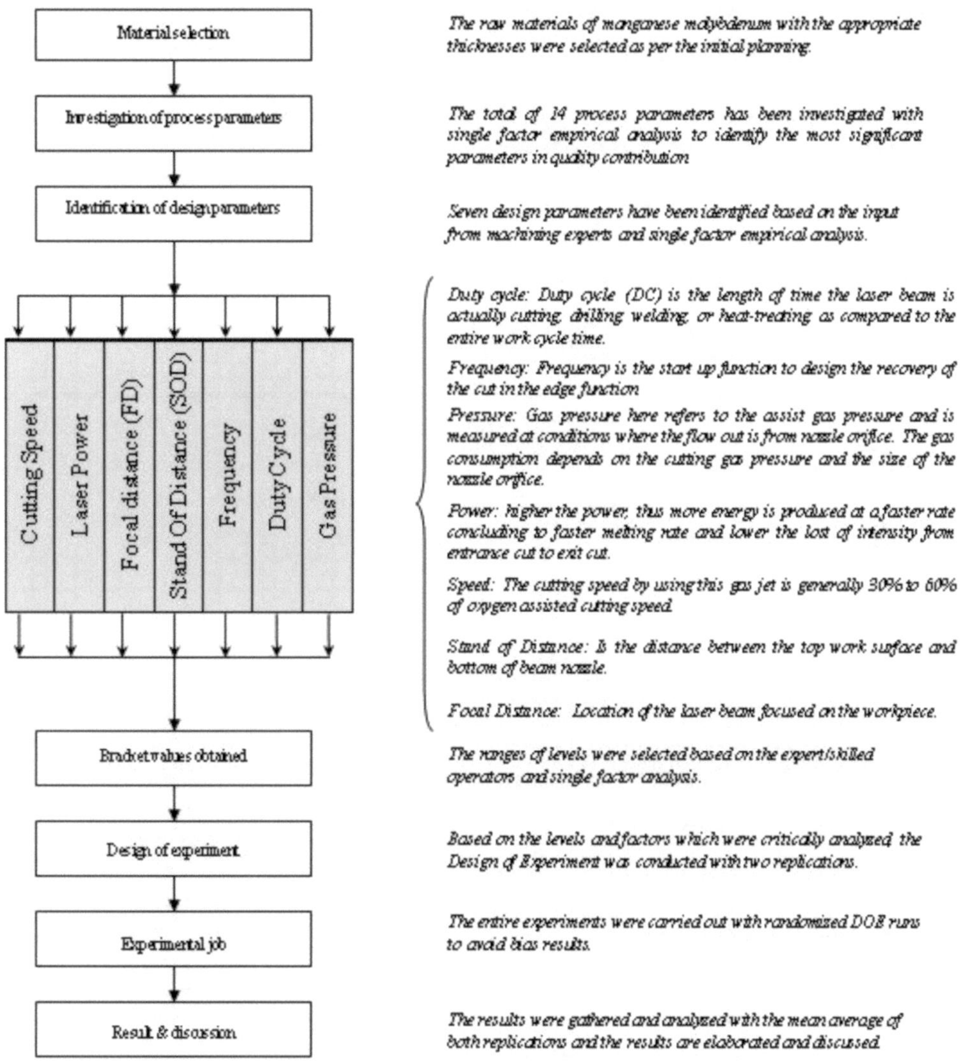

Fig. 1. Research methodology

In laser machining, surface roughness is one of the most important quality evaluation factors. The surface roughness is generally dependent upon the properties of the work material being cut, workpiece thickness, focal length, stand of distance, gas pressure, cutting speed, etc. including the type of cutting gas. Besides the investigation of CO_2 laser cutting parameters investigations are also being studied to further understand the relationship between the gas and the cutting parameters to obtain a good cutting quality.

6. Experimental Setup and Procedure

This scientific investigation is an industry sponsored project in which the kerf width is to be predicted by ANN model to reduce the manufacturing cost and further increase the quality of the end product. In this experiment, seven input parameters were controlled, namely; stand off distance, focal distance, gas pressure, power, cutting speed, frequency and duty cycle. A nozzle diameter of 0.5 mm was used with focused beam diameter of 0.25 mm. Material used in this experiment is grade B, Manganese-Molybdenum pressure vessel plate, with a nominal gauge thickness of 5.0 mm and Tensile Strength of 690 MPa. The plate was cut to the dimension about 1.2 meter length and 0.7 meter width. A cut length of 20mm performed over all the 128 profiles on the plate. Total of 128 experiments have been conducted based on the DOE matrix. All the experimental data sets and the objective function have been trained to develop a sound predictive model. A schematic view of laser machining experimental setup is shown in figure 2.

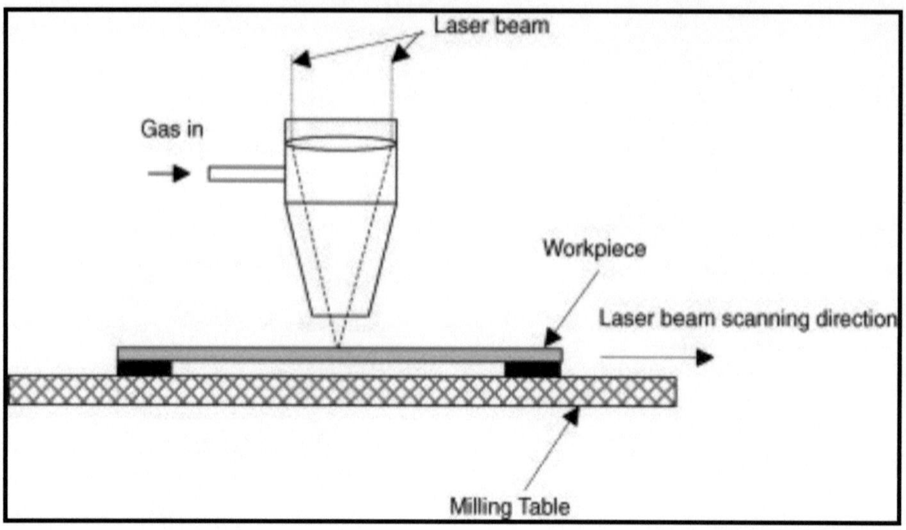

Fig. 2. Schematic of laser machining

7. Experimental Parameters, Machines and Equipments

The workpiece materials, design parameters, laser machine type and its capability together with the entire equipments / apparatus used in this research activity are listed on coming pages. The standards used in data collection and interpretation also stated.

Work Material:

- DIN 17155 HII standard
- 5mm Manganese-Molybdenum
- Grade: B
- Tensile Strength: 550-690 MPa

Controllable parameters:

Variables	Level	
	Low	High
Power (Watt)	2500	2800
Cutting speed (mm/min)	800	1200
Frequency (Hz)	800	1000
S.O.D (mm)	1	1.5
F.D (mm)	0	1
Pressure (Bar)	0.7	1
Duty Cycle (%)	40	80

Laser machine:

- Model: Helius Hybrid 2514 CO_2 Laser Cutting Machine
- Controller: FANUC Series 160 i-L
- Maximum capacity: 4 kW
- Laser source that use to create laser beam is CO_2 gas. The real ingredient is mixture of N_2 (55%), He (40%) & CO_2 (5%) with purity 99.995%.
- Pressure = Max 3 bar

Surf tester:

- Mitutoyo Surftest SJ301
- Sampling length range (0.8 ~ 8)

Data collection and interpretations:

- All the experimental materials, procedures, data collections, analysis, etc. are conducted as per the standard recommendations of 'Laser Cutting of Metallic Materials' German Standard, DIN 2310-5.

- The DIN EN ISO 9013:2000 is referred as it gives the terminological definitions and describes criteria for evaluating the quality of cutting surfaces, quality classifications and dimensional tolerances. It applies in the case of laser beam cuts from material thickness of between 0.5mm and 40mm.

8. Result and Discussion

A quick back-propagation algorithm was employed for a multi-layered perceptron. This has several advantages over the standard BP in that it is much faster in terms of rate of learning and has the ability of adjusting the learning rate and momentum term automatically. Seven input nodes (corresponding to power, speed, pressure, focal distance, stand of distance, frequency, duty cycle) and single output node (corresponding to surface roughness) were used. The best ANN architecture was selected based on the heuristic search and the selected intuitively based on the best fitness value (6.804306) with test error of 0.1469 as shown in table 1 which were developed based on the data live training line as shown in figure 3. The best developed 7-13-1 architecture with single hidden layer is shown in figure 4. The entire data sets was trained and tested based on the Dither Randomization approach. The Quick back propagation coefficient was 1.75 with the learning rate of 0.1 for 500 iterations. The output error method was based on sum-of-square and for the output activation was logistic. The training was done with the speed of 834, 999 967 itr/sec. In precise, the result shown by the network can be considered as very much promising with the prediction error below 0.5%. From the network output, it was found of capable to predict the results of the 128 real experiments to its most accurately possible. The plot of comparative signatures (figure 5) of the trained and tested data show clearly the strength of the developed model in predicting the surface roughness for 5mm Mn-Mo plate by laser cutting. The numeric summary of these results is presented by Table 2, which indicates the network strength by means of statistical analysis, R-square and their respective correlation values.

ID	Architecture	# of Weights	Fitness	Train Error	Validation Error	Test Error	AIC
2	[7-18-1]	163	5.470586	0.133435	0.092195	0.182796	-245.25013
3	[7-11-1]	100	5.840169	0.119474	0.091359	0.171228	-380.97524
4	[7-7-1]	64	5.731579	0.120591	0.090985	0.174472	-452.15644
5	[7-15-1]	136	5.614985	0.125033	0.092011	0.178095	-304.97341
6	**[7 13 1]**	**118**	**6.804306**	**0.094149**	**0.094925**	**0.146966**	**365.9391**
7	[7-14-1]	127	5.789575	0.11389	0.107203	0.172724	-331.18766
8	[7-12-1]	109	5.740716	0.110456	0.097735	0.174194	-369.88190.

Table 1. The summarized data, which were used to support the architecture selection

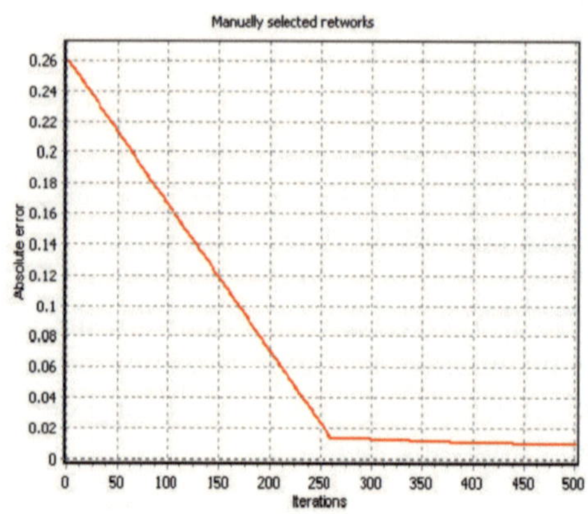

Fig. 3. Iteration vs. error characterization aritecture

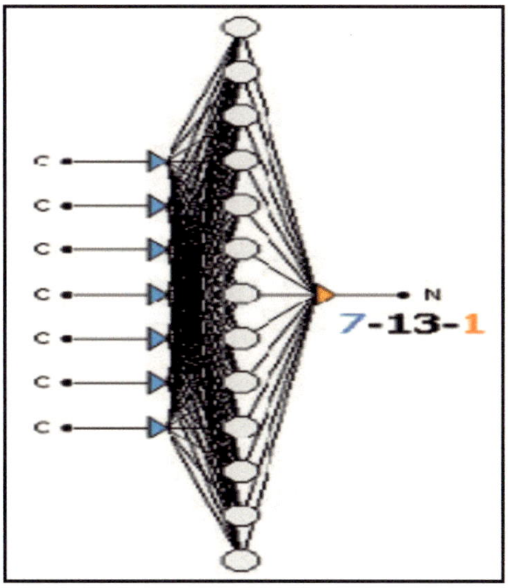

Fig. 4. The 7-13-1 architecture with 7 inputs, 1 hidden layer and singleton output

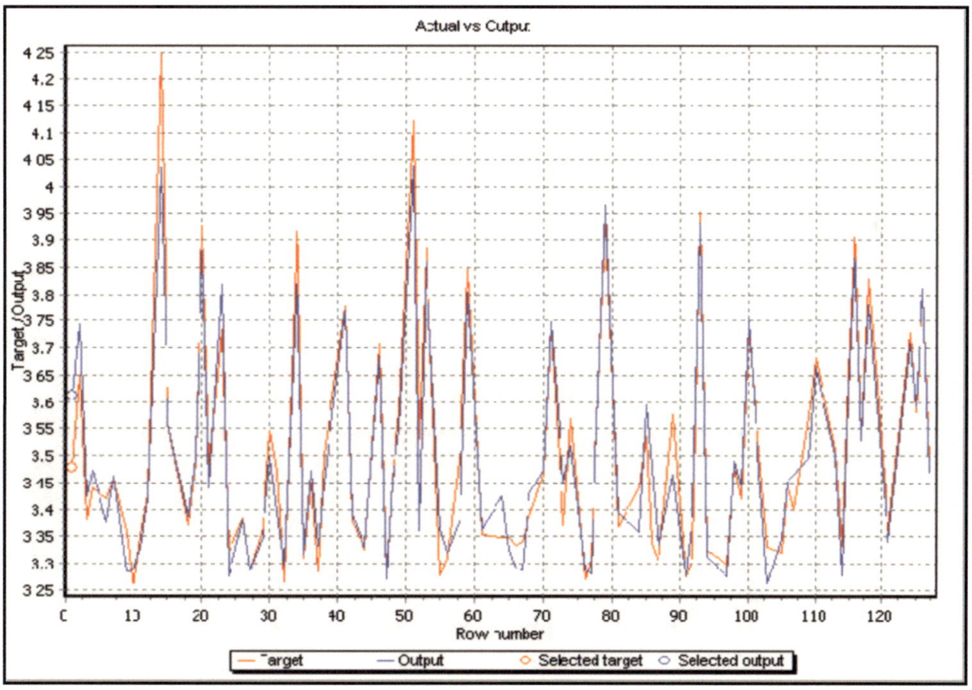

Fig. 5. The comparative signatures of the surface roughness

Summary				
	Target	Output	AE	ARE
Mean:	3.505181	3.496861	0.041733	0.011796
Std Dev:	0.214885	0.200711	0.039975	0.010916
Min:	3.25	3.263643	0.00067	0.000194
Max:	4.25	4.037391	0.216329	0.050901
Correlation: 0.964416				
R-squared: 0.917101				

Table 2. Summary of the ANN modeling - Model strength numeric

9. Acknowledgement

The authors would like to thank Mr. Khor Wong Ghee, Ir. Vijayan & Ir. Segaran, for their sincere guide, advice and expert knowledge sharing in winning this laser machining research project. The authors are also obligated to sincerely thank the top level management of Kara Power Pte. Ltd., (Malaysia) for sponsoring the entire research project including work materials and equipments.

10. References

Abu-Mahfouz, I, (2003). Drilling Wear Detection and Classification Using Vibration Signals and Artificial Neural Network. *Journal of Machine Tools and Manufacture*, Vol. 43, 707-720.

Basem F. Yousef, George K., Evgueni V. (2002). Neural network modeling and analysis of the material removal process during laser machining. *International Journal of Advanced Manufacturing Technology*, Vol. 22, 41–53.

Choudhury, S.K. et al. (1999). On-line Monitoring of Tool Wear in Turning Using a Neural Network. *Journal of Machine Tools and Manufacture*, Vol. 39, 489-504.

Ezugwu, E.O. et al. (1995). Tool-wear Prediction Using Artificial Neural Networks. *International Journal of Materials Processing Technology*, Vol 49, 255-264.

Hao, W. et al. (2006). Prediction of Cutting Force for Self-Propelled Rotary Tool Using Artificial Neural Networks. *Journal of Material Processing Technology*, Vol. 180, 23-29.

Ilhan, R.E. and Akbay, K.S. (1994). Modeling of Overcut with Neural Network Analysis for Electrochemical Surface Grinding (ECG) Processes." *International Journal of Materials Processing Technology*, Vol 38, 125-132.

Jiang, Z. et al. (2007). Prediction on Wear Properties of Polymer Composites with Artificial Neural Networks. *Journal of Composites Science and Technology*, Vol. 67, 168-176.

Jimin, C. et al. (2007). Parameter Optimization of Non-Vertical Laser Cutting. *Journal of Advance Manufacturing Technology*, Vol. 33, 469-473.

Kuo, R. J. (1988). Intelligent tool wear system through artificial neural networks and fuzzy modeling. *Journal of Artificial Intelligence in Engineering*, Vol. 5, 229 - 242.

Lee, J.H. et al. (1996). Application of Neural Network Flank Wear Prediction. *Journal of Mechanical System and Signal Processing*, Vol. 10, 265-276.

Osman, K.A. et al. (1994). Monitoring of Resistance Spot-Welding Using Multi- Layer Perceptrons." *International Journal of Advanced Manufacturing Technology,* Vol. 12, 67–73.

Umbrello, D. et al. (2007). An ANN Approach for Predicting Subsurface Residual Stresses and the Desired Cutting Conditions during Hard Turning. *Journal of Materials Processing Technology,* Vol. 189, 143-152.

Wilkinson, P. et al. (1999). Tool-Wear Prediction from Acoustic Emission and Surface Characteristics via an Artificial Neural Network. *Journal of Mechanical System and Signal Processing,* Vol. 13, 955-966.

5

Using Learning Automata to Enhance Local-Search Based SAT Solvers with Learning Capability

Ole-Christoffer Granmo and Noureddine Bouhmala
University of Agder; Vestfold University College
Norway

1. Introduction

The conflict between exploration and exploitation is a well-known problem in machine learning and other areas of artificial intelligence. Learning Automata (LA) Thathachar & Sastry (2004); Tsetlin (1973) capture the essence of this conflict, and have thus occupied researchers for over forty years. Initially, LA were used to model biological systems, however, in the last decades they have also attracted considerable interest because they can learn the optimal action when operating in unknown stochastic environments. Furthermore, they combine rapid and accurate convergence with low computational complexity.

Recent applications of LA include allocation of polling resources in web monitoring Granmo et al. (2007), allocation of limited sampling resources in binomial estimation Granmo et al. (2007), and optimization of throughput in MPLS traffic engineering Oommen et al. (2007). LA solutions have furthermore found application within combinatorial optimization problems. In Gale et al. (1990); Oommen & Ma (1988) a so-called Object Migration Automaton is used for solving the classical equipartitioning problem. An order of magnitude faster convergence is reported compared to the best known algorithms at that time. A similar approach has also been discovered for the Graph Partitioning ProblemOommen & Croix (1996). Finally, the list organization problem has successfully been addressed by LA schemes. These schemes have been found to converge to the optimal arrangement with probability arbitrary close to unity Oommen & Hansen (1987).

In this chapter we study a new application domain for LA, namely, the Satisfiability (SAT) problem. In brief, we demonstrate how the learning capability of LA can be incorporated into selected classical local-search based solvers for SAT-like problems, with the purpose of allowing improved performance by means of learning. Furthermore, we provide a detailed empirical evaluation of the resulting LA based algorithms, and we analyze the effect that the introduced learning has on the local-search based solvers.

1.1 The Satisfiability (SAT) Problem

The SAT problem was among the first problems shown to be NP complete and involves determining whether an expression in propositional logic is true in *some* model Cook (1971). Thus, solving SAT problems efficiently is crucial for inference in propositional logic. Further, other NP complete problems, such as constraint satisfaction and graph coloring, can be encoded as

SAT problems. Indeed, a large number of problems that occur in knowledge-representation, learning, VLSI-design, and other areas of artificial intelligence, are essentially SAT problems. It is accordingly the case that SAT solver improvements will have a direct impact in all of these areas.

Most SAT solvers use a Conjunctive Normal Form (CNF) representation of propositional logic expressions. In CNF, an expression in propositional logic is represented as a conjunction of *clauses*, with each clause being a disjunction of *literals*, and a literal being a *Boolean variable* or its negation. For example, the expression $P \vee \bar{Q}$ consists of one *single* clause, containing the two literals P and $\bar{Q}$. P is simply a Boolean variable and $\bar{Q}$ denotes the negation of the Boolean variable Q. Thus, according to propositional logic, the expression $P \vee \bar{Q}$ becomes ***True*** if either P is ***True*** or Q is ***False***.

More formally, a SAT problem can be defined as follows. A propositional expression $\Phi = \bigwedge_{j=1}^{m} C_j$ with m clauses and n Boolean variables is given. Each Boolean variable, $x_i, i \in \{1, \ldots, n\}$, takes one of the two values, ***True*** or ***False***. Each clause $C_j, j \in \{1, \ldots, m\}$, in turn, is a disjunction of Boolean variables and has the form:

$$C_j = \left(\bigvee_{k \in I_j} x_k \right) \vee \left(\bigvee_{l \in \bar{I}_j} \bar{x}_l \right),$$

where $I_j, \bar{I}_j \subseteq \{1, ...n\}, I \cap \bar{I}_j = \emptyset$, and $\bar{x}_i$ denotes the negation of x_i.

The task is to determine whether there exists an assignment of truth values to the variables under which Φ evaluates to ***True***. Such an assignment, if it exists, is called a *satisfying assignment* for Φ, and Φ is called satisfiable. Otherwise, Φ is said to be unsatisfiable. Note that since we have two choices for each of the n Boolean variables, the size of the search space S becomes $|S| = 2^n$. That is, the size of the search space grows exponentially with the number of variables.

1.2 Chapter Contributions

Among the simplest and most effective algorithms for solving SAT problems are local-search based algorithms that mix greedy hill-climbing (exploitation) with random non-greedy steps (exploration). This chapter demonstrates how the greedy and random components of such local-search algorithms can be enhanced with LA-based stochastic learning. We will use both pure Random Walk as well as the well-known GSAT algorithm Selman et al. (1994), combined with Random Walk, as demonstration algorithms. The LA enhancements are designed so that the actions that the LA chose initially mimic the behavior of GSAT/Random Walk. However, as the LA explicitly interact with the SAT problem at hand, they learn the effect of the actions that are chosen, which allows the LA to gradually and dynamically shift from random exploration to goal-directed exploitation.

We finally provide a detailed comparative analysis of the new LA based algorithms' performance, showing the effect that the introduced stochastic learning has on the enhanced local-search based algorithms. The benchmark set used contains randomized and structured problems from various domains, including SAT-encoded Bounded Model Checking Problems, Logistics Problems, and Block World Planning Problems.

1.3 Chapter Organization

The chapter is organized as follows. In section 2 we provide a brief overview of selected algorithms for the SAT problem. Furthermore, we take a closer look at the Random Walk and GSAT with Random Walk algorithms, before we in section 3 explain how these latter algorithm can be enhanced with learning capability, using the basic concepts of LA. In section 4, we report the results obtained from testing the resulting new approaches on an extensive test suit of problem instances. Finally, in section 5 we present a summary of our work and provide ideas for further research.

2. Methods for SAT

The SAT has been extensively studied due to its simplicity and applicability. The simplicity of the problem coupled with its intractability makes it an ideal platform for exploring new algorithmic techniques. This has led to the development of several algorithms for solving SAT problems which usually fall into two main categories: systematic algorithms and local search algorithms. We hereby undertake the task of describing selected algorithms from these two categories.

2.1 Systematic Search Algorithms

Systematic search algorithms are guaranteed to return a satisfying truth assignment to a SAT problem if one exists and prove that it is unsatisfiable otherwise. The most popular and efficient systematic search algorithms for SAT are based on the Davis-Putnam (DP)Davis & Putnam (1960) procedure, which enumerates all possible variable assignments. This is achieved by constructing a binary search tree, which is expanded until one either finds a satisfying truth assignment or one can conclude that no such assignment exists. In each recursive call of the algorithm the propositional formula Φ is simplified by means of *unit propagation*. That is, a Boolean variable x_i is selected according to a predefined rule from the n Boolean variables available. Next, all the clauses that include the literal x_i are found, and the literal is deleted from all of these clauses. Let $\mathcal{C} = \{C_1, C_2, ...C_k\}$ be the set of $k(<= m)$ clauses obtained from this process. Similarly, let $\mathcal{D} = \{D_1, D_2, ...D_r\}$ denotes the set of $l(<= m)$ clauses obtained after deleting the literal $\bar{x}_i$ in the same manner. Moreover, let $\mathcal{R} = \{R_1, R_2, ...R_{(m-k-r)}\}$ represent the set (m-k-r) of clauses that does not include any of these two literals. Then, the original proportional formula is reduced to:

$$\Phi_{simpler} = \left(\bigwedge_{i=1}^{k} \bigwedge_{j=1}^{r} (A_i \vee B_j) \right) \bigwedge_{l=1}^{(m-r-k)} R_l.$$

Note that the propositional formula $\Phi_{simpler}$ does not contain the Boolean variable x_i because none of C, D or R does (by way of construction). If thus an empty clause is obtained, the current partial assignment cannot be extended to a satisfying one and backtracking is used to proceed with the search; if an empty formula is obtained, i.e., all clauses are satisfied, the algorithm returns a satisfying assignment. If neither of these two situations occur, an unassigned variable is chosen and the algorithm is called recursively after adding a unit clause containing this variable and its negation. If all branches are explored and no satisfying assignment has been reached, the formula is found to be unsatisfiable. For efficiency reasons, the search tree is explored in depth first search manner. Since we are only interested in whether the SAT problem is satisfiable or not, we stop as soon as the first solution is found. The size of the search tree depends on the branching rule adopted (how to select the branch variable) thereby affecting the overall efficiency of DP. This has led to the development of various improved DP variants which differ in the schemes employed to maximize the efficiency of unit propagation in their branching rules.

2.2 Stochastic Local Search Algorithms (SLS)

The above indicated class of algorithms can be very effective on specific classes of problems, however, when problems scales up, their solution effectiveness typically degrades in an exponential manner. Indeed, due to their combinatorial explosive nature, large and complex SAT problems are hard to solve using systematic search algorithms. One way to overcome the combinatorial explosion is to abandon the goal of systematically conducting a complete search.

2.2.1 Local Search as Iterative Optimization

Local search algorithms are based on what is perhaps the oldest optimization method — *trial and error*. Typically, they start with an initial assignment of truth values to variables, randomly or heuristically generated. The SAT problem can then be reformulated as an iterative optimization problem in which the goal is to minimize the number of unsatisfied clauses (the objective function). Thus, the optimum is obtained when the value of the objective function equals zero, which means that all clauses are satisfied. During each iteration, a new value assignment is selected from the "neighborhood" of the present one, by performing a "move". Most local search algorithms use a 1-flip neighborhood relation, which means that two truth value assignments are considered to be neighbors if they differ in the truth value of *only* one variable. Performing a move, then, consists of switching the present value assignment with one of the neighboring value assignments, e.g., if the neighboring one is better (as measured by the objective function). The search terminates if no better neighboring assignment can be found. Note that choosing a fruitful neighborhood, and a method for searching it, is usually guided by intuition — theoretical results that can be used as guidance are sparse.

2.2.2 GSAT, GSAT with Random Walk, and WalkSAT

One of the most popular local search algorithms for solving SAT is GSAT Selman et al. (1992). Basically, GSAT begins with a random generated assignment of truth values to variables, and then uses a so-called steepest descent heuristic to find the new variable-value assignment, i.e., the 1-flip neighbor with the *least* number of unsatisfied clauses is always selected as the new truth assignment. After a fixed number of such moves, the search is restarted from a new random assignment. The search continues until a solution is found or a fixed number of restarts have been performed. An extension of GSAT, referred to as random-walk Selman et al. (1994) has been realized with the purpose of escaping from local optima. In a random walk step, a randomly unsatisfied clause is selected. Then, one of the variables appearing in that clause is flipped, thus effectively forcing the selected clause to become satisfied. The main idea is to decide at each search step whether to perform a standard GSAT or a random-walk strategy with a probability called the *walk probability*. Another widely used variant of GSAT is the WalkSAT algorithm originally introduced in McAllester et al. (1997). It first picks randomly an unsatisfied clause, and then, in a second step, one of the variables with the lowest *break count*, appearing in the selected clause, is randomly selected. The break count of a variable is defined as the number of clauses that would be unsatisfied by flipping the chosen variable. If there exists a variable with break count equals to zero, this variable is flipped, otherwise the variable with minimal break count is selected with a certain probability. It turns out that the choice of unsatisfied clauses, combined with the randomness in the selection of variables, enable WalkSAT and GSAT with random walk to avoid local minima and to better explore the search space.

2.3 Weight-based Schemes

Recently, new algorithms Gent & T.Walsh (1993); Glover (1989); Hansen & Jaumand (1990); I.Gent & Walsh (1995) have emerged using history-based variable selection strategies in order to avoid flipping the same variable repeatedly. Apart from GSAT and its variants, several clause weighting based SLS algorithms Cha & Iwama (1995)Frank (1997) have been proposed to solve SAT problems. The key idea is to associate the clauses of the given CNF formula with weights. Although these clause weighting SLS algorithms differ in the manner clause weights should be updated (probabilistic or deterministic), they all choose to increase the weights of all the unsatisfied clauses as soon as a local minimum is encountered. In essence, clause weighting acts as a diversification mechanism rather than a way of escaping local minima. Finally, many other generic SLS algorithms have been applied to SAT. These includes techniques such as Simulated Annealing Spears (1993), Evolutionary Algorithms A.E.Eiben & van der Hauw (1997), and Greedy Randomized Adaptive Search Procedures Johnson & Trick (1996).

3. Solving SAT Problems Using Learning Automata

This section demonstrates how the greedy and random components of local-search algorithms can be enhanced with LA-based stochastic learning. We will use both pure Random Walk and GSAT with Random Walk, as demonstration algorithms. We start by defining the basic building block of our scheme — the *Learning SAT Automaton* — before we propose how several such LA can form a *game* designed to solve SAT problems.

3.1 A Learning SAT Automaton

Generally stated, a learning automaton performs a sequence of actions on an *environment*. The environment can be seen as a generic *unknown* medium that responds to each action with some sort of reward or penalty, perhaps *stochastically*. Based on the responses from the environment, the aim of the learning automaton is to find the action that minimizes the expected number of penalties received. Figure 1 illustrates the interaction between the learning automaton and the environment. Because we treat the environment as unknown, we will here only consider the definition of the learning automaton. A learning automaton can be defined in terms of a

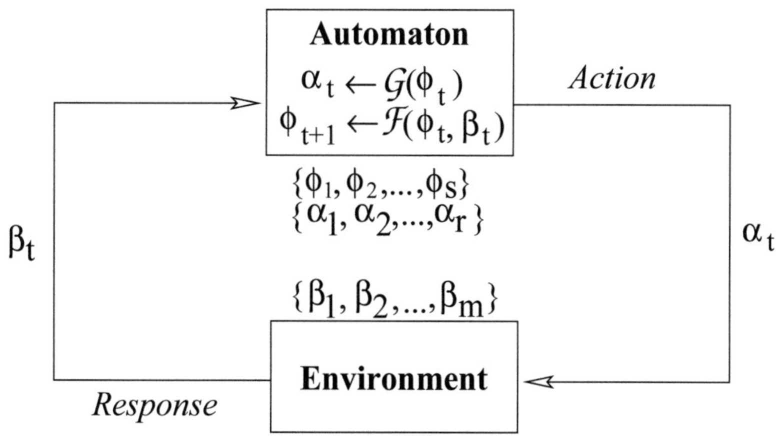

Fig. 1. A learning automaton interacting with an environment

quintuple Narendra & Thathachar (1989):

$$\{\underline{\Phi}, \underline{\alpha}, \underline{\beta}, \mathcal{F}(\cdot,\cdot), \mathcal{G}(\cdot,\cdot)\}.$$

$\underline{\Phi} = \{\phi_1, \phi_2, \ldots, \phi_s\}$ is the set of internal automaton states, $\underline{\alpha} = \{\alpha_1, \alpha_2, \ldots, \alpha_r\}$ is the set of automaton actions, and, $\underline{\beta} = \{\beta_1, \beta_2, \ldots, \beta_m\}$ is the set of inputs that can be given to the automaton. An output function $\alpha_t = \mathcal{G}[\phi_t]$ determines the next action performed by the automaton given the current automaton state. Finally, a transition function $\phi_{t+1} = \mathcal{F}[\phi_t, \beta_t]$ determines the new automaton state from:

1. The current automaton state.
2. The response of the environment to the action performed by the automaton.

Based on the above generic framework, the crucial issue is to design automata that can learn the optimal action when interacting with the environment. Several designs have been proposed in the literature, and the reader is referred to Narendra & Thathachar (1989); Thathachar & Sastry (2004) for an extensive treatment.

We now target the SAT problem, and our goal is to design a team of Learning Automata that seeks the solution of SAT problems. To achieve this goal, we build upon the work of Tsetlin and the linear two-action automaton Narendra & Thathachar (1989); Tsetlin (1973) as described in the following.

First of all, for each literal in the SAT problem that is to be solved, we construct an automaton with

- States: $\underline{\Phi} = \{-N-1, -N, \ldots, -1, 0, \ldots, N-2, N\}$.
- Actions: $\underline{\alpha} = \{\boldsymbol{True}, \boldsymbol{False}\}$.
- Inputs: $\underline{\beta} = \{\mathit{reward}, \mathit{penalty}\}$.

Figure 2 specifies the $\mathcal{G}$ and $\mathcal{F}$ matrices. The $\mathcal{G}$ matrix can be summarized as follows. If the

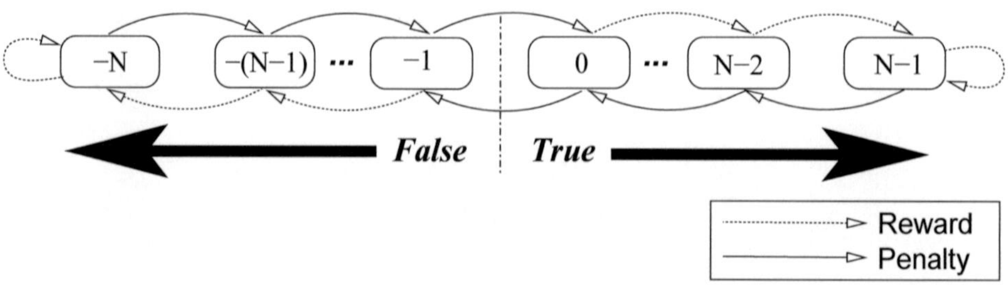

Fig. 2. The state transitions and action selection of the Learning SAT Automaton

automaton state is positive, then action ***True*** will be chosen by the automaton. If on the other hand the state is negative, then action ***False*** will be chosen. Note that since we initially do not know which action is optimal, we set the initial state of the Learning SAT Automaton randomly to either *'-1'* or *'0'*.

The state transition matrix $\mathcal{F}$ determines how learning proceeds. As seen in the graph representation of $\mathcal{F}$ found in the figure, providing a *reward* input to the automaton *strengthens* the currently chosen action, essentially by making it less likely that the other action will be chosen in the future. Correspondingly, a *penalty* input *weakens* the currently selected action by making it more likely that the other action will be chosen later on. In other words, the automaton attempts to incorporate past responses when deciding on a sequence of actions.

3.2 Learning Automata Random Walk (LARW)

```
Procedure learning_automata_random_walk()

Begin
    /* Initialization */
    For i := 1 To n Do
        /* The initial state of each automaton is set to either '-1' or '1' */
        state[i] = random_element({−1, 0});
        /* And the respective literals are assigned corresponding truth values */
        If state[i] == -1 Then x_i = False Else x_i = True;

    /* Main loop */
    While Not stop(C) Do
        /* Draw unsatisfied clause randomly */
        C_j = random_unsatisfied_clause(C);
        /* Draw clause literal randomly */
        i = random_element(I_j ∪ Ī_j);
        /* The corresponding automaton is penalized for choosing the "wrong" action */
        If i ∈ I_j And state[i] < N − 1 Then
          state[i]++;
          /* Flip literal when automaton changes its action */
          If state[i] == 0 Then
            flip(x_i);
        Else If i ∈ Ī_j And state[i] > −N Then
          state[i]−−;
          /* Flip literal when automaton changes its action */
          If state[i] == -1 Then
            flip(x_i);

        /* Draw satisfied clause randomly */
        C_j = random_satisfied_clause(C);
        /* Draw clause literal randomly */
        i = random_element(I_j ∪ Ī_j);
        /* Reward corresponding automaton if it */
        /* contributes to the satisfaction of the clause */
        If i ∈ I_j And state[i] ≥ 0 And state[i] < N − 1 Then
          state[i]++;
        Else If i ∈ Ī_j And state[i] < 0 And state[i] > −N Then
          state[i]−−;
    EndWhile
End
```

Fig. 3. Learning Automata Random Walk (LARW) Algorithm

In addition to the definition of the LA, we must define the environment that the LA interacts with. Simply put, the environment is a SAT problem as defined in Section 1. Each variable of the SAT problem is assigned a dedicated LA, resulting in a team of LA. The task of each LA is to determine the truth value of its corresponding variable, with the aim of satisfying all of the clauses where *that* variable appears. In other words, if each automaton reaches its own goal, then the overall SAT problem at hand has also been solved.

3.3 Learning Automata Random Walk (LARW)

With the above perspective in mind, we will now present the details of the LARW that we propose. Figure 3 contains the complete pseudo-code for solving SAT problems, using a team of LA. As seen from the figure, the LARW corresponds to an ordinary Random Walk, however, both satisfied and unsatisfied clauses are used in the search. Furthermore, the assignment of truth values to variables is indirect, governed by the states of the LA. At the core of the LARW is a punishment/rewarding scheme that guides the team of LA towards the optimal assignment. In the spirit of automata based learning, this scheme is incremental, and learning is performed gradually, in small steps. To elaborate, in each iteration of the algorithm, we randomly select a single clause. A variable is randomly selected from that clause, and the corresponding automaton is identified. If the clause is unsatisfied, the automaton is punished. Correspondingly, if the clause is satisfied, the automaton is rewarded, however, only if the automaton makes the clause satisfied. As also seen, the algorithm alternates between selecting satisfied and unsatisfied clauses.

3.4 Learning Automata GSATRW(LA-GSATRW)

Based on the same underlying principles that motivates the LARW, we will now present the details of the LA-GSATRW that we propose. Figure 4 contains the complete pseudo-code for solving SAT problems, using a team of LA. As seen from the figure, an ordinary GSATRW strategy is used to penalize an LA when it "disagrees" with GSATRW, i.e., when GSATRW and the LA suggest opposite truth values. Additionally, we use an "inverse" GSATRW strategy for rewarding an LA when it agrees with GSATRW. Note that as a result, the assignment of truth values to variables is indirect, governed by the states of the LA. Again, at the core of the LA-GSATRW algorithm is a punishment/rewarding scheme that guides the team of LA towards the optimal assignment. However, in this algorithm, the guidance is based on GSATRW rather than pure RW.

3.5 Comments to LARW and LA-GSATRW

Like a two-action Tsetlin Automaton, our proposed LA seeks to minimize the expected number of penalties it receives. In other words, it seeks finding the truth assignment that minimizes the number of unsatisfied clauses among the clauses where its variable appears.

Note that because multiple variables, and thereby multiple LA, may be involved in each clause, we are dealing with a game of LA Narendra & Thathachar (1989). That is, multiple LA interact with the same environment, and the response of the environment depends on the actions of several LA. In fact, because there may be conflicting goals among the LA involved in the LARW, the resulting game is competitive. The convergence properties of general competitive games of LA have not yet been successfully analyzed, however, results exists for certain classes of games, such as the Prisoner's Dilemma game Narendra & Thathachar (1989).

In our case, the LA involved in the LARW are non-absorbing, i.e., every state can be reached from every other state with positive probability. This means that the probability of reaching

```
Procedure learning_automata_gsat_random_walk()
Input : A set of clauses C; Walk probability p ;
Output : A satisfying truth assignment of the clauses, if found;

Begin
    /* Initialization */
    For i := 1 To n Do
        /* The initial state of each automaton is set to either '-1' or '1' */
        state[i] = random_element({−1,0});
        /* And the respective literals are assigned corresponding truth values */
        If state[i] == -1 Then x_i = False Else x_i = True;

    /* Main loop */
    While Not stop(C) Do
        If rnd(0,1) ≤ p Then
            /* Draw unsatisfied clause randomly */
            C_j = random_unsatisfied_clause(C);
            /* Draw clause literal randomly */
            i = random_element(I_j ∪ Ī_j);
        Else
            /* Randomly select one of the literals whose flipping
               minimizes the number of unsatisfied clauses */
            i = random_element(Best_Literal_Candidates(C));
        /* The corresponding automaton is penalized for choosing the "wrong" action */
        If i ∈ I_j And state[i] < N − 1 Then
            state[i]++;
            /* Flip literal when automaton changes its action */
            If state[i] == 0 Then
                flip(x_i);
        Else If i ∈ Ī_j And state[i] > −N Then
            state[i]−−;
            /* Flip literal when automaton changes its action */
            If state[i] == -1 Then
                flip(x_i);

        If rnd(0,1) ≤ p Then
            /* Draw satisfied clause randomly */
            C_j = random_satisfied_clause(C);
            /* Draw clause literal randomly */
            i = random_element(I_j ∪ Ī_j);
        Else
            /* Randomly select one of the literals whose flipping
               maximizes the number of unsatisfied clauses */
            i = random_element(Worst_Literal_Candidates(C));
        /* Reward corresponding automaton if it */
        /* contributes to the satisfaction of the clause */
        If i ∈ I_j And state[i] ≥ 0 And state[i] < N − 1 Then
            state[i]++;
        Else If i ∈ Ī_j And state[i] < 0 And state[i] > −N Then
            state[i]−−;
    EndWhile
End
```

Fig. 4. Learning Automata GSAT Random Walk Algorithm

the solution of the SAT problem at hand is equal to 1 when running the game infinitely. Also note that the solution of the SAT problem corresponds to a Nash equilibrium of the game.
In order to maximize speed of learning, we initialize each LA randomly to either the state *'-1'* or *'0'*. In this initial configuration, the variables will be flipped relatively quickly because only a single state transition is necessary for a flip. Accordingly, the joint state space of the LA is quickly explored in this configuration. Indeed, in this initial configuration both of the algorithms mimics their respective non-learning counterparts. However, as learning proceeds and the LA move towards their boundary states, i.e., states *'-N'* and *'N-1'*, the flipping of variables calms down. Accordingly, the search for a solution to the SAT problem at hand becomes increasingly focused.

4. Empirical Results

We here compare LARW and LA-GSATRW with their non-learning counterparts — the Random Walk (RW) and the GSAT with Random Walk (GSATRW) schemes. A main purpose of this comparison is to study the effect of the introduced stochastic learning. The benchmark problems we used to achieve this contain both randomized and structured problems from various domains, including SAT-encoded Bounded Model Checking Problems, Graph Coloring Problems, Logistics Problems, and Block World Planning Problems.

4.1 LARW Vs RW

As a basis for the empirical comparison of RW and LARW, we selected a benchmark test suite of 3-colorable graphs that shows so-called *phase transition*. All the instances are known to be hard and difficult to solve and are available from the SATLIB website (http://www.informatik.tu-darmstadt.de/AI/SATLIB). The benchmark instances we use are satisfiable and have been used widely in the literature.
Note that due to the stochastic nature of LARW, the number of flips required for solving a SAT problem varies widely between different runs. Therefore, for each problem, we run LARW and RW 100 times each, with a cutoff (maximum number of flips) which is sufficient (10^7) to guarantee a success rate close to 100%.

4.1.1 Search Trajectory

The manner in which each LA converges to an assignment is crucial for better understanding LARW's behavior. In Figure 5 we show how the best and current assignment progress during the search using a random 3-SAT problem with 150 variables and 645 clauses, taken from the SAT benchmark library.
The plot to the left in Figure 5 suggests that problem solving with LARW happens in two phases. In the first phase, which corresponds to the early part of the search (the first 5% of the search), LARW behaves as a hill-climbing method. In this phase, which can be described as a short one, up to 95% of the clauses are satisfied. The currently best score climbs rapidly at first, and then flattens off as we mount a plateau, marking the start of the second phase. The plateau spans a region in the search space where flips typically leave the best assignment unchanged. The long plateaus becomes even more pronounced as the number of flips increases. More specifically, the plateau appears when trying to satisfy the last few remaining clauses.
To further investigate the behavior of LARW once on the plateau, we looked at the corresponding average state of the LA as the search progresses. The plot to the right in Figure 5 shows the resulting observations. At the start of plateau, search coincides in general with an increase in the average state. The longer the plateau runs, the higher the average state

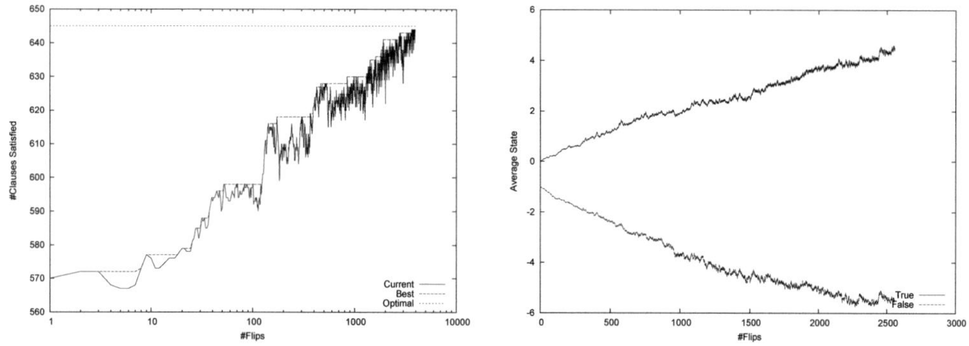

Fig. 5. (Left) LARW's search space on a 150 variable problem with 645 clauses (uf150-645). Along the horizontal axis we give the number of flips, and along the vertical axis the number of satisfied clauses. (Right) Average state of LA. Horizontal axis gives the number of flips, and the vertical axis shows the average state of automaton.

becomes. An automaton with high average state needs to perform a series of actions before its current state changes to either -1 or 0, thereby making the flipping of the corresponding variable possible. The transition between each plateau corresponds to a change to the region where a small number of flips gradually improves the score of the current solution ending with an improvement of the best assignment. The search pattern brings out an interesting difference between LARW and the standard use of SLS. In the latter, one generally stops the search as soon as no more improvements are found. This can be appropriate when looking for a near-optimal solution. On the other hand, when searching for a global maximum (i.e., a satisfying assignment) stopping when no flip yields an immediate improvement is a poor strategy.

4.1.2 Run-Length-Distributions (RLDs)

As an indicator of the behavior of the algorithm on a single instance, we choose the median cost when trying to solve a given instance in 100 trials, and using an extremely high cutoff parameter setting of $Maxsteps = 10^7$ in order to obtain a maximal number of successful tries. The reason behind choosing the median cost rather than the mean cost is due to the large variation in the number of flips required to find a solution. To get an idea of the variability of the search cost, we analyzed the cumulative distribution of the number of search flips needed by both LARW and RW for solving single instances. Due to non-deterministic decisions involved in the algorithms (i.e., initial assignment, random moves), the number of flips needed by both algorithms to find a solution is a random variable that varies from run to run. More formally, let k denotes the total number of runs, and let $f'(j)$ denotes the number of flips for the j-th successful run (i.e, run during which a solution is found) in a list of all successful runs, sorted according to increasing number of flips, then the cumulative empirical RLD is defined by $\hat{P}(f'(j) \leq f) = \frac{|\{j|f'(j) \leq f\}|}{k}$. For practical reasons we restrict our presentation here to the instances corresponding to small, medium, and large sizes from the underlying test-set.
Figures 6 and 7 show RLDs obtained by applying RW and LARW to individual SAT-encoded graph coloring problem instances. As can be seen from the leftmost plot in Figure 6, we observe that on the small size instance, the two algorithms show no cross-over in their corre-

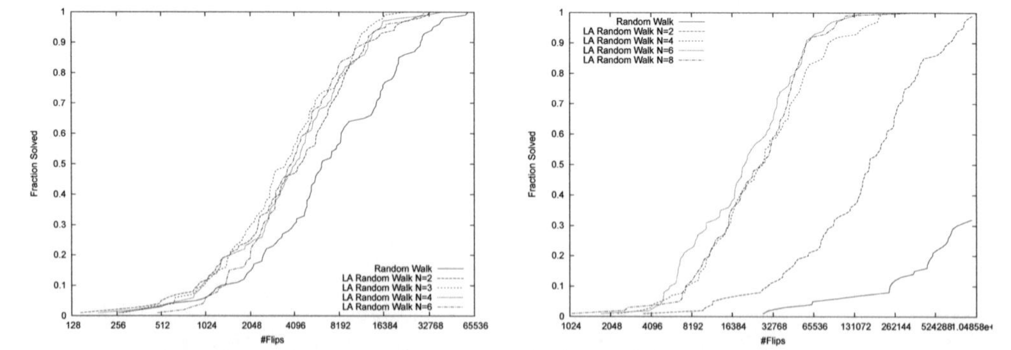

Fig. 6. (Left) Cumulative distributions for a 90-variable *graph coloring* problems with 300 clauses (flat90-300). (Right) Cumulative distribution for a 150-variable *graph coloring* problem with 545 clauses (flat375-1403). Along the horizontal axis we give the number of flips, and along the vertical axis the fraction of problems solved for different values of N.

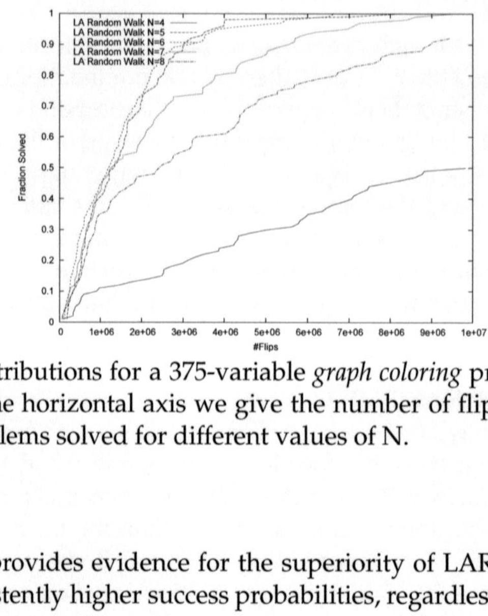

Fig. 7. Cumulative distributions for a 375-variable *graph coloring* problem with 1403 clauses (flat375-1403). Along the horizontal axis we give the number of flips, and along the vertical axis the fraction of problems solved for different values of N.

sponding RLDs. This provides evidence for the superiority of LARW compared to RW (i.e, $N = 1$) as it gives consistently higher success probabilities, regardless of the number of search steps.

On the medium sized instance, to the right in Figure 6, we observe a stagnation behavior with a low asymptotic solution probability corresponding to a value around 0.3. As can be easily seen, both methods show the existence of an initial phase below which the probability for finding a solution is 0. Both methods start the search from a randomly chosen assignment which typically violates many clauses. Consequently, both methods need some time to reach the first local optimum which possibly could be a feasible solution.

The plot in Figure 7 shows that the performance of RW for the large instance (flat375-1403) degrades. Indeed, the probability of finding a feasible solution within the required number of steps is 0. Further, note that the distance between the minimum and the maximum number of search steps needed for finding a solution using RW is higher compared to that of LARW and increases with the hardness of the instance. The learning automaton mechanism pays off as the instance gets harder. Finally, observe that the probability of success gets higher as N increases, to a certain level.

4.1.3 Mean Search Cost

In this section, we focus on the behavior of the two algorithms using 100 instances from a test-set of small and medium sized problem instances. We chose not to include the plot for the large instance (flat375-1403) because RW was incapable of solving it during the 100 trials. For each instance the median search cost (number of local search steps) is measured and we analyze the distribution of the mean search cost over the instances from each test-set. The different plots show the cumulative hardness distributions produced by 100 trials on 100 instances from a test-set.

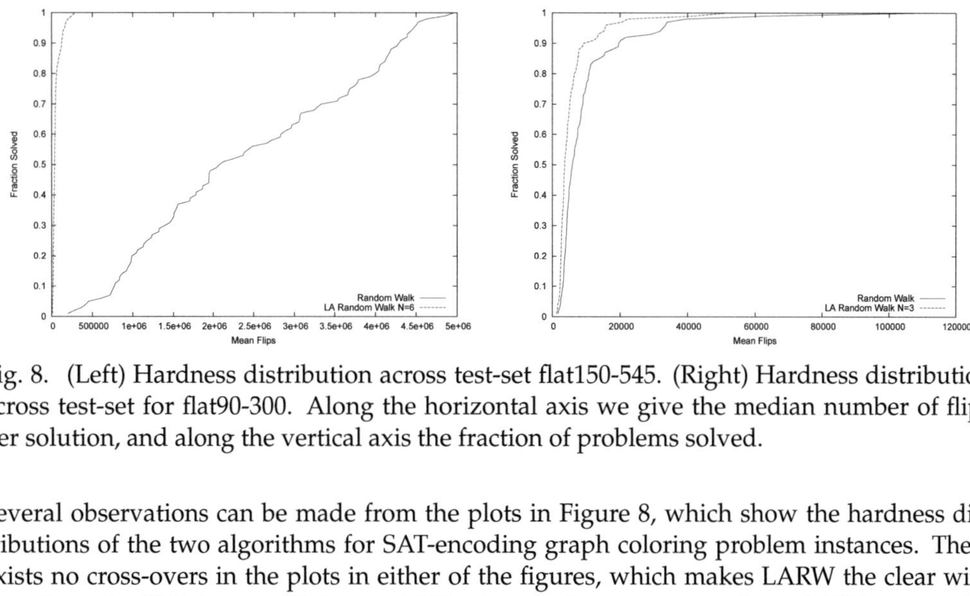

Fig. 8. (Left) Hardness distribution across test-set flat150-545. (Right) Hardness distribution across test-set for flat90-300. Along the horizontal axis we give the median number of flips per solution, and along the vertical axis the fraction of problems solved.

Several observations can be made from the plots in Figure 8, which show the hardness distributions of the two algorithms for SAT-encoding graph coloring problem instances. There exists no cross-overs in the plots in either of the figures, which makes LARW the clear winner. Note also RW shows a higher variability in search cost compared to LARW between the instances of each test-set.

The distributions of the two algorithms confirm the existence of instances which are harder to solve than others. In particular, as can be seen from the long tails of these distributions, a substantial part of problem instances are dramatically harder to solve with RW than with LARW. The harder the instance, the higher the difference between the average search costs of two algorithms (a factor of approximately up to 50). This can be explained by the fact that the automaton learning mechanism employed in LARW offers an efficient way to escape from highly attractive areas in the search space of hard instances leading to a higher probability of success, as well as reducing the average number of local search steps needed to find a solution. The empirical hardness distribution of SAT-encoded graph coloring problems to the right in Figure 8 shows that it was rather easy for both algorithms to find a feasible solution in each trial across the test set flat90-300, with LARW showing on average a lower search cost within a given probability compared to RW. The plot reveals the existence of some instances on which RW suffers from a strong search stagnation behavior.

The plot located to the left in Figure 8 shows a striking poor average performance of RW compared to LARW on the test set flat150-545. Conversely, LARW shows a consistent ability to find solutions across the instances on this test set. For LARW, we observe a small variability in search cost indicated by the distance between the minimum and the maximum number of local search steps needed to find a solution. The differences in performance between these two algorithms can be characterized by a factor of about 10 in the median. The performance differences observed between the two algorithms for small size instances are still observable and very significant for medium size instances. This suggests that LARW in general is considerably more effective for larger instances.

4.2 LA-GSATRW Vs GSATRW

Since LA-GSATRW is more sophisticated and far more effective than LARW, we used larger and harder problem instances to evaluate LA-GSATRW. In brief, we selected a benchmark suite from different domains including problem instances from the Bejing SAT competition held in 1996. Again, due to the random nature of the algorithms, when comparing LA-GSATRW with GSATRW, we run the algorithms 100 times using a maximum number of flips of 10^7 as a stopping criteria (guaranteeing a success rate close to 100%).

4.2.1 Search Space

The manner in which LA converges on assignment is crucial to a better understanding of LA-GSATRW behaviour. In Figure 9, we show how the best found score and the current score progress during the search on a SAT-encoded logistics problem.

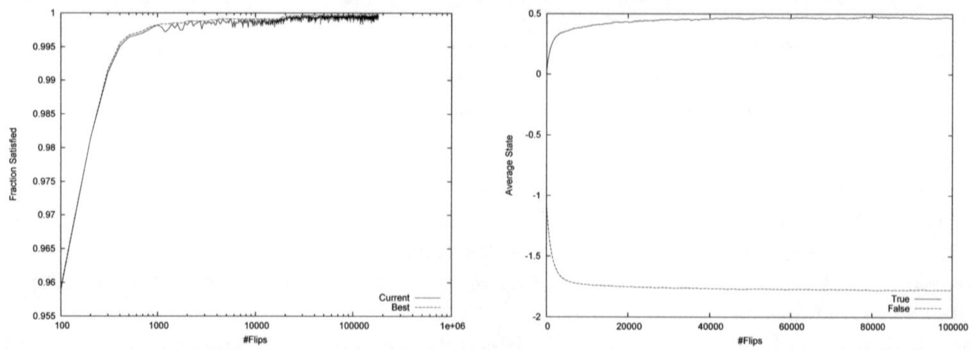

Fig. 9. (Left) LA-GSATRW's search space on a 828 variable problem with 6718 clauses (logistics.a). Along the horizontal axis we give the number of flips, and along the vertical axis the number of satisfied clauses. (Right) Average state of LA. Horizontal axis gives the number of flips, and the vertical axis shows the average state of automaton.

The leftmost plot suggests that problem solving with LA-GSATRW also happens in two phases. Again, in the first phase which corresponds to the early part of the search (the first 5% of the search) LA-GSATRW behaves as a hill-climbing method. In this phase, which can be described as a short one, up to 95% of the clauses are satisfied. The best obtained score climbs rapidly at first, and then flattens off as we reach a plateau, marking the start of the second phase. The plateau spans a region in the search space where flips typically leave the best assignment unchanged. The long plateaus becomes even more pronounced as the number of flips increases, and occurs more specifically in trying to satisfy the last few remaining clauses. To further investigate the behaviour of LA-GSATRW once on the plateau, we looked at the corresponding average state of automaton as the search progresses. The rightmost plot in Figure 9 shows the reported observations. The start of plateau search coincides in general with an increase in the average state. The longer plateau, the higher average state.An automaton with high average state needs to perform a series of actions before its current state changes to either -1 or 0, thereby making the flipping of the corresponding variable possible. The transition between each plateau corresponds to a change to the region where a small number of flips gradually improves the score of the current solution ending with an improvement of the best assignment.

4.2.2 Run-Length-Distributions (RLD)

In order to observe the variability of the search cost of GSATRW and LA-GSATRW, we analyzed the cumulative distribution of the number of search flips needed by the algorithms, as defined in Section 4.1.2.

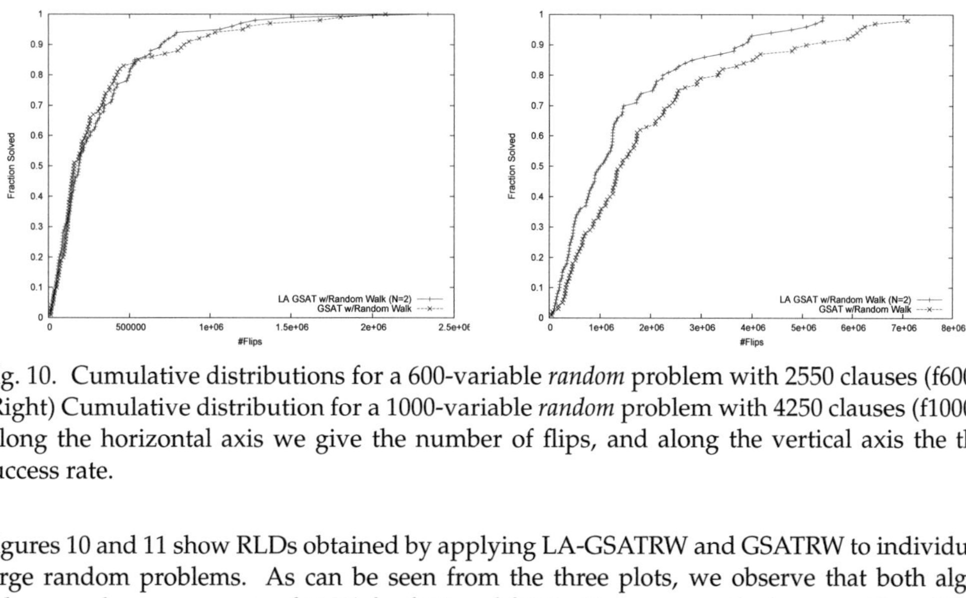

Fig. 10. Cumulative distributions for a 600-variable *random* problem with 2550 clauses (f600). (Right) Cumulative distribution for a 1000-variable *random* problem with 4250 clauses (f1000). Along the horizontal axis we give the number of flips, and along the vertical axis the the success rate.

Figures 10 and 11 show RLDs obtained by applying LA-GSATRW and GSATRW to individual large random problems. As can be seen from the three plots, we observe that both algorithms reach a success rate of 100% for f600 and f1000. However, on the large problem f2000, GSATRW shows a low asymptotic solution probability corresponding to 0.37 compared to 0.45 for LA-GSATRW. Note also, that there is a substantial part of trials that are dramatically hard to solve which explains the large variability in the length of the different runs of the two algorithms. Again, the algorithms show the existence of an initial phase below which the probability for finding a solution is 0. Both methods start the search from a randomly chosen assignment which typically violates many clauses. Consequently, both methods need some time to reach the first local optimum which possibly could be a feasible solution. The two algorithms show no cross-over in their corresponding RLDs even though it is somewhat hard to see for f600 but it becomes more pronounced for f1000 and f2000. The median search cost for LA-GSATRW is 3%, 29%, and 17% of that of GSATRW for f600, f1000 and f2000 respectively. The three plots provides evidence for the superiority of LA-GSATRW compared to GSATRW

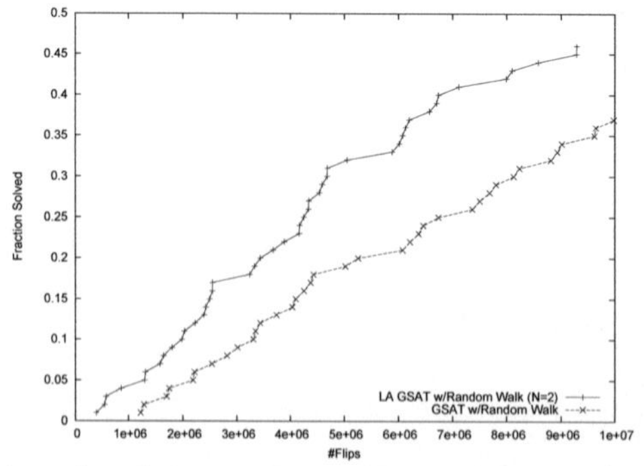

Fig. 11. (Left) Cumulative distributions for a 2000-variables random problem with 8500 clauses (f2000). Along the horizontal axis we give the number of flips, and along the vertical axis the success rate.

as it gives consistently higher success probabilities while requiring fewer search steps than GSATRW.

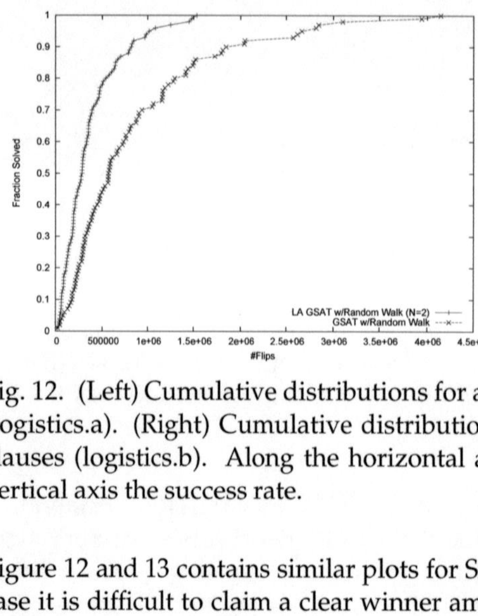

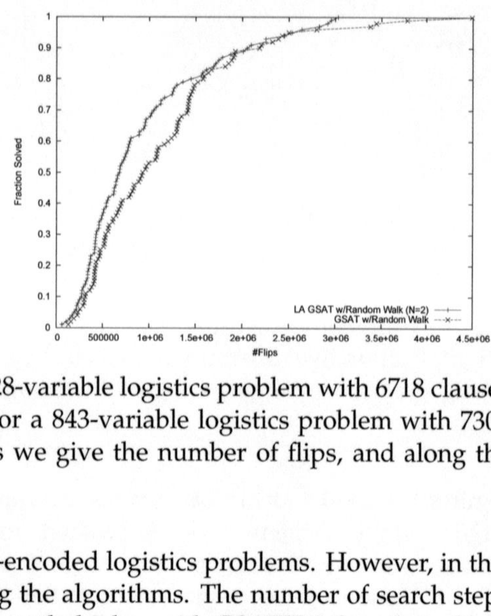

Fig. 12. (Left) Cumulative distributions for a 228-variable logistics problem with 6718 clauses (logistics.a). (Right) Cumulative distribution for a 843-variable logistics problem with 7301 clauses (logistics.b). Along the horizontal axis we give the number of flips, and along the vertical axis the success rate.

Figure 12 and 13 contains similar plots for SAT-encoded logistics problems. However, in this case it is difficult to claim a clear winner among the algorithms. The number of search steps varies between the different trials and is significantly higher with GSATRW than that of LA-GSATRW. However, note that the median search cost for LA-GSATRW is 4%, 29%, 34% and 51% of that of GSATRW for Logistics-d,Logistics-b,Logistics-c, and Logistics-a, respectively. We now turn to single SAT-encoded instances from the Blocks World Planning domain. The crossing of the two RLDs at different points, as shown in figures 1516, indicates that there is no complete dominance of one algorithm over the other when applied to the same problem. Looking at figure 15 and taking the smallest problem (medium) as an example, we notice that for smaller cutoff points, GSATRW achieves higher solution probabilities, while for larger cutoff points LA-GSATRW shows increasingly superior performance.

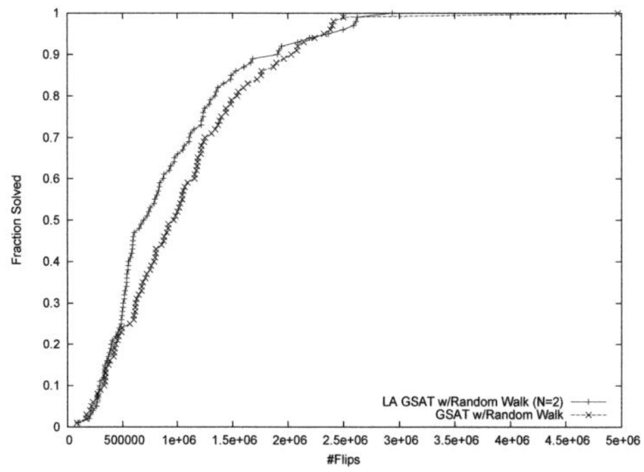

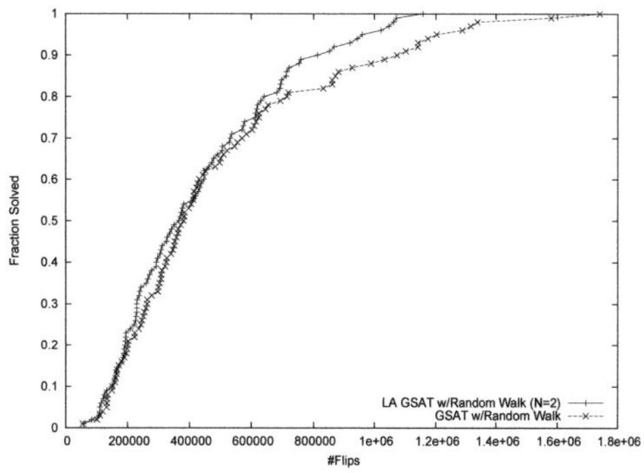

Fig. 13. (Left) Cumulative distributions for a 1141-variable logistics problem with 10719 clauses (logistics.c)). (Right) Cumulative distribution for a 4713-variable logistics problem with 21991 clauses (logistics.d). Along the horizontal axis we give the number of flips, and along the vertical axis the the success rate.

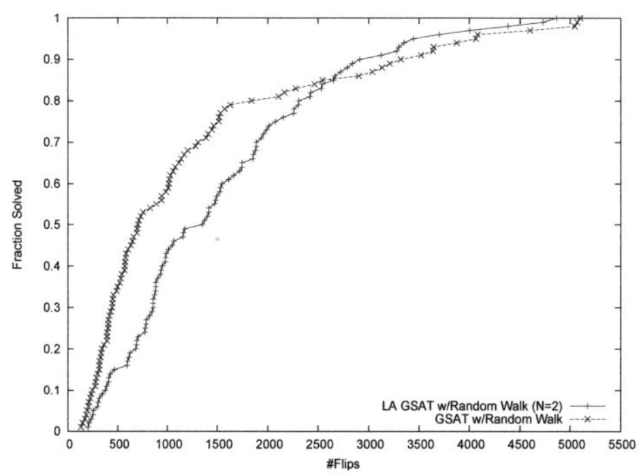

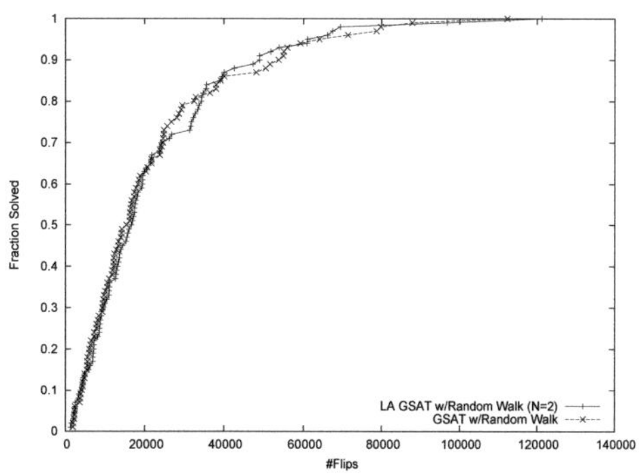

Fig. 14. (Left) Cumulative distribution for a 116-variable *Blocks World* problem with 953 clauses (medium). (Right) Cumulative distribution for a 459 -variable *Blocks World* problem with 4675 clauses (bw-large.a). Along the horizontal axis we give the number of flips, and along the vertical axis the fraction of problems solved for different values of N.

It may be noted that GSATRW performs better than LA-GSATRW for the smallest problem (up to 49% more steps than LA-GSATRW). However this gap is fairly small and is within 5% for medium sized problems (bw-large.a, huge). On the other hand, for the larger problem bw-large.b, the situation is reversed. GSATRW requires 16% more steps than LA-GSATRW. An interesting observation that can be made from the above discussed plots is the ability of both algorithms to show an improved performance when applied to structured problems, such as SAT-encoded Blocks world and logistics problems. Taking for instance the large Block world problem bw-large (1087 variables, 13772 clauses), the median search cost of both methods is around 95% better compared to that measured for Random-3-SAT problem f1000 (1000 variables, 4250 clauses). Finally, the plots in Figures 17 and 18 explore the behaviour of the RLDs when for both algorithms when applied to BMC problems. Both algorithms reach a success rate of 100% with the one exception that,for the medium size problem (bmc-ibm3), the success rate was around 95%. Returning to Figure 17 then, for the smaller problem (bmc-

ibm-2), GSATRW dominates LA-GSATRW on the major part of the runs (i.e, approx 80%), as it reaches high solution probabilities while requiring lower search cost. On the other hand, for the medium sized problem (bmc-ibm-3), the situation is similar, but reversed.
Figure 18 shows the RLD for both algorithms for a larger problem (bmc-ibm-6). As can be seen from the figure, the RLDs for both algorithms have roughly the same shape. The presence of heavy tails in both RLDs indicates that both algorithms get stuck in local minima for a relatively small number of trials. The median search cost for GSATRW is 15% of that of LA-GSATRW for the bmc-ibm-2. However, LA-GSATRW shows a better performance for the medium (improvement of about 8% in the median) and larger problems (improvement of approximately 5%).
Table 1 shows the coefficient of variation (normalised standard deviations) for LA-GSATRW. As can be seen from the previous plots, there is a large variability between the search cost of the different runs. In particular, the long tails of the RLDs show that some of the runs requires much more effort than others. For increasing problem sizes, there is no clear indication that variability increases, as in the case of SAT-encoded BMC problems.

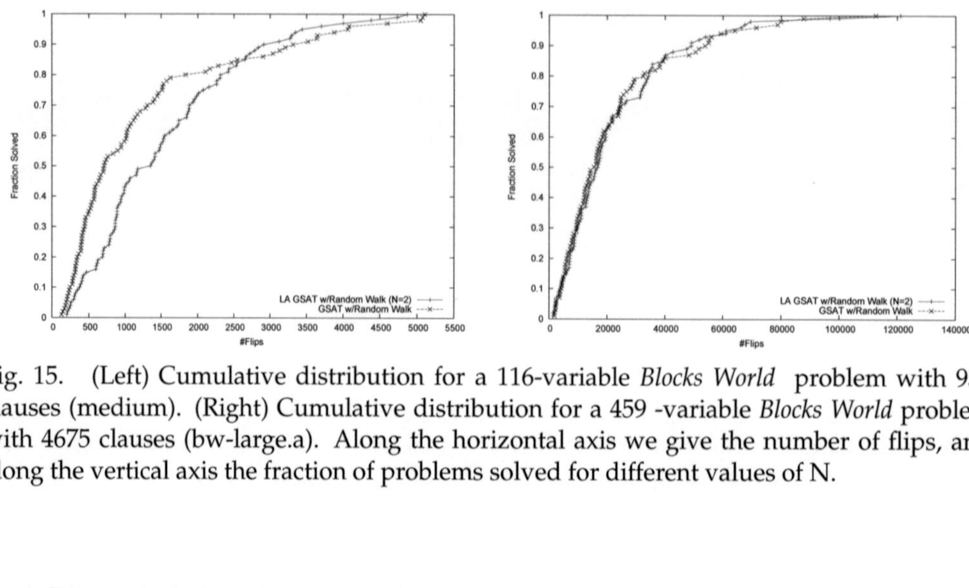

Fig. 15. (Left) Cumulative distribution for a 116-variable *Blocks World* problem with 953 clauses (medium). (Right) Cumulative distribution for a 459 -variable *Blocks World* problem with 4675 clauses (bw-large.a). Along the horizontal axis we give the number of flips, and along the vertical axis the fraction of problems solved for different values of N.

4.2.3 Excess deviation from the solution

Quite often, we observed stagnation behaviour with extremely low asymptotic solution probabilities when applied to SAT-encoded quasigroup problems. The two algorithms were executed to the allowed maximal number of steps and the percentage excess over the solution was recorded. Figures 19 and 20 show the excess deviation over the solution sorted in increasing order. As it can be seen from the plots, both algorithms suffers from severe stagnation indicating incomplete behaviour of the two algorithms when applied to this class of problems. At the exception of the problem qg3-08 where LA-GSATRW achieved a maximal success rate of 0.04% compared to 0.03% for GSATRW, we observe a rapid deterioration of their performance (success rate equals to 0%) with growing problem size. LA-GSATRW appears to have an asymptotic convergence which is better than GSATRW to around 3% – 10% in average excess of the solution.

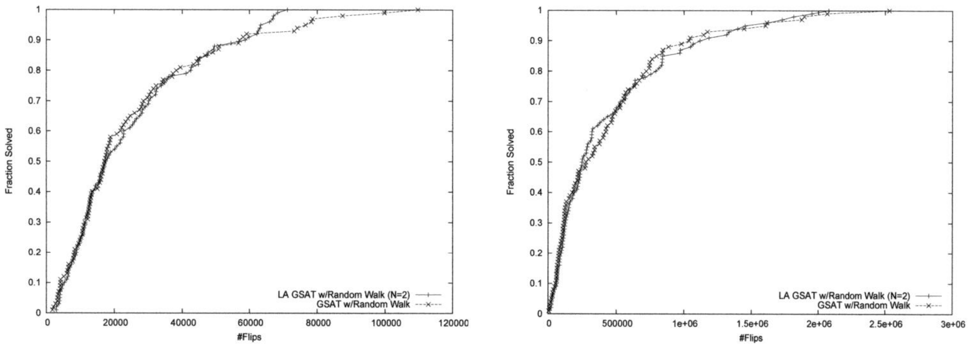

Fig. 16. (Left) Cumulative distributions for a 459-variable *Blocks World* problems with 7054 clauses (huge). (Right) Cumulative distribution for a 1087-variable *Blocks world* problem with 13772 (bw-large.b). Along the horizontal axis we give the number of flips, and along the vertical axis the success rate.

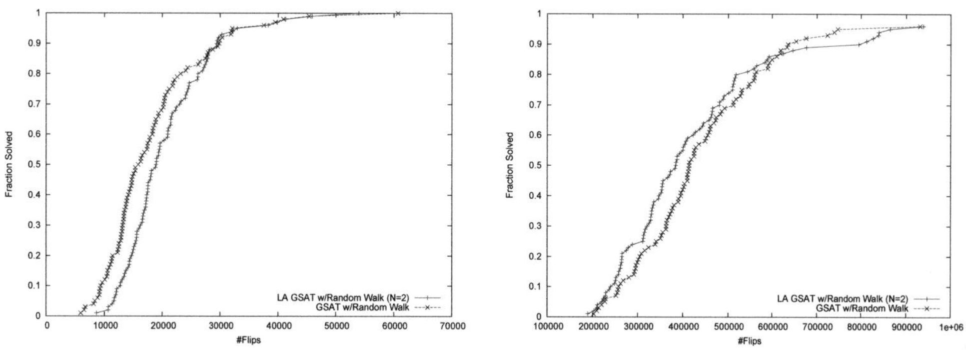

Fig. 17. (Left) Cumulative distributions for a 3628-variable *BMC* problem with 14468 clauses (bmc-ibm2). (Right) Cumulative distribution for a 14930-variable *BMC* problem with 72106 clauses (bmc-ibm3). Along the horizontal axis we give the number of flips, and along the vertical axis the success rate.

4.2.4 Wilcoxon Rank-Sum Test

The number of search flips needed by a meta heuristic to find a feasible solution may vary significantly from run to run on the same problem instance due to random initial solutions and subsequent randomized decisions. As RLDs are unlikely to be normally distributed, we turn to the non-parametric Wilcoxon Rank test in order to test the level of statistical confidence in differences between the median search cost of the two algorithms. The test requires that the absolute values of the differences between the mean search costs of the two algorithms are sorted from smallest to largest and these differences are ranked according to absolute magnitude. The sum of the ranks is then formed for the negative and positive differences separately. As the size of the trials increase, the rank sum statistic becomes normal. If the null hypothesis is true, the sum of ranks of the positive differences should be about the same

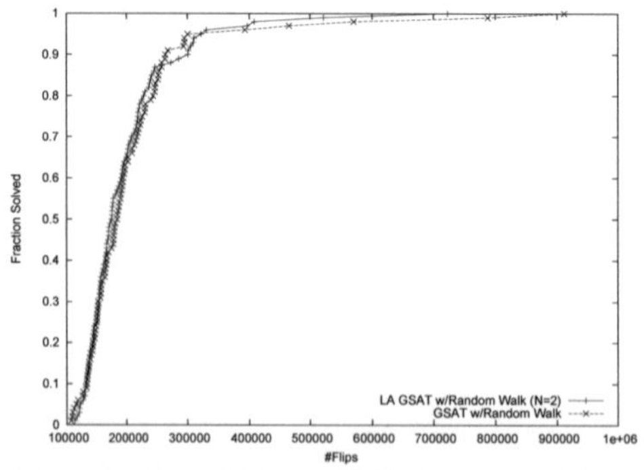

Fig. 18. Cumulative distributions for a 8710-variable *BMC* problems with 8710 clauses (bmc-ibm6). Along the horizontal axis we give the number of flips, and along the vertical axis the success rate.

Test-Problem	LA-GSATRW
f600	11.36
f1000	9.42
f2000	3.90
logistics.a	8.85
logistics.b	7.76
logistics.d	6.14
medium	6.84
bw-large.a	9.12
huge	7.62
bw-large.b	10.49
ibm-bmc2	3.71
ibm-bmc3	3.89
ibm-bmc6	4.30

Table 1. Coefficient of variation.

as the sum of the ranks of the negative differences. Using two-tailed P value, significance performance difference is granted if the Wilcoxon test is significant for $P < 0.05$
An initial inspection of Table 2 reveals two results. Firstly, the success rate of LA-GSATRW was better in 12 problems and the difference in the median search cost was significant in 6 problems. On the other hand, GSASTRW gave better results in 5 problems in terms of success rate but its performance was significant in only 2 cases.

5. Conclusions and Further Work

In this work, we have introduced a new approach based on combining Learning Automata with Random Walk and GSAT w/Random Walk. In order to get a comprehensive overview of the new algorithms' performance, we used a set of benchmark problems containing different problems from various domains. In these benchmark problems, both RW and GSATRW suffers from stagnation behaviour which directly affects their performance. This phenomenon is, however, only observed for LA-GSATRW on the largest problem instances. Finally, the

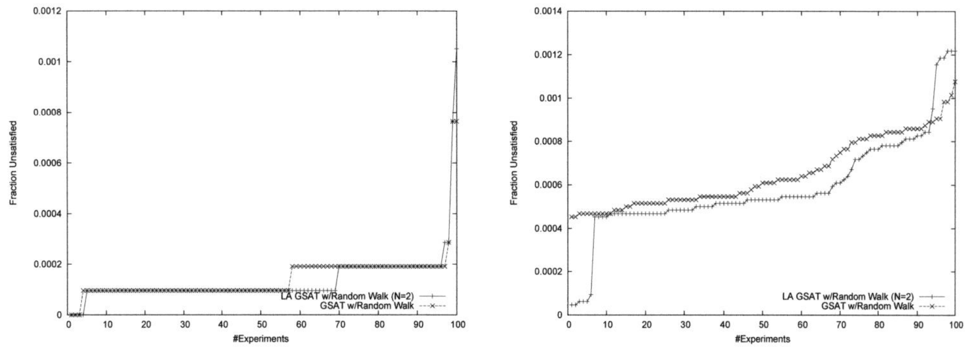

Fig. 19. Excess deviation over the solution for LA-GSATRW and GSATRW. (Left) qg3-08 (512 variables, 10469 clauses). qg5-11 (1331 variables, 64054 clauses). Along the horizontal axis we give the number of trials and along the vertical axis the percentage deviation over the solution.

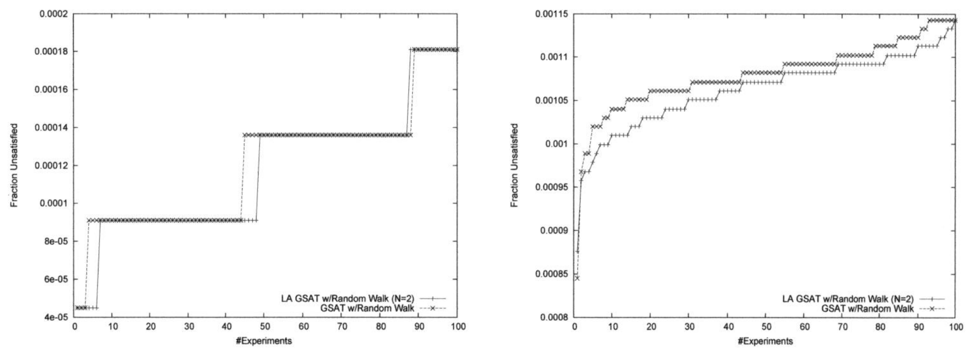

Fig. 20. Excess deviation over the solution for LA-GSATRW and GSATRW. (Left) qg7-09 (729 variables, 22060 clauses). (Right) qg7-13 (2197 variables, 97072 clauses). Along the horizontal axis we give the number of trials and along the vertical axis the percentage deviation over the solution.

success rate of LA-GSATRW was better in 12 of the problems, and the difference in the median search cost was significantly better for 6 of the problems. GSASTRW, on the other hand, gave better results in 5 of the problems in terms of success rate, while its performance was significantly better only in 2 problems.

Based on the empirical results, it can be seen that the Learning Automata mechanism employed in LARW and LA-GSATRW offers an efficient way to escape from highly attractive areas in the search space, leading to a higher probability of success as well as reducing the number of local search steps to find a solution.

As further work, it is of interest to study how Learning Automata can be used to enhance other Stochastic Local Search based algorithms, such as WalkSAT. Furthermore, more recent classes of Learning Automata, such as the Bayesian Learning Automata family Granmo (2009) may offer improved performance in LA based SAT solvers.

Problem	SR: LA-GSATRW	SR: GSATRW	P value	NULL Hypotheis
f600	53%	47%	0.19	Accept
f1000	62%	37%	0.00	Reject
f2000	32%	14%	0.00	Reject
logistic-a	74%	26%	0.00	Reject
logistic-b	54%	46%	0.09	Accept
logistic-c	59%	41%	0.02	Reject
logistic-d	54%	46%	0.29	Accept
bw-medium	36%	64%	0.02	Reject
bw-large-a	49%	51%	0.52	Accept
bw-huge	50%	50%	0.91	Accept
bw-large-b	53%	47%	0.82	Accept
bmc-ibm2	39%	61%	0.01	Reject
bmc-ibm3	52%	44%	0.18	Accept
bmc-ibm6	51%	49%	0.98	Accept
qg-03-08	20%	33%	0.16	Accept
qg-5-11	59%	38%	0.00	Reject
qg-7-9	33%	59%	0.61	Accept
qg-7-13	59%	33%	0.00	Reject

Table 2. Success rate (SR) and Wilcoxon statistical test.

6. References

A.E.Eiben & van der Hauw, J. (1997). Solving 3-sat with adaptive genetic algorithms, *Proceedings of the 4th IEEE Conference on Evolutionary Computation*, IEEE Press, pp. 81–86.

Cha, B. & Iwama, K. (1995). Performance Tests of Local Search Algorithms Using New Types of Random CNF Formula, *Proceedings of IJCAI'95*, Morgan Kaufmann Publishers, pp. 304–309.

Cook, S. (1971). The complexity of theorem-proving procedures, *Proceedings of the Third ACM Symposuim on Theory of Computing*, pp. 151–158.

Davis, M. & Putnam, H. (1960). A computing procedure for quantification theory, *Journal of the ACM* **7**: 201–215.

Frank, J. (1997). Learning short-term clause weights for gsat, *Proceedings of IJCAI'97*, Morgan Kaufmann Publishers, pp. 384–389.

Gale, W., S.Das & Yu, C. (1990). Improvements to an Algorithm for Equipartitioning, *IEEE Transactions on Computers* **39**: 706–710.

Gent, L. & T.Walsh (1993). Towards an Understanding of Hill-Climbing Procedures for SAT, *Proceedings of AAAI'93*, MIT Press, pp. 28–33.

Glover, F. (1989). Tabu search-part 1, *ORSA Journal on Computing* **1**: 190–206.

Granmo, O.-C. (2009). Solving Two-Armed Bernoulli Bandit Problems Using a Bayesian Learning Automaton, *To Appear in International Journal of Intelligent Computing and Cybernetics (IJICC)* .

Granmo, O.-C., Oommen, B. J., Myrer, S. A. & Olsen, M. G. (2007). Learning Automata-based Solutions to the Nonlinear Fractional Knapsack Problem with Applications to Optimal Resource Allocation, *IEEE Transactions on Systems, Man, and Cybernetics, Part B* **37**(1): 166–175.

Hansen, P. & Jaumand, B. (1990). Algorithms for the maximum satisfiability problem, *Computing* **44**: 279–303.

I.Gent & Walsh, T. (1995). Unsatisfied variables in local search, *Hybrid Problems,Hybrid Solutions*, IOS Press, pp. 73–85.

Johnson, D. & Trick, M. (1996). *Cliques, Coloring, and Satisfiability*, Volume 26 of DIMACS Series on Discrete Mathematics and Theoritical Computer Science, American Mathematical Society.

McAllester, D., Selman, B. & Kautz, H. (1997). Evidence for Invariants in Local Search, *Proceedings of AAAI'97*, MIT Press, pp. 321–326.

Narendra, K. S. & Thathachar, M. A. L. (1989). *Learning Automata: An Introduction*, Prentice Hall.

Oommen, B. J. & Croix, E. V. S. (1996). Graph partitioning using learning automata, *IEEE Transactions on Computers* **45**(2): 195–208.

Oommen, B. J. & Hansen, E. R. (1987). List organizing strategies using stochastic move-to-front and stochastic move-to-rear operations, *SIAM Journal on Computing* **16**: 705–716.

Oommen, B. J. & Ma, D. C. Y. (1988). Deterministic learning automata solutions to the equipartitioning pr oblem, *IEEE Transactions on Computers* **37**(1): 2–13.

Oommen, B. J., Misra, S. & Granmo, O.-C. (2007). Routing Bandwidth Guaranteed Paths in MPLS Traffic Engineering: A Multiple Race Track Learning Approach, *IEEE Transactions on Computers* **56**(7): 959–976.

Selman, B., Kautz, H. A. & Cohen, B. (1994). Noise Strategies for Improving Local Search, *Proceedings of AAAI'94*, MIT Press, pp. 337–343.

Selman, B., Levesque, H. & Mitchell, D. (1992). A new method for solving hard satisfiability problems, *Proceedings of AAA'92*, MIT Press, pp. 440–446.

Spears, W. (1993). Simulated Annealing for Hard Satisfiability Problems. Technical Report, Naval Research Laboratory, Washington D.C.

Thathachar, M. A. L. & Sastry, P. S. (2004). *Networks of Learning Automata: Techniques for Online Stochastic Optimization*, Kluwer Academic Publishers.

Tsetlin, M. L. (1973). *Automaton Theory and Modeling of Biological Systems*, Academic Press.

6

Comprehensive and Scalable Appraisals of Contemporary Documents

William McFadden[1], Rob Kooper[1], Sang-Chul Lee[2] and Peter Bajcsy[1]
[1]National Center for Supercomputing Applications, University of Illinois at Urbana-Champaign, Urbana, Illinois, USA
[2]Department of Computer and Information Engineering, Inha University, Incheon, Korea

Abstract

This book chapter describes problems related to contemporary document analyses. Contemporary documents contain multiple digital objects of different type. These digital objects have to be extracted from document containers, represented as data structures, and described by features suitable for comparing digital objects. In many archival and machine learning applications, documents are compared by using multiple metrics, checked for integrity and authenticity, and grouped based on similarity. The objective of our book chapter is to describe methodologies for contemporary document processing, visual exploration, grouping and integrity verification, as well as to include computational scalability challenges and solutions.

1. Introduction

The objective of our work is to design a methodology, algorithms and a framework for document appraisal by (a) enabling exploratory document analyses and integrity/authenticity verification, (b) supporting automation of some analyses and (c) evaluating computational and storage requirements for archival purposes. In order to address the aforementioned criteria, our approach has been to decompose the series of appraisal criteria into a set of focused analyses, such as (a) find groups of records with similar content, (b) rank records according to their creation/last modification time and digital volume, (c) detect inconsistency between ranking and content within a group of records, and (d) compare sampling strategies for preservation of records.

In this work, we had chosen a specific class of electronic documents that (a) correspond to information content found in scientific publications about medical topics, (b) have an incremental nature of their content in time, and (c) contain the types of information representation that are prevalent in contemporary medical environments. Specifically, we narrowed our focus to those electronic documents that contain primarily text, raster and vector graphics as found in typical medical records in office document file formats. Among the file formats, MS Word can be considered as the most widely used file format for creating documents, while Adobe Portable Document Format (PDF) and Ghostscript could be described as the most widely used for exchanging documents. We selected to work with PDF documents since PDF is an open file format, and the open nature of the file format is critical for automated electronic document appraisal and long term preservation.

In order to address the appraisal criteria [1], we adopted some of the text comparison metrics used in [2], image comparison metrics used in [3] and lessons learnt stated in [4]. Then, we designed a new methodology for grouping electronic documents based on their content similarity (text, image and vector graphics), and prototyped a solution supporting grouping, ranking and integrity verification of any PDF files and HTML files [5]. First, text based, vector based and multi-image based comparisons are performed separately. Multiple images in each document are grouped first and then groups of images across documents are compared to arrive to an image-based similarity score. The current prototype is based on color histogram comparison, line count in vector graphics and word frequency comparison. The image colors and word/ integers/ floating numbers can be analyzed visually to support exploratory analyses. Subsets of the undesirable text and image primitives could be filtered out from document comparisons (e.g., omitting conjunctions, or background colors). The results of text, image and vector based comparisons are fused to create a pair-wise document similarity score. The matrix of pair-wise document similarity scores are used for grouping. The other appraisal criteria are approached by ranking documents within a group of documents based either on time stamps or on file name indicating the version number. The inconsistency between ranking and content within a group of records is based on frequency tracking, where the frequency of text, image and vector primitives is monitored over the time/version dimension of the grouped documents.

Currently, we hypothesized that the correct temporal ranking correlates with the content (images, vector and text) in such a way that the content is being modified without sharp discontinuities. Sharp content discontinuities are perceived as significant changes of document descriptors that would correspond, for instance, to large text/image deletions followed by large text/image additions or large text/image additions followed by large text/image deletions. We have experimented with real PDF documents of journal papers to validate the above hypothesis.

The novelty of our work is in designing a methodology for computer-assisted appraisal, in developing and prototyping a mathematical framework for automation of appraisals based on image, vector graphics and text types of information representation, and in designing a scalable solution using the Map and Reduce parallel programming paradigm for using computer clusters.

2. Previous work

<u>*Related work to the proposed framework:*</u> Our work is related to the past work of authors in the area of digital libraries [2], content-based image retrieval [3] and appraisal studies [4]. For example, the authors of [6] analyze PDF document by examining the appearance and geometric position of text and image blocks distributed over an entire document. However, they did not use the actual image and vector graphics information in their analyses. Similarly, the focus in [7] is only on the logical structure of PDF documents but not the

content. The work in [8] and [9] is based on analyses of vector graphics objects only since it is focused on diagrams represented by a set of statistics, e.g., the number of horizontal lines and vertical lines. Other authors also focused only on chart images using a model-based approach [10]. There is currently no method that would provide a comprehensive content-based PDF comparison and appraisal strategy according to our knowledge. In order to prototype a solution for comprehensive document comparisons and clustering, the difficulties lie in dealing with vector graphics objects, fusion of similarities of multiple digital objects, and in providing a scalable solution with the increasing number of documents.

Related work on comparing vector graphics objects: Vector graphics objects are described by the most primitive feature of the graphics object, lines, which are practically useless in meaningful comparisons. Due to this, it is necessary to compare objects at a slightly more sophisticated level by comparing groups of lines and their relationship to each other. However, the manner in which this can be done varies, and many techniques for comparison of simple geometric shapes exist, making it not trivial to choose which graphic comparison to use. Veltkamp [11] showed ten distinct methods for the comparison of polygons and open paths, and it is assumed that more may exist. However, the principle difficulty in implementing almost all of these methods is that they rely on a direct, side-by-side computationally expensive comparison between two graphical objects resulting in a real number comparison value in the range between 0 and 1. In addition, the problem of formulating a metric measuring approximate similarity between visual objects has also been known as an open problem [12, 13]. Finally, there is the problem of the sequential arrangement of the line segments since they could be encoded in the document arbitrarily. This introduces a plethora of problems because there is no guarantee that a visually similar object will be encoded in a document such as an Adobe PDF file in anything like the same way.

Related work on scalability: In the past, the scalability of computations has been approached by using parallel programming paradigms based on message-passing interface[1] (MPI) or open multi-processing[2] (OpenMP). MPI is designed for the coordination of a program running as multiple processes in a distributed memory environment by using passing control messages. MPI could also run in a shared memory system. There are several developed libraries supporting MPI[3]. OpenMP is intended for shared memory machines. It uses a multithreading approach where the master threads forks any number of slave threads. Several known software solutions have also used the hybrid parallel programming paradigm combining the strengths of MPI and OpenMP, for example, WRF[4] or NECTAR[5]. The hybrid approach uses MPI across nodes and OpenMP within nodes, which leads to good utilization of shared memory system resource (memory, latency, and bandwidth).
We have investigated the use of Google's MapReduce[6] and Yahoo!'s Pig[7] framework and its associated PigLatin language. MapReduce is a programming model that allows

[1] http://www-unix.mcs.anl.gov/mpi/usingmpi/examples/simplempi/main.htm
[2] http://software.intel.com/en-us/articles/more-work-sharing-with-openmp
[3] http://www-unix.mcs.anl.gov/mpi/usingmpi/examples/simplempi/main.htm
[4] http://www.wrf-model.org/index.php
[5] http://www.cfm.brown.edu/crunch/ATREE/software.html
[6] http://labs.google.com/papers/mapreduce.html

programmers to focus on the tasks instead of the parallel implementation of the tasks. This lets programmers write simple Map function and Reduce function, which are then automatically parallelized without requiring the programmers to code the details of parallel processes and communications. In the past, the Hadoop users have raised several questions about optimal set up and execution of Hadoop [14], such as:
What are the optimum machine configurations for running a Hadoop cluster?
Should I use a smaller number of high end/performance machines or are a larger number of "commodity" machines?
How does the Hadoop/Parallel Distributed Processing community define "commodity"?

The answers to these questions are of a very high value to the end users and several researchers have searched for solutions. For example, in [15] the authors report a new task scheduler to improve Hadoop's performance for clusters that consist of nodes that are not homogeneous. Similarly, we search for better understanding how to setup and execute Hadoop when multiple types of digital objects have to be analyzed in parallel (e.g., text, images, vector graphics). In addition, in most of the real life applications, the Map and Reduce operations are preceded by input/output (load and transfer) operations that force us to balance the computational gains from Hadoop with the cost of opening files and extracting information.

3. Methodology

This section presents the methodology and theoretical framework for addressing grouping, ranking and integrity verification problems

3.1 Overview

The designed methodology consists of the following main steps: (1) Extract components and properties stored in PDF files/containers. (2) Define text, image and vector graphics primitives, and extract their characteristic features. (3) Group images within each document into clusters based on a pair-wise similarity of image primitives and a clustering similarity threshold. (4) Compute a pair-wise similarity of image clusters across two documents based on their corresponding features. (5) Compute a pair-wise similarity of text & vector graphics primitives across two documents. (6) Calculate fusion coefficients per document to weight the contribution of text-based, image-based and vector-based similarities to the final pair-wise document similarity score. (7) Repeat steps (4-6) for all pairs of documents. (8) Group documents into clusters based on the pair-wise document similarity score and a selected similarity threshold. (9) Assign ranks to all documents based on their time stamps and storage file size. (10) Calculate the second difference of the document characteristic features over time and file size dimensions. Report those documents for which the second difference exceeds a given threshold defining allowed discontinuities in content.

[7] http://incubator.apache.org/pig

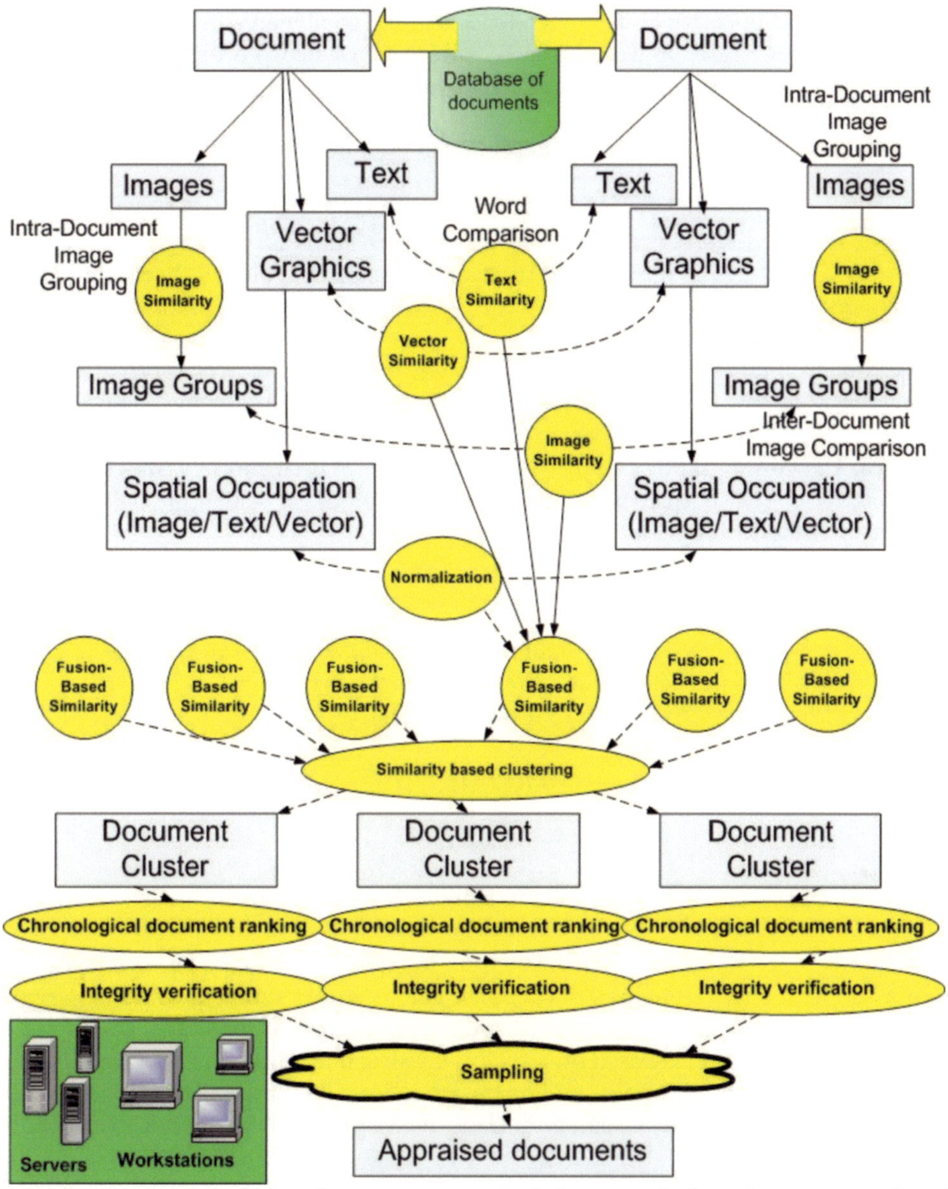

Fig. 1. An overview of the document appraisal framework based on comprehensive comparisons of document's internal digital objects.

3.2 Theoretical Framework

Document grouping problem. Given a set of documents, $\{D_i\}; i = 1, 2, \cdots, N$ compute pair-wise similarity of documents $sim(D_i, D_j)$ and aggregate them into clusters based on the similarity values for further ranking within each cluster.

The similarity of documents is understood as the combined similarity of document components. In our case, it would be the similarity of text, vector and raster (image) graphics components. The three components are decomposed into multiple images I_{ik} and their image primitives e_m^{IMAGE}, vector graphics and their image primitives e_m^{VECTOR}, and text primitives e_m^{TEXT} in textual portions $T_{ik} = T_i$ of a document D_i. The similarity for each component type is derived either directly using the features of its primitives (the case of text) or average features of multiple components of the same type and their primitives (the case of images and vector graphics).

Calculations of Statistical Features. The text feature for the word primitives is the frequency of occurrence of each unique word. The image feature for the color primitive is the frequency of occurrence of each unique color (also denoted a one-dimensional color histogram). The vector graphics feature is the frequency of occurrence of lines forming each vector graphics. The frequency of occurrence provides a statistical estimate of the probability distribution of primitives.

Calculation of Document Similarity. Given two PDF documents D_i, D_j, the similarity is defined as a linear combination of the similarities of the document components. In our case, the formula contains only the text and raster graphics components.

$$\begin{aligned} sim(D_i, D_j) &= w_{TEXT} \cdot sim(T_i, T_j) + \\ & w_{RASTER} \cdot sim(\{I_{ik}\}_{k=1}^{K}, \{I_{jl}\}_{l=1}^{L}) + \\ & w_{VECTOR} \cdot sim(V_i, V_j) \end{aligned} \quad (1)$$

where the $w_{TEXT}, w_{RASTER}, w_{VECTOR}$ are the weighting coefficients.

We have derived the weighting coefficients from the spatial coverage ratio of images, vector graphics and text in two compared documents. The weight assignment could be viewed as the relevance of each PDF component according to the amount of space it occupies in a document. The motivation is based on a typical construction of documents where the space devoted to a textual description or an illustration reflects its importance and hence should be considered in the similarity calculation. Thus, the weighting coefficients are calculated as

$$\begin{aligned} w_{IMAGE}(D_i, D_j) &= \frac{R_{IMAGE}(D_i) + R_{IMAGE}(D_j)}{2}, \\ w_{IMAGE}(D_i, D_j) + w_{VECTOR}(D_i, D_j) &+ w_{TEXT}(D_i, D_j) = 1 \end{aligned} \quad (2)$$

where

$$R_{IMAGE}(D) = \frac{Area_{IMAGE}(D)}{Area_{IMAGE}(D) + Area_{VECTOR}(D) + Area_{TEXT}(D)}, \quad R_{IMAGE}(D) + R_{VECTOR}(D) + R_{TEXT}(D) = 1$$

Calculation of Text Similarity. The similarity of text components from two documents $sim(T_i, T_j)$ is computed using the text features and similarity metric defined according to [2]. The equation is provided below.

$$sim(T_i, T_j) = \sum_{k1,k2} \omega_{i,k1}\omega_{j,k2} \tag{3}$$

where $k1, k2$ are those indices of text primitives that occur in both documents (in other words, there exist $e_{i,k1} = e_{j,k2}$ $e_{i,k1} \in T_i; e_{j,k2} \in T_j$). The ω terms are the weights of text primitives computed according to the equation below.

$$\omega_{ik} = \frac{f_{ik} \log(N / n_k)}{\sqrt{\sum_{l=1}^{L} (f_{il})^2 (\log(N / n_l))^2}} \tag{4}$$

where f_{ik} is the frequency of occurrence of a word e_k in D_i , N is the number of documents being evaluated, *L* is the number of all unique text primitives (words) in both documents, and n_k is the number of documents in the set of all documents being evaluated that contain the word e_k ($n_k = 1$ *or* 2).

Calculation of Raster Graphics (Image) Similarity. In contrary to text that is viewed as one whole component, there are multiple instances of raster graphics components (images) in one document. Thus, the similarity of image components in two documents is really a similarity of two sets of images.

Due to the fact that many documents contain images that are sub-areas or slightly enhanced versions of other images in the same document, we have observed biases in image-based document similarity if all possible image pairs from two documents are evaluated individually and then the average similarity would be computed. The bias is introduced due to large similarity values of one master image in one document with multiple derived images in another document, although many other images would not have any match.

In order to avoid such biases, we approached the similarity calculation by first computing a pair-wise similarity of all images within each document and clustering them. Next, the pair-wise similarity of clusters of images from each document is computed using the average features of clusters.

A. Intra-document image similarity: The similarity of two raster graphics (image) components from one document $sim(I_{ik} \in D_i, I_{il} \in D_i)$ is computed using the one-dimensional color histogram feature and the same similarity metric as defined before for text according to [2]. The equation is provided below.

$$sim(I_{ik} \in D_i, I_{il} \in D_j) = \sum_{k1,k2} \omega_{i,k1}\omega_{i,k2} \tag{5}$$

where $k1, k2$ are those colors that occur in both images (in other words, there exist $e_{i,k1} = e_{i,k2}; e_{i,k1} \in I_{ik}, e_{i,k2} \in I_{il}$). The ω terms are the weights computed the same way as before.

B. Inter-document image similarity: The similarity of two sets of raster graphics (image) components, one from each document, $sim(I_{ik} \in D_i, I_{jl} \in D_j)$ is computed using the average one dimensional color histogram feature of all images in a set and the same similarity metric as defined before for text according to [2]. The equation is provided below.

$$sim(\{I_{ik}\} \in D_i, \{I_{jl}\} \in D_j) = \sum_{k1,k2} \omega_{i,k1}\omega_{j,k2} \tag{6}$$

Calculation of Vector Graphics Similarity. The methodology used text and raster image comparison is based on a statistical comparison technique for comparing large numbers of small information units of precisely defined structure, such as words or colors, which are reused multiple times to construct the document. The difficulty in using this comparison technique with vector graphics is that the most primitive feature of the graphics object, lines, are practically useless in meaningful comparisons. Due to this, it is necessary to compare objects at a slightly more sophisticated level by comparing groups of lines and their relationship to each other. However, the manner in which this can be done varies, and many techniques for comparison of simple geometric shapes exist, making it not trivial to choose which graphic comparison to use.

Several reviews of vector graphics comparison techniques [11, 13, 16] showed distinct methods for the comparison of polygons and open paths. However, the principle difficulty in implementing almost all of these methods is that they rely on a direct, side-by-side computationally expensive comparison between two graphical objects resulting in a real number comparison value in the range between 0 and 1. These types of comparisons would be difficult to integrate into the previously used statistical comparison technique because the current methodology relies on counting exactly reproducible informational units. For example, in a comparison of the text of this document, it would be easy to count the precise number of times the word "text" appears, but if one were to draw many cat graphics whose dimensions were not exactly the same, it would be difficult to count the number of cats because a common definition would not be possible. Instead, it is necessary to develop an approximate characterization of the shape of the graphic, which can then be easily compared with other shape approximations.

In this interest, the algorithm was developed, which binned the angle of each line in any series of connected lines in the document and recorded the binned angles. The angles could be grouped into unordered histograms or stored in the order they are rendered. The angular bin size is also variable. Tests presented in Section 0 were used to find an optimal method. The chosen methodology was unordered grouping with 9 angular bins. Using a textual encoding of the angular description, the algorithm used for text comparison can be used on the vector graphic data.

Finally, rotational and scale invariance of a similarity metric for comparing vector graphics objects has to be considered. For example, defining the angle of a line is simple if the basis axes are taken to be defined by the PDF page, but if this is the case then the comparison technique will not be rotationally invariant. To ensure rotational invariance, there must be a common definition of the basis line against which all the angles can be computed. Since the main feature of the shape is the location of the vertices, it makes sense to find a basis parameter that correlates the individual vertices of each line to each other. To this end, the average of all the vertices in the shape is used to find a center point about which all reference lines can be drawn. The reference line for each angle computation is then drawn through the center point and through the center of the line whose angle is being computed. These two points will always be in the same relation to the line whose angle is being measured despite rotational variance as is clear from Fig. 2. In Fig. 2, the solid black lines are vector graphic lines measured (which constitute a trapezoid in this example). The red dot is the mean of all the vertices of the shape, and the blue dots are the center points of the individual lines. The dotted line is the reference line, which passes through the red dot and the blue dot of the graphic line being measured. The angle (between 0° and 90°) is then computed from the intersection of these two lines which guarantees the rotational invariance.

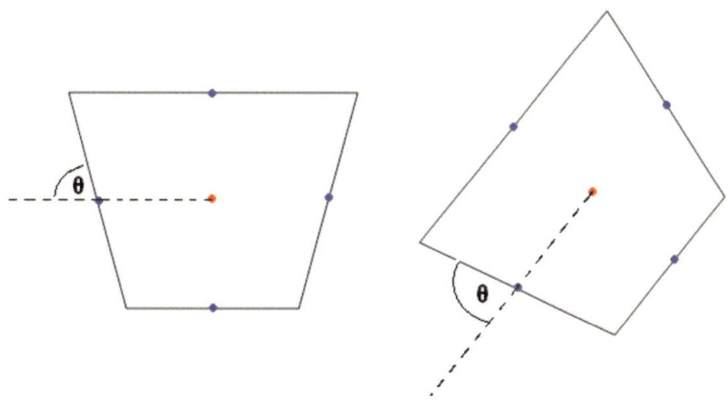

Fig. 2. Rotational invariance of the similarity metric designed for comparing vector graphics objects. The blue points correspond to the middle of each line. The red point is the center of gravity. The angle θ is the angle between each line forming a vector graphics object and the line connecting the center with the midpoint of the vector graphics line. The angle does not change with the rotation of the vector graphics object.

4. Feature Extraction from Adobe PDF Documents

The methodology described earlier is applicable to any set of documents. However, we have chosen to focus on the processing of PDF documents. PDF documents have become almost the defacto standard for information sharing and can be viewed on many different platforms. To be able to compute the similarity of two documents we first need to extract as many features as possible from the PDF documents. In the past we have conducted research to find software toolkits for loading and parsing PDF documents, as well as to identify the cost and functionality tradeoffs of each available software toolkit. The three main toolkits for extracting information from PDF documents are the PDF SDK developed by Adobe, Jpedal developed by IDR and PDFBox an open source SDK (PDFBox has since become a incubation project under the Apache Software Foundation). With these three software toolkits there was a direct relationship between the cost and the completenes of the implementation according to the PDF specification [17]. Jpedal provides a very complete implementation of the PDF specification for a low price. PDFBox has the main advantage of it being open source allowing us to extend the library if needed.

4.1 Feature Extractions

The choice of text primitives could include characters, words, sentences, paragraphs, sections, etc. Given the choice of these primitives, the word feature is mainly used due to relatively high information granularity comparing with characters and robustness for large number of samples comparing with sentences, paragraphs or sections. In particular, we could further divide the words into multiple types such as alphabetical texts, integers, and float (See Fig. 3). The main idea behind this clustering approach is in the fact that a scientific document could include different types of information based on the types of words.

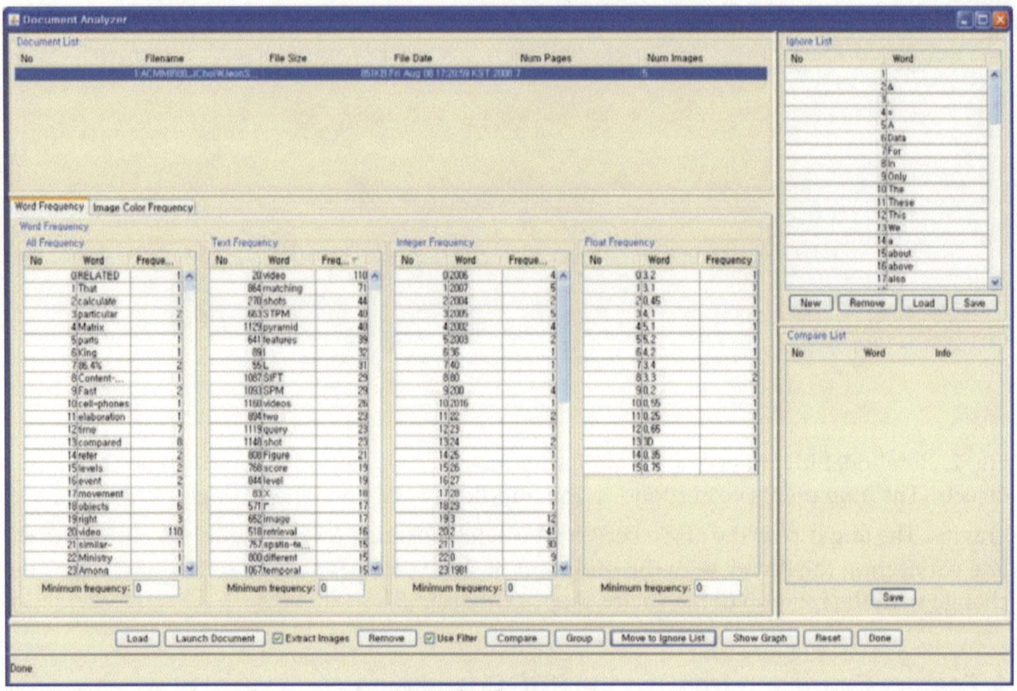

Fig. 3. Example of text features in a scientific document.

Alphabetical words could be further clustered into proper nouns, common nouns, and other frequently used words, e.g., verbs, adjectives, connectives, etc. Analysis on highly frequent common nouns could categorize the document into some scientific topics, and those on proper nouns could label and measure the uniqueness of the document. These classifications could be performed semi- or fully automatically by human or simple dictionary search. In Fig. 3, *text frequency* column shows very high frequency on "video/videos", "matching", and "shots", which implies that the document falls into some apparent topics, such as video matching.

In a scientific document, integer strings could typically represent (a) document numbers, i.e., chapter or page numbers, (b) time information, i.e., years, and/or (c) some data values.

Analyzing the range, i.e., 1900~2009 for years, or non-continuous numerical values, i.e., 2171, 1131400, etc., could give a clue about when the document is written or presence of some data values derived from a study. In Fig. 3, the *integer frequency* column shows some numbers guessed as years and continuous low numerical values guessed as less important information, e.g. page numbers. In addition, due to the fact that the maximum value of the year is 2007, we could also guess that the document was written in or after 2007. The floating point numbers typically appear in a scientific document reporting the measured or derived values from an experiment.The occurrence of these values could provide additional clues about the types of the document.

Similarly, image primitives could become colors at each pixel, shapes of blobs of adjacent pixels with similar color (image segments), color statistics of regular blocks of pixels, etc. In this work, we focused on the statistics of color frequencies in a figure to determine the type of the figures. Fig. 4 shows an example of color frequency analysis on the same scientific document in Fig. 3. Based on the extracted color frequencies after quantification, we could cluster the raster image figures in a typical PDF document into several categories such as charts, natural scenes, or drawings. For example, a chart in Figure 4, shows very high color frequency for the RGB values of [255,255,255] (white), [191,191,255] (cyan), and [255,191,191] (pink). Natural scene would have high color variances in the images depending on the lighting condition, objects in the figure, and zoom level of the scene.

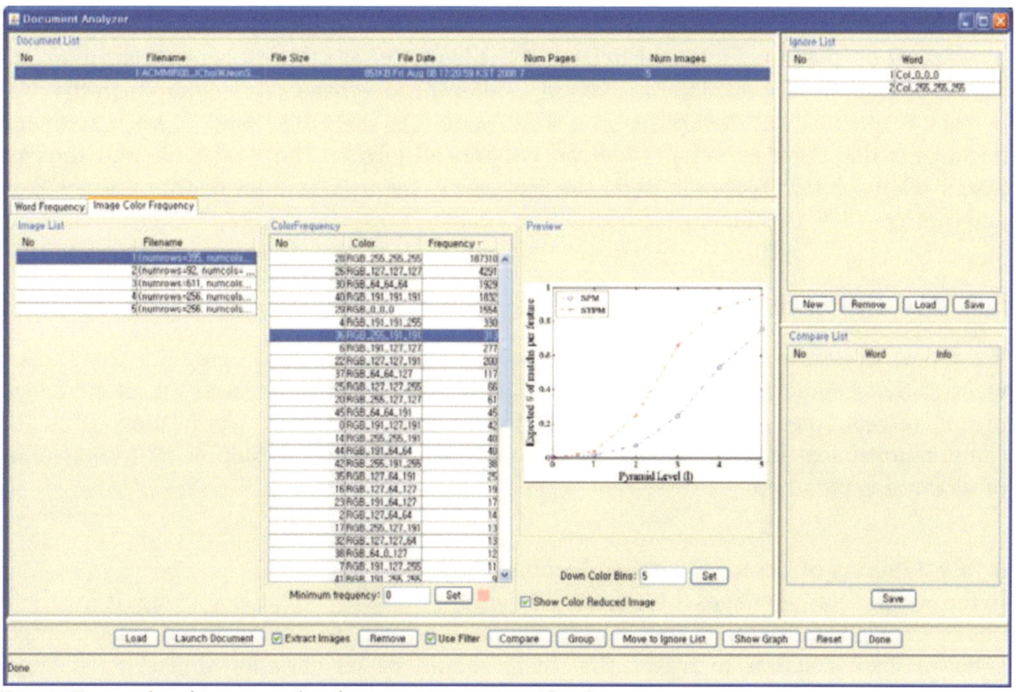

Fig. 4. Example of image color features in a scientific document.

4.2 Scalability of Feature Extractions

To be able to do a better similarity computation of the documents we want a large number of features extracted. The problem becomes that the more features we extract from the PDF

documents, the longer it will take to process a PDF document. The initial approach we took was to store the extracted data for each document so the next time the document is openend we can simply retrieve the cached information. This works well if documents are opened multiple times and not to many complex documents are opened simultanously.
To overcome these problems we have looked at preprocessing the documents. Since we potentially have to preprocess many documents, parallelizing this task is important. The parallelization is achieved by using Apache Hadoop. Each document is preprocessed by our system and the cached information is written to disk. When comparing documents we can simply load the cached information instead of having to process the document.
Hadoop allows us to count occurences in a document. The document is split in smaller pieces (a set of pages) and each page is parsed into objects (text paragraphs, images, vector graphics and in the future other multimedia elements). These objects are sent to a mapping function which will split the object in smaller parts that will be counted. For example text paragraphs are split in words (allowing us to do frequency of occurence of words, dates and numbers) and imaeges are split in pixels (for frequency of occurence of colors). After the map operation the reduce stage will begin which will count the frequency of occurence of the smaller parts generated by the mapper function.
The map and reduce phases of Hadoop can run in parallel, allowing intermediate data to be streamed from the mapper to reducer. This will decrease the time it takes to process a document. In the simple case where we only have one mapper and one reducer we have seen the time be cut in half for parsing the whole document. Since Hadoop codes run in parallel, all the data for a job need to be sent to the processor that will perform the map and reduce operations. For documents that are smaller this overhead can be more than the time it takes to process the document on a local node. On the other hand if we have many documents that need processing we can not run all jobs on the local node and thus no matter what solution is chosen to do the processing, the overhead for distributing the data and results will be the same.

5. Experimental Results

We report experimental results that illustrate the choice of vector graphics comparison metrics, the accuracies of comprehensive document comparisons based on all contained digital objects, the prototype approach to document integrity verification, and the computational scalability achieved using computer clusters and Map & Reduce parallel programming paradigm.

5.1 Evaluations of Vector Graphics Comparisons

In the comparison of images it is standard to ensure that the comparison metric is invariant under translation, rotation, and rescaling. Because the method is based on the angle between lines it stands to reason that there should be no variation under translational variation. Also, as long as rescaling does not distort the image's aspect ratio it should also not make a difference in comparison. To test this, the three documents appearing in Fig. 5 were compared.
Note that the image of the computer in the document on the left has been both translated and rescaled in the center document. The document on the right contains an unrelated image of a CD-ROM drive. The result of a comparison of these three images is 100%

similarity between documents 1 and 2 and 0% similarity between documents 1 and 3 and documents 2 and 3. Therefore the comparison is both translation and scale invariant.
To be sure that this method works a simple test was performed on the three PDF documents shown in Fig. 6.

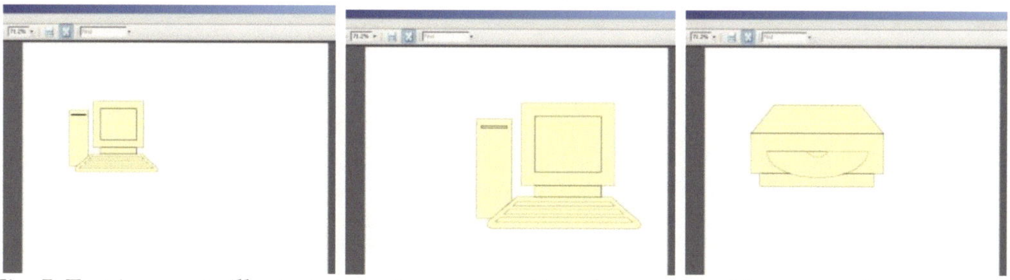

Fig. 5. Test images to illustrate invariance properties of vector graphics comparisons

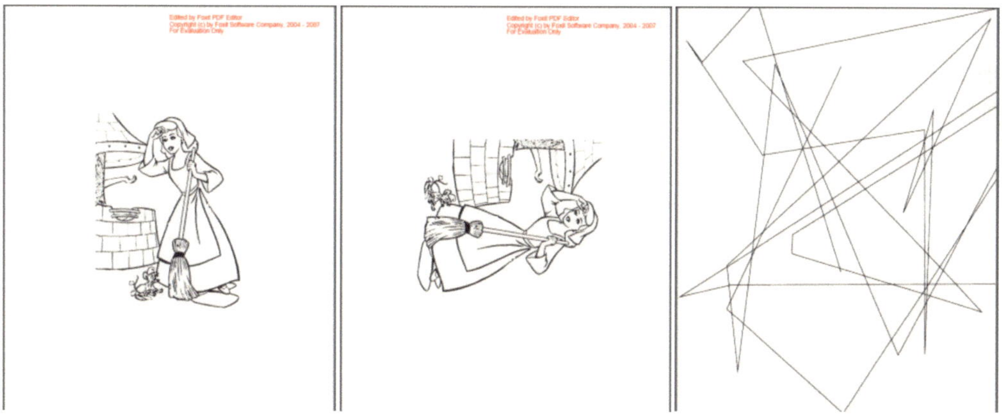

Fig. 6. Three test PDF documents with vector graphics objects. The leftmost document and the center document are just 90° rotations of each other and the rightmost document contains an unrelated set of random lines.

Using the unordered implementation with 9 bins without the rotationally invariant modification, the similarity between the rotated documents is only 0.18, while the similarity between unrelated documents is 0. Using the modification to allow rotational invariance brings the similarity between the rotated documents to 1, while the similarity between the unrelated documents remains at 0. This process was repeated for rotations of 25°, 50°, 75°, and 180°. The 180° rotation also showed a similarity of 1, but when the graphic was rotated by the intermediate angles, the similarity dropped to 0.72. However, the rotations at intermediate angles all showed similarity 1 between other rotations at intermediate angles. This indicates that during partial rotations some line segments may become distorted in the PDF rendering, but this type of problem cannot be rectified because the actual shape is being distorted and there is no way to recover it.

5.2 Evaluations of Comprehensive Document Comparisons and Clustering Results

Using the presented framework, we appraised sets of PDF documents generated during scientific medical journal preparations. The document sample set consisted of 10 documents 4 of which were modified versions of one article and 6 were of a different though related article. The pair-wise comparisons of the features are presented in the following graphs.

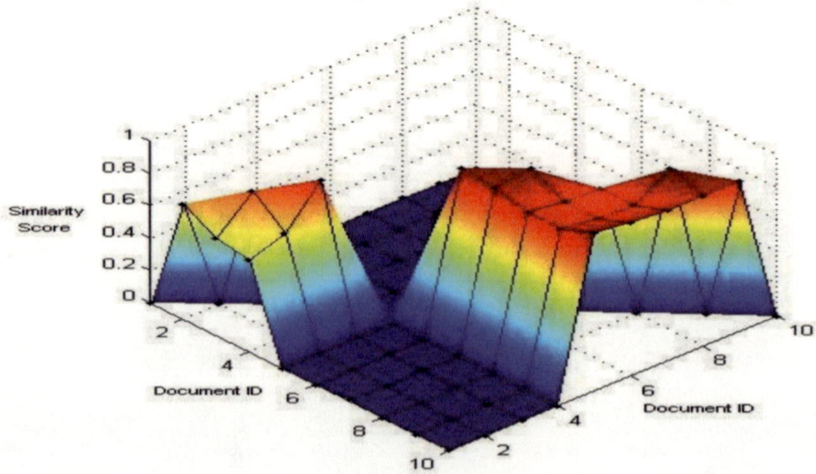

Fig. 7. Word similarity comparison

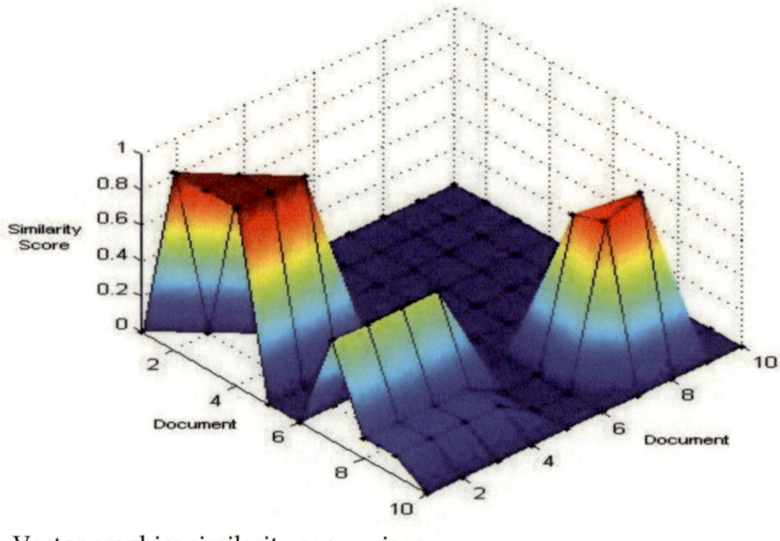

Fig. 8. Vector graphics similarity comparison

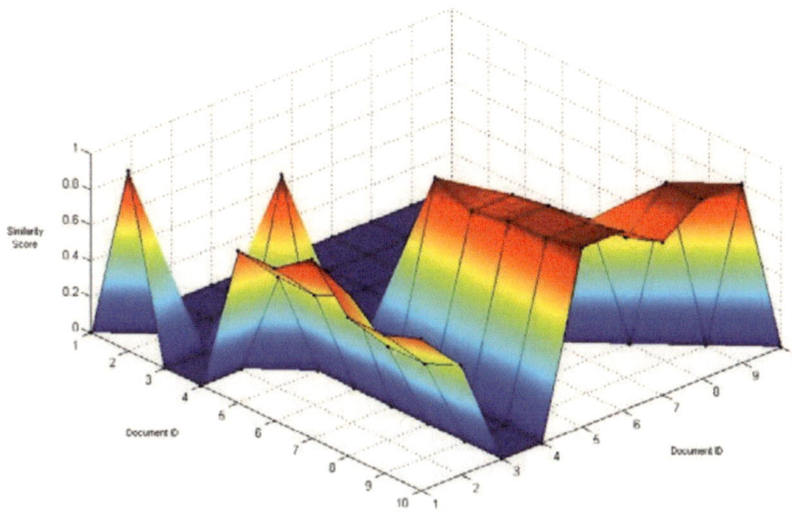

Fig. 9. Raster image similarity comparison

The z values of the graphs in Figures 1-3 represent the similarities between the documents identified with the numbers by the x and y axes. The word similarity comparison clearly shows that the documents 5 through 10 score highly in comparison with each other while they score poorly in comparison to the documents 1 through 4. Likewise, documents 1 through 4 show higher scores for comparison within the group. The vector graphics of documents 1 through 4 are nearly identical while in the second subgroup only documents 7 through 9 are conclusively linked. The raster images within the two subgroups of the documents shows high similarities for the documents 5 through 10 score but the rest are not obvious how they are related. The combination of vector graphics comparison along with word comparison results in a clear consensus about which documents belong together as shown in Figure 4.

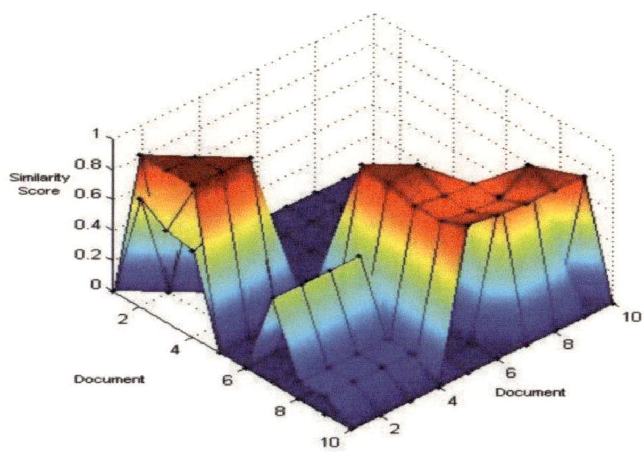

Fig. 10. Vector graphics similarity and word similarity combined

Throughout the documents the relative apportionment of visible space of the three document features varies. Figure 5 shows the fraction of each document covered by words, images and vector graphics.

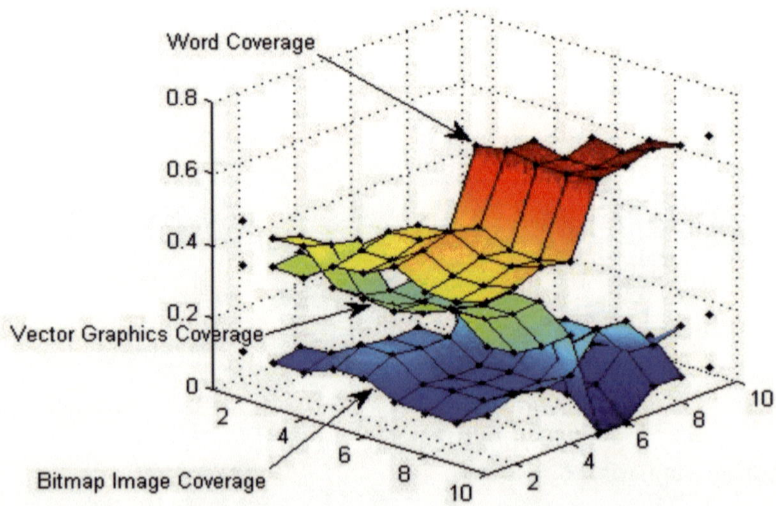

Fig. 11. Portion of document surface allotted to each document feature

Combining the three comparison techniques with weights allotted by the proportion of coverage of the feature represented by that comparison allows for a final similarity score to be established. Figure 6 displays the final comparison matrix, which clearly distinguishes the two subgroups of the original document set.

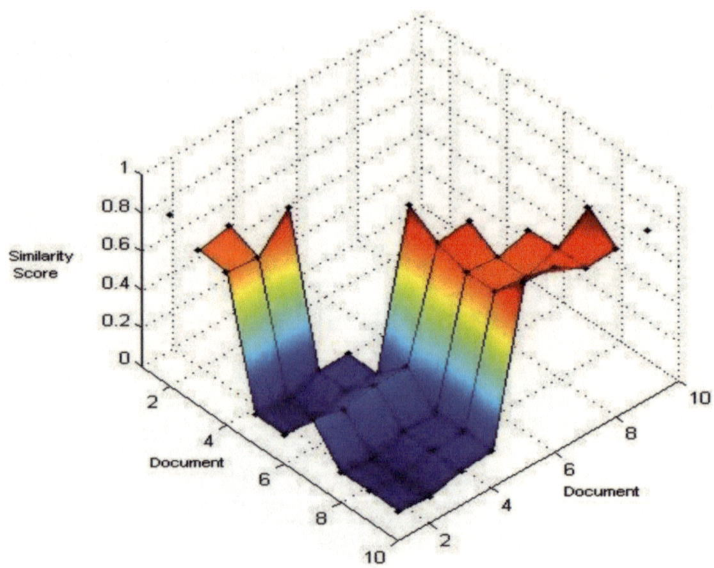

Fig. 12. Comparison using combination of document features in proportion to coverage

5.3 Preliminary Results of Document Integrity Verification

With the documents adequately grouped and ordered by PDF timestamp, the verification process looks for conspicuous editing habits from one document to the next. A successful document order verification relies on multiple failures of the tests displayed in Figures 7 and 8. The current tests conducted search for (a) appearance and disappearance of (1) identical document dates images or (2) identical, and (b) increase or decrease in (1) file size, (2) image count, (3) sentence count, and (4) average date value from one document to the next.

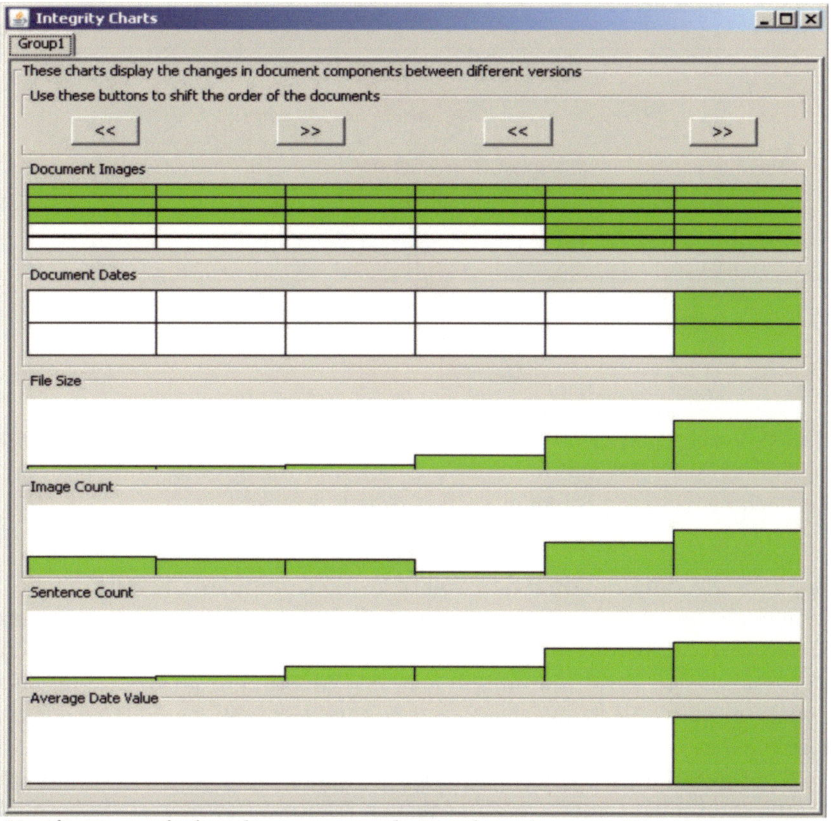

Fig. 13. Verification of the document ordering based upon the time stamps of PDF documents. Documents are aligned from earliest (left) to latest (right). Integrity tests are aligned from top to bottom. These are: (1) appearance or disappearance of document images, (2) appearance and disappearance of dates appearing in documents, (3) file size, (4) image count, (5) number of sentence, and (6) average value of dates found in document.

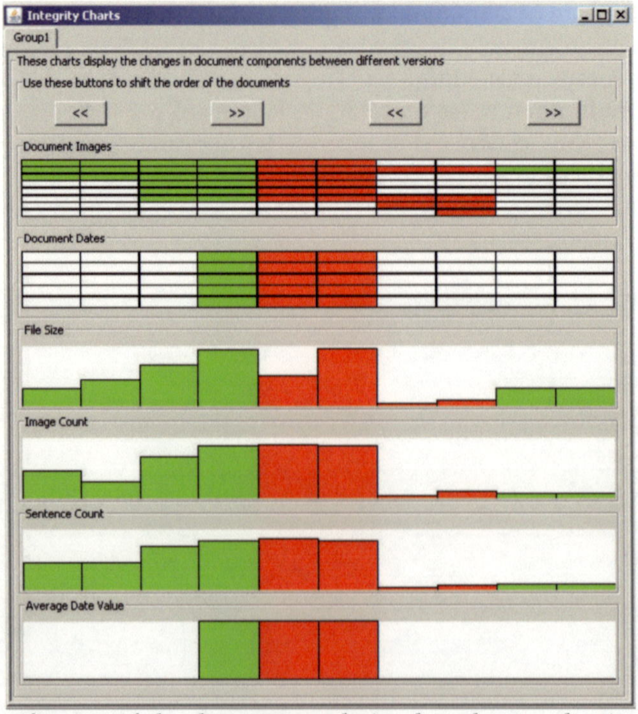

Fig. 14. Failed Verification of the document ordering based upon the time stamps of PDF documents. Green bars indicate reasonable changes to documents while red bars indicate suspicious document editing behavior such as drastic deletions.

5.4 Evaluations of Computational Scalability Using Computer Clusters

Our experimental design focuses on quantifying the speed of the statistical summarization of digital objects in Adobe PDF documents. The choice of statistical summarization is based on the observations that word counting in text, line counting in vector graphics objects and color-based pixel counting in images are all counting operations suitable for distributed computing.

Hardware Configuration: We tested the prototype implementation on several machines that were configured with the Linux operating system (Ubuntu flavor) and Hadoop. There was one cluster at National Center for Supercomputing Applications (NCSA) and one cluster in the Computer Science Department at the University of Illinois at Urbana-Champaign (UIUC) that we used during the last period of performance. The cluster specifications are provided below.

NCSA cluster: The NCSA cluster consisted of four identical desktop machines. Each machine has a Core 2 processor running at 2.4 GHz with 2GB of memory and 100GB of local disk space. The cluster created from these machines was set up to do five Map and one Reduce task per node, resulting in the ability to do 4 * 5 = 20 Map tasks and 4 * 1 = 4 Reduce tasks simultaneously. Each node was also set up to be part of the shared file system with a replication the same as number of nodes in the cluster (resulting in each file being locally on the file system).

Illinois Cloud Computing Testbed cluster: We were given access to the Illinois Cloud Computing Testbed (CCT) in the Computer Science Department, at the University of Illinois at Urbana-Champaign (UIUC). The CCT testbed was funded by Intel, Yahoo! and Hewlett Packard, and provides resources for doing cluster computing research. After arranging the access to the test-bed, we could run jobs on a larger system than the ones at NCSA. However, we did not have control of the CCT system and could not reduce the number of hosts running. Thus, we always run with the maximum number of hosts up equal to 64 nodes. Each node has a dual quad core CPU with 16GB of memory. The cluster created from these machines was set up to do six Map and two Reduce tasks per node, resulting in the ability to do 64*6=384 Map tasks and 64*2=128 Reduce tasks simultaneously. Each node has 2TB of local disk space which is part of the larger distributed file system. Unlike the NCSA clusters this file system has a replication factor of 3 resulting not in each file being locally available.

Software Configuration: For the experiments, we took the NCSA cluster and created two configurations. One configuration had a single machine with both master and slave processes running. The master process is responsible for distributing the jobs and the slaves execute the jobs (the Map and Reduce operations). The second configuration had two machines, where each machine had the slave processes running and one of them had the master process running. The Illinois CCT cluster has a dedicated machine for running the master process and all other machines are running slave processes. The dedicated machine running the master process is not running any slave processes.
We have run experiments with Hadoop on both NCSA cluster and Illinois CCT cluster (also denoted as cloud in the figure below).

Benchmarking: As a reference measurement, we timed the execution without using Hadoop on a single machine. To be able to execute the code with the larger size documents we had to increase the memory to 2GB for the Java VM. The code used to obtain the reference measurement has not been optimized. The reference measurement always corresponds to the blue line in all graphs denoted as SA (stand-alone).
All timing measurements are conducted after the system started and the document to be processed has been uploaded to the distributed file system (in the case of Hadoop). For the case of the stand-alone machine, the timing starts when the document is about to be opened and it stops when the counting is finished (all of this is done in java and averaged over 10 runs so that the Java virtual machine has the time to optimize the code). In the case of Hadoop, the timing starts in the main function when the job is submitted and stops when Hadoop has finished its computation.

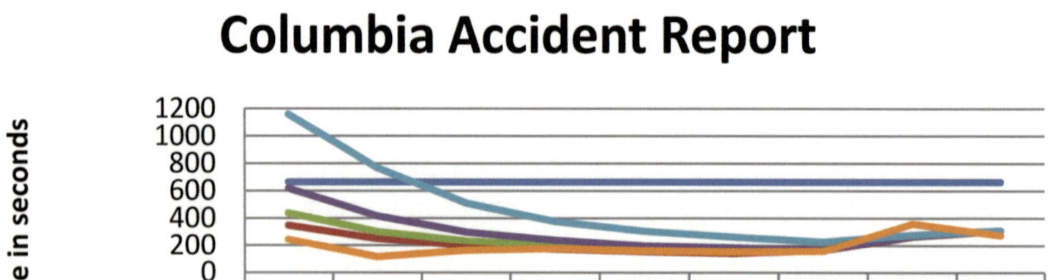

	1 pages	2 pages	4 pages	8 pages	16 pages	32 pages	64 pages	128 pages	256 pages
SA	664	664	664	664	664	664	664	664	664
hadoop1 [4]	347,4	250,4	196,0	170,9	152,5	140,3	162,4	263,8	308,0
hadoop1 [3]	438,0	301,9	233,0	200,7	180,5	154,4	170,4	263,9	309,7
hadoop1 [2]	616,8	416,3	298,4	238,1	197,7	184,7	168,5	265,6	310,3
hadoop1 [1]	1159	768,6	509,8	375,9	304,2	263,1	226,9	277,8	310,8
cloud	242,2	114,4	162,4	174,6	160,2	153,2	157,0	359,0	274,5

Fig. 15. Time to parse the Columbia Investigation PDF document in seconds as a function of the number of pages in each distributed data chunk. The PDF document contains 248 pages, 179.187 words, 236 images, and 30.924 vector graphics; and its size is 10.330.897 bytes. Dark blue curve corresponds to the reference measurement (single machine, no Hadoop). Orange curve (denoted as cloud) corresponds to the Illinois CCT cluster with 64 machines. Other curves correspond to NCSA cluster with a variable number of nodes utilized for the computation (listed in brackets as hadoop1[number of nodes]).

Experimental Results: We have analyzed several documents of various complexity (number of digital objects contained) and various size. The initial experiments took the document and split it up in clusters of 1, 2, 4, 8, ..., 256 pages per map operation (or to the closest power of two larger than the total number of pages in a document). The map operation would take the data from the document and split it up in the smallest possible item. For text it would create a list of words, for images a list of pixels and for vector graphics a list of vector graphic operations (connect points to lines, create a rectangle, etc.). Once these lists are generated, Hadoop would start to reduce these lists by counting how often certain items appeared in the list. Processing time for an example document is shown Fig 15. As it can be seen in Fig 15, the use of Hadoop is definitely advantageous over a stand-alone implementation for complex documents such as the Columbia Investigation report.

6. Summary

We have described a framework for addressing document appraisal criteria. The framework consists of feature extraction from multiple digital objects contained in contemporray documents, pair-wise similarity metrics for comparing digital objects, a comprehensive content-based grouping of documents, ranking based on temporal or file size attributes and verification of document integrity, as well as the parallel algorithms supporting applications with large volumes of documents and computationally intensive processing. Although we selected to work with documents in PDF format, the framework is applicable to any file format as long as the information can be loaded from any proprietary file format. The framework implementation called Document To Learn (Doc2Learn) is available for downloading from http://isda.ncsa.uiuc.edu/.In future, we will be exploring other hypotheses to increase the likelihood of detecting inconsistencies and understanding the high-performance computing requirements of computer-assisted appraisal of electronic records.

7. Acknowledgment

This research was partially supported by a National Archive and Records Administration (NARA) supplement to NSF PACI cooperative agreement CA #SCI-9619019. The views and conclusions contained in this document are those of the authors and should not be interpreted as representing the official policies, either expressed or implied, of the National Science Foundation, the National Archive and Records Administration, or the U.S. government.

8. References

[1] P. Bajcsy, and S.-C. Lee, "Computer Assisted Appraisal of Contemporary PDF Documents," in ARCHIVES 2008: Archival R/Evolution & Identities, 72nd Annual Meeting Pre-conference Programs:, San Francisco, CA, 2008.

[2] G. Salton, J. Allan, and C. Buckley, "Automatic structuring and retrieval of large text files," *in Communication of the ACM,* vol. 37, no. 2, pp. 97-108, 1994.

[3] D. M. Squire, W. Müller, H. Müller *et al.*, "Content-Based query of image databases: inspirations from text retrieval," *Pattern Recognition Letters,* vol. 21, pp. 1193-1198, 2000.

[4] J. A. Marshall, "Accounting For Disposition: A Comparative Case Study of Appraisal Documentation at the NARA in the US, Library and Archives Canada, and the NAA," Dep. of Library and Information Science, Univ. of Pittsburg, 2006.

[5] S.-C. Lee, W. McFadden, and P. Bajcsy, "Text, Image and Vector Graphics Based Appraisal of Contemporary Documents," in The 7th International Conference on Machine Learning and Applications, San Diego, CA., 2008.

[6] W. S. Lovegrove, and D. F. Brailsford, " Document analysis of PDF files: methods, results and implications," *ELECTRONIC PUBLISHING,* vol. 8, no. 2 & 3, pp. 207-220, JUNE & SEPTEMBER 1995, 1995.

[7] A. Anjewierden, "AIDAS: incremental logical structure discovery in PDF documents," in International Conference on Document Analysis and Recognition, 2001.

[8] R. P. Futrelle, M. Shao, C. Cieslik *et al.*, "Extraction, layout analysis and classification of diagrams in PDF documents. Intl. Conf.Document Analysis & Recognition" pp. 1007-1014 year 2003.

[9] M. Shao, and R. P. Futrelle, "Recognition and Classification of Figures in PDF Documents," *Lecture Notes in Computer Science*: Springer Berlin / Heidelberg 2006.

[10] W. Huang, C. L. Tan, and W. K. Leow, "Model-based chart image recognition," in Fifth IAPR International Workshop on Graphics Recognition Computer Vision Center, Barcelona, Catalonia, Spain, 2003, pp. 87-99.

[11] R. C. Veltkamp, and L. J. Latecki, "Properties and Performances of Shape Similarity Measures.," *Data Science and Classification*,. pp. 47-56.

[12] M. Tanase and R. C. Veltkamp, "Part-based Shape Retrieval." In Proceedings of the 13th annual ACM international conference on Multimedia, pages 543–546. ACM New York, NY, USA, 2005.

[13] L. Hess and B.Mayoh. "Graphics and theUnderstanding of Perceptual Mechanisms: Analogies and Similarities". Geometric Modeling and Imaging–New Trends, 2006, pages 107–112, 2006.

[14] Enis. "Machine Scaling," 14th of June 2009; http://wiki.apache.org/hadoop/ MachineScaling.

[15] M. Zaharia, A. Konwinski, A. D. Joseph *et al.*, *Improving MapReduce Performance in Heterogeneous Environments*, UCB/EECS-2008-99, University of California at Berkeley, 2008.

[16] R. C. Veltkamp, "Shape Matching: Similarity Measures and Algorithms." pp. 188-97.

[17] Adobe Systems, "PDF Reference version 1.7," *ISO 32000-1 standard* http://www.adobe.com/devnet/pdf/pdf_reference.html, [June 12th, 2009, 2009].

7

Building an application - generation of 'items tree' based on transactional data

Mihaela Vranić, Damir Pintar and Zoran Skočir
University of Zagreb,
Faculty of Electrical Engineering and Computing
Croatia

1. Introduction

Association rules method is a commonly known and frequently used technique of undirected data mining. One of the commonly known drawbacks of this technique is that it often discovers a very large number of rules, many of which are trivial, uninteresting or simply variations of each other. Domain experts have to go through many of these rules to draw a meaningful conclusion which could be acted upon. Another issue that may arise is that investigation of obtained association ruleswhich cannot provide information about actual distances between items that transactions include (distances being a term describing how often items show up together in same transactions). In this particular case the actual absolute distances are not as important as the relative ones. A feature such as a compact presentation of such distances between items could be used by some business environments to quickly and dynamically produce usable business decisions. Realizing the problem of great quantity of association rules, investigations on redundancy elimination were done and results are presented in (Pasquier et al., 2005) and (Xu, Li, 2007). Here described approach is different from those - final goal is different and acquired structure should be interpreted in specific way.

Driven by issues described above, we have created an application that goes trough presented transactional data multiple times and creates association rules on various levels. The final outcome of created rules is a table that reflects relative distances between items.

Chapter is arranged as follows:

Firstly, in paragraph 2, motivation and problem description is elaborated upon in more detail. Also, some examples of possible usages are given.

Short introduction to the main method used in this article (method of association rules) is given in paragraph 3. Basic terms, measurements used in this method along with examples of its usage are addressed here and certain strengths and weaknesses are elaborated upon.

Paragraph 4 introduces tools bearing relevant connections to the one this chapter deals with.

Chosen technologies for the application realization are discussed in paragraph 5. Application functionality is described in detail in paragraph 6. This paragraph also deals with many issues that emerged with corresponding solutions.

The application was applied on a real life dataset. Its functionality and performance parameters are depicted in paragraph 7. This performance, of course, depends on dataset characteristics, so information about dataset origin is also included. Insight on how certain characteristics of dataset can affect application performance will be given.
There are some fields where the application can be improved. That is left for further investigation and described in paragraph 8.
Finally, paragraph 9 provides concluding thoughts.
Work presented in this chapter concentrates on issues of developing the application core - an algorithm which would in reasonable time provide data which reflects connections between items based on their co-occurrence in same transactions. In subsequent chapters this final data will be referred to as the 'tree data'.
However, visual presentation of the 'tree data' describing the generated tree was also considered. There are some available open source tree presentations based on XML. Even though the application doesn't recognize our generated 'tree data' as input, transformation between our tree data and required XML document should be simple and straightforward.

2. Motivation and Problem Definition

Retail industry, telecommunication industry, insurance companies and other various industries produce and store great quantities of transactional data. For example, in medicine data about patients, therapies, patient reactions etc. is being recorded on daily basis. In this great quantity of data many patterns that could be acted upon are often hidden. If we take retail industry as an example then visual presentation of the distance between items found in the store depending on actual market basket contents could be very helpful. This data could help not only to ensure more effective placement of products on the shelves, but also to provide assistance for customers who could find products they are interested in with more ease. Mentioned findings could also be used to discover some connections which could lead to revelations of hidden causalities.
Transactional data can reveal which items often show up together in some transactions. Certain measure (i.e. aforementioned *distance*) between items could be introduced. Items that very often show up together in same transactions should be considered as close ones, and items that relatively rarely show up together transactions should express greater distance between each other. Based on that distance between items graphical tree presentation containing items could be formed. Close items should be connected very early in a tree (near the tree leaves), while distanced items should connect to each other in a part of a tree closer to the tree root.
Our goal was to find a way to generate data clearly depicting 'closeness' of items with following characteristics:

- data has to be transferable to the graphical tree representation,
- items should be connected if certain proportion of recorded transactions suggests their 'closeness',
- the number of tree levels must be reasonable in order to be manageable by a human analyst (this prerequisite is necessary because of the large number of expected items to be found in transactions).

Certain technologies and available techniques were chosen to construct a solution for the presented problem. Some guidance for that matter is given in (Campos et al., 2005). Decision

was made to use a widely known data mining method of association rules generation. This method has already developed certain measures that could be used to determine item closeness. However, multiple usages of that method will be necessary to construct multiple tree levels.
Attribute distance algorithms were also considered. However, requirement for the application to take into account some measures that reflect ratio in which items appear together and on that bases stop further growth of the item tree encouraged us to use the association rules method instead.

3. General Idea and Theoretical Base of Association Rules

For introduction of association rules and for various explanations (Agrawal et al., 1993) and (Hand et al., 2001) were used.

3.1 Basic terms

Association rules represent local patterns in data. This descriptive data mining method results in a set of probabilistic statements that discover co-occurrence of certain attributes (items). Some basic terms that will be used further on will now be introduced:

Let $I=\{i_1, i_2, ..., i_n\}$ be a set of n binary attributes called *items*.

Let $T=\{t_1, t_2, ..., t_m\}$ be a set of transactions. Each transaction t_j has a unique ID and contains a subset of attributes in I.

A rule has a simple form: if A then B (or simply $A \Rightarrow B$), where $A, B \subseteq I$ and $A \cap B = \emptyset$. *A* and *B* are sets of items (shortly *itemsets*). *A* is called *antecedent*, and *B* is called *consequent* of the rule.

The idea of this widely used and explored method could be easily explained on transactional data concerning purchases in retail - supermarket. In that case I represents a collection of products (items) that could be bought in the store, and every t_j collects some of available products depending on the realized transactions by customers. By analyzing accomplished transactions through a certain time period, some regularities will emerge - for example: transactions that contain bread very often contain milk (bread and milk are items that co-occur in same transactions). Association rule for this relationship looks like: *bread* $\Rightarrow$ *milk*. Example given here depicts one of the most common usages of association rules method - so-called Market Basket Analysis. However, depending of the data at hand, association rules could bring to surface various types of regularities. I could be set of binary attributes that depict some entities or cases of some interest to us. In that case, association rules give us insight that existence of some attribute (attributes) often implicates appearance of some other attribute (attributes). Dataset example is given in Table 1. Rows present transactions, while columns present binary attributes-items. Data should be read like this: items A and B are included in the first transaction.

transaction /item	A	B	C	D
1	1	1	0	0
2	1	1	0	1
3	1	1	1	0
4	1	1	1	1
5	0	1	1	0
6	0	0	0	1
7	0	0	1	0

Table 1. The dataset example

Data given in Table 1, can also be presented in other formats, depending on the requirements of the specific tool used for analysis.
Typical characteristics of transactions are that they don't contain same number of items, and number of items they contain is rather small (comparing to the whole set ***I***). Datasets are consequently very sparse. As stated before, this data mining method is suitable for categorical datasets. Number of items is usually very high as well as the number of possible rules.

3.2 Measurements

All rules that could be formed don't have the same level of interest or significance. That's why certain measurements and constraints on them are introduced. The best known constraints are minimum thresholds on support and confidence. Their definition is:
Support of the itemset A (notice that A could contain one or more items) is the probability of appearance of itemset A in random transaction:

$$\text{supp(A)} = \frac{\text{number of transactions that contain itemset A}}{\text{total number of transactions}} = \text{p(A)} \tag{1}$$

Confidence of a rule $A \Rightarrow B$ is:

$$\text{conf}(A \Rightarrow B) = \frac{\text{number of transactions that contain both itemset A and itemset B}}{\text{number of transactions that contain itemset A}}$$

$$\text{conf}(A \Rightarrow B) = \frac{\text{supp}(A \cap B)}{\text{supp}(A)} = \frac{p(A, B)}{p(A)} \tag{2}$$

In other words confidence is the probability of itemset B appearing in a specific transaction if we know that itemset A is included in it. Most confident rules are generally most valuable ones[1]. However, there are some cases where they work poorly compared to the random choice of transaction where certain item appears. That is the reason for introducing a new measure: rule lift.

[1] Support is sometimes called coverage, while synonym for confidence is accuracy.

$$\text{lift}(A \Rightarrow B) = \frac{\text{rule confidence}}{\text{probability of appearance of B in random transaction}}$$

$$\text{lift}(A \Rightarrow B) = \frac{p(A,B)}{p(A)} * \frac{1}{p(B)} \qquad (3)$$

Association rules are required to satisfy a user-specified minimum support and minimum confidence. Algorithms first find all itemsets that satisfy given support, and then rules that could be formed from this itemsets are examined to satisfy minimum confidence. Real issue in terms of processing time and capacity is the first step since number of candidate itemsets grows exponentially with number of items. Many algorithms for generating association rules were presented over time. One of the most used one is Apriory algorithm, which is also implemented in the tools that are to be used in application described in this book chapter.

3.3 Common usage, strengths and weaknesses

Rule structure is quite simple and interpretable. However, one has to be careful since these rules don't have to describe causal relationships but only state the fact of co-occurrence of items in transactions.

As stated before, this descriptive data mining method lets data tell its own story. Depending on the adapted parameters, rules with support and confidence greater that specified minimum are generated. Previous knowledge and some experimentation is required to tweak the parameters in such manner so the algorithm yields the best possible results - so not to end up with an extremely low number of rules or to get thousands of them. Furthermore, it is common to get a large number of rules that present fairly obvious facts (like connecting certain attributes which is predetermined before and not really a revelation), and special attention has to be taken to distinct such results apart from the new, potentially useful information. It is often hard for the analyst to get a clear picture of connections between items (attributes) since one connection is expressed with many rules (e.g. A ⇒ B; B ⇒ A; A,C ⇒ B; B,C ⇒ A...). Furthermore, it is often difficult to distinguish which connections are stronger than others.

Application described in this chapter resulted from seeking a way to present rules in a manner which would enable better understanding and faster reaction of business analyst responsible for rule interpretation and forming of actable business decisions.

4. Available Viewer Applications

The problem of interpreting high quantities of association rules emerged early with usage of given method and algorithms. Many tools tried to resolve this issue by providing various graphical representations of constructed rules. Some tools enable the analyst to pick an antecedent or consequent which results in rules that satisfy this condition being displayed (e.g. *Oracle Data Miner*). Other tools incorporate modules like 'Association Rules Tree Viewer' (e.g. *Orange* - component-based data mining software). Those applications enable tree-like association rules presentation. Rules antecedents appear as tree roots while

consequents form branches. If multiple antecedent elements are present then second antecedent element forms a new branch. This branch is further expanded to leaves (consequents) or more complex branches (further antecedent elements).
Main goal of the existing software solutions is to enable better representation of rules generated in one step - algorithm applied once and producing rules satisfying thresholds of minimal support and confidence.
One drawback of such presentation is that the same rule - connection between two attributes appears in more than one place in a tree which results in basic problem of difficult readability not being resolved by those applications and/or tools. Our main goal is to form a tree where an item will always appear only once.

5. Technologies and Tools

Association rules as a data mining technique is pretty demanding when it comes to processing time and power. We wanted to distance our application from the ETL process and enable it to work with the data that is already in the database. That is why we decided to use database inbuilt data mining functionalities. Those functionalities are available in Oracle Database 11g Enterprise Edition and known as ODM (*Oracle Data Mining*). Choice of this technology brought us certain important advantages: data mining models are treated as objects inside the database and data mining processes use database inbuilt functions to maximize scalability and time efficiency. Furthermore, security is resolved by the database which makes it relatively simple to update the data (this usually depends on actual data sources, organization business rules, etc.). ODM offers a few application programming interfaces which could be used to develop the final application, such as PL/SQL and Java API. Decision to use PL/SQL and direct access to database objects that keep various information on final association rules model was made, due to flexibility it offers and opportunity to tweak the finally developed algorithm to best suit our needs. Algorithm was stored as a script containing both PL/SQL blocks and DDL instructions. Java was chosen to further develop the aforementioned developed algorithm and tweak parameters for every step of tree level generation.

6. Application Functionality

6.1 'Tree representation' data

For better understanding of following steps a clarification of the goal and its data representation must be presented. As stated before, final goal of the application is to generate a tree-like structure that reflects co-occurrence of items in the same transactions (or co-occurrence of attributes in the observations). A presentation that corresponds to structure is presented in Fig. 1 (on the left). This tree-like structure has to be mapped to the data in some way. Expected characteristics of the data model are:

- to be straightforward and easily transferable to the tree-like structure
- to be easily readable
- preference that every algorithm step (which generates one tree level) corresponds to one data structure (for example column in a relational table).

Decision to adopt the data model corresponding to the one presented in Fig. 1 (on the right) was made. Final data model consist of one relational table where every row presents one item (making the column of item ID necessary), and other columns which reflect item's belonging to certain groups on various levels.

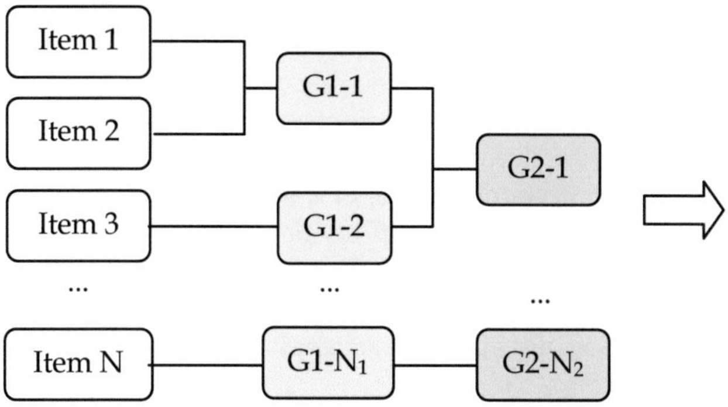

ITEM	Level 1	Level2
Item 1	1	1
Item 2	1	1
Item 3	2	1
...	...	...
Item N	N_1	N_2

Fig. 1. Final tree-like structure and its data representation

Level column interpretation works like this: items having the same number in a certain column belong to the same group on that level and are connected in a tree structure (in that level). If there are items that on a certain level don't have items to be grouped with (on certain criteria) then they have a unique group number in that column - i.e. there are no other items to share their group number with (in Fig. 1 - *Item 3* on *level 1* has a unique group number 2). Numbers (group marks) N_1, N_2... depend on number of group identification on certain level and identified groups on previous levels. If a binary tree is created formulas for N_1 and general N_j are provided below:

$$N_1 = N - \frac{G_1}{2}$$

$$N_j = N_{j-1} - \frac{G_j}{2}$$

Where:
- N - total number of items
- N_j - maximum group number on level j
- G_j - number of formed groups on level j

It is important to emphasize that some groups consist of only one element from previous level (e.g. G1-2). The existence of this group is not necessary and in final graphical representation it doesn't have to be displayed.

6.2 Overall algorithm

To generate the tree representation data described in the previous paragraph, multiple level data generation (further called one step creation) must be preformed and acceptably saved to the whole model. Items present the tree leaves of the final model. Data mining method of association rules will be used for generation of each level - one model per tree level. Generation of each level will further in the text be addressed as *one step creation* - or 'OSC'.
Level 1 will capture items that are most closely related (closest in the terms described in paragraph 2 of this chapter). For every following level parameters of association rules generation will be loosened to the extent permitted by the analyst. Depending on the

starting dataset and enforced parameters certain number of levels will be created. Level presenting the tree root doesn't have to be reached.
Data has to be adjusted for each OSC activity (except for the first one where certain characteristics of input data are presumed). After performing each OSC, model results have to be extracted and tree representation data has to be updated. OSC activity is realized by SQL script containing both PL/SQL blocks and SQL DDL commands (further referred as OSC script).
Because of the necessary DDL commands, OSC can't be encapsulated in a PL/SQL procedure. Therefore a custom Java class was used for creation of user interface and orchestration of the entire process, taking into account parameter inputs made by the user (analyst). Java class is the one responsible for running the OSC script (of course depending on certain conditions).
Fig. 2 presents the overall application functionality. One can notice that the process of data input (with all checkups that go with it) is left in care of other applications. User is only required to name the table containing input transactional data.
Java class functionality is presented by functional blocks in red colour, while the basic functionalities of OSC script are presented in green. Final result of the main Java class method is development of *tree representation data*. Graphical presentation of developed data model is not the focus of this text and is left for further investigation. Technology to present it is left to final user preferences. However, researches on this matter were also made. There are some open-source solutions that enable interactive graphical presentations of tree-like structures through Internet browsers (e.g. *Google Interactive Treeview*). Transformation of the generated relational tree representation data into a (for example) XML file - which mentioned tool uses as its input - is rather straightforward.

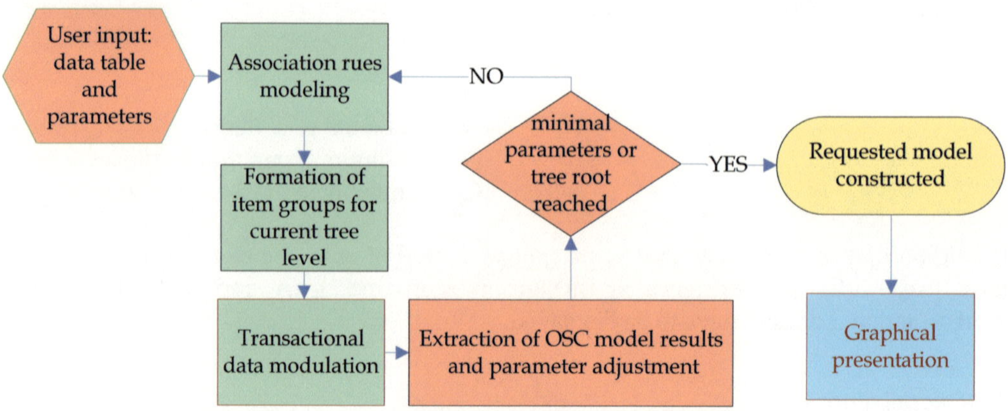

Fig. 2. Developed algorithm shown through main functionality blocks

Input data parameters and its adjustment through algorithm should be elaborated in more detail. At algorithm start-up, analyst is required to specify the following boundaries: top and bottom support and confidence (measures used in association rules methods) together with acceptable number of tree levels (L). Top boundaries are used to form the first level of item tree. All items included in generated association rules with support and confidence greater than parameters used as input for certain step are connected. Through following

steps those starting measures are being lowered until they reach bottom support and confidence.
The actual purpose of bottom support and confidence is based on the fact that analyst is not interested in connections between items which are not supported by certain proportions of transactions. If analyst wants to utilize even minimal number of transactions supporting certain connections (so no item is left unconnected except the ones that appear in transactions containing only one item) than bottom support and confidence should be set to value near zero.
At this moment, algorithm that adjusts parameters between OSC steps in linear way is developed (distance between bottom and top parameters is divided by (L-1) and parameters through whole process are tweaked to reach from top levels to bottom ones through (L-1) steps). It is possible for the algorithm to reach the tree root even earlier - but that depends on the actual data being analyzed.

6.3 Generation of one tree level – recurring step in detail

This paragraph will present the developed OSC script in more detail and elaborate the decisions made during its construction.
Decision to use some database structures directly (i.e. tables which keep data about generated model in the specific step) was made. Usage of PL/SQL data mining API when forming groups of items would slow the whole process down. The most important parts of OSC script are:

A) **view creation**
   Database inbuilt data mining functions require certain presentation of transactional data.
B) **setup of model parameters**
   For this, a special table is created. This table is named *settings table.*
C) **model generation**
   PL/SQL data mining API is used to perform model generation.
   Input parameters are:
   a. model name
   b. mining function (association rules with only one available algorithm - Apriory)
   c. data table name (view in our case)
   d. column which identifies each transaction specification
   e. settings table name.
D) **created database structures**
   As a consequence of the previous step certain tables that keep information about generated model (association rules) are created. This step is implicit and doesn't require custom coding. Most important tree tables are:
   T1: encloses information of antecedent and consequent itemsets IDs along with measurements connected with the rule
   T2: reflects structure of each itemset
   T3: presents all items in separated rows.

E) **rules ordering**
Multiple connections among few items may appear. To ensure that the most significant ones are presented in level groupings, rules are ordered and confidence is chosen as an order criteria. In the future only one PL/SQL instruction has to be altered to change this criterion (if the analyst needs such a change).

F) **elimination of itemsets and rules**
To take into account only those rules which only concern two-way connections, all itemsets containing more than one item are eliminated together with the corresponding rules. There are a few reasons for that step: final tree is intended to present structure where relative distance between two items can be compared with a distance between other two items. Rules which have more elements in antecedent or consequent can't be properly depicted in intended tree structure.

G) **formation of item groups**
Items that are not already occupied by some group in a certain level are grouped together on the basis of sequential reading of ordered rules. They are being assigned the next unused number - group mark.

H) **population of group column**
A certain number of items is expected not to take part in any groups on specific level. They will have NULL values in certain table cells. Group column must be populated with unused numbers – group marks.

I) **storing of the tree level information**
Finally, useful information about performed groupings is saved to the special table which is to be used outside of the OSC step.

J) **transactional data modulation**
To be able to perform the next level generation, transactional data needs to be altered. In the next step association rule modelling must be performed on groups formed on previous level.

K) **index creation**
On certain phases of the OSC step indexes have to be created to speed up the whole process (without them required time for some steps may exceed required time for model generation).

L) **cleansing of some structures**
Every OSC step generates structures that are to be used in the next OSC step. For that reason cleansing of those structures must be preformed.

6.4 Possible issues

Major issues and questions that emerged during OSC script creation are described in this chapter.

(A) TRANSACTIONAL DATA MODULATION AND ITS CONSEQUENCES

First issue is the one concerning the changes of transactional data. Data is changed to enable performing each consecutive step and to avoid losing information about item 'connections'. The real question is whether the final measures (produced by models after transactional data change) are acceptable and how the tree structure should be interpreted.
Implemented algorithm in each transaction replaces original item ID with the newly assigned group mark. Since association rules measures are important for the next level of

tree structure generation, a question may arise regarding the consequence of replacing a group of items with one sole item which will represent the entire group.
To best depict the problem, transactional data presented in Table 1 is used as an example to make a tree structure model. Certain measures for the input data can be calculated (equations (2) and (3)). Support of items and item pairs is presented in Table 2. This table is orthogonally symmetric since supp(A,B)=supp(B,A) which is a consequence of a support definition.

	A	B	C	D
A	4/7	4/7	2/7	2/7
B	4/7	5/7	3/7	2/7
C	2/7	3/7	4/7	1/7
D	2/7	2/7	1/7	3/7

Table 2. Calculated support for dataset example

Table 3 presents calculated confidence of possible binary rules for the same example data. Items presented at row beginnings represent antecedents and columns present consequents (e.g. conf(B⇒A)=4/5). Since generally conf(A⇒A)=1, these measures were not marked in the table.

consequent antecedent\	A	B	C	D
A		1	1/2	1/2
B	4/5		3/5	2/5
C	1/2	3/4		1/4
D	2/3	2/3	1/3	

Table 3. Calculated confidence for possible binary rules

If parameters for first level creation are set in such a way that only items A and B are connected in a group called X (conf(A⇒B)=1), than one of the possible representations of final model is depicted on Fig.3.

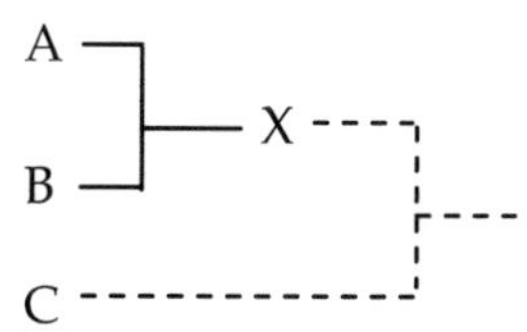

Fig. 3. Possible formation of a tree structure based on example data

Two important questions may arise concerning the replacement of A and B with a group/item named X:

- what happens to the relationships of items unaffected by this new group?
- what happens to the measures of possible rules which include 'new item' X?

Regarding relationships between items unaffected by formed group, the following facts stand:

- support of those items remains the same
- support of itemsets that don't contain X remains the same (e.g. supp(C,D))

- previous two entries result in no effect on the possible rules not containing X.

Depicted features are desirable and welcome.

Regarding possible rules which include 'new item' X, measure calculations show the following:

- supp(X)>=max(supp(A), supp(B))
- supp(X)<supp(A)+supp(B)
- support of itemsets that include X increases: (supp(X,C)=supp((AvB),C)>= max(supp(A,C), supp(B,C))
- confidence of rules that incorporate X as an antecedent will fall somewhere between conf(A⇒C) and conf(B⇒C).
- confidence of rules that incorporate X as a consequent will be greater than conf(C⇒A) and conf(C⇒B) (support of (X,C) is equal or greater than supp(A,C) or supp(B,C) while support of antecedent remains the same).

From these observations, following reasoning could be made: item X will display closeness to some other item (e.g. item C) in the case that both of its components (A and B) display closeness to C. If A is 'close' to C but B isn't, than the appearance frequency of A and B in transactional data has to be taken into account. If appearance of A is frequent, while B is rare, than measure of closeness (conf(X⇒C)) will be more influenced by item A and X would be relatively close to C. That means that X (as antecedent) exposes more average (or tenderer) features than its components with the number of supporting transactions also affecting the outcome. Explained and depicted features of grouping item X are also desirable and acceptable.

When examining X as a consequent, it can be stated that it can more easily be connected to other items than can solely items A and B, which is also logical consequence of grouping.

Final tree representation should be interpreted in the following way: based on transactional data, items A and B are close i.e. connected. If X is further connected to C then we can say that item group of A and B exposes closeness to C. However, direct connection between A and C cannot be stated (likewise for items B and C).

(B) ELIMINATION OF TRANSACTIONS CONTAINING ONLY ONE ITEM

In real life datasets which the authors have encountered many transactions exist which contain only one item. These cases also emerge in our application usage. After making certain groups and modulating transactional data for the new step, it is possible that some transactions exist which include only one item which is result of grouping (e.g. first transaction in Table 1, after replacing A and B with X, contains only one item). Such transactions seemingly do not contribute to further analysis and could potentially be eliminated.

However, it is worth to consider the impact of these eliminations on further rules development. To demonstrate consequences of transaction elimination, first example is used and then ratios are generalized. Example of transactional data presented in Table 1 is used, where on level 1 of a tree structure items A and B are connected and form 'new item' X. Renewed transactional data is presented in Table 4.

transaction /item	X	C	D
1	1	0	0
2	1	0	1
3	1	1	0
4	1	1	1
5	1	1	0
6	0	0	1
7	0	1	0

Table 4. Example - transformed data after first level creation

For analysis, three general cases are recognized. All possible combinations of item relationships belong to one of them:

- rules where X is antecedent
- rules where X is consequent
- rules not containing X;

where X is the single item in eliminated transaction.

Measures for given example:

- before elimination of first transaction:

$$\text{supp}(X)=\frac{5}{7};\ \text{supp}(C)=\frac{4}{7};\ \text{supp}(D)=\frac{3}{7};\ \text{supp(X,C)}=\frac{3}{7};\ \text{supp(C,D)}=\frac{1}{7}$$

$$\text{conf}(\text{X}\Rightarrow C)=\frac{3}{5};\ \text{conf}(\text{C}\Rightarrow X)=\frac{3}{4};\ \text{conf}(\text{C}\Rightarrow D)=\frac{1}{4}$$

- after elimination of the first transaction:

$$\text{supp}'(X)=\frac{4}{6};\ \text{supp}'(C)=\frac{4}{6};\ \text{supp}'(D)=\frac{3}{6};\ \text{supp}'(\text{X,C})=\frac{3}{6};\ \text{supp}'(\text{C,D})=\frac{1}{6}$$

$$\text{conf}'(\text{X}\Rightarrow C)=\frac{3}{4};\ \text{conf}'(\text{C}\Rightarrow X)=\frac{3}{4};\ \text{conf}'(\text{C}\Rightarrow D)=\frac{1}{4}$$

To generalize - if m transactions are eliminated because they contained only one item, measures change in the following way:

- before elimination of first transaction:

$$\text{supp}(X)=\frac{\text{x}}{\text{t}} \qquad \text{supp(X,C)}=\frac{\text{g}}{\text{t}}$$

$$\text{supp}(C)=\frac{\text{c}}{\text{t}} \qquad \text{supp(C,D)}=\frac{\text{h}}{\text{t}}$$

$$\text{supp}(D)=\frac{\text{d}}{\text{t}}$$

$$\text{conf}(X \Rightarrow C) = \frac{g}{x} \tag{4}$$

$$\text{conf}(C \Rightarrow X) = \frac{g}{c} \tag{5}$$

$$\text{conf}(C \Rightarrow D) = \frac{h}{c} \tag{6}$$

- after elimination of *m* transaction:

$$\text{supp}'(X) = \frac{x - m}{t - m} \qquad \text{supp}'(X,C) = \frac{g}{t\text{-}m}$$

$$\text{supp}'(C) = \frac{c}{t - m} \qquad \text{supp}'(C,D) = \frac{h}{t\text{-}m}$$

$$\text{supp}'(D) = \frac{d}{t - m}$$

$$\text{conf}'(X \Rightarrow C) = \frac{g}{x - m} \tag{7}$$

$$\text{conf}'(C \Rightarrow X) = \frac{g}{c} \tag{8}$$

$$\text{conf}'(C \Rightarrow D) = \frac{h}{c} \tag{9}$$

Comparing (4), (5) and (6) with (7), (8) and (9) the following conclusion can be made: confidence of rules containing X as consequent and confidence of rules not containing X remains the same but confidence of rules containing X as antecedent increases. Therefore elimination of transactions containing only one item on various levels should not be performed since it could skew the real relationships between items.
This decision could also be supported by an extreme case example where item X is the only item appearing in many transactions, with only one transaction where it appears with another item - C. If we eliminate transactions which include only one item then conf(X⇒C) would be 1, which is very far from the true relationship.

(C) DIFFERENT TREE STRUCTURES DEPICTING THE SAME TRANSACTIONAL DATA AS A CONSEQUENCE OF DIFFERENT PARAMETER INPUT

For the same transactional data, various final tree presentations could be made depending on parameter input. Two extremes would be:

- very loose parameters
- strict parameters with slight changes from one step to another.

Fig. 4 presents two outcomes depending on the input parameters.

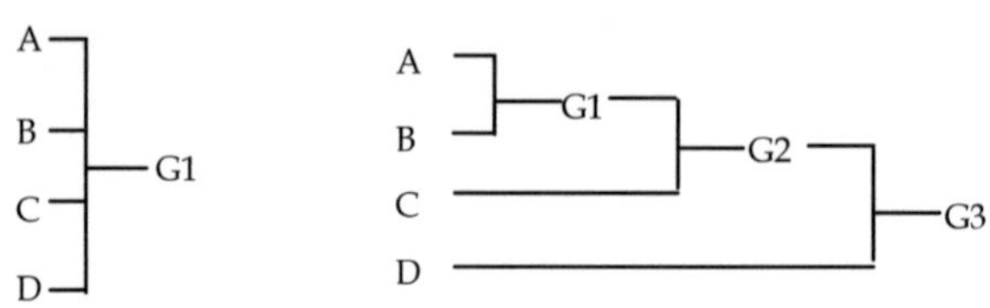

Fig. 4. Two tree-like structure outcomes depending on input parameters

What is loose and what is strict usually depends on characteristics of the input dataset. This is an issue best left to analyst's discretion; analyst should tweak the parameters to get the structure he/she feels is the most informative and could most easily be acted upon.

7. Results on Real-life Dataset

7.1 Data set Characteristics

Datasets can vary in great extent when their various characteristics are in question. These characteristics influence overall performance of the generated application. Therefore some characteristics of dataset at hand used for verification of application performance will be presented first.

Number of transactions and **number of items** are the most obvious characteristics of dataset and usually the most important ones. Example dataset presented in Table 1 includes 7 transactions and 4 items.

Data density could be presented by a ratio between realized appearances of items in transactions compared to the case where every transaction includes all items. Density is for the most datasets very low and therefore is often multiplied by 100 to form 'modified data density' (i.e. if average transaction includes every hundredth item the density results in 1). Data density for example data is 15/(7*4)=0,53 (53% of table cells are populated with value '1'). It could be useful to notice the **most** frequently **appearing item** and what is number of transactions where it could be found (e.g. item B appears in most transactions, 5 of them).

Average number of items per transaction gives a good insight on the input dataset (for given example this ratio is 2,29).

Application performance was examined on few real-life datasets. The one which clearly demonstrates the performance of generated application was chosen. It holds data of market basket contents in one computer store. Characteristics of chosen dataset are given in Table 5.

Dataset characteristic	Value
Number of transactions	940
Number of items	14
Data density	0,21
Number of transactions where the most frequently appearing item appeared	303 (32%)
Average number of items per transaction	2,98

Table 5. Characteristics of examined real-life dataset

First step is the most critical one, so it will be examined in more detail.
12 rules were found with parameters set to values:

- minimal support: 0,1
- minimal confidence: 0,1.

Those rules resulted in 2 item groups: one containing 4 items and one containing 2 items (Table 6). Two groups that satisfied first setting chosen by the analyst resulted in a pretty good score comparing to 12 association rules those groups stemmed from and which analyst doesn't have to read. Of course, this concise presentation resulted in some information loss, but it happened in accordance with analyst decision of parameter setting.

After updating transactional data[2], a number of items are represented as one item in further analysis. Therefore there are some duplicate entries of items belonging to certain transactions that could be eliminated. For example, let items A and B belong to transaction t_i, and they are grouped and their group is presented by 'item X', then duplicate recording of item X belonging to transaction t_i is not necessary. Immediate benefit is that data for transaction representation is reduced from 2804 rows to 2345 rows. In the following steps this reduction is reiterated resulting in shorter execution time for every subsequent level creation.

Application performance could be demonstrated by setting following input parameters:

- minimal support: 0,1-0,08;
- minimal confidence=0,1
- expected levels=3.

Resulting model is presented in Table 6. As it can be observed, there are some items that relatively rarely show up together with any other item in transactions and they stay as solitary leaves. If we take a look at the real items that are connected, some combinations of items are quite logical, for instance: *External 8X CD-ROM* and *CD-RW, High Speed Pack of 5.*

Final model data presentation, given in Table 6, shows that our data representation can easily be converted to a graphical tree-like structure. Readability can be improved simply by sorting the columns data – going from the levels closest to the root towards those nearer to the leaves.

Item_id	Name	Level_1	Level_2	Level_3
12	18" Flat Panel Graphics Monitor	3	2	1
9	SIMM- 16MB PCMCIAII card	3	2	1
8	Keyboard Wrist Rest	8	2	1
7	External 8X CD-ROM	2	3	1
10	CD-RW, High Speed Pack of 5	2	3	1
11	Multimedia speakers- 3" cones	9	3	1
3	Standard Mouse	1	1	
4	Extension Cable	1	1	
14	Model SM26273 Black Ink Cartridge	4	1	
2	Mouse Pad	4	1	
1	Y Box	5		
5	Envoy Ambassador	6		
6	Envoy 256MB - 40GB	7		
13	O/S Documentation Set - English	10		

Table 6. Resulting model for real-life dataset

Each following step data characteristics change: number of items decreases, data density increases and number of items per transaction decreases.

[2] Every realization of item's appearance in transaction is presented in a separate row.

Application testing showed that not only data characteristics influenced final model structure (number of groupings per level and level numbers) but also the nature of data in question. For the optimal use of application analyst should be closely acquainted with business problem, available data and usability of final model.

8. Further work

There are some areas in application functioning that could be improved. The most important one concerns parameter adjusting since it has great effect on application functionality and final outcome. Dataset characteristics play the most important role here so in the future application should give the analyst suggestions for parameter setup based on input dataset. It would prevent analyst from straying and would offer him a priori guidance on what choices could potentially be the most effective. Some researches regarding usage of data density in mining association rules have already been undertaken. Its usage is even further investigated in (Cheung et al., 2007) where new measures of data density for quantitative attributes are introduced.

In some cases analysts will want to investigate on how some specific item groups are connected to other items, for example illness symptoms that are somehow connected to diseases or other symptoms.Insight in belonging tree structure could bring upon some new notions. For that matter a feature to bundle some items in advance will be offered by application.

The bottleneck of implemented algorithm is the need for repeated creation of association rules in each step. However, some time improvements could be made by optimizations of SQL commands and PL/SQL blocks.

9. Conclusion

New approach to well known data mining method of association rules is developed and elaborated. In a nutshell, an application was created which generates a tree-like structure representing an interpretation of relationship between items based on their co-occurrence in transactional data.Survey of existing applications' functionalities using association rules is presented, along with motivation to make rather different solution. Way of interpretation of developed solution is clearly elaborated.

Application was realized with Java technology and uses database in-built data mining functions. This technology bundle gave us both flexibility and advantages of optimizations through direct in-base data structure manipulation. One more benefit of such approach is that data doesn't have to be transferred from its original source. Although association rules are quite resource exhausting method, with reasonable parameters input for specific dataset, good performance characteristics were accomplished.

During application development some issues emerged. They were examined and most important decisions along with reasoning are presented in this chapter.

There are many possible usages of developed tool and data model. It is quite easy to interpret it and exploit it. However, like with every data mining method, final functionality and benefits depend on quality of input data and analyst acquaintance with business problem, the data and application itself.

10. References

Agrawal, R.; Imielinski, T. & Swami, A. (1993).: Mining Association Rules Between Sets of Items in Large Databases, Proceedings of the 1993 ACM SIGMOD international conference on Management of data, pp 207-216, 0-89791-592-5, May 25-28, 1993, Washington, D.C., United States

Campos, M.M.; Stengard, P.J.& Milenova, B.L. (2005).: Data-centric automated data mining, Proceedings of the Fourth International Conference on Machine Learning and Applications, pp. 97-104, 0-7695-2495-8, December 15-17 2005, IEEE Computer Society, Washington, DC

Cheung, D. W. ; Wang, L.; Yiu, S. M. & Zhou B. (2007). Density-Based Mining of Quantitative Association Rules, In: *Knowledge Discovery and Data Mining. Current Issues and New Applications,* 257-268, Springer Berlin/Heidelberg, 978-3-540-67382-8, Germany

Hand, D.; Mannila, H.; Smyth, P. (2001). Principles of Data Mining, The MIT Press, ISBN: 026208290, USA

Orange - component-based data mining software
Available: http://www.ailab.si/orange/ (accessed on 20.05.2009.)

Pasquier, N.; Taouil, R.; Bastide, Y.; Stumme, G. & Lakhal, L. (2005).: Generating a condensed representation for association rules. *Journal of Intelligent Information Systems,* Vol. 24, No. 1. (January 2005), pp 29-60, 0925-9902

Xu, Y. & Li, Y. (2007).: Mining Non-Redundant Association Rules Based on Concise Bases. *International Journal of Pattern Recognition and Artificial Intelligence,* Vol. 21, No. 4. (June 2007), pp 659-675, 0218-0014

8

Applications of Support Vector Machines in Bioinformatics and Network Security

Rehan Akbani and Turgay Korkmaz
University of Texas at San Antonio
San Antonio, Texas, USA

1. Introduction

Support Vector Machines (SVM) were introduced by Vapnik and colleagues (Vapnik, 1995) and they have been very successful in application areas ranging from image retrieval (Tong & Chang, 2001) and handwriting recognition (Cortes, 1995) to text classification (Joachims, 1998). However, when faced with imbalanced datasets where the number of negative instances far outnumbers the positive instances, the performance of SVM drops significantly (Wu & Chang, 2003). There are many applications in which instances belonging to one class are heavily outnumbered by instances belonging to another class. Such datasets are called imbalanced datasets, since the class distributions are not evenly balanced. Examples of these imbalanced datasets include the human genome dataset and network intrusion datasets. In the human genome dataset, only a small proportion of the DNA sequences represent genes, and the rest do not. In network intrusion datasets, most of the nodes in a network are benign; however, a small number may have been compromised. Other examples include detecting credit card fraud, where most transactions are legitimate, whereas a few are fraudulent; and face recognition datasets, where only some people on a watch list need to be flagged, but most do not. An imbalance of 100 to 1 exists in fraud detection domains, and it approaches 100,000 to 1 in other applications (Provost & Fawcett, 2001).

Although it is crucial to detect the minority class in these datasets, most off-the-shelf machine learning (ML) algorithms fail miserably at this task. The reason for that is simple: Most ML algorithms are designed to minimize the classification error. They are designed to generalize from sample data and output the simplest hypothesis that best fits the data, based on the principle of Occam's razor. This principle is embedded in the inductive bias of many machine learning algorithms, such as decision trees, which favour shorter trees over longer ones. With imbalanced data, the simplest hypothesis is often the one that classifies all the instances as the majority class.

Consider the scenario where a network consists of 1000 nodes, 10 of which have been compromised by an attacker. If the ML algorithm classifies all of these nodes as uncompromised, it misclassifies only 10 out of 1000 nodes, resulting in a classification error of only 1%. In most cases, an accuracy of 99% is considered very good. However, such a classifier would be useless for detecting compromised nodes.

Therefore, for many imbalanced datasets, the ML classifier ends up classifying everything as the majority class. Artificial Neural Networks (ANNs) use gradient descent with the objective of minimizing the classification error, which usually occurs when the minority class is completely ignored. In K Nearest Neighbours, the vicinity of the test instance is more likely to be dominated by the majority class resulting in a majority class prediction. Decision Trees perform pruning to reduce the risk of over fitting. In most cases, they prune out the leaf with the minority class, leaving only a decision stump at the root with the majority class. Even Support Vector Machines (SVM) fall prey to imbalanced datasets.

The second factor that causes ML algorithms to ignore the minority class is that many of them are designed to ignore noise in the dataset. As a result, they end up treating the minority class as noise and discard them. Many algorithms modify the behaviour of existing algorithms to make them more immune to noisy instances, such as IB3 (Aha, 1992) for kNN, or pruning of decision trees, or soft margins in SVM (Vapnik, 1995). While these approaches work well for balanced datasets, they fail when dealing with highly imbalanced datasets having ratios of 50 to 1 or more (Akbani et al., 2004).

In this chapter, we highlight the reasons why SVM, in particular, fails and what can be done to overcome this. We specifically chose SVM to attack the problem of imbalanced data because SVM is based on strong theoretical foundations (Vapnik, 1995) and it performs well with moderately imbalanced data even without any modifications (Akbani et al., 2004). SVM has its strengths in that the final model is only dependent on the support vectors, whereas the rest of the instances are discarded. Its unique learning mechanism makes it an interesting candidate for dealing with imbalanced datasets, since SVM only takes into account those instances that are close to the boundary, i.e. the support vectors. This means that SVM is unaffected by non-noisy negative instances far away from the boundary even if they are huge in number. Another advantage is that even though there may be more majority class support vectors than minority class, because of Karush-Kuhn-Tucker conditions, the weights of the minority class support vectors would be higher, resulting in some offsetting.

We use the human genome dataset and the network security dataset as illustrative examples. The major difference between the properties of these datasets is that the imbalance ratio for the human genome dataset is very large, but we know what that ratio is at the time of training. Both the training and test sets are derived from the same distribution (the human genome), so the imbalance ratio in the train and test sets would be the same. For network security, however, we do not know at the time of training what the imbalance ratio in a real network would be. To make matters worse, that ratio is not expected to remain constant and would vary as attackers compromise more nodes, or are detected and removed from the network. The imbalance ratio is expected to change dynamically and any algorithm needs to adapt to that change. In this chapter, we present techniques to deal with these changes.

2. Effects of Imbalance on SVM

In order to combat the effects of imbalance, we need to understand exactly why SVM's performance deteriorates with high imbalance ratios. To do that, we need to look at how soft margin SVMs work. Given a set of labelled instances $X_{train} = \{x_i, y_i\}^n_{i=1}$ and a kernel function

K, SVM finds the optimal a_i for each x_i to maximize the margin γ between the hyper plane and the closest instances to it. The class prediction for a new test instance x is made through:

$$sign\left(f(x) = \sum_{i=1}^{n} y_i \alpha_i K(x, x_i) + b \right) \tag{1}$$

where b is the threshold. 1-norm soft-margin SVMs minimize the primal Lagrangian:

$$L_p = \frac{\|w\|^2}{2} + C\sum_{i=1}^{n} \xi_i - \sum_{i=1}^{n} \alpha_i \left[y_i \left(w \cdot x_i + b \right) - 1 + \xi_i \right] - \sum_{i=1}^{n} r_i \xi_i \tag{2}$$

where $a_i \geq 0$ and $r_i \geq 0$ (Cristianini & Shawe-Taylor, 2000). The penalty constant C represents the trade-off between the empirical error ξ and the margin. In order to meet the Karush-Kuhn-Tucker (KKT) conditions, the value of a_i must satisfy:

$$0 \leq \alpha_i \leq C \quad \text{and} \quad \sum_{i=1}^{n} \alpha_i y_i = 0 \tag{3}$$

2.1 Reasons for performance loss with imbalanced data

1. *Weakness of Soft-Margins.* The most significant factor for the loss in performance of SVMs is the weakness of soft margin SVMS. Mathematically, we can see from eq. 2 that minimizing the first term on the right hand side $||w||^2/2$, is equivalent to maximizing the margin γ, while minimizing the second term $C \sum \xi$ minimizes the associated error. The constant C specifies what trade-off we are willing to tolerate between maximizing the margin and minimizing the error. If C is not very large, SVM simply learns to classify everything as negative because that makes the margin the largest, with zero cumulative error on the abundant negative examples. The only trade-off is the small amount of cumulative error on the few positive examples, which does not count for much. This explains why SVM fails completely in situations with a high degree of imbalance.

2. *Positive points lie further from the ideal boundary.* Wu and Chang (Wu & Chang, 2003) point out this factor as one source of boundary skew. They mention that the imbalance in the training data ratio means that the positive instances may lie further away from the "ideal" boundary than the negative instances. This is illustrated by way of example that if we were to draw n randomly chosen numbers between 1 to 100 from a uniform distribution, our chances of drawing a number close to 100 would improve with increasing values of n, even though the expected mean of the draws is invariant of n. As a result of this phenomenon, SVM learns a boundary that is too close to and skewed towards the positive instances.

3. *Imbalanced Support Vector Ratio.* Another source of boundary skew according to Wu and Chang (Wu & Chang, 2003) is the imbalanced support vector ratio. They found that as the training data gets more imbalanced, the ratio between the positive and negative support vectors also becomes more imbalanced. They hypothesize that as a result of this imbalance, the neighbourhood of a test instance close to the boundary is more likely to be dominated by negative support vectors and hence the decision function is more likely to classify a boundary point negative. We would like to point out however, that because of the KKT conditions in eq. 3, the sum of the a's associated with the positive support vectors must be

equal to the sum of the a's associated with the negative support vectors. Because there are fewer positive support vectors with correspondingly fewer a's, each positive support vector's a must be larger than the negative support vector's a on average. These a's act as weights in the final decision function (eq. 1) and as a result of larger a's the positive support vectors receive a higher weight than the negative support vectors which offsets the effect of support vector imbalance to some extent. This shows why SVM does not perform too badly compared to other machine learning algorithms for moderately skewed datasets.

3. Applying SVM to Bioinformatics

To illustrate the degree of imbalance encountered in bioinformatics, we use the example of trying to identify parts of genes in human DNA. Human DNA consists of 23 pairs of chromosomes. The Human Genome Project sequenced these chromosomes and we now have almost the entire DNA sequence of 3 billion base pairs. However, not all of the 3 billion base pairs in DNA code for proteins. In fact, the vast majority of DNA does not code for proteins. Portions of DNA that code for proteins are called genes. Genes have several components which are illustrated in Figure 1.

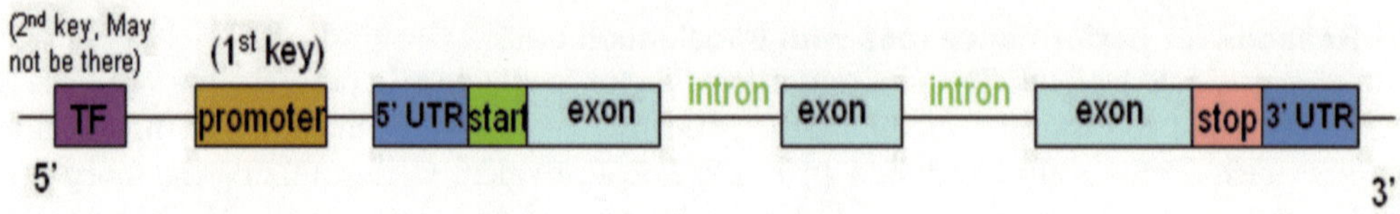

Fig. 1. Components of a typical gene

1st and 2nd keys (promoters): These regions aid in initiating gene expression (i.e. protein production). They may be absent.
5' UnTranslated Region (UTR): This is the point where mRNA transcription begins.
Start (Translation Initiation Site - TIS): This is the position where translation begins i.e. proteins start to be coded from this site.
Exon: This is region of DNA that codes for the protein.
Intron: This region of DNA is interspersed between two exons and it does not code for proteins. It is spliced out from the mRNA before translation begins.
Donor Site (not shown): The junction where an exon meets an intron.
Acceptor Site (not shown): The junction where an intron meets an exon.
Together the donor and acceptor sites are called **splice sites**.
Stop: This is the termination site where protein synthesis stops. It always consists of one of three possible codons, TGA, TAA or TAG.
3' UTR: This is the region after the stop codon that does not code for a protein but it forms the tail of the mRNA that is produced by the gene.

The problem of gene finding is to identify the locations of each of these components on the DNA sequence. For our example, we only try to identify the start and stop codons. Almost all start codons have the sequence ATG, while all stop codons consist of either TAA, TAG or TGA. But not all ATG sequences are start codons and not all TAA, TAG and TGA sequences are stop codons or else the problem would become trivial. We counted the number of times

ATG occurs in the entire human genome and found that it occurs approximately 104 million times. Note that if the DNA sequence was random then ATG would occur $(1 / 4^3) \times 3 \times 10^9 = 47$ million times. By contrast, there are an estimated 23,000 confirmed and unconfirmed genes that have ATG as the start codon. So assuming 23,000 genes the estimated degree of imbalance in predicting when an ATG sequence is a start codon, (henceforth called positive instances), and when it is not (negative instances) is:

ATG is a start codon : ATG is not a start codon
23,0000 : 104,000,000
1 : 4,522

Looking at the problem of identifying stop codons independently of other predictions poses an even greater degree of imbalance. We have found that there are about 300 million TAG, TAA or TGA sequences in the human genome. Only 23,000 of them are suspected to be actual stop codons. The imbalance ratio for stop codons is therefore:

23,000 : 300,000,000
1 : 13,043

Unfortunately, ordinary machine learning algorithms are incapable of handling this extremely high degree of imbalance.

4. Related Work

Several researchers have approached the problem of trying to identify the start codon, or translation initiation site (TIS). Stormo et al. (Stormo et al., 1982) use a perceptron and train it using DNA sequences obtained from E. coli. They used a feature vector containing four bit encodings of the nucleotide sequence as their training data. The window size of the feature vector was up to 101 base pairs.

Pedersen and Nielsen (P&N) (Pedersen & Nielsen, 1997) constructed their famous dataset from eukaryotic DNA data. They removed the introns and joined together the resulting exons. They used only those sequences that had the TIS annotated, with at least 10 upstream and 150 downstream nucleotides. They also removed redundant sequences. This dataset has been used by several researchers for TIS prediction. Their dataset contains 3312 ATG sites that are TIS and 10063 sites that are not TIS, giving an imbalance of only around 1:3. Pedersen and Nielsen used a 3-layer neural network and a window size of 203 base pairs to predict the TIS. They obtained a sensitivity score of 78%, specificity of 87% and an accuracy of 85%. Their program is called NetStart and is available for public use.

Zien et al. (Zien et al., 2000) use a modified Support Vector Machine kernel to predict the TIS. They engineer the SVM kernel to incorporate prior biological knowledge in the learning scheme. Essentially they modified the kernel so that nucleotides that are close together have a greater impact on the outcome rather than those that are further apart. They achieved a sensitivity of 70%, specificity of 94% and an accuracy of 88% using the P&N dataset.

Zeng et al. (Zeng et al., 2002) and Li et al. (Li et al., 2004) focus on feature selection rather than a specific ML algorithm. They construct a huge variety of features from the P&N dataset and then use standard feature selection algorithms to decide which features to keep.

Zeng et al. used 9 different features for use in training. They claim that their technique is independent of the base classifier used and outperforms any other classifier.
Salamov et al. (Salamov et al., 1998) used the linear discriminant function to train their classifier using a set of 6 features constructed from the P&N dataset. They achieved an accuracy of 89%. Hatzigeorgiou (Hatzigeorgiou, 2002) used two feed-forward neural networks and a ribosome scanning rule to obtain a classifier with an accuracy of 94%.
It should be noted, however, that none of these methods deal directly with the entire chromosome. Most of them use the P&N dataset that has an imbalance of only 1:3. As mentioned earlier the amount of imbalance in the human genome is about 1:4522. The author suspects that these methods will fail when applied to the entire genome.
The problem of imbalanced datasets has been approached from two main directions. The first approach is to preprocess the data by under sampling the majority instances or oversampling the minority instances. Kubat and Matwin (Kubat & Matwin, 1997) proposed a one-sided selection process which under sampled the majority class in order to remove noisy, borderline, and redundant training instances. But if we use SVM as our classifier, removing redundant (far away) instances has no effect and removing borderline instances may adversely affect the accuracy of the learned hyper plane.
Japkowicz (Japkowicz, 2000) evaluated the oversampling and under sampling techniques for skewed datasets and concluded that both methods were effective. Ling and Li (Ling & Li, 1998) combined oversampling with under sampling, but this combination did not provide significant improvement in the "lift index" metric that they used. Chawla et al. (Chawla et al., 2002) devised a method called Synthetic Minority Oversampling Technique (SMOTE). This technique involved creating new instances through "phantom-transduction." For each positive instance, its nearest positive neighbours were identified and new positive instances were created and placed randomly in between the instance and its neighbours.
The other approach to dealing with imbalanced datasets using SVM biases the algorithm so that the learned hyper plane is further away from the positive class. This is done in order to compensate for the skew associated with imbalanced datasets which pushes the hyper plane closer to the positive class. This biasing can be accomplished in various ways. In (Wu & Chang, 2003) an algorithm is proposed that changes the kernel function to develop this bias, while in (Cristianini, 2002) the kernel matrix is adjusted to fit the training data. Veropoulos et al. (Veropoulos et al., 1999) suggested using different penalty constants for different classes of data, making errors on positive instances costlier than errors on negative instances.

5. Our Method

Since an imbalance ratio of over 1:1000 is well beyond the performance capabilities of any ML algorithm, we decided to generate the TIS data from the human genome with an imbalance of 1:100 for our current scheme. Even this ratio causes most ML algorithms to perform very poorly. This ratio is still much higher than the P&N dataset which has an imbalance ratio of only 1:3.
Our first strategy was to construct a dataset containing sequences from the human genomic data and then use it to generate several candidate features for our algorithm. We then used feature selection algorithms to select the best attributes from among them. This technique was originally proposed by Zeng et al. (Zeng et al., 2002). To begin with, we randomly chose

known ATG TIS sites from the NCBI database for our positive examples. Then we randomly picked ATG sites from the genome that are not known to be TIS sites, for our negative examples. We maintained a ratio of 1:100 for positive to negative examples. A window of 200 nucleotides was chosen for every example, running from 100 bps upstream of the ATG to 100 bps downstream of the ATG. This set constituted our raw dataset.

From this raw dataset, we generated several features. Every position in the raw data was used as a candidate feature. In addition, we generated the frequency of occurrence of all possible monomers, dimers, trimers, all the way up to hexamers that lie upstream of the ATG and also for those that lie downstream of the ATG. This gave us a total of 11120 features. Then we ran several different feature selection algorithms on this large set of attributes to determine the top attributes. We ran the Correlation Feature Selection (CFS) algorithm, which prefers those set of attributes that have a high correlation with the class label, but low correlation among themselves, and also Information Gain, Gain Ratio, and chi-squared test. By observing their results, we were able to choose the top 15 of the 11120 attributes, which were found to be the following (in order of importance): dn-CG, dn-TA, dn-AT, up-AT, up-CG, dn-GC, dn-G, up-TA, dn-CGG, up-CGG, dn-T, dn-ATT, pos -3, pos -1, pos +4, where dn-CG means the frequency of occurrence of CG downstream of the ATG, and up-CG means the frequency of CG upstream of the ATG, pos -3 means the nucleotide at position -3. Although we found pos -3, pos -1 and pos +4 to be the most important positions, the relevance score for these was much lower than the relevance score for the frequency counts, but we included them in our experiments nevertheless. It should also be noted that these positions correspond to the Kozak consensus sequence (Kozak, 1996). Our final dataset consisted of these 15 selected features. We used a similarly generated separate test set for evaluation.

We needed to modify the basic SVM algorithm to overcome some of the problems mentioned in Section 2. One of those problems is that with imbalanced datasets, the learned boundary is too close to the positive instances. We need to bias SVM in a way that will push the boundary away from the positive instances. Veropoulos et al. (Veropoulos et al., 1999) suggest using different error costs for the positive (C^+) and negative (C^-) classes. Specifically, they suggest changing the primal Lagrangian (eq. 2) to:

$$L_p = \frac{\|w\|^2}{2} + C^+ \sum_{\{i|yi=+1\}}^{n_+} \xi_i + C^- \sum_{\{j|yj=-1\}}^{n_-} \xi_j - \sum_{i=1}^{n} \alpha_i \left[y_i (w \cdot x_i + b) - 1 + \xi_i \right] - \sum_{i=1}^{n} r_i \xi_i \quad (4)$$

The constraints on a_i then become:

$$0 \le \alpha_i \le C^+ \text{ if } y_i = +1 \quad \text{and} \quad 0 \le \alpha_i \le C^- \text{ if } y_i = -1 \quad (5)$$

Furthermore, we note that $\xi_i > 0$ only when $a_i = C$ (Liu et al., 2004). Therefore non-zero errors on positive support vectors will have larger a_i while non-zero errors on negative support vectors will have smaller a_i. The net effect is that the boundary is pushed more towards the negative instances. However, a consequence of this is that SVM becomes more sensitive to the positive instances and obtains stronger cues from the positive instances about the orientation of the plane than from the negative instances. If the positive instances are sparse, as in imbalanced datasets, then the boundary may not have the proper shape in the input space as illustrated in Figure 2.

The solution we adopted to remedy the problem of sparse positive instances was to generate several synthetic minority instances, in line with Chawla et al's technique (Chawla et al., 2002). We repeatedly randomly selecting two neighbouring positive instances using the Euclidean distance measure and then generated a new instance that lies somewhere randomly in between these instances. The underlying assumption was that the space between two positive neighbouring instances was assumed to be positive. We found this assumption to hold for our dataset. We found that over sampling the minority class in this way was much more effective than the traditional over sampling technique of generating multiple identical copies of existing minority instances. Simply resampling the minority instances merely overlaps the instances on top of each other and does not help in "smoothing out" the shape of the boundary. We synthetically generated new instances between two existing positive instances which helped in making their distribution more well-defined. After this over sampling, the input space may look like Figure 3.

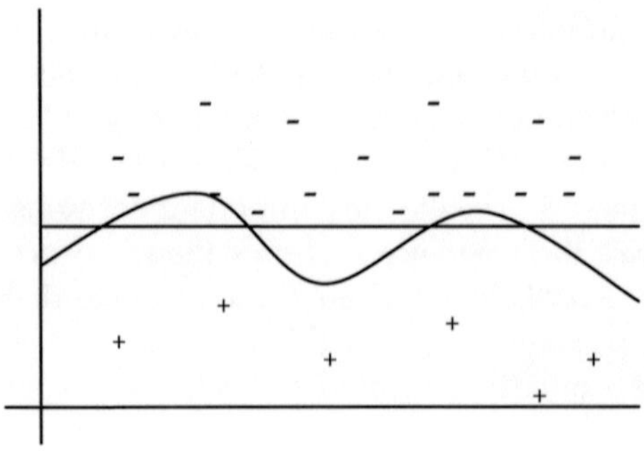

Fig. 2. The learned boundary (*curved line*) in the input space closely follows the distribution of the positive instances. The ideal boundary is denoted by the horizontal line

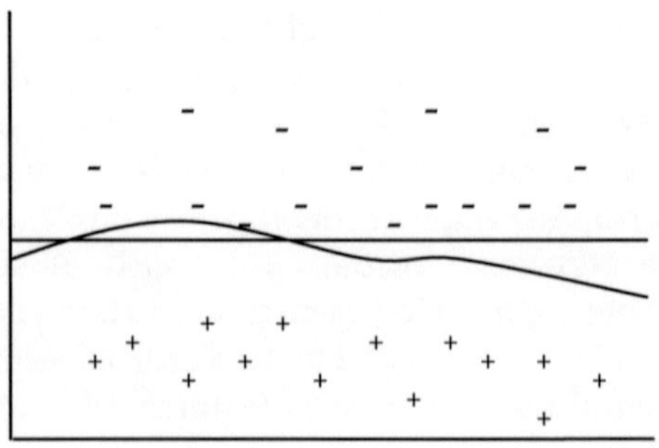

Fig. 3. After oversampling, the positive instances are now more densely distributed and the learned boundary (*curved line*) is more well defined

Synthetic oversampling also alleviates the problem of soft margins, since now the cost of misclassifying minority instances is significant. This, together with higher costs of misclassifying minority instances levels the playing field for both classes.

To summarise, our method consists of:

1. Generating and selecting the most relevant features for the problem.
2. Using different error costs for different classes to push the boundary away from the positive instances and overcome soft margin weakness.
3. Generating synthetic minority instances to make the positive instances more densely distributed in order to make the boundary more well defined.

6. Results

We compared our algorithm with several other standard ML algorithms for predicting TISs in the human genome. We also compared our technique with the common approach of over sampling the minority class or under sampling the majority class in order to reduce the

Algorithm	F-Measure
Voted Perceptron	0
ZeroR	0
SVM	0
SVM with Under Sampling	0.041
SVM with Over Sampling	0.082
Neural Network	0.133
AdaBoost with C4.5	0.148
3 Nearest Neighbours	0.182
Decision Tree	0.2
Naive Bayes	0.205
Bagging with C4.5	0.25
Our Algorithm	0.44

Table 1. Performance of various ML algorithms vs. our algorithm on the TIS dataset

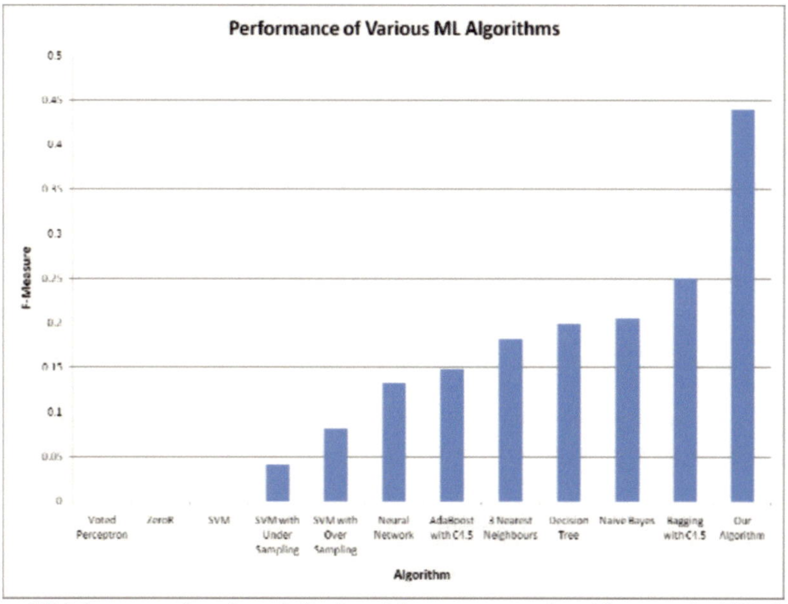

Fig. 4. Plotted F-Measure of various ML algorithms vs. our algorithm on the TIS dataset

imbalance ratio in the dataset prior to training. For evaluation, we used the F-measure as our metric, which is the harmonic mean of the recall and precision. The results are shown in Table 1 and plotted in Figure 4. They illustrate how poorly standard ML approaches perform for predicting TISs at the genomic level due to the high imbalance ratio. Our approach improves the performance significantly. By varying the parameters of our algorithm we are able to obtain different recall and precision values. Some examples of recall/precision obtained respectively are: 15%/100%, 29%/95%, 85%/4%. Thus, depending on the application the algorithm parameters can be varied to obtain the desired level of recall vs. precision.

While the results are encouraging, we must bear in mind that the TIS dataset we generated was a watered down version with 1:100 imbalance ratio, compared to the 1:4522 imbalance ratio found in the human genome. The search for algorithms that can deal with such large imbalances is far from over. However, we suggest using heuristics based on domain knowledge to discard those ATG codons which are unlikely to be TISs, instead of directly feeding them into the ML classifier. These heuristics may include ATG codons that are too far from, or too close to stop codons or splice sites. This will reduce the imbalance ratio to some extent and may improve performance.

7. Applying SVM to Network Security

In network intrusion detection, the goal is to identify compromised nodes in the network. One approach towards accomplishing this is to monitor the behaviour of nodes in order to detect anomalous or malicious behaviour. Reputation Systems, such as seller ratings on eBay, rely on the postulate that past behaviour can be used to predict future behaviour. If a node has behaved maliciously in the past, it will likely behave maliciously in future. The objective is to detect nodes that behave maliciously and avoid interacting with them a priori. In general, we can summarize existing RSs found in the literature (Jiang & Baras, 2006; Srivatsa et al., 2005; Kamvar et al., 2003; Josang & Ismail, 2002) within a general framework as shown in Figure 5. According to this framework, a node that needs to decide whether to transact with another node or not must first gather historical data about that node (e.g., the proportion of good vs. bad transactions in the last x minutes). Then it applies a customized mathematical equation or statistical model to the data to produce an output score. For example, the RS in (Kamvar et al., 2003) is based on using Eigen values from Linear Algebra, the one in (Srivatsa et al., 2005) is based on using derivatives and integrals, whereas the one in (Josang & Ismail, 2002) is based on Bayesian systems utilizing the Beta distribution. Depending on the output of the equation or model, the system then decides how to respond. In most cases, the equation or model is customized to detect specific types of malicious behaviour only. For instance, the algorithm in (Srivatsa et al., 2005) is designed to detect malicious behaviour that alternates with good behaviour and varies over time.

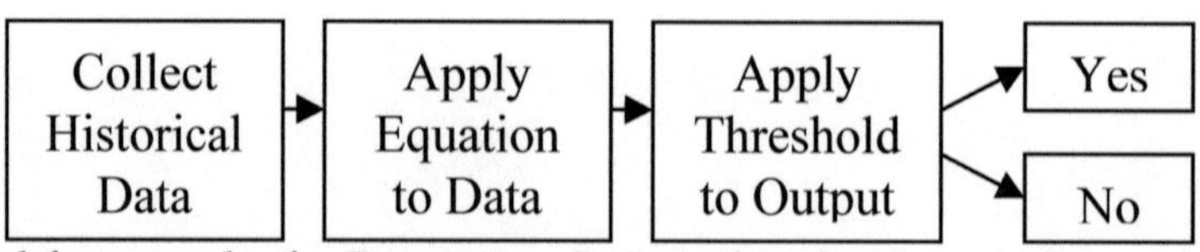

Fig. 5. General framework of a Reputation System that decides whether to transact with a given node or not.

In contrast to developing a separate module for each attack pattern, we can employ Machine Learning, specifically Support Vector Machines (SVM), to build a flexible and dynamic RS that can be trained to thwart a multitude of attack patterns easily and efficiently. It can also be retrained to detect new, previously unknown attack patterns.

8. Basic Machine Learning Approach

Using Figure 5, we can redefine the problem of designing Reputation Systems (RS) into one of finding the optimal set of input features and equations (steps 1 and 2 in Fig. 5) that allow us to distinguish between malicious and benign nodes with high accuracy. Machine Learning (ML) is of particular significance in this context since many ML algorithms are able to determine and approximate the optimal equation needed to classify a given set of data. We envision the problem of RS as a time series prediction problem, which states: Given the values of the dependent variable at times (*t*, *t-1*, *t-2*, ..., *t-n*), predict the value of the variable at time (*t* + *1*) (Baras & Jiang, 2005; Jiang & Baras, 2004). The dependent variable in this case is the proportion of good transactions conducted by a node in a given time slot. Predicting this variable at time (*t* + *1*) gives us the probability that the node will behave well if we choose to transact with it at time (*t* + *1*). Therefore, we opted to use Support Vector Machines (SVM) as our ML algorithm because it has been shown to successfully approximate mathematical functions (Abe, 2005) and make time series predictions (Camastra & Filippone, 2007).

In our scheme, we build SVM models against different types of malicious behaviours offline, and then upload those models to the nodes in the network. The nodes can use those models to classify new nodes and predict if a new node is malicious or not. Constructing models is computationally expensive so it is done offline, possibly by a third party. However, the classification step is not very expensive and can be done on the node in real time. When a new type of attack is discovered, a new model can be constructed against it. This is similar to how anti-virus systems work where the anti-virus is developed offline and then uploaded to clients. Similarly, in our scheme the vendor of the RS might update its subscribers with SVM models against new attacks.

An implied assumption is that after a transaction has taken place, a node can determine if the transaction was good or bad with a certain high probability. This is true in many cases, such as in commercial transactions on eBay, as well as in file downloads (where a corrupted or virus infected file would be considered bad), or in providing network services (Baras & Jiang, 2005; Jiang & Baras, 2004). Another assumption is that the feedbacks can be reliably transmitted without being tampered with. This can be accomplished by a node digitally signing every feedback it sends. These assumptions are made by many researchers in the field (Jiang & Baras, 2006; Srivatsa et al., 2005; Kamvar et al., 2003) and we also make the same assumptions in our study. However, a few transactions might be incorrectly labelled good or bad. SVM can handle fair amounts of such "noise" in the dataset (Abe, 2005).

9. Building the Core SVM based Reputation System

If all the participants in a network gave honest and correct feedbacks about the transactions they conducted, then it would be trivial to spot malicious nodes since all the good nodes would have 100% positive feedbacks, whereas the malicious nodes would not. But in reality, this is not the case and we have to deal with three principle challenges:

i. Dishonest feedback given by malicious nodes against other nodes they have transacted with.

ii. Incorrect feedback from legitimate nodes by mistake (noise).

iii. Fake feedback given by malicious nodes about transactions that never really occurred.

Our goal is to use SVM to tackle problems *i* and *ii*. However, SVM cannot detect if a feedback was fake, but digitally signed certificates can be used to solve problem *iii* (Akbani et al., 2008). We assume that the proportion of dishonest to honest feedbacks given by malicious nodes is much higher than the proportion of incorrect to correct feedbacks given by legitimate nodes. This is how we can distinguish between inadvertent noise and deliberately false feedbacks. If malicious nodes reduce the proportion of dishonest feedbacks to match those of incorrect feedbacks, we have still succeeded in our goal of reducing malicious behaviour.

We have to take into account several factors when building the SVM based RS that will deal with problems *i* and *ii*. The most important factor is the set of features to use. We divide time into regular intervals called time slots. The network administrator can choose and fix a time slot that is a few minutes to a few hours long, depending on how frequently nodes in the network transact on average. The features in our experiments consist of the proportion of positive vs. negative feedbacks assigned to a node during a given time slot by the nodes it has transacted with. To collect features for a test node, we need to query all the nodes in the network and ask them to provide us any feedbacks they have about the node for a given slot. The fraction of positive feedbacks versus total feedbacks for that slot forms a single feature. Each time slot then corresponds to one feature. This is in accordance with (Srivatsa et al., 2005), and is also based on features used in time series prediction problems (Camastra & Filippone, 2007). The number of features is also important. Using too few features might not provide sufficient information to the classifier, whereas using too many might result in the "Curse of Dimensionality" (Abe, 2005) and spurious overheads. We can vary the number of features by varying the number of time slots used. We use 15 time slots for our core SVM.

Next, we need to consider the proportion of malicious nodes vs. good nodes for the training set, called the imbalance ratio. In an actual setting, we would not know the proportion of malicious nodes in the network, so the testing should be done with varying imbalance ratios. However, the training set can only have one imbalance ratio since we need to build just one SVM model. We use a malicious node proportion of about 60% since that ratio yields good results.

For SVM, the kernel used is another key factor. We decided to use the linear kernel since it performs well and it is computationally less expensive to build and test than other kernels. The size of the training dataset used to train the classifier was 1,000 instances.

10. Evaluation of SVM based Reputation System

In order to evaluate the SVM based RS, we generated several datasets using simulations of a network consisting of 1,000 nodes. Time was divided into slots and in each time slot, several transactions were conducted between two randomly chosen pairs of nodes. Each node would then label the transaction as good or bad and store that label. The label may or may not reflect the true observation of a node, i.e. a node may lie about a transaction and give dishonest feedback (problem *i*).

Good Behaviour: Good behaviour is characterized as a node conducting a normal transaction and giving honest feedback about it.

Bad Behaviour: Bad behaviour is characterized as a node conducting a malicious transaction and/or giving dishonest feedback.

In addition, we introduced a random error of 5% to account for the fact that a node may incorrectly detect a transaction and mistakenly label it good or bad. This corresponds to problem *ii* described above.

The simulation was allowed to run for several time slots and then data about each node was gathered. To gather data about a node x, all the other nodes in the network were queried and asked to give information about x going back a certain number of time slots. The total number of good and bad transactions conducted by x in a given time slot were accumulated and the proportion of positive feedback was computed. This computation was repeated for each time slot of interest. In this way a concise, aggregate historical record of x was obtained. The correct label of malicious or benign was assigned to x by us, based on its role in the simulation, for testing purposes only. The adversarial model was as follows.

10.1 Adversarial Model

All the malicious nodes in the network behaved in one of four different ways. A quarter of the malicious nodes behaved maliciously all the time. Another quarter oscillated their behaviour, alternating between good and bad with a randomly chosen frequency and duty cycle. The third quarter also oscillated their behaviour, but they colluded with other malicious nodes and left positive feedbacks about each other whenever they interacted. The last quarter had oscillating behaviour with lots of collusion where malicious nodes conducted multiple transactions with each other. In a real world setting we would not know which, if any, attack was being launched by any given node, so the performance of the RS in this attack scenario would tell us what would happen if similar attacks were conducted simultaneously.

10.2 Experiments and Results

We evaluated our core SVM based RS against two other algorithms, TrustGuard Naïve and TrustGuard TVM (Trust Value based credibility Measure) (Srivatsa et al., 2005). We set the same parameters for TrustGuard that their authors used in their paper. TrustGuard's authors have shown that it performs very well compared to eBay's reputation system, which is commonly used as a benchmark in the literature for RSs. Therefore, we decided to directly compare our performance with TrustGuard, instead of eBay.

In the initial set of experiments, we collected data going back 15 time slots for each simulation run. For oscillating behaviour, the period of oscillations was kept less than 15 to ensure it was distinguishable from legitimate behaviour. For SVM, a separate set of training data was also generated and SVM was trained on it. The training data had a fixed proportion of malicious nodes (about 60%).

For each node, its transaction history for the last 15 slots was fed into each RS. Then using the output of the RS, a determination was made about whether the node was malicious or benign. For SVM this was done by looking at the distance between the test node and the decision boundary. If this distance was greater than a threshold, the node was considered benign. Larger thresholds result in fewer false positives, but also fewer true positives. This might be desirable in critical applications where we want to be sure that a node that is given access to a resource is indeed good, even if that means denying access to some legitimate nodes. TrustGuard also outputs a score that can also be compared against a threshold and access can be granted if the score is greater than the fixed threshold.

Classification Error: In the first set of experiments, the thresholds were fixed at their midpoint values so that the results were not artificially biased either towards increasing true positives (lower thresholds) or decreasing false positives (higher thresholds) but were halfway. Since the range of thresholds for SVM is $(-\infty, \infty)$, its threshold was set to 0. The range for TrustGuard is $[0, 1]$, so its threshold was set to 0.5. Then the percentage of malicious nodes in the network was varied. The proportion of nodes that were misclassified, or the classification error, was measured. The results are illustrated in Figure 6. The results show that SVM significantly outperforms TrustGuard's Naïve and TVM algorithms, even if the proportion of malicious nodes is very large (i.e. 80%). It is also interesting to note that there is not much difference between TrustGuard's TVM and Naïve algorithms, even though TVM is much more complex.

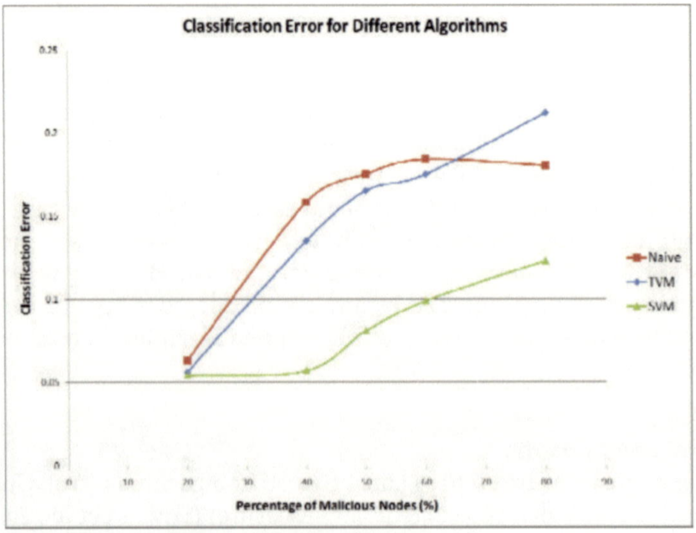

Fig. 6. Classification Error vs. Proportion of malicious nodes

ROC Curves: To obtain more in depth evaluations, we ran hundreds of more simulations in order to generate ROC curves for all three RSs. ROC curves are commonly used in Machine Learning to evaluate classifiers, irrespective of the thresholds used. The curve is obtained by varying the threshold, so that we can compare how the true positive rate varies with the false positive rate. The area under the ROC curve shows how good a classifier is. Classifiers with larger areas under the curve are better. The ideal ROC curve is an upside down L-shaped curve, containing the point (0, 1) that corresponds to 100% true positive rate and 0% false positive rate.

Each point on the curve was obtained by running 30 simulations with different random number seeds, and then taking their mean. Confidence Intervals were taken around each point to ensure that the curve of SVM did not overlap with that of TrustGuard (the confidence intervals are too small to be visible on the graphs). The results are shown in Figure 7, along with the diagonal random "guessing" line which corresponds to randomly guessing the label of the given nodes. The results show that SVM again outperforms TrustGuard, regardless of the thresholds used. The area under the curve is greater for SVM than TrustGuard.

11. Dynamic Thresholds with SVM

The major problem with network intrusion datasets is that we do not know the imbalance ratio at the time of training. We do not know how many malicious nodes there will be in a real network and we cannot expect their proportion to remain constant. However, the classification error could be greatly improved if we knew the imbalance ratio in the network at any given point in time. We could, for instance, vary the bias that SVM uses in order to obtain better classification accuracy.

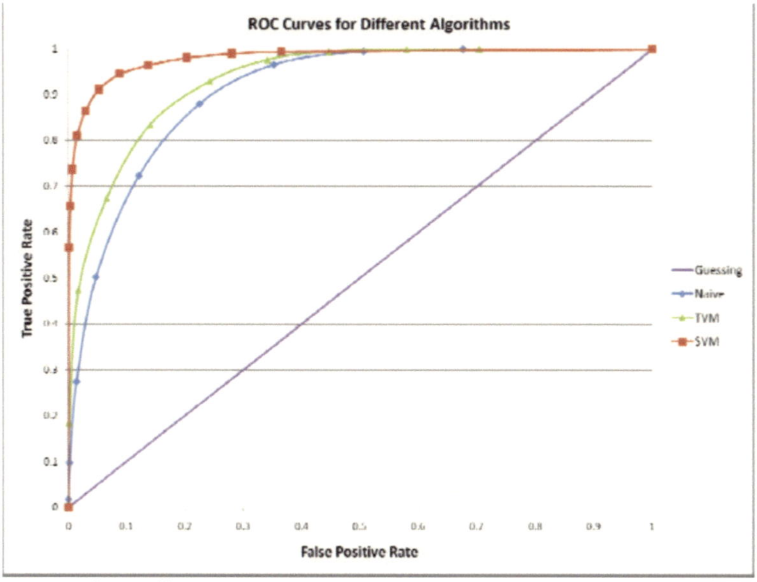

Fig. 7. ROC Curves for Different Algorithms

The general equation of a linear SVM is (Abe, 2005):

$$w.x + b \geq 0 \quad \text{for positive class}$$
$$w.x + b < 0 \quad \text{for negative class}$$

Where x is the instance vector, w is the normal to the SVM hyper plane, and b is the bias threshold. The reason why SVM's performance degraded at high malicious node proportions was because it was misclassifying the positive (non-malicious) instances. Therefore, we can increase the threshold, b, slightly so that those instances close to the SVM boundary are classified as positive. In other words, by increasing b we can effectively trade false negatives with false positives.

The bias pays off at higher proportions of malicious nodes when there are more false negatives than false positives. However, it costs us when the proportion of malicious nodes is small since there are more false positives than false negatives. This increases the error for small proportions. This observation led us to the idea that if we could know the proportion of malicious nodes in the network, we could adjust the bias threshold accordingly to optimize accuracy. The threshold would be decreased for fewer malicious nodes, and increased for more malicious nodes. We propose a scheme called "Dynamic Thresholds" that utilizes this idea.

To begin with, we determine what the ideal thresholds are for given proportions of malicious nodes using brute force trial and error. The ideal threshold is defined as that threshold which maximizes accuracy. We expect the threshold curve to be specific for a given SVM model, and each model would have its own associated curve. The ideal thresholds curve for our dataset is given in Figure 8.

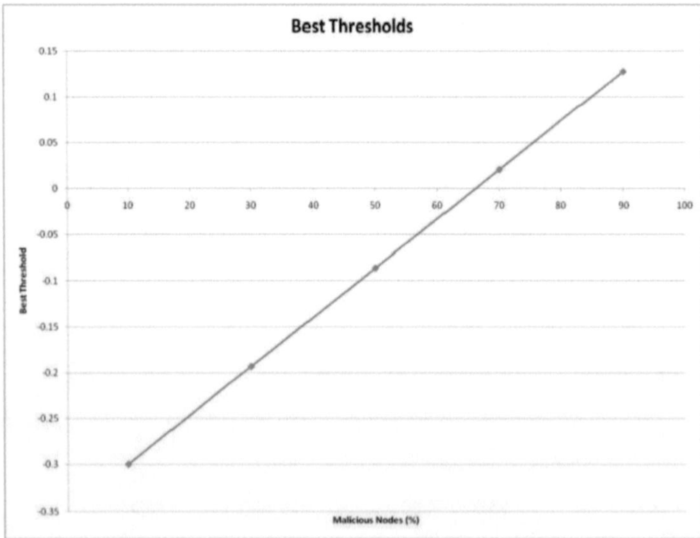

Fig. 8. SVM's best threshold vs. Malicious Nodes percentage

In our simulations, all the *w.x* values were normalized between the range (-1, 1). The threshold value, *b*, is with reference to this range. We generated more datasets and introduced greater variations in the duty cycles and frequencies of the oscillating behaviour of malicious nodes. As expected, this degraded the performance of the default SVM model. Then we used the best thresholds to determine the difference in error. Figure 9 shows the reduction in error achieved using the optimum thresholds versus using the default threshold of zero.

The results clearly show that dynamic thresholds can be very useful for significantly reducing the error. However, the challenge is that in a real world setting, we do not know the proportion of malicious nodes in the network and therefore, we cannot decide what threshold to use. To overcome this, we propose estimating the proportion of malicious nodes through sampling.

The idea is that a new node that joins the network would initially use the default threshold of zero. It would conduct transactions as usual and estimate the proportion of malicious nodes from all the nodes it has interacted with or received feedback about. A node is considered malicious if either the Reputation System classifies it as malicious, or if a transaction is conducted with the node and the transaction is deemed to be malicious. Once a large enough sample is collected by the node, it can use that sample to estimate the proportion of malicious nodes in the network and then dynamically adjust its threshold to improve the RS's accuracy.

We conducted experiments to determine what a good sample size would be before adjusting the threshold. We determined that once about 20 to 25 samples have been collected, a fairly good estimate of the actual proportion can be obtained. We therefore recommend that nodes should obtain a sample of at least 20 to 25 before adjusting their thresholds.

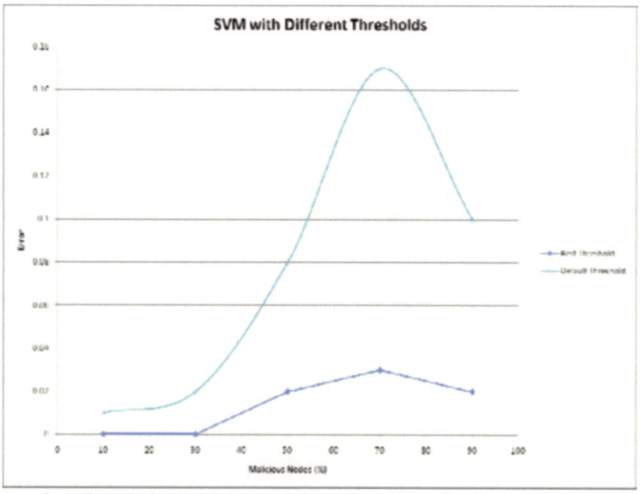

Fig. 9. SVM error under the default threshold and under the best thresholds

Figure 10 shows the reduction in error when Dynamic Thresholds are put into practice. Sample sizes of 20 and 25 are used. These samples are randomly collected and classified, based on a node's interactions with other nodes, and used to estimate the proportion of malicious nodes in the network. The threshold is adjusted based on the estimated proportions. The results show a significant reduction in error even at high proportions. Once the threshold has been adjusted, the sample is discarded and a fresh sample is started. In this way, the node can continuously monitor the proportion of malicious nodes and adjust its threshold as the proportion changes over time.

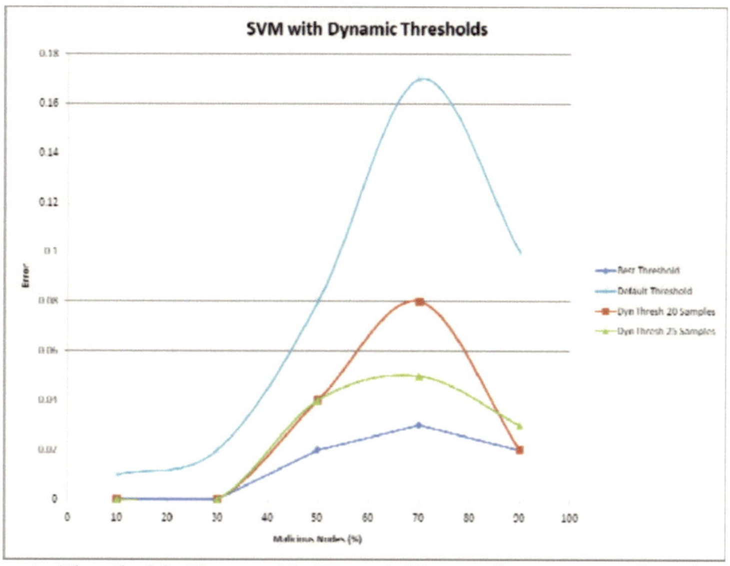

Fig. 10. Dynamic Thresholds Error with 20 and 25 samples compared to the default error and the minimum possible error

12. Conclusions and Future Work

This chapter discusses the issues faced when trying to train SVM on imbalanced datasets. The main reason why SVM performs poorly for such datasets is because of the weakness of soft margins. Soft margins were introduced in order to make SVM resilient against non-separable datasets. The idea was to tolerate some classification error as a trade off for maximizing the margin between the support vectors. But this has an adverse effect when it comes to imbalanced datasets. SVM ends up with a hyper plane that is far from the entire cluster of instances. Any instance that is on the same side of the plane as the cluster is classified as the majority class. Having the hyper plane further from the instances maximizes the margin, at the cost of misclassifying the minority class. But since there are only a few instances of the minority class, the error is rather small and the benefit of larger margins overcomes this. Therefore, everything is classified as the majority class.

Some solutions to this problem are presented in the chapter and evaluated against human genome and network intrusion datasets. The imbalance ratio in the genome dataset can be as high as 1:4500. This is well beyond the capability of traditional ML algorithms. However, we can use under sampling of the majority class and heuristics to reduce the imbalance ratio. Then we can use the techniques presented in this chapter to improve the performance of SVM on this dataset. These techniques include generating and selecting good features, using different error costs for majority and minority instances, and generating synthetic minority instances to even out the imbalance.

Then we discussed datasets where the imbalance ratio is not known at the time of training. Network intrusion is one such application domain where the number of malicious nodes in the network is unknown at the time of training. We introduced dynamic thresholds to try to estimate this proportion and then adjust the SVM model's parameters to significantly improve its performance. We also showed that building Reputation Systems and automatically determining their rule sets using Machine Learning is not only feasible, but yields better results than some of the manually generated rule sets found in the literature.

Although the techniques presented in this chapter have been shown to significantly improve SVM's performance on imbalanced datasets, there are still limitations on what degrees of imbalance SVM can handle. We have tested SVM on imbalance ratios of 1:100, however, bioinformatics datasets have imbalances of 1 to several thousands. In future, researchers need to invent better algorithms that are capable of handling such huge imbalances.

13. Acknowledgments

This work was supported by US Dept. of Defence Infrastructure Support Program for HBCU/MI, Grant: 54477-CI-ISP (Unclassified), and by the National Science Foundation under grant CRI - 0551501. We would like to thank Dr. G.V.S. Raju and Dr. Stephen Kwek for their assistance and input towards this research.

14. References

Abe, S. (2005). Support Vector Machines for Pattern Classification (Advances in Pattern Recognition), Springer, ISBN 1852339292, Chp 6, 11, London, UK

Aha, D. (1992). Tolerating noisy, irrelevant and novel attributes in instance-based learning algorithms. International Journal of Man-Machine Studies, Vol. 36, 267-287

Akbani, R.; Kwek, S. & Japkowicz, N. (2004). Applying Support Vector Machines to Imbalanced Datasets, Proceedings of the 15th European Conference on Machine Learning (ECML), pp. 39-50, Pisa, Italy, Sept. 2004, Springer-Verlag, Germany

Akbani, R.; Korkmaz, T. & Raju, G.V.S. (2008). Defending Against Malicious Nodes Using an SVM Based Reputation System, Proceedings of MILCOM 2008, Sponsored by Raytheon, IEEE, AFCEA, San Diego, California, USA, 2008

Baras, J. S. & Jiang, T. (2005). Managing trust in self-organized mobile ad hoc networks, Workshop NDSS, Extended abstract, 2005

Camastra, F. & M. Filippone (2007). SVM-based time series prediction with nonlinear dynamics methods. Knowledge-Based Intelligent Information and Eng. Systems, LNCS, Springer, Vol. 4694, 2007, pp 300-307

Chawla, N.; Bowyer, K.; Hall, L. & Kegelmeyer, W. (2002). SMOTE: Synthetic Minority Over-sampling Technique. Journal of Artificial Intelligence Research, Vol. 16, 2002, pp. 321-357

Cortes, C. (1995). Prediction of Generalisation Ability in Learning Machines. PhD thesis, Department of Computer Science, University of Rochester

Cristianini, N. & Shawe-Taylor, J. (2000). An Introduction to Support Vector Machines and other kernel-based learning methods, Cambridge University Press, ISBN 0521780195, Cambridge, UK

Cristianini, N.; Kandola, J.; Elisseeff, A. & Shawe-Taylor, J (2002). On Kernel Target Alignment. Journal of Machine Learning Research, Vol. 1, 2002

Hatzigeorgiou, A. G. (2002). Translation initiation start prediction in human cDNAs with high accuracy. Bioinformatics 18, pp. 343-350, 2002

Japkowicz, N. (2000). The Class Imbalance Problem: Significance and Strategies, Proceedings of the 2000 International Conference on Artificial Intelligence: Special Track on Inductive Learning, Las Vegas, Nevada, 2000

Jiang, T. & Baras, J. S. (2004). Ant-based adaptive trust evidence distribution in MANET, Proceedings of the 24th International Conference on Distributed Computing Systems, Tokyo, Japan, March, 2004

Jiang, T. & Baras, J. S. (2006). Trust evaluation in anarchy: A case study on autonomous networks, Proceedings of the 25th Conference on Computer Communications, 2006

Joachims, T. (1998). Text Categorization with SVM: Learning with Many Relevant Features, Proceedings of the 10th European Conference on Machine Learning (ECML), 1998

Josang, A. & Ismail, R. (2002). The beta reputation system, Proceedings of the 15th BLED Electronic Commerce Conference, Slovenia, June, 2002

Kamvar, S. D.; Schlosser, M. T. & Garcia-Molina, H. (2003). The EigenTrust algorithm for reputation management in P2P networks, Proceedings of the International World Wide Web Conference, WWW, 2003

Kozak, M. (1996). Interpreting cDNA sequences: Some insights from studies on translation. Mammalian Genome 7, 1996, pp. 563-574

Kubat, M. & Matwin, S. (1997). Addressing the Curse of Imbalanced Training Sets: One-Sided Selection, Proceedings of the 14th International Conference on Machine Learning, 1997

Ling, C. & Li, C. (1998). Data Mining for Direct Marketing Problems and Solutions, Proceedings of the Fourth International Conference on Knowledge Discovery and Data Mining, New York, NY, USA, 1998

Liu, H.; Han H.; Li J. & Wong, L. (2004). Using amino acid patterns to accurately predict translation initiation sites. In Silico Biology 4, Bioinformation Systems, 2004

Pedersen, A. & Nielsen, H. (1997). Neural network prediction of translation initiation sites in eukaryotes: perspectives for EST and genome analysis, Proceeding of the International Conference on Intelligent Systems for Molecular Biology, pp. 226-233, 1997

Provost, F. & Fawcett, T. (2001). Robust Classification for Imprecise Environments. Machine Learning, Vol. 42, No. 3, pp. 203-231

Salamov, A.; Nishikawa, T. & Swindells, M. A. (1998). Assessing protein coding region integrity in cDNA sequencing projects. Bioinformatics 14, pp. 384-390, 1998

Srivatsa, M.; Xiong, L. & Liu, L. (2005). TrustGuard: Countering vulnerabilities in reputation management for decentralized overlay networks, Proceedings of the International World Wide Web Conference, WWW, 2005

Stormo, G.; Schneider, T.; Gold, L. & Ehrenfeucht, A. (1982). Use of the 'Perceptron' Algorithm to Distinguish Translational Initiation Sites in E.coli. Nucleic Acids Res., Vol. 10, pp. 2997–3011

Tong, S. & Chang, E. (2001). Support Vector Machine Active Learning for Image Retrieval, Proceedings of ACM International Conference on Multimedia, pp. 107-118

Vapnik, V. (1995). The Nature of Statistical Learning Theory. Springer, ISBN 0387987800, New York, NY, USA

Veropoulos, K.; Campbell, C. & Cristianini, N. (1999). Controlling the sensitivity of support vector machines, Proceedings of the International Joint Conference on AI, pp. 55–60, 1999

Wu, G. & Chang, E. (2003). Class-Boundary Alignment for Imbalanced Dataset Learning, Proceedings of ICML 2003 Workshop on Learning from Imbalanced Data Sets II, Washington DC, USA

Zeng, F.; Yap, H. C. & Wong, L. (2002). Using feature generation and feature selection for accurate prediction of translation initiation sites, Proceedings of 13th Workshop on Genome Informatics, Universal Academy Press, pp. 192-200, 2002

Zien, A.; Ratsch, G.; Mika, S.; Scholkopf, B.; Lemmen, C.; Smola, A.; Lengauer, T. & Muller, K. R. (2000). Engineering support vector machine kernels that recognize translation initiation sites. Bioinformatics, Vol. 16, pp. 799-807, 2000

9

Machine learning for functional brain mapping

Malin Björnsdotter
Institute of Neuroscience and Physiology
University of Gothenburg
Sweden

1. Introduction

Human brain activity – the product of multiple neural networks encoding a multitude of concurrent cognitive states and responses to various stimuli – is a prime example of highly complex data. Irrespective of measuring technique, acquired brain signals are invariably exceedingly noisy, multivariate and high-dimensional. These inherent properties produce analysis difficulties traditionally overcome by utilization of descriptive statistical methods averaging across numerous time-fixed events, and conclusions about brain function are thus typically based on mean signal variations in single measuring points. It is, however, commonly believed that neural network activity responsible for cognitive function is distributed across time, frequency and space – aspects that traditional descriptive statistics inevitably fail to capture. Machine learning approaches do, in contrast, supply tools for detection of single, subtle signal patterns, rather than characteristic univariate, average activity. The field of pattern recognition harbors great potential in answering research questions fundamentally relevant for understanding the functional organization of the human brain where conventional methods fail.

Machine learning techniques are, consequently, being increasingly used by the neuroimaging community for a variety of data analyses. In functional magnetic resonance imaging (fMRI; described in section 2), where neural activity is estimated through measuring changes in blood flow and oxygenation (collectively called 'hemodynamics') at an excellent spatial resolution, for example, brain activation magnitudes are minute – at a magnetic field of 1.5 Tesla, for example, the hemodynamic change in response to a stimulation is typically only about 2% of the total amplitude Buxton (2002). This effect, nonetheless, provides researchers a non-invasive window into the human brain, and can be utilized to localize regions activated by various conditions in an attempt to understand the functional organization of the cortex. Conventionally, regional activity is estimated by fitting a spatially invariant model of the expected hemodynamic change at each individual measuring point (voxel) and, subsequently, testing for differences in signal levels between two experimental conditions Friston et al. (1994a). This massively univariate (voxel-by-voxel) analysis produces statistical maps highlighting brain locations that are "activated" by the condition in an appealing fashion (see figure 1E). Although this analytical scheme has proven tremendously useful in functional brain mapping, it is limited to revealing average stimuli - single location relationships and cannot reflect individual events or effects in distributed activation patterns.

In recent years, state-of-the-art machine learning methods allowing identification of subtle, spatially distributed single-trial fMRI signal effects not detectable using conventional analysis have instead won substantial ground Haynes & Rees (2006); Norman et al. (2006). Typically, a classifier model is trained to identify signal patterns related to a given experimental condition by integrating information across multiple voxels, thus allowing detection of information which only produce weak single-voxel effects. Subsequently, the trained classifier is applied to new data samples and attempts to predict the experimental condition to which each sample belongs. This approach, termed multivoxel pattern analysis (MVPA; Norman et al. (2006); or more seductively 'brain reading'), was initiated with a breakthrough fMRI study of the vision pathway Haxby et al. (2001). Volunteers were shown a number of visual stimuli from various object categories (cats, faces, houses, etc.), and the researchers found that fMRI responses evoked by each object category was associated with a distinct spatial signal pattern which could be identified ('decoded') by a classification scheme. The authors concluded that information is encoded across spatially wide and distributed patterns of fMRI responses, undetectable by conventional approach designed to detect voxel-by-voxel statistically significant activations. Since then, numerous studies have utilized multivoxel pattern analysis for exploring human brain function with outstanding results (see e.g. Björnsdotter et al. (2009); Cox & Savoy (2003); Formisano et al. (2008); Haynes & Rees (2005a;b); Howard et al. (2009); Kamitani & Tong (2005)).

The variety of machine learning approaches utilized in fMRI spans a vast range: from classical linear discriminant analysis Carlson et al. (2003) to state-of-the-art particle swarm optimization Niiniskorpi et al. (2009). This chapter introduces machine learning concepts in the context of functional brain imaging, with focus on classification based fMRI brain mapping. First, the fMRI technique for measuring brain activity is presented, including technical background and a number of considerations for subsequent analysis. Second, the essential steps required for effective machine learning classification analysis are described, and, ultimately, an example of our work utilizing evolutionary algorithms for mapping human brain responses to pleasant touch is presented.

2. Functional magnetic resonance imaging

Functional magnetic resonance imaging (fMRI) derives from magnetic resonance imaging (MRI), which is utilized for obtaining structural (as opposed to functional) images of tissue (see figure 1A and B). Magnetic resonance imaging is made possible by intrinsic physical properties of atoms in matter, including magnetism and nuclear spin. Measurable effects in such inherent properties due to local blood oxygenation changes in response to neural activity provide an effective, albeit indirect, entirely non-invasive measure of brain activation. Below follows a description of the technical MRI and fMRI background as well as the conventional approach to fMRI signal processing and analysis (see also e.g. Buxton (2002) or Norris (2006) for more details).

2.1 Magnetic resonance imaging

In magnetic resonance imaging (MRI), the magnetism and nuclear spin of atoms are utilized to obtain information about the environment in which the they are contained (e.g. brain tissue; see Buxton (2002) for more technical details on MRI). The spin refers to the inherent angular momentum possessed by all atomic nuclei with an odd number of protons or neutrons, and, fundamentally important for brain imaging, only one substance abundantly found in organic tissue possesses such a spin – the hydrogen atom. Due to the spin, the hydrogen atom also has a magnetic dipole moment and, therefore, behaves like a small magnet.

When there is no external magnetic field, the magnetic dipole moments are randomly orientated and there is a net magnetization of approximately zero. When an external magnetic field is applied, a majority of the magnetic moments will gradually align with the magnetic field (a process referred to as longitudinal relaxation) with a time constant T_1 (typically around 1 s), and a net magnetization in the direction of the field is produced. Also, the nuclei will change the direction of the axis of rotation around the field axis in a process called *precession*. The frequency of precession, v_0, is called the *Larmor* (or nuclear magnetic resonance) frequency. The Larmor frequency is proportional to the strength of the external magnetic field: $v_0 = \gamma B_0$, where B_0 (measure in Tesla, T) is the external magnetic field strength and γ (units: MHz/T) is the gyromagnetic ratio. The latter is a physical property of the given element, and for hydrogen the ratio is 42.58 MHz/T. Magnetic fields used for human fMRI are typically in the range of 1.5 T (approximately 30 000 times the earth's magnetic field) to 9 T.
The precession of the nuclei could potentially induce a current in a receiver coil placed nearby, and thus be measured. However, although the nuclei precess with the same frequency, their phase is different and the net magnetism is zero – thus no current would be induced in the coil. The phase of the precessing nuclei must therefore be coordinated. This is achieved by applying a rapidly oscillating magnetic radio frequency (RF) pulse at the precession frequency (v_0) to the nuclei. The rapid oscillations of the RF pulse gradually nudge the magnetic moments away from their initial axis of precession. The RF pulse can be applied to rotate all the magnetic moments 90 degrees, and thus change the net magnetization from being aligned with the external magnetic field to pointing perpendicular to the field – still, however, precessing around the field. As a result, the magnetic moments are in phase, producing a precessing net magnetization which can be registered by a receiver coil. The induced current, alternating with the Larmor frequency, is informative about the physical environment, such as the number of nuclei (spins) in the sample.
Notably, the current induced in the coil decays over time (a process called *relaxation*). This decay is partly due to thermal motion on the molecular level, realigning the net magnetic moments with the external magnetic field (T_1 relaxation), partly to that the random interactions of nuclei result in a loss of coherence of the precession which reduces the net magnetization (T_2 relaxation). Moreover, inhomogeneities in the magnetic field cause dephasing, since the precession frequency of the nuclei is proportional to the strength of B_0. This effect in combination with the random nuclei interactions is referred to as T_2^* relaxation.
Fundamentally important for functional and structural imaging, the relaxation times differ between various tissues (such as muscle and bone, gray and white brain matter, and so on). Using an MRI scanner, structural images (akin to X-rays) can therefore be reconstructed from the acquired relaxation signals (figure 1A).

2.2 BOLD functional imaging

In addition to structural images, magnetic resonance techniques can also be utilized for acquiring *functional* data, that is, signals related to some sort of active function of the brain. Functional magnetic resonance imaging (fMRI) is based on the presence of hemoglobin (the molecule in red blood cells which contains oxygen) combined with various hemodynamic changes (such as blood flow, blood volume, oxygen consumption etc). Hemoglobin is diamagnetic when oxygenated and paramagnetic when deoxygenated and, therefore, possesses different magnetic characteristics depending on oxygenation state. This phenomenon, in combination with the measured T_2^* (transversal) relaxation (see the section on Magnetic resonance imaging above), is used in fMRI to detect magnetic differences between oxygenated and de-

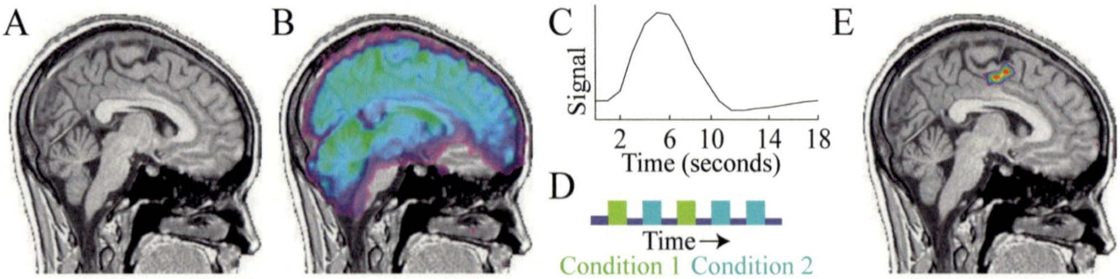

Fig. 1. **A**. MRI structural image. **B**. fMRI functional image. **C**. Hemodynamic response function (in arbitrary units). **D**. Schematic of experimental paradigm with two conditions. **E**. General linear model (GLM) statistical activation map.

oxygenated blood in the brain. Specifically, blood-oxygen-level dependent (BOLD) fMRI is the technique used to identify temporal and spatial variations in the proportion of oxygenated to deoxygenated blood, which, in turn, is an indication of blood flow changes Ogawa et al. (1990). A relative increase in blood flow results in a positive signal, and vice versa.

For brain function related studies, the BOLD signal is acquired volume by volume, and each volume element is referred to as a 'voxel' (see figure 1B). The minimum time required for one whole brain volume is typically in the range of 2-3 seconds, and each voxel is in the range of 2-4 mm per side. Thus, fMRI has comparatively poor temporal resolution and excellent spatial resolution.

2.3 Neural correlates of BOLD

It was observed as early as in the 1890s that nerve cell activation level is positively correlated with blood flow Roy & Sherrington (1890). The temporal pattern of blood flow changes in response to activated nerve cells is called the hemodynamic response function (HRF; see figure 1C), and different brain areas respond differently Leoni et al. (2008). The full course of the blood flow response to a briefly presented stimulus is about 20 s and a maximum is obtained at approximately 6 s. As a result, the temporal resolution of fMRI is limited due to the inherent delay in the hemodynamic response. Capillaries, small arteries and veins, as well as large arteries and veins all contribute to the registered BOLD signal.

Although it is generally assumed that changes in blood flow (and supply of oxygenated blood) is prompted by increased oxygen consumption by activated nerve cells, the exact relationship between neural activity and the BOLD signal is not fully understood. In fact, the measurable (highest in amplitude) portion of the HRF appears to be a substantial over-compensation (supplying more blood than is required by metabolic demands) and the mechanisms for this are unknown. Moreover, the BOLD signal is an indirect measure of brain activity, and is susceptible to influence by physical parameters of non-neural nature, and, can, in fact, potentially represent increased blood flow into an area despite no local neural activity (see e.g. Sirotin & Das (2008)). Concurrent intracortical recordings of neural signals and fMRI responses in the visual cortex in monkeys have shown, however, that local field potentials are significantly correlated to the hemodynamic response (Logothetis et al. (2001); see also Goense & Logothetis (2008) for a review).

3. Conventional brain mapping analysis

The aim of conventional analysis is typically to identify regions of the brain which are activated by the processing of a given stimulation or condition. In order to achieve effective analysis, a number of steps are required. First, the experimental paradigm must be carefully designed in order ensure that the actual effect of interest is analyzed. Second, the acquired data must be pre-processed, followed by a statistical analysis which estimates significantly activated regions. A variety of softwares exist for both pre-processing and statistical analysis, including the freely available Neurolens (neurolens.org), SPM (fil.ion.ucl.ac.uk/spm; Frackowiak et al. (1997)) and ANFI (afni.nimh.nih.gov), as well as commercial software such as BrainVoyager (brainvoyager.com). The required analysis steps are described in detail below.

3.1 Experimental paradigm

Careful attention needs to be paid to the type and organization of conditions presented during the experiment (the experimental paradigm) in order to isolate the effect of interest (as opposed to noise or other cognitive process). Typically, paradigms involve a number of stimulus conditions which are contrasted in subsequent analysis to remove confounding variables (such as attentional effects). During the scanning session, the conditions are presented in a predetermined fashion in one of a number of ways. Influenced by positron emission tomography (PET) imaging where extended stimulation periods are required in order to produce stable activations Muehllehner & Karp (2006), fMRI studies often utilize experimental paradigms which alternate extended periods of stimuli being 'on' or 'off' (see figure 1D; Turner et al. (1998)). This so called *block design* is appealing due to ease of presentation and analysis, as well as to the relatively high signal-to-noise ratios achieved. Brief stimuli can, however, produce a measurable BOLD response (e.g. 34 ms; Rosen et al. (1998)), and such are applied in *event-related designs*. Various types of conditions unsuitable for study with block designs, such as the oddball paradigm McCarthy et al. (1997), are instead made possible by event-related studies. Also, more dynamic responses, suitable in situations where habituation is a concern, are produced, and, given similar scanning times, more stimulus repetitions can be applied (see e.g. Kriegeskorte et al. (2008) for a study utilizing numerous stimuli applications). A draw-back of even-related paradigms is, however, the lower functional signal-to-noise ratio than in block design paradigms Bandettini & Cox (2000).

3.2 Pre-processing

In order to reduce noise, the acquired fMRI data is subjected to a series of pre-processing operations. The following steps are typically applied, although all are not necessarily required and further steps can be included to improve the analysis (see e.g. Friston et al. (2007) or Henson (2003) for more details, and note that virtually all fMRI analysis software include functions for these corrections).

- *Slice-time correction*: The acquisition of an entire brain volume generally takes in the order of 2-3 seconds (depending on MRI scanner parameters), during which slices of brain tissue are scanned consecutively. The resulting shift in acquisition time between slices is typically corrected by resampling the time courses with linear interpolation such that all voxels in a given volume represent the signal at the same point in time.
- *Motion correction*: The excellent spatial resolution of fMRI means that slight movements of the head can affect the signal analysis substantially, and head movement effects must

therefore be corrected. A variety of more or less sophisticated algorithms are available in any of the software packages mentioned above.

- *Signal filtering*: Temporal drifts which can significantly affect the results are typically removed using temporal high-pass filtering. Noise can further be reduced by temporal low pass filtering.
- *Spatial smoothing*: In order to reflect some spatial integration, spatial smoothing is typically applied on the volume time series using a Gaussian kernel with the parameter FWHM (full width at half maximum) in the range of 3-12 millimeters. Spatial smoothing increases subsequent mapping sensitivity when two conditions differ in terms of their regional mean activation levels. In these cases, local signal differences coherently point in the same direction and are enhanced by spatial averaging. However, if two conditions differ in terms of their fine-grained spatial activation patterns, spatial smoothing has a destructive effect and cancels out the discriminative information, which can be detected by pattern recognition methods (see the section on Machine learning brain mapping analysis below).
- *Spatial normalization*: Individual brains are highly anatomically and functionally variable. Thus, for group analysis and comparison with brain atlases, the fMRI data must be projected into a standard brain space such as Talairach Talairach & Tournoux (1988) or so called MNI (Montreal Neurological Institute; Evans et al. (1993)) space. This is performed with a number of different algorithms (see e.g. Collins et al. (1994), and see Crinion et al. (2007) for issues with spatial normalization).

3.3 General linear modelling and activation detection

Numerous variations of fMRI analysis techniques are widely used, and the field is under active research. The most lucrative approach thus far, however, includes statistical analysis to produce images (statistical parametric maps) which identify brain regions that show significant signal changes in response to the conditions present during scanning (see e.g. Henson (2003)). Typically, a spatially invariant model of the expected blood oxygenation level dependent (BOLD) response is fitted independently at each voxel's time course and the differences between estimated activation levels during two or more experimental conditions are tested Friston et al. (1994a). Parametric tests, assuming that the observations are drawn from normal populations, are typically applied. Most such parametric modeling techniques are versions of the general linear model (GLM). The GLM aims to explain the variation of the time course $y_1...y_i...y_n$, in terms of a linear combination of explanatory variables and an error term. For a simple model with only one explanatory variable $x_1...x_i...x_n$, the GLM can be written as:

$$y_i = x_i\beta + \epsilon_i \tag{1}$$

where β is the scaling (slope) parameter, and ϵ_i is an error term. The model is also often written in matrix form when containing more variables:

$$Y = X\beta + \epsilon \tag{2}$$

where Y is the vector of observed voxel values, β is the vector of parameters and ϵ is the vector of error terms. The matrix X is termed the design matrix, containing one row per time point and one column per explanatory variable in the model (e.g. representing the presence or absence of a specific condition). In order to detect activations, the magnitude of the parameter in

β corresponding to these vectors are computed. β can be determined by solving the following equations:

$$X^T Y = (X^T X)\hat{\beta} \tag{3}$$

where $\hat{\beta}$ corresponds to the best linear estimate of β. Given that $X^T X$ is invertible, $\hat{\beta}$ can be estimated as:

$$\hat{\beta} = (X^T X)^{-1} X^T Y \tag{4}$$

These parameter estimates are normally distributed, and since the error term can be determined, statistical inference can be made as to whether the β parameter corresponding to the model of an activation response is significantly different from the null hypothesis. A number of additional parameters (regressors) can be included in the GLM analysis, such as drift, respiration, motion correction parameters or other information of interest.
Importantly, the massively univariate testing results in one statistic per voxel, and thus produces a classical problem of multiple comparisons which requires correction Friston et al. (1994a). Depending on the number of voxels included for analysis, the threshold for which a voxel can be considered significant varies – for smaller regions the threshold is lower. While whole-brain analyses might not yield any significant results, directed searches in carefully, a priori identified regions of interests can potentially yield significantly activated voxels. Thus, in combination with methods for mitigating the multiple comparisons problem, this massively univariate analysis produces statistical maps of response differences, highlighting brain locations that are activated by a certain condition dimension (see figure 1E; Friston et al. (1994a)). As such, univariate activation detection maps average single-voxel responses to experimental conditions, and does not reflect direct relationships between distributed patterns of brain processing and single condition instances.

4. Machine learning brain mapping analysis

Contrary to conventional univariate analysis (described above), where average voxel-by-voxel signal increases or decreases are estimated using statistical techniques, machine learning approaches utilize information distributed across multiple voxels. Specifically, classifier-based machine learning algorithms attempt to identify and distinguish the specific spatial activity patterns produced by single experimental conditions.
To this end, multivoxel fMRI activity patterns (samples) can be represented as points in a multidimensional space where the number of dimensions equals that of voxels. In the simplified situation of a two-voxel volume, each pattern can be considered as a point in a plane corresponding to the magnitude measured in each voxel (see figure 2). The aim of a classifier is to distinguish the conditions, that is, to separate the points belonging the each of the condition classes. As shown in the figure, the method of doing so depends on the structure of the data – if the conditions are sufficiently different (figure 2A) this can be done on a single voxel level (with conventional univariate statistics), whereas if the voxel distributions overlap (figure 2B and C) multiple voxels must be taken into account to distinguish the conditions.
After initial pre-processing and estimation of single condition responses, application of classifier-based machine learning techniques to fMRI generally entails a number of steps (see figure 3). The data is partitioned into datasets – one for training the classifier (that is, estimating classifier parameters), and one exclusively used in conjunction with the trained classifier to evaluate the classification performance. Voxel selection, aiming at reducing the complexity of

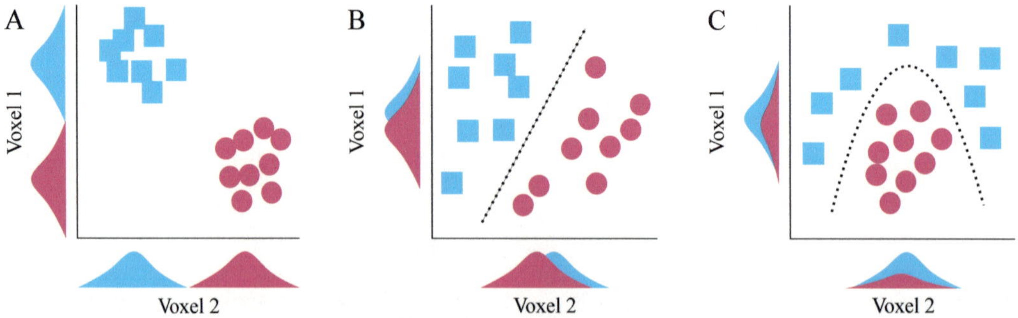

Fig. 2. Two-voxel illustration of the multivoxel analysis approach, where blue and purple represent two different experimental conditions. In **A**, the response distributions to the conditions (the Gaussian curves) are separable in each single voxel and a univariate statistical approach is feasible to distinguish the conditions. In **B**, however, the two conditions can not be separated in each individual voxels due to the overlap of the distributions, and a univariate measure would fail in distinguishing the conditions. A linear decision boundary (dotted line) can, however, separate the conditions. Similarly, in **C**, the conditions can be separated but a non-linear decision boundary is required.

the dataset and improving classification performance, is performed, often in intimate conjunction with classifier training. During classifier training, several processing and voxel selection cycles may therefore be explored. After voxel selection and classifier training, discriminative maps are produced indicating regions encoding information regarding the conditions. Finally, the capability of the trained classifier to accurately discriminate the experimental conditions when presented with data from the hitherto unused partition is tested to assess classifier generalization ability.

4.1 Experimental paradigm

The experimental paradigm considerations for machine learning based analysis are typically the same as for conventional approaches, including those for block-design (see e.g. Björnsdotter et al. (2009)) and event-related (see e.g. Beauchamp et al. (2009); Burke et al. (2004)) paradigms. For machine learning analysis, event-related designs have the benefit of producing more independent datapoints, which, in turn, yields less contaminated estimations of the spatial pattern related to each condition. In theory, this can improve the machine learning algorithm's sensitivity in detecting information contained in the spatial patterns. However, rapid-event related designs risk temporal overlap of hemodynamic responses, although various techniques can be applied to reduce this effect (see e.g. Beauchamp et al. (2009)).

4.2 Pre-processing

The pre-processing steps required for machine learning analysis are essentially identical to conventional analysis pre-processing, with the notable exception of spatial smoothing – if the conditions differ in terms of their fine-grained spatial activation patterns, spatial smoothing will reduce the discriminative information content. Moreover, without smoothing the highest possible spatial resolution offered by the fMRI scanner is preserved, and small differences in location can be maximally resolved. Smoothing may, nonetheless, have a beneficial impact on classification performance (LaConte et al., 2003)

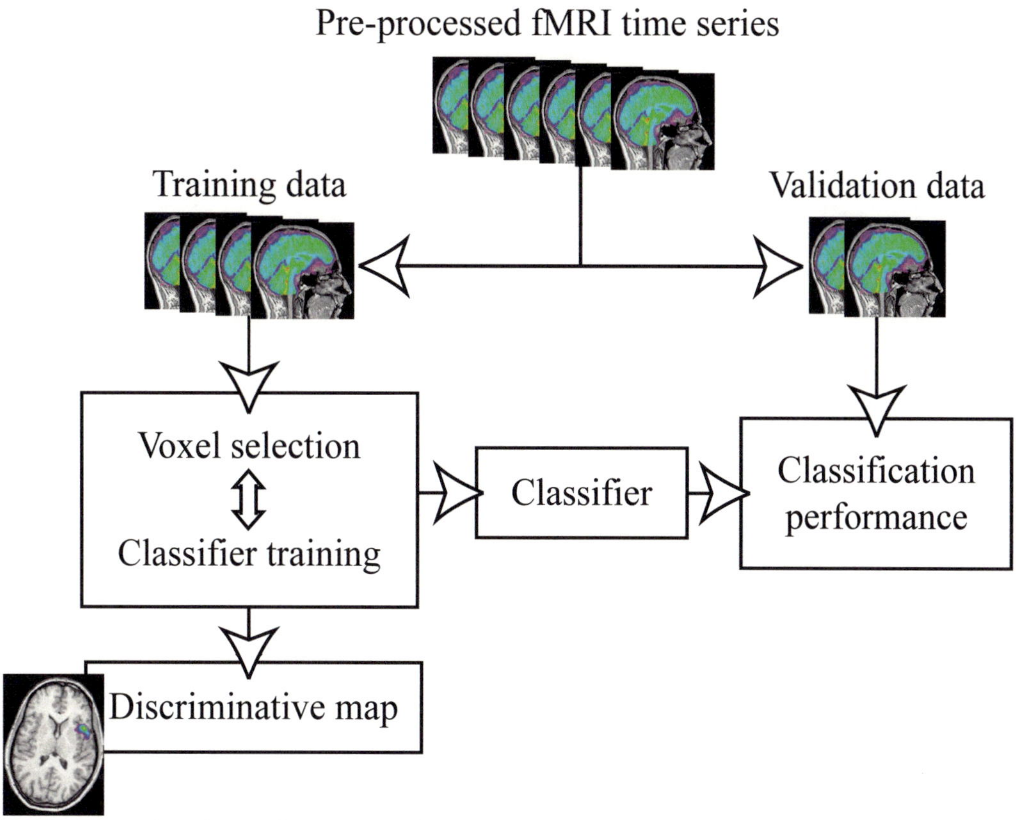

Fig. 3. General multivoxel pattern analysis (MVPA) workflow.

4.3 Condition response estimation

The continuous fMRI brain activity signal, consisting of a series of intensity values for each voxel across the scanning time course, must be re-represented as single condition responses per time unit for subsequent analysis. Generally, one time-measure (volume) is used as a sample, but as outlined in the section on BOLD fMRI above, the hemodynamic response (with delays of approximately 6 s after onset of stimulation) must be accounted for when estimating temporal single-trial responses. A number of activation representations have been used in multivoxel fMRI studies, including the following:

1. *Single-volume intensities*: The intensity at a single acquisition volume can be used to represent a condition Haynes & Rees (2005a); Mourão-Miranda et al. (2005), given appropriate hemodynamic lag compensation. A simple approach to compensating for hemodynamic lag is to simply shift the data labels the corresponding amount of acquisition time points (typically around 6 s).
2. *Volume-average intensities*: When the conditions are applied during multiple volumes (e.g. in a block design study), the average intensity across the volumes Björnsdotter et al. (2009); Kamitani & Tong (2005); Mourão-Miranda & Reynaud (2006) can be used. Typically the first few volumes are also discarded. This approach has the added benefit of increased signal-to-noise ratio.

3. *Single-trial GLM fitting*: A third option is to directly estimate the single-trial response based on the hemodynamic response function De Martino et al. (2008); Formisano et al. (2008); Staeren et al. (2009). Here, a trial corresponds to one application of the stimulus, or, in the block design case, the duration of the 'on' block. A trial estimate of the voxel-wise response is obtained by fitting a general linear model (GLM) with one predictor coding for the trial response and one linear predictor accounting for a within-trial linear trend to each single trial. The trial-response predictor can be obtained by convolution of a boxcar with a double-gamma hemodynamic response function (HRF; Friston et al. (1998)). At every voxel, the corresponding regressor coefficient (beta) is taken to represent the trial response.

4.4 Data partitioning

In order to avoid classifier overfitting and unsound prediction accuracies (see e.g. Kriegeskorte et al., 2009 for a review of this problem in functional brain imaging), care is required when partitioning the data samples into training (used for any aspect of establishing the classifier, including classifier parameter estimation and voxel selection) and validation (exclusively used in the validation of the already established classifier) data.

Potential dependencies between datasets must be carefully avoided – the inherent temporal sluggishness of the hemodynamic response producing temporal dependencies is of particularly concern when fMRI is considered. Thus, any randomization of training and validation samples must be preceded by a condition response estimation (see section above) ensuring no temporal dependencies between samples (or the prediction accuracies will be biased towards the higher end of the spectrum). Another possibility is to select a temporally independent validation sample from samples collected towards the end of the scanning session.

4.5 Classifiers

Classifiers employed for multivoxel pattern analysis of fMRI data range from various versions of linear discriminant analysis Carlson et al. (2003); Haynes & Rees (2005a;b); Kriegeskorte et al. (2006); O'toole et al. (2005), correlation-based classification Haxby et al. (2001); Spiridon & Kanwisher (2002) linear Cox & Savoy (2003); De Martino et al. (2008); Formisano et al. (2008); Kamitani & Tong (2005); LaConte et al. (2005); Mitchell et al. (2004); Mourão-Miranda et al. (2005); Mourão-Miranda & Reynaud (2006); Staeren et al. (2009) and non-linear Cox & Savoy (2003); Davatzikos et al. (2005) support vector machine (SVM), artificial neural networks (ANNs; Hanson et al. (2004); Polyn et al. (2005)) and gaussian naive bayes (GNB) classifiers Mitchell et al. (2004). See e.g. Duda et al. (2000) for details on these classifiers.

Despite the theoretical superiority of non-linear classifiers, linear classifiers have by far been most popular in fMRI multivoxel research (see citations above). A highly appealing advantage of linear classifiers is the direct relation between classifier weights and voxels, providing a means to understand which regions of the brain are multivariately informative De Martino et al. (2008); Mourão-Miranda et al. (2005). Although linear discriminant analysis and linear support vector machines have dominated the field, there appears to be little practical difference between linear classifiers Ku et al. (2008).

4.6 Performance metrics

The performance metrics indicates the ability of the classifier to predict the condition categories to which previously unseen samples belong. Typically, the performance metric is expressed in terms of classification performance (e.g. proportion correctly or incorrectly labelled instances of the validation data, or area under the receiver operating characteristic curve). Due to the limited number of samples available in fMRI studies, various data partitioning schemes such as cross-validation are utilized in order to obtain a good estimate of the performance Duda et al. (2000).

4.7 Voxel selection

As is well-known from other areas of machine learning, classification performance degrades as the number of irrelevant features increases (party due to the curse of dimensionality; Bellman (1961); Guyon & Elisseeff (2003)). Given the excessive number of voxels in a typical brain volume (in the order of tens to hundreds of thousands) compared to the limited number of available volumes (typically in the range of tens to hundreds), voxel selection is an acute issue (as also pointed out by Norman et al. (2006)). Selection of an adequate subset of voxels is not only of critical importance in order to obtain classifiers with good generalization performance, but also to provide insight into what brain regions encode information relevant to the conditions under investigation ("brain mapping"). Moreover, fMRI voxel selection deviates from conventional feature selection in the sense that the smallest possible subset of voxels which is *sufficient* for maximal classification is not necessarily desired. In fact, *all* voxels which potentially contain relevant information are interesting, as is the relative degree of information content (see Sato et al. (2009) for a discussion on this topic).

In early stages of fMRI multivoxel analysis, the feature selection problem was resolved by region-of-interest (ROI) based methods where classifiers were applied to voxels in anatomically or functionally pre-defined areas Cox & Savoy (2003); Haynes & Rees (2005a); Kamitani & Tong (2005). Coarse brain maps can be obtained, given that some ROIs produce higher classification results than others. Although this approach can be of high utility provided previously determined ROIs, only testing of a highly limited set of spatial hypotheses is possible and no information regarding which number and combination of voxels form a discriminative pattern can be obtained.

Another popular early method is voxel ranking and selection according to various univariate measures. These include estimations of activation magnitude due to any condition, as measured using an F-test (activation-based voxel selection) or the ability to differentiate the conditions, as quantified by parametric (t) or non-parametric (Wilcoxon) statistical tests (discrimination-based voxel selection; Haynes & Rees (2005a); Mitchell et al. (2004); Mourão-Miranda & Reynaud (2006)). The univariate ranking is either used directly (selecting a number of the highest ranked voxels for classification), or for initial, fast but coarse ranking for improved speed and accuracy in subsequent multivariate voxel selection (see e.g. De Martino et al. (2008); Niiniskorpi et al. (2009)). Such activation- and discrimination-based voxel selection, however, disregards any distributed aspects of the brain processing and is thus sub-optimal in the processing pipe-line of multivariate analysis.

A second generation of voxel selection methods which utilize the multivariate nature of fMRI data can be categories into two distinct classes – locally multivariate analysis, where information is integrated across multiple voxels in a small neighborhood of adjacent spatial locations (see for example Kriegeskorte et al. (2006)) and globally multivariate, where voxels are jointly analyzed in spatially remote regions or across the entire brain volume (see e.g. De Martino et al. (2008); Mourão-Miranda et al. (2005)).

Although not strictly a voxel selection approach, the locally multivariate method termed "the searchlight" introduced by Kriegeskorte and colleagues (2006) scans the brain with a fixed-size sphere to identify regions which encode information regarding the experimental conditions. This method relies on the assumption that the discriminative information is encoded in neighboring voxels within the sphere. Such locally-distributed analysis might, however, be suboptimal when no hypothesis is available on the size of the neighborhood and might fail to detect discriminative patterns jointly encoded by distant regions (e.g. bilateral activation patterns). Other locally multivariate, fixed-size search approaches have followed suit Björnsdotter & Wessberg (2009). The evolutionary algorithm described in more detail below belongs to the class of locally multivoxel methods. However, the evolutionary algorithm is fundamentally different in that it optimizes voxel cluster size, shape and location in a more traditional feature selection sense Björnsdotter Åberg & Wessberg (2008). The evolutionary algorithm thus produces highly sensitive maps specifically tailored to the spatial extent of the informative region and is suitable in studies where low contrast-to-noise ratio, single optima are expected (such as in the somatotopy study described below; Björnsdotter et al. (2009)).

Global multivoxel selection schemes taking any number of spatially separate regions into account is represented by recursive feature elimination (RFE; De Martino et al. (2008); Formisano et al. (2008); Staeren et al. (2009)) which is initiated by a massively multivariate, whole-brain classification approach Mourão-Miranda et al. (2005). This method requires the use of a linear classifier, where the contribution of each voxel to the classification can be estimated by the classifier weights. The ranking obtained from the classifier weights is subsequently used for iterative elimination of voxels until a voxel subset which maximally discriminate the conditions is obtained. This approach is appropriate when the discrimination of the experimental conditions is reflected by widely distributed activation patterns that extend and include a number of separate brain regions.

In summary, the various voxel selection schemes used in multivoxel pattern analysis for brain mapping differ in scope and sensitivity, and care is required when choosing a voxel selection scheme suitable for the given fMRI study. In all voxel selection cases, group maps describing informative voxels across a number of individuals can be formed using various statistical techniques (see Wang et al. (2007) for details).

5. Brain mapping using evolutionary algorithms

As mentioned above, a key issue in the analysis of fMRI data is the identification of brain areas involved in the processing of given conditions, and, consequently, selection of voxels which can be used to effectively classify the conditions. Given a typical brain volume of $64 \times 64 \times 25$ voxels and the combinatorial explosion of possible voxel combinations, however, voxel selection is a daunting task, and the excessive number of possible voxel combinations renders any exhaustive search virtually impossible (but see the discussion of locally-multivariate mapping above). To address this issue, we developed a machine learning optimization method based on evolutionary algorithms Reeves & Rowe (2002), that extracts voxels yielding optimal brain state classification results in an intelligent and efficient fashion. In the following section we illustrate the evolutionary algorithm in detail, and subsequently demonstrate the utility of machine learning in general and our evolutionary algorithm in particular for highly sensitive mapping of an authentic physiological problem – that of the body-map representation of pleasant touch in the posterior insular cortex.

5.1 Evolutionary algorithms

An evolutionary algorithm is an optimization scheme inspired by Darwinian evolution, where potential problem solutions are encoded as individuals in a population Reeves & Rowe (2002). Various genetic schemes, including mutation operators, selection and reproduction (sexual or

asexual) are subsequently applied in order to improve the over-all fitness of the population and eventually find an individual which fulfills the required fitness. Importantly, biologically interpretable maps require spatial consistency - that is, where a few single, distributed voxels might be sufficient for good classification results (see e.g. Åberg et al. (2008)), from a neuroimaging perspective it is more interesting to identify *all* informative voxels in a given region (again, see Sato et al. (2009) for a discussion on this topic). Our evolutionary algorithm was therefore designed to identify a spatially coherent voxel cluster of unrestricted size which optimally differentiated the conditions.
Below follows details on the implementation of the algorithm, and pseudo-code for the algorithm is presented in figure 4.
Representation: One chromosome representing one voxel cluster was encoded per individual. Due to the exceedingly high dimensionality of fMRI data (in the order of tens to hundreds of thousands of features), we chose to encode the clusters sparsely as indexed lists (and not as typical binary strings).
Initialization: The population of individuals was initialized in a stochastic fashion, where, for each individual, one seed voxel was randomly selected. The voxel cluster was then constructed by the addition of random voxels which neighbor the seed voxel, or, subsequently, any voxel already in the cluster. We have also obtained excellent results from covering the entire brain volume with randomized clusters and subsequently selecting a population of individuals from the best-performing random clusters.
Mutation operations: The following mutation operations were implemented in the algorithm: the addition of a number of voxels, the deletion of a number of voxels, and the substitution of a voxel with another voxel. All voxel additions and substitutions were performed on neighboring voxels, that is, voxels within the 26 voxel cube surrounding any voxel already contained in the cluster. Also, deletions or substitutions resulting in voxels disconnecting from the clusters were disallowed. The frequency of mutation was regulated by a constant mutation rate parameter for each mutation operation. Also, a voxel cluster in the population was occasionally substituted for a new, randomly generated cluster to add fresh genetic material and aid in escaping potential local maxima.
Selection and reproduction: A standard tournament scheme was used for parent selection. In order to retain a variety of the genetic material and maintain searches in widespread regions of the brain, the proportion of parents to discarded individuals was set high. It should be noted, however, that the suitable proportion of parents depends on the expected signal-to-noise-ratio of the data as well as the number of regions of interest. Since all individuals in the population represent different locations and crossover thus would destroy the spatial integrity of the voxel clusters, reproduction was asexual and the new generation was formed by cloning the parents.
Fitness computation: The fitness value, that is, the condition classification success, of each individual cluster was computed using a classifier. Any classifier can be applied (including non-linear schemes; see the discussion on Classifiers above), and we used linear support vector machines Suykens et al. (2002). To ensure high generalization capability, the algorithm is supplied with three datasets. The first was used in classifier training (training data, 35% of the total volumes) while the second was used for fitness estimation (testing data, 45%). The third dataset was exclusively used with the already trained and optimized classifier and voxel cluster (validation data, 20%). Any fitness measure indicative of classification performance can be used, including proportion correctly classified instances or the area under the receiver operating characteristic curve (see the discussion on Performance metrics above).

Termination criterium: The algorithm was run for either a pre-determined maximum number of generations or until a cluster yielding testing data classification rates above a given threshold was obtained. The algorithm can, however, overtrain when allowed to run the full course. We therefore used the cluster with the best result on the mean of the training and testing data performance for validation classification.

```
BEGIN
 Initialize population;
 While (termination criteria not met);
        For (each individual);
                Apply mutation operations;
                        1. Add n_a random voxels;
                        2. Remove n_r random voxels;
                        3. Substitute n_s random voxels;
        End For
        Select parents;
        Reproduce;
        generation = generation + 1;
 End While
END
```

Fig. 4. Pseudo-code for evolutionary voxel selection (Åberg & Wessberg, 2008).

5.2 Example: Somatotopic organization of the insular cortex due to pleasant touch

Machine learning in general and the evolutionary algorithm described above in particular have been of high utility in our research on how the brain processes pleasant touch. In the study described here we specifically used the advantages of the superior sensitivities of multi-voxel pattern analysis to demonstrate that a specific region of the cortex is activated differently depending on what body part is stimulated.

The brain receives information about touch through two fundamentally different systems – one network of thick, myelinated fibers, termed Aβ afferents, which transmit discriminative aspects of touch (e.g. what type of texture am I touching?), and a parallel network of thin, unmyelinated so called C-tactile fibers, which are primarily activated by gentle types of touch and signal hedonic, pleasant features of the tactile sensation Löken et al. (2009); Olausson et al. (2002); Vallbo et al. (1999; 1993). The C-tactile system was recently discovered in humans, and is currently under intense research Edin (2001); Löken et al. (2007); Nordin (1990); Vallbo et al. (1999).

The C-tactile system is difficult to study in relation to brain processing, mainly since it cannot be activated selectively – any mechanical stimulation of the skin invariably co-activates thick, myelinated fibers in healthy subjects. C-tactile physiology has, nevertheless, been successfully explored in a patient (GL) with neuronopathy syndrome Sterman et al. (1980), who lacks large myelinated Aβ afferents but whose C fibers are intact Olausson, Cole, Rylander, McGlone, Lamarre, Wallin, Krämer, Wessberg, Elam, Bushnell & Vallbo (2008); Olausson et al. (2002). Due to the lack of Aβ fibers, GL has no sensation of touch. We demonstrated, however, that she can detect the light stroking of a brush and reports a pleasant sensation in response to the stimuli Olausson et al. (2002). Surprisingly, we recently found that she can not only detect the stimulus, but also distinguish the body quadrant to which it was applied at an accuracy of 72% Olausson, Cole, Rylander, McGlone, Lamarre, Wallin, Krämer, Wessberg, Elam, Bushnell & Vallbo (2008). GL's performance suggests that the C-tactile system projects some, albeit crude, information about stimulus location.

The C-tactile system belongs to a class of fibers (C afferents) which projects various information about the physiological condition of the body, including temperature and pain, from the periphery to the brain (see Craig (2002) for a review of this system). As opposed to Aβ fibers, which project directly to brain regions specifically processing tactile information (the somatosensory cortices), C afferents have been shown to connect from the thalamus to a part of the brain called the insular cortex on the opposite side of the brain to which the stimulation was applied Craig et al. (2000; 1994); Hua le et al. (2005). Similarly, functional imaging in GL and a similarly deafferented subject (IW) revealed that C-tactile stimulation also activates the insular cortex Olausson, Cole, Vallbo, McGlone, Elam, Krämer, Rylander, Wessberg & Bushnell (2008); Olausson et al. (2002). Moreover, for pain and temperature stimulation, the posterior part of the insular cortex has been shown to be organized in a particular fashion – upper body stimulation stimulations project anterior (closer to the nose) than lower body part stimulations Brooks et al. (2005); Henderson et al. (2007); Hua le et al. (2005). This type of organization is referred to as somatotopic and is observed in several brain regions where the physical location of the stimulation is important, such as the primary somatosensory and motor cortices.

A corresponding somatotopic organization of the insular cortex due to pleasant touch could potentially explain GL's surprisingly good localization performance. However, as opposed for example painful stimuli, C-tactile activations are typically weak and often difficult to identify using conventional statistical methods. In order to investigate whether posterior insular cortex projections due to pleasant touch are organized in a body-map similar to that of painful and temperature stimulation, we therefore applied the evolutionary algorithm to data acquired as described below.

6. Data acquisition

Participants: Informed consent was obtained from six healthy subjects, as well as one subject (GL) with sensory neuronopathy syndrome Sterman et al. (1980). At the age of 31, GL suffered permanent loss specifically of thick myelinated afferents (the so called $A\beta$ fibers), leaving unmyelinated and small-diameter myelinated afferents intact Forget & Lamarre (1995). She can detect temperature and pain normally Olausson, Cole, Rylander, McGlone, Lamarre, Wallin, Krämer, Wessberg, Elam, Bushnell & Vallbo (2008); Olausson et al. (2002), but denies any ability to sense touch below the level of the nose Forget & Lamarre (1995). In a forced choice task she could, however, perceive light touch, and she failed to detect vibratory stimuli (which poorly excite C-tactile afferents; Olausson, Cole, Rylander, McGlone, Lamarre, Wallin, Krämer, Wessberg, Elam, Bushnell & Vallbo (2008)). Moreover, in a four-alternative forced choice procedure, she identified 72% of soft brush stimuli to the correct extremity (at chance level of 25%). Healthy subjects, on the other hand, detect light touch as well as vibration without fail, and can localize point indentation on the skin to an accuracy in the range of two centimeters Norrsell & Olausson (1994). The Ethical Review Board at the University of Gothenburg approved the study, and the experiments were performed in accordance with the Declaration of Helsinki.

Stimulation: Light stimulation, known to vigorously activate C-tactile afferents in humans as well as in other species Bessou et al. (1971); Douglas & Ritchie (1957); Edin (2001); Kumazawa & Perl (1977); Nordin (1990); Vallbo et al. (1999; 1993); Zotterman (1939), was delivered using a seven centimeter wide soft brush with an indentation force 0.8 N. The experimenter manually stroked the brush in a proximal to distal direction on the right forearm or thigh.
Scanning protocol: The experimenter applied the tactile stimulation according to timing cues from the scanner, and all subjects were instructed to focus on the stimulus throughout the fMRI scanning session. In the healthy subjects, the distance covered was 16 centimeters for a duration of three seconds, whereas in the case of GL the distance was 30 centimeters and the duration four seconds. Three-volume blocks of forearm brushing, thigh brushing or no brushing (rest) were alternated in a pseudo-random order with equal numbers of each of the three conditions. The condition order remained fixed throughout each scan and across participants, and the scanning session consisted of one anatomical and six functional scans. During each functional scan, 13 blocks were obtained in the healthy subjects and 10 in GL, totaling in 78 and 60 three-volume blocks per condition respectively. A 1.5 T fMRI scanner (healthy subjects: Philips Intera; GL: Siemens Sonata) with a SENSE head coil (acceleration factor 1) was used to collect whole brain scans.
Pre-processing: The standard pre-processing steps described previously were applied to the data. Motion correction was performed using the Neurolens software package (www.neurolens.org; developed at the Neurovascular Imaging Lab, UNF Montreal, Canada), whereas the remaining pre-processing steps were performed using custom-coded scripts in Matlab (The Mathworks, Natick, MA). To offset hemodynamic delay and minimize within-trial variability, the first volume in each block was discarded and an average over the remaining two volumes was obtained (leaving a total of 78 volumes per stimulus for the healthy subjects and 60 for GL). The posterior contralateral (left) insula, containing a subject mean of 222 (range 177-261) voxels for the healthy participants and 97 voxels for GL, was subsequently identified using an anatomical reference Naidich et al. (2004) and previous multivoxel analysis (see Björnsdotter et al. (2009) for further details on the identification of the ROI). All analysis was performed in original individual space, and the resulting maps were transformed into MNI (Montreal Neurological Institute) standard stereotactic space Evans et al. (1993) using SPM5 Friston et al. (1994b) with the supplied EPI brain as template. For data visualization, the programs MRIcron (by Chris Rorden, `www.sph.sc.edu/comd/rorden/mricron/`) and Cartool (by Denis Brunet, `http://brainmapping.unige.ch/Cartool.htm`) were used.
Conventional analysis: A general linear model (GLM) whole-brain analysis was performed on smoothed data (Gaussian filter FWHM 6 mm). A fixed effect model was used to generalize healthy subject activations to the group level. The resulting activation maps were thresholded to a false discovery rate (FDR) of < 0.01).
Machine learning analysis: In order to compare the forearm and thigh brushing projections, the evolutionary clustering scheme was applied to the forearm/rest and thigh/rest datasets separately within the region of interest (ROI) in the posterior insular cortex. The number of voxels allowed in the cluster was fixed in order to obtain directly comparable classification performances within and between individuals. In GL, seven voxels was empirically determined to be a suitable cluster size for high classification performance. The corresponding volume in the healthy subjects, due to the higher spatial sampling frequency of the functional data, was 20 voxels. The algorithm was iterated 200 times, and the clusters which maximally differentiated the forearm and thigh stimuli from rest were identified. The magnitude of condition separabil-

ity (classification score) was quantified by the area under the receiver operating characteristic (ROC) curve (AUC).

7. Results

Conventional analysis: The whole-brain general linear model approach identified a variety of expected activated regions in the healthy subjects, including the contralateral postcentral gyrus (the primary somatosensory cortex; T-value peak at MNI [X, Y, Z] coordinates 5.2 [-26, -42, 64] for forearm stimulation and 6.9 [-16, -48, 70] for thigh stimulation) and bilateral parietal operculum (secondary somatosensory cortex). No significant activations were identified in the insular cortex, however, and for the neuronopathy patient GL no significantly activated voxels were identified in any region of the brain.
Machine learning analysis: The evolutionary multivoxel pattern recognition approach was substantially more successful, however, and the condition discrimination performance of the identified clusters were highly significant in GL as well as for the healthy volunteers. Forearm and thigh tactile stimulation were found to project to distinctly separate locations in GL, with a substantial euclidean distance between cluster centroids of 8.9 mm (figure 5A). The forearm cluster centroid was located at MNI (X, Y, Z) coordinates (-34, -10, 4), and the thigh cluster was found at (-34, -18, 0). The distance between clusters was thus maximal in the anterior-posterior (Y) plane at 8 mm, whereas the location differences in the remaining planes were non-existent or small (X: 0 mm, Z: 4 mm). Validating the pattern observed in GL, the healthy subject insular projections were also arranged in a clear somatotopic fashion. The individual forearm and thigh cluster centroid locations are shown in figure 5B, illustrating the consistency in activation pattern across all individuals including GL. The difference in location was significant only in the Y-plane (anterior-posterior; two-tailed paired t-test, $p < 0.05$). The subject mean euclidean distance between the cluster centroids equaled that of GL at 9.3 (range 6.6-12) mm. Our evolutionary machine learning algorithm was able to identify the subtle fMRI pattern produced by pleasant touch, invisible to conventional univariate analysis. Moreover, we demonstrated that such pleasant touch projects to different regions of the insular cortex depending on what part of the body was stimulated.
The observation of the body-map topology has important physiological consequences, mainly in strengthening the suggestion that C-tactile afferents are organized in a fashion similar to that of the pain and temperature systems. Also, our study suggests that, although the Aβ system is clearly dominant for touch discrimination and localization, there is some localization functionality to the C-tactile system. It appears improbable that the C-tactile system plays a significant role in discriminative touch, yet it can be presumed that the general stimulus location significantly modulates *affective* sensations which are intimately related to C-tactile activity Löken et al. (2009). Propagation of such affective information is of fundamental importance in preparing appropriate actions in response to emotionally relevant stimuli. Thus, we hypothesize that the crude localization capacity of the C-tactile system serves an affective function, where, for example, a gentle stroke on the cheek evokes a different motivational and hedonic response than that on the leg, thus signaling various emotional aspects with corresponding social consequences.

8. Concluding remarks

In contrast to conventional statistical techniques based on average voxel-by-voxel activations, machine learning-based multivoxel pattern analysis utilizes the inherent multivariate nature

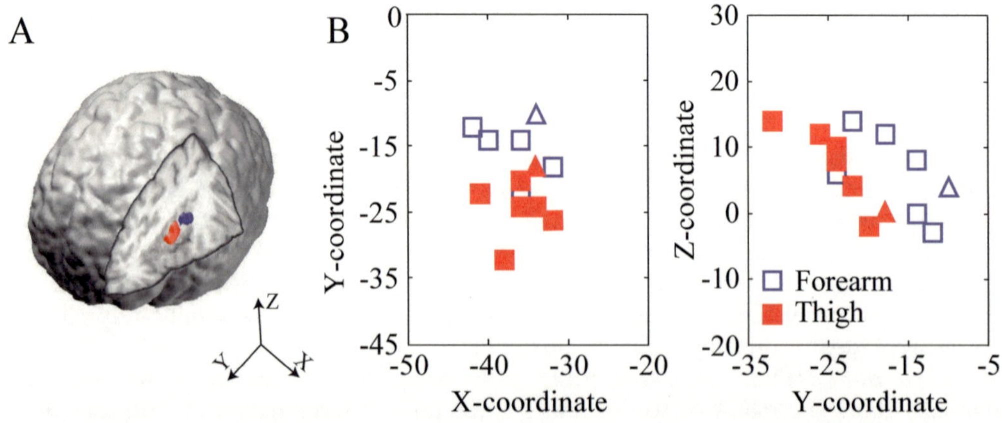

Fig. 5. Insular somatotopy of the contra-lateral posterior insular cortex due to pleasant touch identified using the evolutionary voxel selection scheme. **A**, The voxel clusters maximally differentiating forearm (red) and thigh (blue) stimulation from rest in the neuronopathy syndrome patient GL, reflecting the projection of pleasant touch afferents. A similar somatotopic organization was consistently identified also in neurologically intact subjects, as demonstrated in panel **B**, showing the forearm (red/filled) and thigh (blue/empty) cluster centroid MNI coordinates for each of the healthy subjects (□) and the neuronopathy syndrome patient GL (△). There was a significant difference between forearm and thigh cluster centroid location in the Y-plane only (two-tailed paired t-test, $p < 0.05$).

of brain activity and highlight informative spatial patterns. As such, these state-of-the-art analysis methods outperform conventional techniques in terms of brain mapping sensitivity, but also provides a direct link between brain state and brain activity patterns. Moreover, brain responses to conditions are treated as independent - as opposed to average - evoked activation patterns, allowing interesting and highly novel studies of functional representation Kriegeskorte et al. (2008). Also, as the spatial resolution is continuously improved with advances in high field imaging Yacoub et al. (2008), issues such as reduced signal-to-noise ratio and escalating multiple comparison problem will render univariate analysis less feasible and pave the way for multivoxel analyses Kriegeskorte & Bandettini (2007).
The utility of machine learning in neuroimaging is evidenced by the recent surge of studies taking advantage of the appealing benefits of multivoxel analysis – despite the fact that appropriate application of machine learning concepts to fMRI analysis currently requires not only an understanding of brain physiology, but also solid technical and mathematical knowledge. Further interdisciplinary research aiming to refine, develop and integrate machine learning techniques for standard fMRI analysis promises exciting possibilities for improved insight into the inner workings of the human brain.

9. Acknowledgments

This research was supported by the Swedish Research Council (grant K2007-63X-3548, Dr. J. Wessberg) and the Sahlgrenska University Hospital (grant ALFGBG 3161). The fMRI data was acquired in collaboration with Line Löken, Karin Rylander, Linda Lundblad, Dr. Håkan

Olausson and Dr. Catherine Bushnell. I am highly grateful to GL for her invaluable contribution, and to Dr. Johan Wessberg and Dr. Federico De Martino for continuous support and expert comments on the manuscript.

10. References

Åberg, M., Löken, L. & Wessberg, J. (2008). An evolutionary approach to multivariate feature selection for fMRI pattern analysis, *Proceedings of the International Conference on Bio-inspired Systems and Signal Processing* .

Bandettini, P. A. & Cox, R. W. (2000). Event-related fMRI contrast when using constant inter-stimulus interval: theory and experiment., *Magnetic Resonance in Medicine* **43**(4): 540–548. **URL:** *http://view.ncbi.nlm.nih.gov/pubmed/10748429*

Beauchamp, M., Laconte, S. & Yasar, N. (2009). Distributed representation of single touches in somatosensory and visual cortex., *Human Brain Mapping* **(in press)**.

Bellman, R. E. (1961). *Adaptive Control Processes*, Princeton University Press, Princeton, NJ.

Bessou, P., Burgess, P. R., Perl, E. R. & Taylor, C. (1971). Dynamic properties of mechanoreceptors with unmyelinated (c) fibers, *Journal of neurophysiology* **34**(1): 116–31.

Björnsdotter Åberg, M. & Wessberg, J. (2008). An evolutionary approach to the identification of informative voxel clusters for brain state discrimination, *IEEE Journal of Selected Topics in Signal Processing* **2**(6): 919–928.

Björnsdotter, M., L. S. Löken, H. Olausson, A. B. Vallbo, and J. Wessberg (2009). Somatotopic organization of gentle touch processing in the posterior insular cortex. Journal of Neuroscience 29(29): 9314-9320.

Björnsdotter, M. & Wessberg, J. (2009). Particle swarm voxel clustering for multivariate fmri mapping, *Organization for Human Brain Mapping Annual Meeting, San Fransisco, USA* .

Brooks, J. C. W., Zambreanu, L., Godinez, A., Craig, A. B. & Tracey, I. (2005). Somatotopic organisation of the human insula to painful heat studied with high resolution functional imaging, *Neuroimage* **27**: 201–209.

Burke, D., Murphy, K., Garavan, H. & Reilly, R. (2004). Pattern recognition approach to the detection of single-trial event-related functional magnetic resonance images., *Medical and Biological Engineering and Computing* **42**(5): 604–9.

Buxton, R. B. (2002). *An introduction to functional magnetic resonance imaging*, Cambridge University Press, Cambridge, United Kingdom.

Carlson, T. A., Schrater, P. & He, S. (2003). Patterns of activity in the categorical representations of objects., *Journal of Cognitive Neuroscience* **15**(5): 704–717. **URL:** *http://www.mitpressjournals.org/doi/abs/10.1162/jocn.2003.15.5.704*

Collins, D. L., Neelin, P., Peters, T. M. & Evan, A. C. (1994). Automatic 3d intersubject registration of MR volumetric data in standardized Talairach space., *Journal of Computer Assisted Tomography* **18**(2): 192–205.

Cox, D. D. & Savoy, R. L. (2003). Functional magnetic resonance imaging (fMRI) 'brain reading': detecting and classifying distributed patterns of fMRI activity in human visual cortex., *Neuroimage* **19**(2 Pt 1): 261–270.

Craig, A., Chen, K., Bandy, D. & Reiman, E. (2000). Thermosensory activation of insular cortex., *Nature Neuroscience* **3**(2): 184–190.

Craig, A. D. (2002). How do you feel? interoception: the sense ofthe physiological condition of the body, *Nature Reviews Neuroscience* **3**(8): 655–666.

Craig, A. D., Bushnell, M., Zhang, E. & Blomqvist, A. (1994). A thalamic nucleus specific for pain and temperature sensation., *Nature* **372**(6508): 770–3.

Crinion, J., Ashburner, J., Leff, A., Brett, M., Price, C. & Friston, K. (2007). Spatial normalization of lesioned brains: Performance evaluation and impact on fMRI analyses, *Neuroimage* **37**(3): 866–875.

Davatzikos, C., Ruparel, K., Fan, Y., Shen, D., Acharyya, M., Loughead, J., Gur, R. & Langleben, D. (2005). Classifying spatial patterns of brain activity with machine learning methods: Application to lie detection., *Neuroimage* **28**: 663–668.

De Martino, F., Valente, G., Staeren, N., Ashburner, J., Goebel, R. & Formisano, E. (2008). Combining multivariate voxel selection and support vector machines for mapping and classification of fMRI spatial patterns, *Neuroimage* **43**(1): 44–58.
URL: *http://dx.doi.org/10.1016/j.neuroimage.2008.06.037*

Douglas, W. W. & Ritchie, J. M. (1957). Nonmedullated fibres in the saphenous nerve which signal touch., *Journal of Physiology* **139**(3): 385–99.

Duda, R. O., Hart, P. E. & Stork, D. G. (2000). *Pattern Classification*, Wiley-Interscience Publication.

Edin, B. (2001). Cutaneous afferents provide information about knee joint movements in humans., *Journal of Physiology* **531**(Pt 1): 289–97.

Evans, A. C., Collins, D. L., Mills, S. R., Brown, E. D., Kelly, R. L. & Peters, T. M. (1993). 3d statistical neuroanatomical models from 305 MRI volumes, *Proceedings of the IEEE-Nuclear Science Symposium and Medical Imaging Conference* pp. 1813–1817.

Forget, R. & Lamarre, Y. (1995). Postural adjustments associated with different unloadings of the forearm: effects of proprioceptive and cutaneous afferent deprivation., *Canadian Journal of Physiology and Pharmacology* **73**(2): 285–94.

Formisano, E., De Martino, F., Bonte, M. & Goebel, R. (2008). "who" is saying "what"? brain-based decoding of human voice and speech., *Science* **5903**(322): 970–3.

Frackowiak, R., Friston, K., Frith, C., Dolan, R. & Mazziotta, J. (1997). *Human Brain Function.*, Academic Press.

Friston, K., Ashburner, J., Kiebel, S., Nichols, T. & Penny, W. (eds) (2007). *Statistical Parametric Mapping: The Analysis of Functional Brain Images*, Academic Press.
URL: *http://books.elsevier.com/neuro/?isbn=9780123725608&srccode=89660*

Friston, K. J., Fletcher, P., Josephs, O., Holmes, A., Rugg, M. D. & Turner, R. (1998). Event-related fMRI: Characterizing differential responses, *Neuroimage* **7**(1): 30–40.
URL: *http://dx.doi.org/10.1006/nimg.1997.0306*

Friston, K. J., Holmes, A. P., Worsley, K. J., Poline, J. P., Frith, C. D. & Frackowiak, R. S. J. (1994a). Statistical parametric maps in functional imaging: A general linear approach, *Human Brain Mapping* **2**(4): 189–210.
URL: *http://dx.doi.org/10.1002/hbm.460020402*

Friston, K. J., Holmes, A. P., Worsley, K. J., Poline, J. P., Frith, C. D. & Frackowiak, R. S. J. (1994b). Statistical parametric maps in functional imaging: A general linear approach, *Human Brain Mapping* **2**(4): 189–210.

Goense, J. B. & Logothetis, N. K. (2008). Neurophysiology of the BOLD fMRI signal in awake monkeys, *Current Biology* **18**(9): 631–640.

Guyon, I. & Elisseeff, A. (2003). An introduction to variable and feature selection, *Journal of machine learning research* **3**(1): 1157–1182.

Hanson, S. J., Matsuka, T. & Haxby, J. V. (2004). Combinatorial codes in ventral temporal lobe for object recognition: Haxby (2001) revisited: is there a "face" area?, *Neuroimage* **23**(1): 156–66.

Haxby, J. V., Gobbini, M. I., Furey, M. L., Ishai, A., Schouten, J. L. & Pietrini, P. (2001). Distributed and overlapping representations of faces and objects in ventral temporal cortex., *Science* **293**: 2425–2430.

Haynes, J. & Rees, G. (2005a). Predicting the orientation of invisible stimuli from activity in human primary visual cortex, *Nature Neuroscience* **8**(5): 686–691.
URL: *http://www.nature.com/neuro/journal/v8/n5/abs/nn1445.html*

Haynes, J. & Rees, G. (2005b). Predicting the stream of consciousness from activity in human visual cortex., *Current Biology* **15**: 1301–1307.

Haynes, J. & Rees, G. (2006). Decoding mental states from brain activity in humans, *Nature Reviews Neuroscience* **7**(7): 523–534.
URL: *http://dx.doi.org/10.1038/nrn1931*

Henderson, L., Gandevia, S. & Macefield, V. (2007). Somatotopic organization of the processing of muscle and cutaneous pain in the left and right insula cortex: A single-trial fMRI study, *Pain* **128**: 20–30.

Henson, R. (2003). Analysis of fMRI time series, *in* R. Frackowiak, K. Friston, C. Frith, R. Dolan, K. Friston, C. Price, S. Zeki, J. Ashburner & W. Penny (eds), *Human Brain Function*, 2nd edn, Academic Press.

Howard, J., Plailly, J., Grueschow, M., Haynes, J. & Gottfried, J. (2009). Odor quality coding and categorization in human posterior piriform cortex., *Nature Neuroscience* **(In press)**.

Hua le, H., Strigo, I. A., Baxter, L. C., Johnson, S. C. & Craig, A. D. (2005). Anteroposterior somatotopy of innocuous cooling activation focus in human dorsal posterior insular cortex., *American Journal of Physiology - Regulatory, Integrative, and Comparative Physiology* **289**(2): 319–325.

Kamitani, Y. & Tong, F. (2005). Decoding the visual and subjective contents of the human brain, *Nature Neuroscience* **8**(5): 679–685.
URL: *http://www.nature.com/neuro/journal/v8/n5/abs/nn1444.html*

Kriegeskorte, N. & Bandettini, P. (2007). Combining the tools: activation- and information-based fmri analysis, *NeuroImage* **38**: 666–668.

Kriegeskorte, N., Goebel, R. & Bandettini, P. (2006). Information-based functional brain mapping, *PNAS* **103**: 3863–3868.

Kriegeskorte, N., Mur, M., Ruff, D. A. A., Kiani, R., Bodurka, J., Esteky, H., Tanaka, K. & Bandettini, P. A. A. (2008). Matching categorical object representations in inferior temporal cortex of man and monkey., *Neuron* **60**(6): 1126–1141.
URL: *http://dx.doi.org/10.1016/j.neuron.2008.10.043*

Ku, S. P., Gretton, A., Macke, J. & Logothetis, N. K. (2008). Comparison of pattern recognition methods in classifying high-resolution bold signals obtained at high magnetic field in monkeys., *Magnetic resonance imaging* **26**(7): 1007–1014.
URL: *http://dx.doi.org/10.1016/j.mri.2008.02.016*

Kumazawa, T. & Perl, E. (1977). Primate cutaneous sensory units with unmyelinated (C) afferent fibers., *Journal of Neurophysiology* **40**(6): 1325–38.

LaConte, S., Strother, S., Cherkassky, V., Anderson, J. & Hu, X. (2005). Support vector machines for temporal classification of block design fMRI data., *Neuroimage* **26**(2): 317–29.

Leoni, R., Mazzeto-Betti, K., Andrade, K. & de Araujo, D. (2008). Quantitative evaluation of hemodynamic response after hypercapnia among different brain territories by fMRI., *Neuroimage* **41**(4): 1192–8.

Logothetis, N. K., Pauls, J., Augath, M., Trinath, T. & Oeltermann, A. (2001). Neurophysiological investigation of the basis of the fmri signal., *Nature* **412**(6843): 150–157.
URL: *http://dx.doi.org/10.1038/35084005*

Löken, L., Wessberg, J., Morrison, I., McGlone, F. & Olausson, H. (2009). Coding of pleasant touch by unmyelinated afferents in humans., *Nature Neuroscience* **12**(5): 547–8.

Löken, L., Wessberg, J. & Olausson, H. W. (2007). Unmyelinated tactile (CT) afferents are present in the human peroneal and radial nerves, *Society for Neuroscience 38th Annual Meeting, San Diego, USA* (827.2).

McCarthy, G., Luby, M., Gore, J. & Goldman-Rakic, P. (1997). Infrequent events transiently activate human prefrontal and parietal cortex as measured by functional mri., *Journal of Neurophysiology* **77**(3): 1630–1634.

Mitchell, T. M., Hutchinson, R., Niculescu, R. S., Pereira, F., Wang, X., Just, M. & Newman, S. (2004). Learning to decode cognitive states from brain images, *Machine Learning* **57**(1-2): 145–175.

Mourão-Miranda, J., Bokde, A. L., Born, C., Hampel, H. & Stetter, M. (2005). Classifying brain states and determining the discriminating activation patterns: Support vector machine on functional MRI data, *Neuroimage* **28**(4): 980–95.

Mourão-Miranda, J. & Reynaud, E., M. F. C. G. B. M. (2006). The impact of temporal compression and space selection on SVM analysis of single-subject and multi-subject fMRI data., *Neuroimage* **33**(4): 1055–65.

Muehllehner, G. & Karp, J. S. (2006). Positron emission tomography, *Physics in Medicine and Biology* **51**(13): R117–R137.
URL: *http://dx.doi.org/10.1088/0031-9155/51/13/R08*

Naidich, T., Kang, E., Fatterpekar, G., Delman, B., Gultekin, S., Wolfe, D., Ortiz, O., Yousry, I., Weismann, M. & Yousry, T. (2004). The insula: anatomic study and MR imaging display at 1.5 T., *American Journal of Neuroradiology* **25**(2): 222–32.

Niiniskorpi, T., Björnsdotter Åberg, M. & Wessberg, J. (2009). Particle swarm feature selection for fmri pattern classification, Proceedings of the International Conference on Bio-inspired Systems and Signal Processing, Porto, Portugal.

Nordin, M. (1990). Low-threshold mechanorecepetive and nociceptive units with unmyelinated C fibres in the human supraorbital nerve, *Journal of Physiology* **426**(310): 229–240.

Norman, K. A., Polyn, S. M., Detre, G. J. & Haxby, J. V. (2006). Beyond mind-reading: multi-voxel pattern analysis of fMRI data, *Trends in Cognitive Sciences* **10**(9): 424–430.

Norris, D. G. (2006). Principles of magnetic resonance assessment of brain function, *Journal of Magnetic Resonance Imaging* **23**(6): 794–807.
URL: *http://dx.doi.org/10.1002/jmri.20587*

Norrsell, U. & Olausson, H. (1994). Spatial cues serving the tactile directional sensibility of the human forearm., *Journal of Physiology* **478**(Pt 3): 533–40.

Ogawa, S., Lee, T. M., Kay, A. R. & Tank, D. W. (1990). Brain magnetic resonance imaging with contrast dependent on blood oxygenation., *PNAS* **87**(24): 9868–9872.
URL: *http://dx.doi.org/10.1073/pnas.87.24.9868*

Olausson, H., Cole, J., Rylander, K., McGlone, F., Lamarre, Y., Wallin, B., Krämer, H., Wessberg, J., Elam, M., Bushnell, M. & Vallbo, Å. (2008). Functional role of unmyelinated tactile afferents in human hairy skin: sympathetic response and perceptual localization., *Experimental Brain Research* **184**(1): 135–40.

Olausson, H., Cole, J., Vallbo, Å., McGlone, F., Elam, M., Krämer, H., Rylander, K., Wessberg, J. & Bushnell, M. (2008). Unmyelinated tactile afferents have opposite effects on insular and somatosensory cortical processing., *Neuroscience Letters* **436**(2): 128–32.

Olausson, H., Lamarre, Y., Backlund, H., Morin, C., Wallin, B. G., Starck, G., Ekholm, S., Strigo, I., Worsley, K., Vallbo, Å. B. & Bushnell, M. C. (2002). Unmyelinated tactile afferents signal touch and project to insular cortex., *Nature Neuroscience* **5**(9): 900–904.

O'toole, A. J., Jiang, F., Abdi, H. & Haxby, J. V. (2005). Partially distributed representations of objects and faces in ventral temporal cortex, *Journal of Cognitive Neuroscience* **17**(4): 580–590.

Polyn, S. M., Natu, V. S., Cohen, J. D. & Norman, K. A. (2005). Category-specific cortical activity precedes retrieval during memory search, *Science* **310**(5756): 1963–6.

Reeves, C. & Rowe, J. E. (2002). *Genetic Algorithms - Principles and Perspectives: A Guide to GA Theory*, Kluwer Academic Publishers, Norwell, MA, USA.

Rosen, B. R., Buckner, R. L. & Dale, A. M. (1998). Event-related functional MRI: Past, present, and future, *PNAS* **95**(3): 773–780.
URL: *http://dx.doi.org/10.1073/pnas.95.3.773*

Roy, C. S. & Sherrington, C. S. (1890). On the regulation of the blood-supply of the brain., *Journal of Physiology* **11**(1-2).
URL: *http://view.ncbi.nlm.nih.gov/pubmed/16991945*

Sato, J., Fujita, A., Thomaz, C., Martin Mda, G., Mourão-Miranda, J., Brammer, M. & Amaro Junior, E. (2009). Evaluating SVM and MLDA in the extraction of discriminant regions for mental state prediction., *Neuroimage* **46**(1): 105–14.

Sirotin, Y. B. & Das, A. (2008). Anticipatory haemodynamic signals in sensory cortex not predicted by local neuronal activity, *Nature* **457**(7228): 475–479.
URL: *http://dx.doi.org/10.1038/nature07664*

Spiridon, M. & Kanwisher, N. (2002). How distributed is visual category information in human occipito-temporal cortex? an fMRI study., *Neuron* **35**: 1157–1165.

Staeren, N., Renvall, H., F., D., Goebel, R. & Formisano, E. (2009). Sound categories are represented as distributed patterns in the human auditory cortex., *Current Biology* **19**(6): 498–502.

Sterman, A. B., Schaumburg, H. H. & Asbury, A. K. (1980). The acute sensory neuronopathy syndrome: a distinct clinical entity., *Annals of Neurology* **7**(4): 354–8.

Suykens, J., Gestel, T. V., Brabanter, J. D., Moor, B. D. & Vandewalle, J. (2002). *Least Squares Support Vector Machines*, World Scientific.

Talairach, J. & Tournoux, P. (1988). *Co-Planar Stereotaxic Atlas of the Human Brain: 3-Dimensional Proportional System : An Approach to Cerebral Imaging*, Thieme Medical Publishers.
URL: *http://www.amazon.co.uk/exec/obidos/ASIN/0865772932/citeulike-21*

Turner, R., Howseman, A. & Friston, K. (1998). Functional magnetic resonance imaging of the human brain: Data acquisition and analysis., *Experimental Brain Research* **123**: 5.

Vallbo, Å., Olausson, H. & Wessberg, J. (1999). Unmyelinated afferents constitute a second system coding tactile stimuli of the human hairy skin, *Journal of Neurophysiology* **81**(310): 2753–2763.

Vallbo, Å., Olausson, H., Wessberg, J. & Norrsell, U. (1993). A system of unmyelinated afferents for innocuous mechanoreception in the human skin, *Brain Research* **628**(310): 301–304.

Wang, Z., Childress, A., Wang, J. & Detre, J. (2007). Support vector machine learning-based fmri data group analysis., *Neuroimage* **15**(36): 1139–51.

Yacoub, E., Harel, N. & Ugurbil, K. (2008). High-field fMRI unveils orientation columns in humans., *PNAS* **105**(30): 10607–12.

Zotterman, Y. (1939). Touch, pain and tickling: an electro-physiological investigation on cutaneous sensory nerves., *Journal of Physiology* **95**(1): 1–28.

10

The Application of Fractal Concept to Content-Based Image Retrieval

An-Zen SHIH
Jin-Wen University of Science and Technology
Taiwan

1. Introduction

The saying 'a picture is worth a thousand words' conveys the idea that images transmit information more efficiently than words can. Furthermore, it is increasingly true that images are an important feature of our daily lives. Because of progress in computer technology, people tend to rely on computers to handle this image data. However, significant problem is that computers are far less adept than people are interpreting this data.
The problem lies in the difficulty that computers have in understanding the image data. This vision process is something most humans take for granted - computers however need to be programmed both to progress the image data and to extract an understanding. Vision implies not only seeing but also understanding the contents of an image. For a computer, an image is just an array of numbers. When people look at an image, they see beyond the array of numbers to the semantics of the data, the visual content of the image. This is why people can easily distinguish different pictures but computers can't.
Nevertheless, a human's eyes can be deceived. In addition, it is tedious for people to look at lots of images, or to concentrate on performing tasks based on image content. Therefore, programming computers to distinguish different images or to select interesting image from a welter of them become an important task.
To date, many image processing methods have been proposed and tested to solve the problem of reading and selecting image data. Fractal, which is a new concept found in last century, suggest a way around the problem. Fractals are patterns that exhibit self similarity. Self similarity means the fractal patterns can be subdivided recursively into smaller non-overlapping parts and each part is a small replica of the whole. Many natural structures exhibit fractal characteristics. By extension fractal patterns will also appear in images. These fractal patterns interested people because that they could be used as a powerful tool in image retrieval.
The application of fractal concept to content-based image retrieval is classified into two groups: fractal dimension approach and fractal compression approach. In this chapter we will describe the idea how to use fractal compression technique in image retrieval.
This chapter is arranged as following. In the next section we will introduce the concept of

fractal and fractal compression. And then a introduction section of content-based image retrieval is followed. After that a whole section will be used to describe the idea how to use fractal compression technique in image retrieval. Finally, a brief summary can be found in the end of this chapter.

2. Fractal Concept

2.1 Self Similarity and Self Affinity

Mandelbrot invented the word 'fractal' and described it as[1]

'Mathematical and natural fractals are shapes whose roughness and fragmentation neither tend to vanish, nor fluctuate up and down, but remain essentially unchanged as one zooms in continually and examination is refined.'

From the above words, we notice that fractal presents a strong similarity in its shape. This similarity is defined as self-similarity.[2] In other words, the meaning of self-similarity is that each part is a linear geometric reduction of the whole, with the same reduction ratios in all directions.

Self-similarity can be deterministic self-similarity or statistical self-similarity. Deterministic self-similarity means the self-similarity object can be derived into non-overlapping parts and each non-overlapping part is exactly similar to the whole. A good example is the Sierpinski triangle.(see figure 1) Statistical self-similarity means that the self-similarity object can be derived into non-over-lapping parts and each non-overlapping part only looks similar to the whole but is not exactly similar. The difference is that there is a small difference between the divided part and the entire patter. However, the difference is so small we can usually ignore it. A good example is a cauliflower head. Each part of a cauliflower head is "statistically" look like the whole cauliflower head with a little distortion.

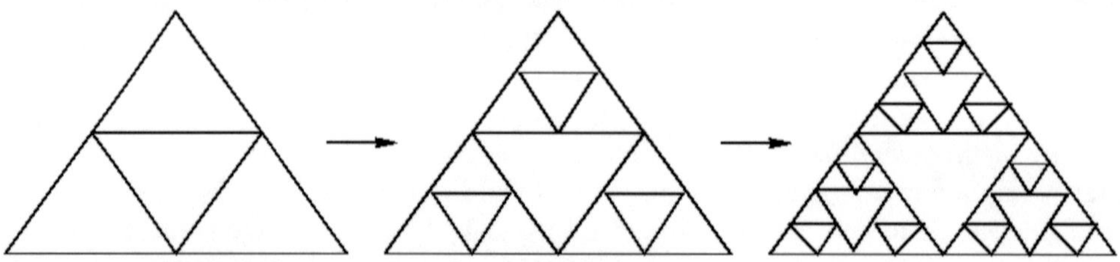

Fig. 1. Sierpinski Triangle - an example of self-similarity

There is also another form of similarity called self-affinity. A self-affinity object is that different ratio will be applied to different direction.. That is, different ratio is applied in different direction continuously to generate a pattern. In Figure 1, if we reduce the Sierpinski triangle one third in horizontal direction but by one half in the vertical direction, then we have a Sierpinski triangle of self affinity.

2.2 Iterated Function System

Iterated Function System (IFS) were first described by Michael Barnsley in 1985 as a tool to create deterministic fractals. The advantage of IFSs is that IFS itself is very straightforward in form but it is capable of generating complex functions.

The IFS code can be represented in matrix form as follows. Assume that a coordinate system in the place is given and that all the maps ω_i are affine. Where a transformation ω is affine if it may be represented by a matrix M and translation t as $\omega(x) = Mx+t$, or

$$\omega\begin{bmatrix} x \\ y \end{bmatrix} = \begin{bmatrix} a & b \\ c & d \end{bmatrix}\begin{bmatrix} x \\ y \end{bmatrix} + \begin{bmatrix} e \\ f \end{bmatrix} \tag{1}$$

For application to an image, the above matrix needs to change to

$$W\begin{bmatrix} x \\ y \\ z \end{bmatrix} = \begin{bmatrix} a & b & 0 \\ c & d & 0 \\ 0 & 0 & s \end{bmatrix}\begin{bmatrix} x \\ y \\ z \end{bmatrix} + \begin{bmatrix} e \\ f \\ o \end{bmatrix} \tag{2}$$

Here z is the grey level of the image. The parameter a, b, c, d e and f control the spatial transformation, s controls contrast and o controls brightness.

Not only fractal pattern can be constructed by an IFS system, but also that this procedure can be inverted. That is, for a specific fractal images, we can determine the IFS and store that instead of the whole image.

Fractal image compression is based on IFS theory. It was based on affine transformations acting locally rather than globally. An image to be encoded is partitioned into non-overlapping range blocks R. The task of a fractal encode is to find a large block of the same image (a domain block D) for every range block such that a transformation of the block W(D) is a good approximation of the range block. This transformation can be written as Equation 2 which is a combination of geometrical transformation and luminance transformation.

In the decoding period, the transformation of each range block needs to be transmitted to the decoder. This code, when applied to the initial image, will generate a simulation of the original image.

There are two different kinds of IFS compression. The first is IFS compression and the other is PIFS compression. The PIFS compression is also called local iterated function system. Because the image is usually not perfectly fractal, it is hard to find a global self-similarity or self-affinity spreading the whole image. Instead, we should try to find parts of the image which are self-similar.

2.3 The PIFS Compression Method.

We will begin our description of PIFS with a simple illustration. An image of size 32 · 32pixels is divided into 16 non-overlapping sub-images called ***ranges*** with size 8 ·8 pixels. Next a window of size 16 ·16 pixels is moved line by line horizontally then vertically in the same image to choose a sub-image called the ***domain***. The total numbers of domains in the image will be 16 ·16.

For each range we will find a domain which contains the same pattern inside the range. We use a window to select the domain and to execute the IFS transformation shown in equation

(2) on the domain. Then we can compare the transformed domain and the range. After searching for all the possible domains in the image, we can possibly find the domain that is considered to have same pattern on the range. If we cannot find the domain we want, then we divide the image into smaller sub-image 8 ·8 and search the image again. This procedure continues until every range on the image has found a domain with the same pattern.
As a real image is composed of many fractal patterns, it is natural way of thinking to divide the image according to the different fractal patterns and then try to find different IFS code for each of then. However, it is very difficult to implement this in an automatic algorithm.
There are many ways to partition the image. The most popular method is quadtree partitioning method. The essential idea of quadtree partitioning is that the image is broken up into four equal-sized sub-squares. Each sub-image can be broken up into a further four equal-sized sub-images if necessary. Finally the image is composed of different sized squares.
It should be pointed out that the procedure of dividing the image can't repeat beyond a specific bound. Before we execute the quadtree partitioning, we should set up the smallest size of the square. The division will stop if the square size is smaller than the above pre-defined size.
The implementation of PIFS is very similar to the above simple illustrated sample. Firstly, the image is divided into 16 ranges by using the quadtree portioning method. Then for each range we will find a domain which will look like the range after transformation. If a range can't be mapped onto a suitable domain, then this range is divided into four parts using quadtree partitioning. For each sub-image we again try to find a domain containing the same pattern as the range. If a sub-image still can't find a good domain then this sub-image has to be divided into four parts yet again. The process continues until every part of the image finds a domain somewhere in the same image.
To sum up, we can describe PIFS algorithm as below. An image can be viewed as a three dimension function. That is, the grey level represented as $z = f(x, y)$ where x and y are the locations of the pixels in the image. The total image then is represented as $F = (x, y, f(x, y))$. The image can tiled into subsets, $D_1, D_2, \dots, D_n$ and $R_1, R_2, \dots, R_n$ where D_n and R_n are called domains and ranges respectively. On each range and domain, it is possible to find a set of mapping, $\omega_1, \omega_2, \dots, \omega_n$, which will transform ranges to domains. The transformations, $\omega_1, \omega_2, \dots, \omega_n$, compose The PIFS system of the image. In other words, we have transformed the image into several matrix$\omega_1, \omega_2, \dots, \omega_n$.

3. Content-Based Image Retrieval Concept

Content-based image retrieval (CBIR) is any technology which can help us to organize digital picture archives by their visual content. The term "content-based" implies that computers have to analyze the content of an image during the search and the term "content" refers to colors, shapes, textures, or any other information which can be extracted from the image. By this definition, anything ranging from an image similarity function to a robust image annotation engine falls under the purview of CBIR. People from different fields, such as, computer vision, machine learning, information retrieval, human-computer interaction, database systems, Web and data mining, information theory, statistics, and psychology contributing and becoming part of the CBIR community.[3]
Two problems exist in CBIR. The first is how to mathematically describe an image. The

second is how to access the similarity between images based on description. The first problem lies in the difficulty of .computers have in understanding the image data. When an image is presented, people can usually see beyond the shapes and colors on the image to the real content of that image. However, computers can't understand the content of the image if we don't program the computers. This is because an image data is just an array of numbers for the computers. So we hope to find a mathematic description of the image, which is sometimes called signature, in order that computers can understand the semantic meaning of an image. After we find the mathematic description of an image, computers can possibly use the signature to compare different images and select interesting ones.

The general algorithm of CIBR begins with extraction of features such as color, texture, shapes, etc. Then these features are analysis to acquire mathematical descriptions of the image. Because it is often impossible that an image is composed with only one pattern, people begin to shift from finding a global feature representation of image, such as color histogram or a global shape, to local features. This is helped with image segmentation, which is critical for characterizing shapes within images. In other words, good image segmentation is toward better image understanding. To date, precise segmentation of an image is, however, still remained an open problem.

All methods of mathematical description extraction have their advantage and limitations.

4. Application of Fractal Concept to CIBR

4.1 Background

In 1848, Shannon suggested that digital data set is made up of information and redundancy. Redundancy means duplicated or unnecessary information in the data set. His theory implies a way of data compression.

Data compression is preformed to decrease redundancy for data storage and data communication. This can be done by transforming the raw data into a new representation while the data, or most of the data, is the same and the length of the new representation will be as small as possible. Because of the way in which data compression tries to use a new representation to shorten the data, sometimes the data compression is called coding.

Compression efficiency can be measured in two ways: algorithm complexity and amount of compression. Algorithm complexity means the time required to compress the data. The amount of compression can be calculated by redundancy, average message length, and compression ratio.

Instead of what is suggested by 'compression', it is important to get another point of view of data compression. By preserving the essential data and removing the duplicate and unnecessary data, data compression gives not only an efficient storage method but also a new representation of the data. This new representation, while still having the essential properties of the raw data, can become an index into the original data. This 'index' can be very useful for selecting the data with similar characteristics in large collections of data. Thus we argue that the compression not only solves the problem of storage but also can become a classification method.

An image is a kind of digital data. It is precisely on such grounds that Shannon's compression theory can be applied onto images. So it is possible to compress an image and remove redundancy while preserving the important feature in the image. That is, image compression suggests itself to be a way around the problem of image retrieval. These

important features are clearly captured in the compressed code.
An important property of the compressed code therefore is that it can be used in image recognition because (somehow) represent the 'essence' of the image. This property is often neglected. Since the compression code contains the 'essential' information of an image, it is reasonable to differentiate images by comparing their compressed codes. Thus if two compressed codes are identical or almost identical, then we can say these two images are identical or similar. Alternatively, if two compression codes are different, then the images are different.
With the help of compressed codes, it is possible that computers can be given a limited 'understanding' of the essential difference between images.
However, there are a number of compression methods on the world. Among these methods, fractal compression method suggests itself to be a good algorithm to retrieve images.
As mentioned in Section 2, fractal image compression is based on IFS theory. It can be classified into two main groups: IFS compression and PIFS compression. IFS compression compress the whole image with one IFS function while PIFS divides the image into several parts then compress different parts with different IFS functions. Nevertheless, most real images are not fractal patterns. We may consider them a composition of several fractal patterns. It is obvious that the IFS method is not applicable to real images. Only with PIFS can we hope to compress ordinary images.
The advantage of PIFS compression is that it can use a very simple form to represent the image. This simple form, in turn, can be a classification criterion in selecting images. In addition, because it will occupy less memory space than the original images, it can solve the memory problem and same on CPU time.

4.2 Literature review

Describing and extracting image's feature is always a key question in content-based image retrieval system. An image can be characterized by its fractal codes, and fractal codes can be used as the image's feature to retrieve the images effectively.
Many people have found that fractal coding is a very promising way in image retrieval. Here we just select some of their works to give a global view of application of fractal compression in image retrieval.
In 1995, Cheng et al. used fractal coding to index image content for a digital library. They conducted experiment on some natural images as well as biomedical images. Their method is that they convert all images to fractal codes before adding to the database. After that they compute the measure on the fractal codes and organize then into indices.[4]
Two years later, Mari-Julie et al. proposed a new method, based on fractal transformation, which can quickly pick up a image pattern from 100 images. They convert texture and edge of pattern into fractal code and then use it for searching process.[5]
In 1998, in his PhD thesis, Shih used fractal compression technique to search specific gamma images from nucleus dataset. In addition, he found that a-priori knowledge of the data can help the computer to recognize images more efficient.[6]
Tien, in his master dissertation, used fractal code to select images. He used Fisher's discrimination function to judge whether the selected image is similar to the one wanted or not.[7]
Then in 2008, Fan et al. suggested to use fractal code to select images. In order to shorten the time of selection, they organized the fractal code into several index and used those index to

search the data. They found that this could accelerate the period of image retrieval.[8]
The same year in 2008, Zhang et al. used IFS code for image retrieval on the compression domain. Their experiment result showed that compared with the direct image pixels similar matching strategy, the algorithm using fractal compression code shortens the retrieval times of compression domain greatly and guarantees the retrieval accuracy.
The above works make it clear that the essence of an image can be captured in the compression code and the code is very useful is querying the specific image from images.
4.3 Algorithm of Fractal Coding of Image Retrieval
If we took a closer look at how people use fractal code to select images, we will find there are two ways of selection. The first is that, we have a specific image and we want to pick up same images, or similar images, from the data set. The second is that, with a-priori knowledge, we know there are some images are different with others and we want to pick them up. Nevertheless, we can preprocess the second with part of the image data set and find the specific image as the target image.
The algorithm that using fractal compression codes in image retrieval is as below.

Algorithm
begin
read target image
get PIFS transformation ω_i
set tolerance ε
while not end-of-file
{
  read tested images
  get PIFS transformation ω_i
  compare with target image
  if (comparison value $\leq \varepsilon$)
    image found
  else
    discard
}
end

4.3 Discussion of the problems

In this section, we want to talk some problems might occurred when using fractal compression code in image retrieval.
In section 4.2 we have found that many people have tested the fractal compression method on different images. In section 2 we have mentioned that there are two kinds of fractal compression methods: the IFS compression and the PIFS (partitioned IFS) compression. The IFS method is good for describing classic fractal patterns but not real images. That is why people use PIFS of image retrieval.
Unlike the IFS compression method which explores the self similarity of the entire image, the PIFS compression methods try to explore the self similarity on sub-image. During the compression process PIFS method recursively divides the image and tries to find sub-images containing the same pattern. In this way, the PIFS compression method records self similarity patterns into the set of coefficients of the compression code.

The partitioning method chosen for implementation was important. It can determine whether the compression result is good or bad. When we partition an image, we are looking for two sub-images containing the same pattern. Thus it is important that the sub-image will contain a pattern. A good partitioning method can do this.
The documents listed in the literature review section confirmed that the PIFS method does code the essential information in an image. Different images have been used as tested data and their results indicated that the method can compress and decompress the image without losing key feature of the image.
Another advantage of PIFS method is that, since we are looking for the same pattern in two sub-images, it could help us to find the pattern if we can confine the search area to where the pattern might appear. We don't need detailed a-priori knowledge of where this pattern is, all we need is a possible target area where the pattern might be found. This can be defined arbitrarily by the user.
We can speed the image recognition process by the use of parallel processing. Usually, the problem of PIFS method is that it is time consuming. However, if we use distributed work station for each of the different parts of the same image, we could save a lot of time.
Nevertheless, several weakness of PIFS method is discovered. Firstly, usually there is more or less background noise on real images. This might affect the compression results. That is, a pattern could mix with noise so that it becomes difficult to be detected. De-noising method is a need before we execute PIFS method on the image.
Another weakness is the comparison method. We should choose a proper comparison method to detect the intensity difference between two sub-images. If the difference is small, then they might contain smaller features. However, the difficulty is to set a threshold value on to the computed comparison value to decide how small the intensity can be tolerated. This threshold value has empirically determined. However, the danger is that this empirical value might not be suitable for every kinds of image.
The full PIFS compression code might be very long. Thus to analyze this data and to extract meaningful information is not easy. However, the code set could be modified to classify images.

5. Summary

In the beginning of this chapter we noted that images are a key information resource and while processing them in computers is straightforward, understanding them is not so simple.
Image recognition suggests a solution to this problem. To compress an image is to remove the redundancy, i.e. unnecessary information, and transform the essential information into compressed codes. Because the compressed codes contain the essential information of the image, it should be possible to use the compression code to compare and recognize the images themselves.
Among many image recognition methods, fractal compression method proves itself to be a promising method. It provides good compression and arguably the most concise codes for image recognition. This method is based on fractal theory. In section 2 we noted that fractals are patterns which exhibit self similarity, which means fractal patterns can be sub-divided recursively into smaller non-overlapping parts and each part is a smaller replica of the entire pattern. Thus, no matter how complicated a fractal pattern looks, it is actually composed of

the same pattern at a different size.
The principle of fractal compression is to compress an image by exploring the possible fractal patterns in the image. The principle of the IFS approach is that we can use a set of coefficients to describe the self similarity of a fractal pattern. This set of coefficients then can be used to re-constructed fractal patterns. Alternatively, if there is fractal pattern in an image, it should be possible to use IFS coefficients to represent it. Thus an image can be compressed by simply storing the IFS coefficients rather than the original image. The advantage of the IFS approach is it is simple in form but it can represent complicate 3d structure.
These PIFS codes are a very promising tool in image retrieval. We have illustrated some people's works It shows that fractal is a good tool to be develop in image retrieval. In addition, constrains of using fractal in image retrieval are mentioned and discussed.

6. Reference

[1] D. J. Tildesley M Fleischmann and R.C.Ball. editors. Fractal in the Natural Science
[2] B. Mandelbrot. Fractals-forms, chance and dimension. W. H. Freeman and Company. 1997
[3] Ritendra Datta, Dhiraj Joshi, Jia Li, and James Z. Wang, Image Retreival :Ideas, Influence, and Trends of New Age, ACM Computing Survey, Vol. 40 No. 2, Article 5, April 2008
[4] Biao Cheng, Aidong Zhang, Raj Acharya, and Claudio Sibata Using Fractal Coding to Index Image Content for a Digital Library, Tachnical Report, University of Buffalo, 1995.
[5] Jean Michel Marie-Julie, Hassane Essafi Image Database Indexing and Retieval Using the Fractal Transform, Multimedia Applications, Services and Techniques -ECMAST '97, p169-p182, Springer Berlin / Heidelberg, 1997
[6] Tien Fu-Ming, Fractal-based Image Database Retrieval, Master dissertation, Zhong Shan University, Taiwan, 2001
[7] Ce Fan, Dongfa Gao, Xiaorong Wu and Ying Li, Retrieval based on Indexing for Compressed Domain, 2008 International Conference on Computer Science and Software Engineering, p1291-p1294, 2008
[8] Liangbin Zhang, Yi Wang, Lifeng Xi, Kun Gao and Tianyun Hu, New Method of Image Retrieval using Fractal Code on the Compression Domain, WSEAS Transaction on System, Issue 12, Volume 7, Dec. 2008

11

Gaussian Processes and its Application to the design of Digital Communication Receivers

Pablo M. Olmos, Juan José Murillo-Fuentes
and Fernando Pérez-Cruz
University of Seville, Signal Theory and Communications Department. Spain.
University of Princeton, Princeton (NJ), Electrical Engineering Department. USA.
University Carlos III in Madrid, Department of Signal Theory and communications.
Leganes (Madrid), Spain

Abstract

In this chapter, we introduce Gaussian processes for machine learning and their application to designing digital communication receivers. Gaussian processes for machine learning are Bayesian nonlinear tools for solving regression and classification problems. Gaussian processes for regression (GPR) were introduced in the mid-nineties to solve nonparametric estimation problems from a Bayesian perspective. They place a Gaussian process (GP) prior over the possible regressors and use the available data to obtain a posterior regressor, which it is able to explain the observations without overfitting. The covariance matrix of the GP prior describes the different solutions that can be achieved, e.g. linear, polynomial, or universal regressors. The solution of GPR is analytical given its covariance function and, besides providing point estimates, it also assigns confidence intervals for the predictions. Furthermore, the covariance function can be optimized by maximum likelihood to better represent the data, which adds additional flexibility to our regression approximation.

GPR can be generalized to solve classification problems, namely Gaussian processes for classification (GPC). GPC extends the idea of GPR for a classification likelihood model. For this likelihood, the GPC posterior is no longer analytically tractable and we need to approximate it. Expectation Propagation (EP), which matches the mean and covariance of the GP posterior to a Gaussian distribution, is the most widely used approximation. Unlike most state-of-the-art classifiers, GPC does not return point-wise decisions, but it provides an accurate posterior probability for each classification decision. This is a major advantage to be exploited by subsequent applications for reducing the base error produced by our nonlinear classifiers.

Nonlinear regression and classification techniques have been widely used for designing digital communication receivers for nonlinear channels or whenever there is little information about the channel model or for nonlinear model. These nonlinear tools must use short training sequences to learn the channel and to adapt to a wide range of scenarios, from linear minimum phase to nonlinear and non-minimum phase and from single to multi-user

scenarios. In this framework, Gaussian processes for machine learning can be used instead of other nonlinear tools, such as neural networks or support vector machines, providing several advantages to these widespread techniques. First, their structure can be learnt by maximum likelihood. Hence, we avoid cross-validation techniques; which reduces the number of training samples needed to provide accurate predictions. And, at the same time, we may learn more parameters compared to other state-of-the-art techniques, i.e., we have more flexible models that can easily resort from linear to intricate nonlinear solutions. Second, they provide accurate posterior probability estimates that can be exploited by the channel decoder to reduce the overall error rate of our communication system.
We analytically study how Gaussian processes for machine learning can replace other nonlinear techniques for designing the all-important digital communication receiver. We also present some covariance matrices suitable for general digital communication channels. We illustrate our theoretical results by showing how GPR provides accurate solutions to the channel equalization and multi-user detection problems with very short training sequences and how a low-density parity-check (LDPC) channel decoder might benefit from a GPC equalizer that provides accurate posterior probability estimates.

1. Introduction

Gaussian processes are typically used to characterize the noise component in digital communication systems, as it is mainly caused by thermal noise fluctuations (Salehi & Proakis, 2002). In this chapter, we propose the Gaussian processes (GPs) framework to design nonlinear receivers in digital communication systems. GPs were initially presented as a nonlinear estimation technique in 1978 (O'Hagan & Kingman, 1978) and were rapidly forgotten due to its computation complexity. In the mid-nineties, they were independently rediscovered (Williams & Rasmussen, 1996). Since then, they have been shown to fit many different applications (Williams & Rasmussen, 2006) and nowadays their computational complexity is no longer a limiting issue (Quiñonero-Candela & Rasmussen, 2005).
There is a vast literature on machine learning techniques for designing digital communication systems. The channel equalization problem has been addressed with different machine learning tools, such as multilayered perceptrons (MLPs) (Gibson & Cowan, 1991), radial basis function networks (RBFNs) (Chen et al., 1991), recurrent RBFNs (Cid-Sueiro et al., 1994), self-organizing feature maps (SOFMs) (Kohonen et al., 1991), wavelet neural networks (Chang & Wang, 1995), GCMAC (González-Serrano et al., 1998), kernel adaline (KA) (Mitchinson & Harrison, 2002), or support vector machines (SVMs) (Pérez-Cruz et al., 2001), among many others. Other digital communication systems that have also benefited from nonlinear detection and estimation algorithms are multiuser detection (Cruickshank, 1996), (Tanner & Cruickshank, 1997), (Caffery & Stuber, 2000), and (Pham et al., 2007), multiple-input multiple-output systems (Sánchez-Fernández et al., 2004), beamforming (Martínez-Ramón et al., 2007), predistortion (González-Serrano et al., 2001), and plant identification (Arenas-García et al., 2006) to name a few.
For these machine learning approaches, it is necessary to prespecify the hyperparameters (structure), since standard methods for searching the optimal hyperparameters, i.e., cross validation (Kimeldorf, G.S. & Wahba, 1971), (Bishop, 1995) require immense computational resources, which are not available in most communication receivers, and also their training

time is highly variable. As a result, they use a suboptimal structure that requires longer training sequences for ensuring optimal receiver performance.

Gaussian processes for machine learning are rooted in Bayesian statistics (Williams & Rasmussen, 2006), and consequently allow building a likelihood function for its hyperparameters given the training examples. This likelihood can be optimized to set the hyperparameters. This property makes GPs an attractive tool for designing nonlinear digital communication receivers, compared to other nonlinear machine learning tools, because the hyperparameters can be optimally set for each instantiation of our problem with a single optimization procedure. For short training sequences, hyperparameter mismatch significantly affects the performance of digital communication receivers, while for longer training sequences, this performance is not sensitive to variations in the hyperparameters. Most papers applying nonlinear machine learning for designing digital communication receivers propose fixed hyperparameters and sufficiently long training sequences. Our proposal is to introduce GPR with optimally trained hyperparameters to reduce the length of the training data sequence. We experimentally illustrate that previous fixed hyperparameters machine learning tools clearly underperforms the GPR. In addition, we show that GPR can be understood as a nonlinear MMSE estimator. Therefore GPR achieves optimal results from the MMSE viewpoint, a quite extended criterion in digital communications.

Gaussian processes can be extended for solving classification problems, namely GPC. In this case, the posterior is no longer tractable and we need to use approximations to compute the prediction for each class label (Williams & Rasmussen, 2006). A Gaussian distribution is typically used to approximate the GPC posterior, either using Laplace (Williams & Barber, 1998) or Expectation Propagation methods (Kuss & Rasmussen, 2005), because the posterior is unimodal for a large enough training set. GPC is a Bayesian tool that provides the posterior probability for each decision. This property makes it unique among the nonlinear methods for channel equalization. A soft equalizer allows the channel decoder to significantly reduce its error rate, because it has individual information about which bits might be in error. GPC outperforms the SVM with a probabilistic output (Platt, 2000). This method passes the SVM output through a sigmoid, which is not quite principled, as Platt himself explains in (Platt, 2000), but it typically provides good predictions. However, in some cases, its probability predictions are not accurate, as shown in (Kuss & Rasmussen, 2005), because we cannot know a priori how good this fit would be.

The GPR can also be used to design linear and nonlinear multiuser detectors (MUDs) in CDMA communications. The GPR solution for MUD receivers is advantageous in several ways, when compared to other nonlinear machine learning tools (e.g. MLPs, RBFNs and SVMs). First, the GPR solution is analytical, given its parameters. There is no need for solving a complex optimization problem at this stage. Second, given a training dataset, a likelihood function for the GPR parameters can be stated and, hence, its parameters can be optimally set (in maximum likelihood sense). MLPs, RBFNs or SVMs need to specify beforehand its structure or parameters, which can be suboptimal for each individual instantiation of our problem. These characteristics translate to shorter training sequences and improved convergence for GPR-based CMDA receivers.

The rest of the chapter is organized as follows. In Section 0 we describe the equalization and multi-user detection problems and we introduce the channel model considered through this chapter. We present the design of digital communication receivers as an optimization problem in Section 0 and show how different nonlinear machine learning tools can be fitted in this framework. Section 0 and Section 0 are devoted to presenting Gaussian processes for regression and classification. The optimization of the GP hyperparameters is proposed in Section 0. We deal with the equalization problem using Gaussian processes in Section 0. The GPR multi-user detector is analyzed in the next section. We conclude in Section 0 with some final comments.

2. Equalization and multi-user detection.

2.1 Channel model

We consider throughout the chapter the following deterministic channel model:

$$\mathbf{x} = \mathbf{H}\mathbf{s} + \mathbf{z}, \tag{1}$$

where $\mathbf{s}$ is a random variable column-vector representing the transmitted symbols, $\mathbf{H}$ corresponds to the deterministic channel gains, unknown to both the transmitter and receiver, $\mathbf{z}$ is zero-mean Gaussian noise, and $\mathbf{x}$ represents the received symbols. This model is general enough to capture most standard communication systems. We can also combine different $\mathbf{H}$ matrices to accommodate other communication systems.

I. *Intersymbol interference:* each element in $\mathbf{s}$ is a symbol transmitted at a different time instant. $\mathbf{H}$ is a row vector that represents the channel impulsive response.

II. *Multiple-input multiple-output:* $\mathbf{H}_{ij}$ represents the gain from the i-th receiving antenna to the j-th transmitting antenna and $\mathbf{s}$ represents the symbols transmitted by the antenna array.

III. *Fading:* $\mathbf{H}$ is a diagonal matrix with the fading coefficients and $\mathbf{s}$ represents the symbols transmitted at each time instant.

IV. *CDMA:* the columns of $\mathbf{H}$ collect each user's spreading code and each element of $\mathbf{s}$ represents the symbol transmitted by the user.

2.2 Equalization in digital communication receivers

In Fig. 1, we depict a simple band-based model to describe a nonlinear dispersive Single Input-Single Output (SISO) communication channel. In this case, $\mathbf{H}$ is a row vector representing the coefficients of the impulse response of the channel:

$$\begin{aligned} h(z) &= \sum_{i=0}^{n_C-1} h_i z^{-i}, \\ \mathbf{H} &= \begin{bmatrix} h_0 & h_1 & \cdots & h_{n_C} \end{bmatrix}, \end{aligned} \tag{2}$$

where n_C denotes the channel length. The nonlinearities in the channel, due to amplifiers and converters in the receiver can be modeled as (Mitchinson & Harrison, 2002):

$$x[j] = g(r[j]) + z[j] = g\left(\mathbf{H}\mathbf{s}_j\right) + z[j], \tag{3}$$

where $g(\cdot)$ is the nonlinear function the inputs face at the receiver (amplifiers and converters) and $\mathbf{s}_j$ is a column vector where each element is a symbol transmitted at a different time instant:

$$\mathbf{s}_j = \left[s[j] \;\; s[j-1] \;\; \cdots \;\; s[j-n_C+1] \right]^\top. \tag{4}$$

The equalizer collects a set of n_{EQ} consecutive received symbols:

$$\mathbf{x}_j^{EQ} = \left[x[j+\tau], x[j-1+\tau], \ldots, x[j-n_{EQ}+1+\tau] \right], \tag{5}$$

to predict each symbol $s_j = s[j]$, where n_{EQ} and τ represents, respectively, the length and the delay of the equalizer. In Section 0, we propose the use of GPC and GPR for channel equalization.

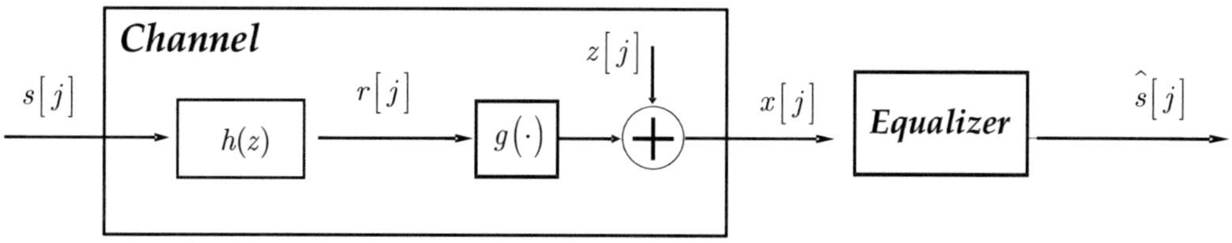

Fig. 1. Simple discrete-time SISO transmission channel model.

2.3 Multi-user detection in CDMA communications

In this chapter we focus on synchronous DS-CDMA, (Verdú, 1998), and we assume all users transmit at the same symbol rate using a BPSK modulation. The obtained results can be generalized to other scenarios, as asynchronous DS-CDMA, different rates, or modulations. The discrete chip-rate-sampled baseband synchronous DS-CDMA model proposed in (Verdú, 1998) is illustrated in Fig. 2. In this model, k symbols are transmitted (one per user) at instant j:

$$\mathbf{u}_j = [\mathrm{s}_j(1), \mathrm{s}_j(2), \ldots, \mathrm{s}_j(\mathrm{k})]^\top. \tag{6}$$

Each user's symbol, $s_j(l)$, is multiplied by its spreading code, $\mathbf{c}_l$, which is a sequence of n_S pseudorandom binary values regarded as chips. The resulting signal is amplified by a different gain, a_l, i.e., in the downlink of a mobile (cellular) communication system larger amplitudes are assigned to users further away, causing the near-far problem to users closest to the base station. The n_S-chip signal at the receiver end yields:

$$\mathbf{x}_j^{mud} = \mathbf{H}_m \begin{bmatrix} \mathbf{H}_S\mathbf{A} & 0 & \dots & 0 \\ 0 & \mathbf{H}_S\mathbf{A} & \ddots & \vdots \\ \vdots & \ddots & \ddots & 0 \\ 0 & \dots & 0 & \mathbf{H}_S\mathbf{A} \end{bmatrix} \cdot \begin{bmatrix} \mathbf{u}_j \\ \mathbf{u}_{j-1} \\ \vdots \\ \mathbf{u}_{j-M+1} \end{bmatrix} + \mathbf{z} = \mathbf{H}\mathbf{v}_j + \mathbf{z}, \tag{7}$$

where $\mathbf{H}_S$ is an $n_S \times k$ matrix whose columns contains the spreading codes, $\mathbf{A}$ is a $k \times k$ diagonal matrix containing the user amplitudes and $\mathbf{z}$ is an $n_S M$ dimensional column-vector with additive white Gaussian noise (AWGN) of variance $\sigma_{\mathbf{z}}^2\mathbf{I}$.

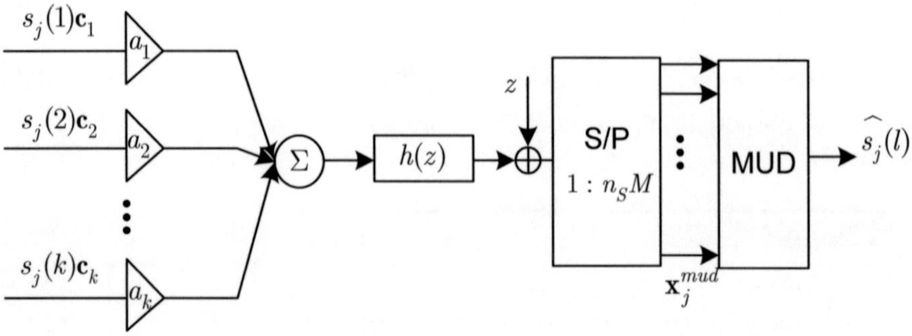

Fig. 2. System model for DS-CDMA.

We have pre-multiplied the received chips by $\mathbf{H}_m$ to incorporate the effect of a multipath channel in the CDMA system (Chen et al., 2001). $\mathbf{H}_m$ is a Toeplitz matrix, in which each row represents the channel impulsive response. We consider a time-invariant channel with inter-symbolic interference (ISI) characterized by its discrete channel impulsive response $h(z)$ of length n_C in chip periods. The length of the channel response times the chip period is the maximum delay considered in our multipath model. The matrix $\mathbf{H}$ in (7) summarizes the effect of the channel, the spreading codes and the different amplitudes for each user, where $\mathbf{v}_j = \begin{bmatrix} \mathbf{u}_j^\top & \mathbf{u}_{j-1}^\top & \cdots & \mathbf{u}_{j-M+1}^\top \end{bmatrix}^\top$ is a kM dimensional vector including the transmitted bits.

The objective for the DS-CDMA multi-user detector (MUD) receiver is to recover the transmitted bit for a particular user, the *UoI*. Linear MUDs are useful when the ISI is negligible and the codes are quasi-orthogonal. When the multipath effect and the near-far problem are strong, the optimal detector becomes highly nonlinear. The nonlinearity of the detector is significantly more disruptive for short spreading codes. In these scenarios nonlinear detectors are useful. Nonlinear MUDs for DS-CDMA estimate the symbol of the UoI as $\widehat{s_j}(l) = f(\mathbf{x}_j)$. If we knew all the 2^{kM} possible received noise free states, we could derive a MUD by studying a Bayes-optimal classifier (Chen et al., 2001). This optimal one-shot detector is given by:

$$\widehat{s}_j(l) = \operatorname{sign}\left(\sum_{i=1}^{2^{kM}} \frac{\tilde{s}^{(i)}(l)}{\sqrt{2\pi}\sigma_{\mathbf{z}}} \exp\left(-\frac{\| \mathbf{x}_j^{mud} - \mathbf{H}\mathbf{v}^{(i)} \|^2}{2\sigma_{\mathbf{z}}^2}\right)\right), \tag{8}$$

where $\tilde{s}^{(i)}(l) = \{\pm 1\}$ is the class label for the i-th noise free state $\mathbf{H}\mathbf{v}^{(i)}$. This structure resembles that of the Gaussian used in (Mitra & Poor, 1994), and suggests Gaussian kernels in SVM, as proposed in (Chen et al., 2001). But its complexity is exponential in the number of users and the length of the channel response, provided we have the 2^{kM} possible free states.

3. Nonlinear optimization for communication receivers

3.1 Minimum mean squared error detector

Given the channel model in (1), we can estimate, in the receiver, the transmitted vector using a minimum mean squared error (MMSE) detector (Kay, 1993):

$$f_{mmse}(\mathbf{x}) = \underset{f(\cdot)}{\operatorname{argmin}}\, E\left[\left\| \mathrm{s} - f(\mathbf{x})\right\|^2\right]. \tag{9}$$

The function $f_{mmse}(\mathbf{x})$ is the mean value of s given the received vector $\mathbf{x}$, $E[\mathrm{s} \mid \mathbf{x}]$, which is a linear function of $\mathbf{x}$ if s is a Gaussian distribution. Practical structural constraints dictate the use of discrete constellations, such as PSK and QAM, which depart from the optimal Gaussian distributions. Although linear detectors cannot achieve $E[\mathrm{s} \mid \mathbf{x}]$ if s is a discrete random variable, and thus the MMSE is only a proxy for minimizing the probability of misclassification. Still digital communication receivers use linear MMSE detectors for estimating the transmitted vector, because they can be easily implemented and hopefully their performance is not severely degraded. The linear MMSE, $f(\mathbf{x}) = \mathbf{w}^\top \mathbf{x}$, detector can be expressed as a Wiener filter:

$$\mathbf{w}_{mmse} = \underset{\mathbf{w}}{\operatorname{argmin}}\, E\left[\left(s - \mathbf{w}^\top \mathbf{x}\right)^2\right] = \left(E\left[\mathbf{x}\mathbf{x}^\top\right]\right)^{-1} E\left[\mathbf{x}s\right]. \tag{10}$$

3.2 Machine learning for digital communication receivers

The design of digital communication receivers can be readily understood as a supervised classification problem (Gibson et al, 1991) in which the receiver constructs a classifier for deciding over the incoming symbols. Machine learning tools optimize the risk of misclassification:

$$f_{opt}(\mathbf{x}) = \underset{f(\cdot)}{\operatorname{argmin}}\, E\left[L\left(s, f(\mathbf{x})\right)\right] = \underset{f(\cdot)}{\operatorname{argmin}} \int L\left(s, f(\mathbf{x})\right) p(s, \mathbf{x}) ds d\mathbf{x}, \tag{11}$$

where $L(\cdot)$ is a loss function that measures the penalty for wrongly classifying a pattern, and $f(\mathbf{x})$ is the nonlinear model to predict s.

The joint density, $p(s,\mathbf{x})$, is typically unknown and thus we use a training sequence $\{\mathbf{x}_i, s_i\}_{i=1}^n$ and the empirical risk minimization (ERM) inductive principle (Vapnik, 1998) to obtain the optimal solution:

$$\hat{f}_{opt}(\mathbf{x}) = \underset{f(\cdot)}{\operatorname{argmin}} \left\{ \sum_{i=1}^{n} L(s_i, f(\mathbf{x}_i)) + \lambda\Omega(\| f \|) \right\}, \tag{12}$$

where we have included a regularization term, $\lambda\Omega(\| f \|)$, to avoid overfitting and to ensure that the minimum of the empirical risk converges to the minimum risk (Vapnik, 1998) as the number of training samples increases.

If we choose $f(\mathbf{x}) = \mathbf{w}^\top\phi(\mathbf{x})$, $L(s, f(\mathbf{x})) = (s - \mathbf{w}^\top\phi(\mathbf{x}))^2$ and $\Omega(f) = \| \mathbf{w} \|^2$ we get a convex functional,

$$\mathbf{w}_{nl\_mmse} = \underset{\mathbf{w}}{\operatorname{argmin}} \left\{ \sum_{i=1}^{n} (s_i - \mathbf{w}^\top\phi(\mathbf{x}_i))^2 + \lambda \| \mathbf{w} \|^2 \right\}, \tag{13}$$

which can be analytically solved,

$$\mathbf{w}_{nl\_mmse} = \left(\boldsymbol{\Phi}^\top\boldsymbol{\Phi} + \lambda\mathbf{I}\right)^{-1} \boldsymbol{\Phi}^\top\mathbf{s}, \tag{14}$$

where $\boldsymbol{\Phi} = [\phi(\mathbf{x}_1),\ldots,\phi(\mathbf{x}_n)]^\top$ and $\mathbf{s} = [s_1,\ldots,s_n]^\top$. We denote this solution as nonlinear MMSE, since it is a nonlinear extension of (10) in which we have replaced $\mathbf{x}$ by $\phi(\mathbf{x})$ and the expectations by sample averages.

In the next section we show (14) is equivalent to the mean solution provided by Gaussian processes for regression with a Gaussian likelihood function and that it can be solved using kernels (Pérez-Cruz & Bousquet, 2004).

4. Gaussian Processes for Regression

In a nutshell, Gaussian processes for regression (GPR) assume that a GP prior governs the set of possible regressors. Consequently, the joint distribution of training and test data is given by a multidimensional Gaussian density function, and the predicted distribution for each test point is estimated by conditioning on the training data.

We mainly present GPR from the Bayesian generalized linear regression viewpoint. Although from this opening we lose the GPs interpretation. We believe it is a simpler way to understand GPR. This approach mimics how most machine learning textbooks introduce nonlinear regression (Bishop, 1995), (Schölkopf & Smola, 2001) and (Haykin, 1999) and it helps understanding GPR as a nonlinear MMSE estimation. Therefore, practitioners in signal processing for digital communications can readily relate to this new tool for estimation and detection. Another point of view is that of the function space. Both interpretations are described in (Williams, 1999), where they are shown to be identical for Gaussian likelihood models. There is more about GPs than what we introduce in this summary, for interested readers, GPs extensions can be found in (Williams & Rasmussen, 2006).

4.1 Weight-space view

A generalized linear regressor expresses the input-output relation as

$$s = \mathbf{w}^\top \phi(\mathbf{x}) + \nu, \tag{15}$$

where $\phi(\cdot)$ is a nonlinear transformation to a higher dimensional feature space and ν is a random variable that measures the deviation between s and its estimate. In Bayesian machine learning, given a labeled training sequence, $\mathcal{D} = \{\mathbf{x}_i, s_i\}_{i=1}^n$ where the input $\mathbf{x}_i \in \mathbb{R}^d$ and the output $s_i \in \mathbb{R}$, and a statistical model for ν, $\mathbf{w}$ is considered to be a random variable and, to predict the outcome of $\mathbf{x}_*$, we use its conditional density given the training data set, $p(\mathbf{w} \mid \mathcal{D})$. This conditional density, known as the posterior of $\mathbf{w}$, can be computed through Bayes rule,

$$\begin{aligned} p(\mathbf{w} \mid \mathcal{D}) = p(\mathbf{w} \mid \mathrm{s}, \mathbf{X}) = \frac{p(\mathrm{s} \mid \mathbf{X}, \mathbf{w}) p(\mathbf{w})}{p(\mathrm{s} \mid \mathbf{X})} = \\ = \frac{p(\mathbf{w})}{p(\mathrm{s} \mid \mathbf{X})} \prod_{i=1}^{n} p(s_i \mid \mathbf{x}_i, \mathbf{w}), \end{aligned} \tag{16}$$

where $p(s_i \mid \mathbf{x}_i, \mathbf{w})$ is the likelihood function of $\mathbf{w}$, $p(\mathbf{w})$ its prior distribution, $\mathbf{X} = [\mathbf{x}_1, \ldots, \mathbf{x}_n]^\top$ and $p(\mathrm{s} \mid \mathbf{X})$ is the evidence of the model. To predict the output for a new test point $\mathbf{x}_*$ we integrate out $\mathbf{w}$:

$$p(s_* \mid \mathbf{x}_*, \mathcal{D}) = \int_{\mathbf{w}} p(s_* \mid \mathbf{x}_*, \mathcal{D}, \mathbf{w}) p(\mathbf{w} \mid \mathcal{D}) d\mathbf{w}, \tag{17}$$

in which the conditional density of each s_* (the likelihood of $\mathbf{w}$) is weighted by the posterior of $\mathbf{w}$ and is summed over all possible $\mathbf{w}$. As a result, we get a full statistical description of s_*, given all the available information ($\mathbf{x}_*$ and $\mathcal{D}$). In this setting, we predict the value of s_* using the full statistical model of $\mathbf{w}$, not only its maximum likelihood estimate. This setting is quite general, as we can use any model for the likelihood and prior for solving the regression estimation problem. Gaussian likelihood, $p(s \mid \mathbf{x}, \mathbf{w}) = \mathcal{N}(\mathbf{w}^\top \phi(\mathbf{x}), \sigma_\nu^2)$, leads to the MMSE criterion; and a zero-mean Gaussian prior, $p(\mathbf{w}) = \mathcal{N}(\mathbf{0}, \sigma_{\mathbf{w}}^2 \mathbf{I})$, allocates probability mass to every possible $\mathbf{w}$ and allows solving (17) analytically. The posterior distribution in (16) is then a Gaussian density function, $p(\mathbf{w} \mid \mathcal{D}) = \mathcal{N}(\mu_{\mathbf{w}}, \Sigma_{\mathbf{w}})$, where

$$\mu_{\mathbf{w}} = \sigma_{\mathbf{w}}^2 \left(\sigma_{\mathbf{w}}^2 \mathbf{\Phi}^\top \mathbf{\Phi} + \sigma_\nu^2 \mathbf{I} \right)^{-1} \mathbf{\Phi}^\top \mathbf{s}, \tag{18}$$

$$\Sigma_{\mathbf{w}}^{-1} = \frac{1}{\sigma_\nu^2} \mathbf{\Phi}^\top \mathbf{\Phi} + \frac{1}{\sigma_{\mathbf{w}}^2} \mathbf{I}. \tag{19}$$

Actually, the posterior mean in (18) is identical to the maximum a posteriori (MAP) of (16):

$$\begin{aligned} \mu_{\mathbf{w}} &= \mathbf{w}_{MAP} = \underset{\mathbf{w}}{\operatorname{argmax}} \left\{ p(\mathbf{w} \mid \mathbf{s}, \mathbf{X}) \right\} \\ &= \underset{\mathbf{w}}{\operatorname{argmax}} \left\{ \log p(\mathbf{s} \mid \mathbf{X}, \mathbf{w}) + \log p(\mathbf{w}) \right\} \\ &= \underset{\mathbf{w}}{\operatorname{argmax}} \left\{ -\frac{1}{\sigma_\nu^2} \sum_{i=1}^{n} (s_i - \mathbf{w}^\top \phi(\mathbf{x}_i))^2 - \frac{1}{\sigma_{\mathbf{w}}^2} \| \mathbf{w} \|^2 \right\}, \end{aligned} \tag{20}$$

which is identical to (12) for $\lambda = \sigma_\nu^2 / \sigma_{\mathbf{w}}^2$. We can also check that (18) is equal to (14) and, therefore the GPR mean prediction can be regarded as a nonlinear MMSE estimation for the nonlinear mapping $\phi(\cdot)$. The prediction for s_* in (17) is a Gaussian density function $p(s_* \mid \mathbf{x}_*, \mathcal{D}) = \mathcal{N}(\mu_{s_*}, \sigma_{s_*})$:

$$\mu_{s_*} = \phi^\top(\mathbf{x}_*) \mu_{\mathbf{w}} = \phi^\top(\mathbf{x}_*) \frac{1}{\sigma_\nu^2} \Sigma_{\mathbf{w}} \mathbf{\Phi}^\top \mathbf{s}, \tag{21}$$

$$\sigma_{s_*}^2 = \phi^\top(\mathbf{x}_*) \Sigma_{\mathbf{w}} \phi(\mathbf{x}_*) = \phi^\top(\mathbf{x}_*) \left(\frac{1}{\sigma_\nu^2} \mathbf{\Phi}^\top \mathbf{\Phi} + \frac{1}{\sigma_{\mathbf{w}}^2} \mathbf{I} \right)^{-1} \phi(\mathbf{x}_*). \tag{22}$$

4.2 Alternative formulation

There is an alternative formulation for μ_{s_*} and $\sigma_{s_*}^2$, in which we do not need to know the nonlinear mapping $\phi(\cdot)$ and we only need to work with its inner product or kernel, defined as:

$$k(\mathbf{x}_i, \mathbf{x}_j) = \sigma_{\mathbf{w}}^2 \phi^\top(\mathbf{x}_i)\phi(\mathbf{x}_j). \tag{23}$$

To obtain this alternative formulation, we first define the covariance matrix $\mathbf{C}$ as

$$(\mathbf{C})_{ij} = k(\mathbf{x}_i, \mathbf{x}_j) + \sigma_\nu^2 \delta_{ij}, \tag{24}$$

which can be related to $\Sigma_{\mathbf{w}}$ as follows:

$$\Sigma_{\mathbf{w}}^{-1}\mathbf{\Phi}^\top = \left(\frac{1}{\sigma_\nu^2}\mathbf{\Phi}^\top\mathbf{\Phi} + \frac{1}{\sigma_{\mathbf{w}}^2}\mathbf{I}\right)^\top \mathbf{\Phi}^\top = \frac{1}{\sigma_\nu^2\sigma_{\mathbf{w}}^2}\mathbf{\Phi}^\top\mathbf{C}. \tag{25}$$

Now if we premultiply (25) by $\Sigma_{\mathbf{w}}$ and postmultiply it by $\mathbf{C}^{-1}$, we obtain the following equivalency: $\Sigma_{\mathbf{w}}\mathbf{\Phi}^\top / \sigma_\nu^2 = \sigma_{\mathbf{w}}^2\mathbf{\Phi}^\top\mathbf{C}^{-1}$, which can be used to simplify (22) and express the GPR prediction mean as

$$\mu_{s_*} = \phi^\top(\mathbf{x}_*)\sigma_{\mathbf{w}}^2\mathbf{\Phi}^\top\mathbf{C}^{-1}\mathbf{s} = \mathbf{k}^\top\mathbf{C}^{-1}\mathbf{s}, \tag{26}$$

where

$$\mathbf{k} = \sigma_{\mathbf{w}}^2\phi^\top(\mathbf{x}_*)\mathbf{\Phi}^\top = [k(\mathbf{x}_*, \mathbf{x}_1), \ldots, k(\mathbf{x}_*, \mathbf{x}_n)]^\top. \tag{27}$$

To compute the prediction for any vector $\mathbf{x}_*$, we do not need to know the nonlinear mapping $\phi(\cdot)$, only its kernel. The complexity of computing μ_{s_*} in (26) is linear in the number of training examples, because we can pre-compute the vector $\mathbf{C}^{-1}\mathbf{s}$ that does not depend on $\mathbf{x}_*$ and we only need to filter $\mathbf{k}$ with it for each new test pattern.

We can also define the variance of our predictor using kernels as follows:

$$\sigma_{s_*}^2 = k(\mathbf{x}_*, \mathbf{x}_*) - \mathbf{k}^\top\mathbf{C}^{-1}\mathbf{k}, \tag{28}$$

which is achieved after applying to (19) the matrix inversion lemma (Scharf, 1990). Equations in (26) and (28) represent the predictions for $\mathbf{x}_*$ given by the Gaussian processes view of GPR. The matrix $\mathbf{C}$ is the covariance matrix of a multidimensional Gaussian distribution, hence its name, that describes the training data, and the vector $\mathbf{k}$ represents the covariance vector between the training dataset and the test vector. Therefore, the function

$k(\cdot,\cdot)$ has to be a positive-definite function to ensure that the Gaussian processes covariance matrix $\mathbf{C}$ is also positive definite.

4.3 Function-space view

An equivalent and alternative way of reaching similar results is to consider inference directly in the so-called function space, where we use a Gaussian process to describe a distribution over functions. If $f(\mathbf{x}) = \mathbf{w}^\top \phi(\mathbf{x})$ we may rewrite (17) as

$$p(s_* \mid \mathbf{x}_*, \mathcal{D}) = \int p(s_* \mid \mathbf{x}_*, \mathcal{D}, f_*) p(f_* \mid \mathbf{x}_*, \mathcal{D}) df_*, \tag{29}$$

where $f_* = f(\mathbf{x}_*)$ and proceed in a similar way to estimate (16) and solve it for a Gaussian prior on $f(\mathbf{x})$ and Gaussian likelihood $p(s \mid \mathbf{x}, f) = \mathcal{N}(f(\mathbf{x}), \sigma_\nu^2)$:

$$p(f_* \mid \mathbf{x}_*, \mathcal{D}) = \int p(f_* \mid x_*, \mathbf{x}, \mathbf{f}) p(\mathbf{f} \mid \mathcal{D}) d\mathbf{f}, \tag{30}$$

where

$$p(\mathbf{f} \mid \mathcal{D}) = p(\mathbf{f} \mid \mathbf{X}, \mathrm{s}) = \frac{\prod_i p(\mathrm{s}_i \mid f_i) p(\mathbf{f} \mid \mathbf{X})}{p(\mathrm{s} \mid \mathbf{X})}. \tag{31}$$

5. Gaussian processes for classification

Gaussian process for classification is a bit trickier than the regression counterpart, because we cannot rely on a Gaussian likelihood function to predict the labels of each class as the outcomes come from a discrete set (Williams & Rasmussen, 2006). Thereby to predict the class labels we need to resort to numerical integration or approximations to tractable density models. A generalized linear binary classifier predicts the class label for an input $\mathbf{x}$ as follows:

$$p(s = +1 \mid \mathbf{w}, \mathbf{x}) = p(s = +1 \mid f(\mathbf{x})) = \sigma(f(\mathbf{x})), \tag{32}$$

where $f(\mathbf{x}) = \mathbf{w}^\top \phi(\mathbf{x})$ is an underlying continuous function, $\sigma(\cdot)$ is a sigmoid that squashes $f(\mathbf{x})$ between 0 and 1, and $p(s = -1 \mid f(\mathbf{x})) = 1 - p(s = +1 \mid f(\mathbf{x}))$. Function $\sigma(\cdot)$ is typically the logistic function or the cumulative density function of a Gaussian (Williams & Rasmussen, 2006).

Given a labeled training sequence $\mathcal{D} = \{\mathbf{x}_i, s_i\}_{i=1}^n$, where the input $\mathbf{x}_i \in \mathbb{R}^d$ and the output $s_i \in \{\pm 1\}$, we can compute the posterior over the underlying function

$\mathbf{f} = [f(\mathbf{x}_1),\ldots,f(\mathbf{x}_2)]^\top$ using Bayes rule, as we did in the last section for GPR with $\mathbf{w}$, and we can integrate out $\mathbf{f}$ to predict the class label for any new test point $\mathbf{x}_*$. We can compute the class label for the test samples as follows:

$$p(s_* = +1 \mid \mathbf{x}_*, \mathcal{D}) = \int \sigma(f_*) p(f_* \mid \mathbf{x}_*, \mathcal{D}) df_*. \tag{33}$$

Now, equations (30) and (31) are intractable due to the likelihood model employed for $f(\mathbf{x})$ in (32). GPC typically relies on a Gaussian approximation for the posterior density $p(\mathbf{f} \mid \mathcal{D})$, to analytically solve (30), and (33) is a one-dimensional integral that can be easily solved numerically. The standard approximations to the posterior $p(\mathbf{f} \mid \mathcal{D})$ are Laplace or Expectation Propagation, as explained in (Kuss & Rasmussen, 2005). Further details on how to approximate the posterior can be found in (Williams & Rasmussen, 2006).

6. Hyperparameter optimization

If either $\phi(\cdot)$ or $k(\cdot,\cdot)$ are known, we can predict the output of any incoming sample in a regression (26) or a classification problem (33). But for most estimation problems, the best nonlinear transformation (or its kernel) is unknown. Therefore, it is usually defined in a parametric form as function of the so-called *hyperparameters*. The optimal setting of the hyperparameters could be obtained by cross-validation, similarly to any other nonlinear machine learning method. From the point of view of Bayesian machine learning, we can proceed as we did for the parameters $\mathbf{w}$ in Section 0. First, we compute the likelihood of the hyperparameters of the kernel given the training dataset:

$$p(\mathrm{s} \mid \mathbf{X}, \theta) = \int p(\mathrm{s} \mid \mathbf{f}, \mathbf{X}, \theta) p(\mathbf{f} \mid \mathbf{X}, \theta) d\mathbf{f}, \tag{34}$$

where θ represents the hyperparameters of the covariance function or kernel. We have added to explicitly indicate the dependence on the kernel's hyperparameters. This was omitted in the GPR and GPC presentations in Sections 0 and 0 for clarity purposes.

Second, we can define a prior for the hyperparameters, $p(\theta)$, that can be used to construct its posterior:

$$p(\theta \mid \mathcal{D}) = \frac{p(\mathrm{s} \mid \mathbf{X}, \theta) p(\theta)}{p(\mathrm{s} \mid \mathbf{X})}. \tag{35}$$

Third, we can integrate out the hyperparameters to obtain the predictions:

$$p(s_* \mid \mathbf{x}_*, \mathcal{D}) = \int p(s_* \mid \mathbf{x}_*, \mathcal{D}, \theta) p(\theta \mid \mathcal{D}) d\theta. \tag{36}$$

However, in this case, the likelihood of the hyperparameters does not have a conjugate prior and the posterior is non-analytical. Hence the integration has to be done either by sampling or approximations. Although this approach is well principled, it is computational intensive and it demands a high number of samples. Thereby it is not feasible for digital communications receivers.

Alternatively, we can use the likelihood function in (34) of the hyperparameters and compute its maximum to obtain its optimal setting (Williams & Rasmussen, 1996), which is used to describe the kernel for the test samples. Although setting the hyperparameters by maximum likelihood is not a purely Bayesian solution, it is fairly standard in the community and it allows using Bayesian solutions in time-sensitive applications. The maximum likelihood hyperparameters are given by

$$\theta_{ML} = \underset{\theta}{\operatorname{argmax}}\ p(\mathbf{s} \mid \mathbf{X}, \theta). \quad (37)$$

This optimization is nonconvex (Mackay, 2003). But as we increase the number of training samples, the likelihood becomes a unimodal distribution around the maximum likelihood hyperparameters and the ML solution can be found using gradient ascent techniques. See (Williams & Rasmussen, 1996) for further details.

6.1 Covariance matrix

To optimize the kernel hyperparameters in (37), we need to describe a kernel in a parametric form. Kernel design is one of the most challenging open problems in machine learning, as it is mainly driven by each particular application. We need to incorporate our prior knowledge into the kernel, but, at the same time, we want the kernel to be flexible to explain previously unknown trends in the data. In (Williams & Rasmussen, 1996), a list of flexible kernels (e.g., linear, Gaussian, neural networks, Matérn, among others) is presented along with their properties.

For example, if we know the optimal solution to be linear, we could use the linear kernel: $k(\mathbf{x}, \mathbf{x}') = \sigma_{\mathbf{w}}^2 \mathbf{x}^\top \mathbf{x}'$. In general, kernel functions are more complex and they incorporate several hyperparameters. For example, the Gaussian kernel with automatic relevance determination (ARD) proposes one nonnegative weight, γ_ℓ, per input dimension:

$$k(\mathbf{x}_i, \mathbf{x}_j) = \alpha_1 \exp\left(-\sum_{\ell=1}^{d} \gamma_\ell \left(x_{i\ell} - x_{j\ell} \right)^2 \right) + \alpha_2 \mathbf{x}_i^\top \mathbf{x}_j + \alpha_0 \delta_{ij}, \quad (38)$$

where we have added a linear kernel to use this covariance function for designing digital communication receivers. For this kernel function we define the hyperparameters as $\theta = [\log \alpha_0, \log \alpha_1, \log \alpha_2, \log \gamma_1, \cdots, \log \gamma_d]$, because these hyperparameters need to be positive to ensure that $k(\cdot,\cdot)$ is a positive semi-definite function. Hence, we can apply unconstrained optimization tools when we optimize over θ. The covariance function in (38) is a good kernel for designing digital communication receivers using GPR and GPC, because it contains a linear and a universal nonlinear part.

The linear part can mimic the best linear decision boundary and the nonlinear part modifies it, where the linear explanation is not optimal to obtain the expectation of s given $\mathbf{x}$. If the channel is linear, then the ML solution sets $\alpha_1 = 0$ and there is no interference of the nonlinear term with the linear one in the solution. Also, using Gaussian kernel, also denoted as radial basis function (RBF) kernel, for the nonlinear part seems an appropriate choice to achieve nonlinear decisions for digital communication receivers, because the received symbols form a constellation of clouds of points with Gaussian spread around its centers. Due to the symmetry in communication problems and to avoid overfitting, we use the same length scale for all dimensions: $\gamma = \gamma_1 = \cdots = \gamma_d$.

7. Equalization with Gaussian processes.

We return to the system model described in Fig. 1. In this section, we face the experimental study of the Gaussian processes based equalizer. We can apply either regression (GPR) (Pérez-Cruz et al., 2008) or classification (GPC) (Pérez-Cruz et al., 2007). The GPR solution has the advantage of being analytical, which makes it easy to compute, while to obtain the GPC solutions we need to use approximations for its posterior distribution, which can be time consuming. However, the GPR solution cannot be interpreted as posterior probabilities for each output, because it assumes it is solving a regression problem with Gaussian noise. And that is not the case for channel equalization, which can be cast as a classification problem.

The GPR input is a set of n_{EQ} consecutive received symbols. It is first trained with a set $\mathcal{D} = \{\mathbf{x}_i^{EQ}, s_i\}_{i=1}^n$, where $\mathbf{x}_i^{EQ} \in \mathbb{R}^{n_{EQ}}$. The solution of the GPR process for a new input $\mathbf{x}_*$ is the posterior mean μ_{s_*} (26) and variance $\sigma_{s_*}^2$ (28). The decision about the s_* symbol is based on the μ_{s_*} parameter. In the binary case, $s \in \{\pm 1\}$, the GPR-equalizer decides which the transmitted bit was according to:

$$\widehat{s_*} = \text{sign}(\mu_{s_*}) = \text{sign}(\mathbf{k}^\top \mathbf{C}^{-1}\mathbf{s}). \tag{39}$$

A GPC equalizer is also trained with a training set $\mathcal{D} = \{\mathbf{x}_i^{EQ}, s_i\}_{i=1}^n$, to predict the probability $p(s_* = +1 \mid \mathbf{x}_*^{EQ}, \mathcal{D})$ for a new input $\mathbf{x}_*^{EQ}$. The symbol s_* can be estimated by

$$\widehat{s_*} = \begin{cases} +1 & p(s_* = +1 \mid \mathbf{x}_i^{EQ}, \mathcal{D}) > 0.5 \\ -1 & p(s_* = +1 \mid \mathbf{x}_*^{EQ}, \mathcal{D}) < 0.5 \end{cases}. \tag{40}$$

In the next section, we show that the Bit Error Rate (*BER*) performance obtained with GPR and GPC equalizers in (39) and (40), is similar. If the information bits $m[j]$, see Fig. 3, are encoded into a binary sequence $s[j]$ using a channel code, the resulting *BER* will be further reduced if the channel decoder takes as input the GPC posterior probability estimates $p(s_* = +1 \mid \mathbf{x}_*, \mathcal{D})$ instead hard decisions using (39) or (40). Any state of-the-art procedure as Low-Density Parity-Check (LDPC) codes or Repeat and Accumulate (RA) codes (Mackay, 2003) will provide BER bellow 10^{-5} for snr close to capacity. In the experimental section, we compare the performance obtained with the receiver in Fig. 3 when both GPC and SVM are used as equalizer. As we mentioned in the introduction, SVM soft-output can be transformed into posterior probability by using the method proposed by Platt (Platt, 2000).

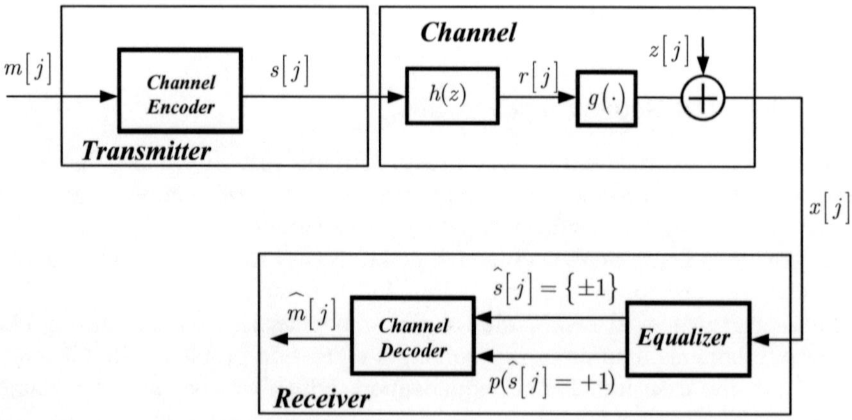

Fig. 3. Discrete time channel model, together with the transmitter and receiver proposed, including the channel coder and decoder.

7.1 Experimental results

In the next experiments, we deal with the equalization problem in nonlinear channels. The results in these experiments allow drawing some general conclusions about the advantages of GPs for designing digital communication receivers. The channel model is given by:

$$h(z) = 0.3482 + 0.8704z^{-1} + 0.3482z^{-2}. \tag{41}$$

We add a memoryless nonlinearity to the receiver that transforms each received signal as follows:

$$g(r) = r + 0.2r^2 - 0.1r^3 . \tag{42}$$

This channel was proposed in (Mitchinson & Harrison, 2002) for modeling radio communication channels and nonlinear amplifiers in wireless communication receivers. To construct the equalizers, we use six received samples to predict each transmitted symbol with a delay of two samples. For the GPC and GPR equalizers, we use the kernel proposed in (38)and SVM is trained with two different kernels: one of them is a linear kernel and the other one is a Gaussian kernel (Pérez-Cruz & Bousquet, 2004). We use a simpler kernel for SVM, because (38) has far too many parameters that cannot be learned with short training sequences. This topic is discussed in detail in (Pérez-Cruz & Murillo-Fuentes, 2008). For the SVMs we train a set of receivers with different hyperparameters and we report the best

result. Thereby, the comparison is biased in favor of the SVM when compared to the GPR and GPC solutions.
In Fig. 4, we show the BER versus the snr for all equalizers and $n = 512$. For snr less than 22 dB, the nonlinear GPR equalizer achieves the minimum BER with a gain larger than 3 dB for BER around 10^{-3}. For larger snr, the performance of this nonlinear equalizer degrades and the linear equalizers perform significantly better. The nonlinear SVM equalizer performs as the GPR equalizer for snr lower than 17 dB, but for larger snr the training sequence is not long enough and its solution degrades (overfitting). For snr larger than 20 dB, the nonlinear SVM equalizer is not able to reduce the achieved BER. The nonlinear SVM and the GPR as the snr increases are not able to get optimal equalizers, because there is not enough diversity in the training sequence and they overfit to it. The GPR performance is better than the SVM for large snr, because it uses a covariance function in (28) that incorporates a linear term. Although it overfits the nonlinear part, the linear component allows the GPR to reduce the BER for large snr. If we had increased the training sequence, the SVM and GPR would perform better than the linear methods for larger values of the snr.

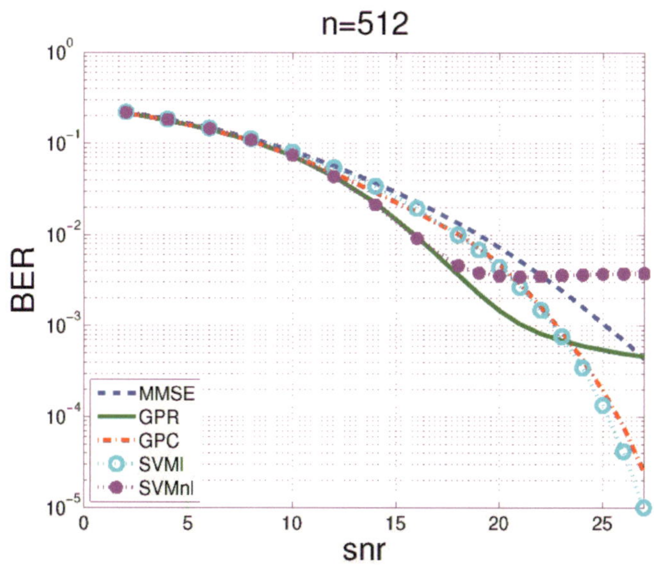

Fig. 4. We report the BER versus snr for a channel equalization problem with the channel model in (41) and (42). The dashed line represents the linear MMSE receiver, the solid line the GPR, the dash dotted line the GPC, the dotted line with circles the linear SVM, and the dotted line with bullets the nonlinear SVM.

The GPC shuts down the nonlinear part and performs as the linear SVM. They are both able to perform significantly better than the linear MMSE, because the channel model is nonlinear. For a nonlinear channel, the received constellation is no longer symmetric, and penalizing the squared error is suboptimal, as it forces that all the detected symbols to be equally far from its optimal value (Pérez-Cruz & Murillo-Fuentes, 2008). The SVM and GPC equalizers only care, if the points are correctly classified, and they only focus on those that

might not be, which explains the BER gap between the linear MMSE equalizer and the GPC and linear SVM ones. In any case, for the snr between 10 and 20 dB, the GPR receivers (and nonlinear SVM) are significantly better than the linear methods and the GPC.
As mentioned before, the channel decoding process can take advantage of the GPC posterior estimation. The GPR solution cannot be interpreted as posterior probabilities for each output bit, because it assumes it is solving a regression problem with Gaussian noise. We illustrate that the novel approach based on GPC provides accurate predictions for posterior probabilities. We consider a linear channel with a simpler transfer function that will actually allow us to compare the true posterior probability and the one provided by the GPC equalizer:

$$h(z) = 1 + 0.5z^{-1}\,. \tag{43}$$

We have shown in Fig. 5-Fig. 7, the calibration curves for the GPC equalizer compared to the optimum posterior probabilities for 10^4 test samples. Training sequences with 100, 200 and 800 samples are considered. In the horizontal axis we report the true posterior probability and in the vertical axis the probability predicted by the GPC equalizer. In these plots we can see that, as we increase the number of training samples, the points concentrate on the diagonal axis, which represents the perfect fit between GPC equalizer and the optimum. Hence, the longer the training sequence is the better the match between the predicted and true posterior probabilities will be.

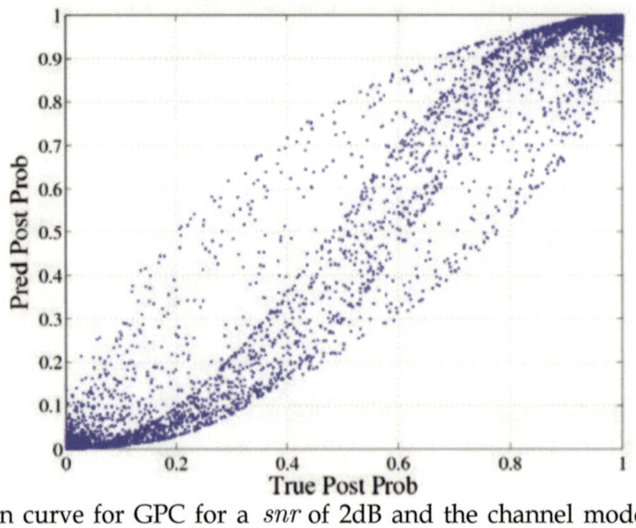

Fig. 5. Calibration curve for GPC for a snr of 2dB and the channel model in (43) for 100 training samples.

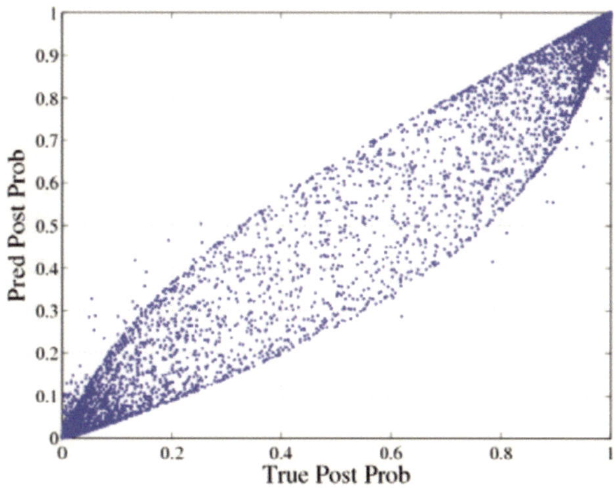

Fig. 6. Calibration curve for GPC for a snr of 2dB and the channel model in (43) for 200 training samples.

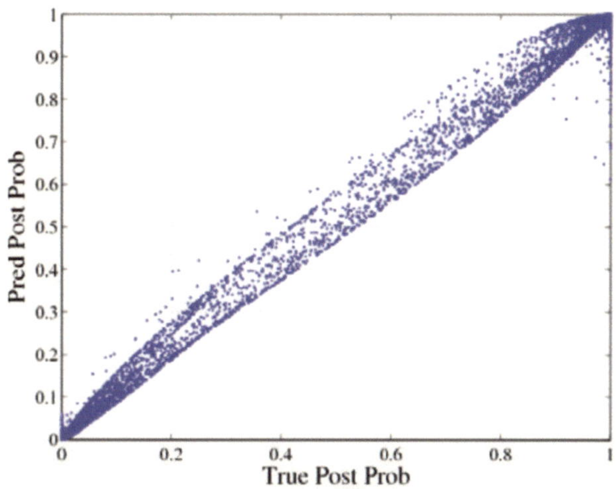

Fig. 7. Calibration curve for GPC for a snr of 2dB and the channel model in (43) for 800 training samples.

8. The GPR Multi-user detector

The GPR mean prediction in (26) can be directly used as a nonlinear multi-user detector (Murillo-Fuentes & Pérez-Cruz, 2009). This GPR estimate resembles that of a linear detector. It has a weight vector, either $\mu_{\mathbf{w}_j}$ or $\mathbf{C}^{-1}\mathbf{s}$, multiplied by a nonlinear transformation, either $\phi^{\top}(\mathbf{x}_*)$ or $\mathbf{k}^{\top}$, of the input to be predicted. The output of the GPR detector is the prediction of the bit transmitted by the *UoI*. The input to the GPR is a vector with n_Q consecutives samples from the channel:

$$\mathbf{y}_j = \left[\left(\mathbf{x}_j^{mud}\right)^\top, \left(\mathbf{x}_{j-1}^{mud}\right)^\top, \ldots, \left(\mathbf{x}_{j-n_Q+1}^{mud}\right)^\top \right]^\top, \tag{44}$$

where $\mathbf{x}_j$ are the n_S chips received at time step j in (7). If the codes of the other users are available, we could first project the received chips onto them as follows,

$$\mathbf{y}_j = \left[\left(\mathbf{x}_j^{mud}\right)^\top \mathbf{H}_S, \left(\mathbf{x}_{j-1}^{mud}\right)^\top \mathbf{H}_S, \ldots, \left(\mathbf{x}_{j-n_Q+1}^{mud}\right)^\top \mathbf{H}_S \right]^\top. \tag{45}$$

The GPR equalizer is trained with a set $D = \left\{\mathbf{y}_i, s_i\right\}_{i=1}^n$. For a new input $\mathbf{y}_*$, the *UoI* symbol is estimated as

$$\widehat{s_*}(l) = \text{sign}(\mu_{s_*}) = \text{sign}(\mathbf{k}^\top \mathbf{C}^{-1}\mathbf{s}), \tag{46}$$

where

$$\mathbf{k} = [k(\mathbf{y}_*, \mathbf{y}_1), \ldots, k(\mathbf{y}_*, \mathbf{y}_n)]^\top. \tag{47}$$

As mentioned earlier, the Gaussian processes framework can be extended for solving classification tasks. Gaussian process for classification (GPC) solution is non-analytical and we need to approximate its posterior distribution to make posterior probability predictions for the new samples and to train its hyperparameters. These approximations are computationally intensive and make GPC harder to train than GPR. Moreover, as detailed in (Williams & Rasmussen, 2006) and illustrated in Fig. 4 in the last section, in many cases GPR performs equally well to GPC, if we are only interested in minimizing the misclassification rate. Therefore, although GPC seems the natural tool for solving this task, we decided to use GPR because it is less computationally demanding and its misclassification rate is similar to that of GPC.

8.1 Experimental results

In our first experiment, we employ Gold spreading codes with 31 chips per user, because they have favorable cross correlation properties that limit the interferences by other users and their delayed replicas (Cover & Thomas, 1991). We report results for systems operating with 3 and 16 users and we assume the user of interest is 50 dB bellow the other users. This is a fairly standard scenario when one of the users is close to the base station and it is assigned little power. We use the received 31 chips to detect each transmitted symbol. The channel model is the one described in (41) and (42) in Section 0.

We show the bit error rate (BER) versus the *snr* for 16 users in Fig. 8 with 512 training symbols. The effect of the 16 users can be approximated by white noise. Therefore, the optimal solution will be closed to a linear detector. All the receivers perform similarly well except for the nonlinear SVM. The training sequence for the nonlinear SVM with 16 users is not long enough, and hence the nonlinear SVM is unable to detect the transmitted bits and reports chance-level performances. The GPR solution is quite similar to the MMSE solution, because it almost shuts down its nonlinear part in (38). As we show in Section 0, the GPR with a linear kernel and the linear MMSE provide equivalent solutions in this case. This result is quite relevant, as we do not tell the GPR receiver that the solution is linear. GPR finds it out on its own, when it maximizes the hyperparameters' likelihood. The GPC also cancels its nonlinear part and it is able to avoid overfitting. The linear SVM detector presents the worse performance among the proposed methods that converge in both cases, although it is barely noticeable in the figures.

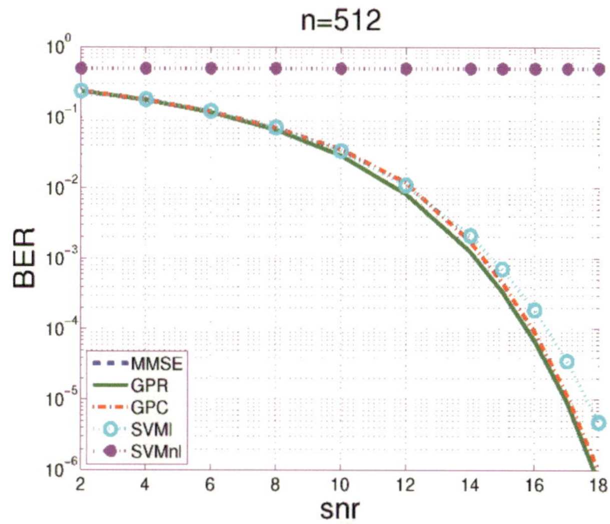

Fig. 8. We report the BER versus the *snr* for a multiuser detector with 16 users. The dashed line represents the linear MMSE receiver, the solid line the GPR, the dash-dotted line the GPC, the dotted line with circles the linear SVM, and the dotted line with bullets the nonlinear SVM.

The optimal solution is almost linear and all the proposed procedures perform equally well, once the training sequence is long enough. The training sequence of 512 symbols is not long enough for the nonlinear SVM with 16 users and it is unable to correctly tune its multiuser detector. If we had increased the training sequence to several thousand samples, the nonlinear SVM would converge and it would provide a solution close to the other algorithms. The differences in BER are not significant to decide which method is best, but the differences in training time might lead us to choose one over the others, as we discuss in short.

We report the BER as a function of the training examples for 16 users and $snr = 16\,\text{dB}$ in Fig. 9. These results are more meaningful than the BER versus *snr* reported in Fig. 8, because there is a significant disparity between the performances of the different methods.

The GPR receiver presents the fastest learning curve closely followed by the linear MMSE and linear SVM solutions. We conjecture this is due to the GPR optimal training of its hyperparameter, because it is able to adjust them for each training sequence, while the linear SVM uses a constant setting, which might be good for a long training sequence, but not as good for shorter ones.

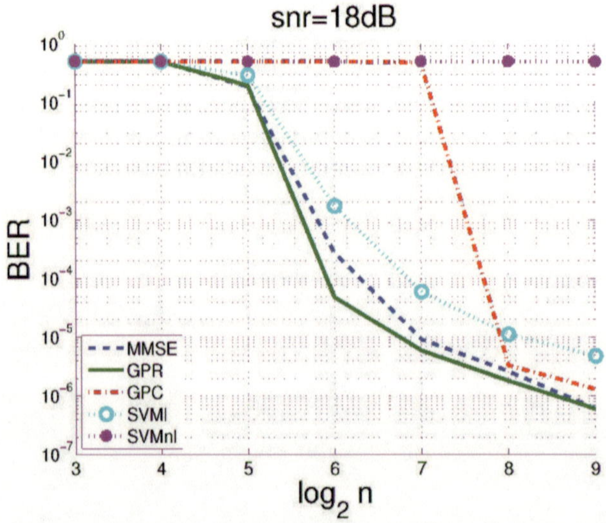

Fig. 9. We report the BER versus the length of the training sequence for a multiuser detector with 16 users and $snr = 16$ dB. The dashed line represents the linear MMSE receiver, the solid line the GPR, the dash-dotted line the GPC, the dotted line with circles the linear SVM, and the dotted line with bullets the nonlinear SVM.

We repeat Experiment 2 in (Chen et al, 2001), in which 3 users transmit with an orthogonal 8-dimension spreading code. The solution for user 2 is highly nonlinear and we report the BER versus the snr in Fig. 10. The linear SVM and MMSE clearly underperform compared to the nonlinear methods. The GPR and nonlinear SVM achieve almost identical results. The GPC for low snr mimics the results of the nonlinear methods ($snr < 14$ dB) and for high snr, it reports the same results as the linear receivers ($snr > 16$ dB). This behavior is explained by the length and diversity of the training sequence. If the training sequence is long enough, the GPC receiver provides the best nonlinear decision function, otherwise it reports the best linear decision function to avoid overfitting. For low snr, 512 symbols are long enough for the GPC to achieve the best nonlinear decision function and the GPC receiver trains its hyperparameters to obtain this nonlinear detector. For high snr, there is not enough diversity in a training sequence with 512 symbols and it is only able to report the best linear detector, as it shuts down its nonlinear part to avoid overfitting.
With these two experiments, we are able to show that the GPR with the covariance function in (38) is able to obtain the best results in both scenarios. If the solution is linear, it performs as the linear MMSE, needing shorter-training sequences. If the solution is nonlinear, the GPR receiver builds a nonlinear detector that significantly improves the MMSE solution.

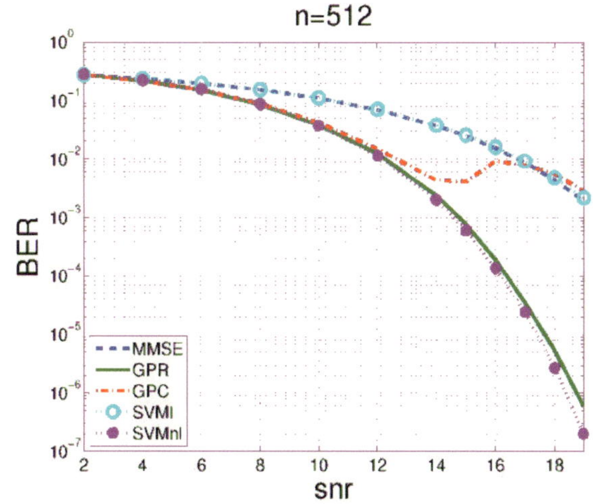

Fig. 10. We report the BER versus *snr* for a multiuser detector with 3 users and a training sequence of 512 symbols. The dashed line represents the linear MMSE receiver, the solid line the GPR, the dash-dotted line the GPC, the dotted line with circles the linear SVM and the dotted line with bullets the nonlinear SVM. The linear SVM is on top of the linear MMSE line.

9. Conclusions

We have proposed GPR and GPC for designing digital communication receivers. GPR follows a wide range of machine learning tools that have been successfully applied to the design of digital communication receivers. GPR can be viewed as a nonlinear MMSE. MMSE is the standard criterion used for designing digital communication receivers, as it trades off inverting the channel and not amplifying the noise. GPR solution is analytical given the nonlinear function, while most machine-learning methods need to perform an optimization problem to achieve their solution. On the other hand, GPC provides extra information for each one of its decisions, i.e. the posterior probability of being in the correct class. This information can be used by the channel decoder to significantly reduce the BER for low signal to noise ratio. This characteristic is not shared by the other nonlinear machine learning tools, as they can only provide hard decisions as outputs. We have shown that, as the number of samples increases, the predicted probabilities tend to the true posterior probabilities. To highlight the advantages of GPs as digital communications receivers we compare their performances to that of SVM. SVM provides solutions as good as GPR does, but it needs more training samples. These tools have been compared in two typical scenarios in digital communications: equalization and multiuser detection. In both experiments GPs exhibit an outstanding behavior.

10. Acknowledgements

This work was partially funded by Spanish government (Ministerio de Educación y Ciencia TEC2006-13514-C02-{01,02}/TCM, Consolider-Ingenio 2010 CSD2008-00010) and the

European Union (FEDER). Fernando Pérez-Cruz is supported by Marie Curie Fellowship 040883-AI-COM

11. References

Arenas-García, J., Martínez-Ramón, M., Navia-Vázquez, A. & Figueiras-Vidal, A. (2006). Plant identification via adaptive combination of transversal filters, *Signal Processing*, Vol. 86, No. 9, pp. 2430–2438. ISSN 01651684.

Bishop, C. M. (1995). *Neural Networks for Pattern Recognition*, Clarendon Press, Oxford, UK. ISBN 0198538642.

Caffery, J. & Stuber, G.L. (2000). Nonlinear multiuser parameter estimation and tracking in CDMA systems, *IEEE Transactions on Communications*, Vol. 48, No. 12, pp. 2053-2063. ISSN 00906778.

Chang, P. R. & Wang, B. C. (1995). Adaptive decision feedback equalization for digital satellite channels using multilayer neural networks, *IEEE Journal on Selected Areas in Communications*, Vol. 13, No. 2, pp. 316–324. ISSN 07338716.

Chen, S., Gibson, G. J, Cowan C. N. & Grant P.M. (1991). Reconstruction of binary signals using an adaptive radial basis-function equalizer, *Signal Processing*, Vol. 22, No. 1, pp.77–93. ISSN 01651684.

Chen, S., Samingan, A. K. & Hanzo, L. (2001). Support vector machine multiuser receiver for DS-CDMA signals in multipath channels, *IEEE Transactions on Neural Networks*, Vol. 12, No. 3, pp. 604–611. ISSN: 10459227.

Cid-Sueiro, J., Artés-Rodríguez, A. & Figueiras-Vidal, A. (1994). Recurrent radial basis function networks for optimal symbol by-symbol equalization, *Signal Processing*, Vol. 40, No. 1, pp. 53–63. ISSN 01651684.

Cover, T. M. & Thomas, J. A. (1991). *Elements of Information Theory*, John Wiley & Sons. New York. USA. ISBN 0471241954.

Cruickshank, D. (1996). Radial basis function receivers for DS-CDMA, *Electronics Letters*, Vol. 32, No. 3, pp. 188–190. ISSN 00135194.

Gibson, G. J., Siu S. & Cowan C. N. (1991). The application of nonlinear structures to the reconstruction of binary signals, *IEEE Transactions on Signal Processing*, Vol. 39, No. 8, pp. 1877–1884. ISSN: 1053587X.

González-Serrano, F. J., Murillo-Fuentes, J. J. & Artés-Rodríguez, A. (2001). GCMAC-Based predistortion for digital modulations, *IEEE Transactions on Communications*, Vol. 49, No. 9, pp. 1679–1689, 2001. ISSN 0090-6778.

González-Serrano, F. J., Pérez-Cruz, F. & Artés-Rodríguez, A. (1998). Reduced-complexity equalizer for nonlinear channels, *Electronics Letters*, Vol. 34, No. 9, pp. 856–858. ISSN 00135194.

Haykin, S. (1999). *Neural Networks: A Comprehensive Foundation*, Prentice-Hall, Upper Saddle River, NJ, USA, 2nd edition. ISBN 0132733501.

Kay, S. M. (1993). *Fundamentals of Statistical Signal Processing: Estimation Theory*. Prentice Hall. pp. 344-350. ISBN 0130422681.

Kimeldorf, G. S. & Wahba, G. (1971). Some results in Tchebycheffian
spline functions, *Journal of Mathematical Analysis and Applications*, Vol. 33, No. 1, pp. 8295. ISSN 0022247X.

Kohonen, T., Raivio, K., Simula, O., Venta, O. & Henriksson, J. (1990). Combining linear equalization and self-organizing adaptation in dynamic discrete-signal detection, *Proceedings of the International Joint Conference on Neural Networks (IJCNN '90)*, Vol.1, pp. 223–228, San Diego, California, USA, June.

Kuss, M. & Rasmussen, C. E. (2005). Assessing approximate inference for binary Gaussian process classification, *The Journal of Machine Learning Research*, Vol. 6, pp. 1679-1704. ISSN 15337928.

MacKay, D. J. (2003). *Information Theory, Inference and Learning Algorithms*, Cambridge University Press, Cambridge, UK. ISBN 0521642981.

Martínez-Ramón, M., Rojo-Álvarez, J. L., Camps-Valls, G. & Christodoulou, C. G. (2007). Kernel antenna array processing, *IEEE Transactions on Antennas and Propagation*, Vol. 55, No. 3, pp. 642-650. ISSN 0018926X.

Mitchinson, B. & Harrison, R. F. (2002). Digital communications channel equalization using the Kernel Adaline, *IEEE Transactions on Communications*, Vol. 50, No. 4, pp. 571-576. ISSN 00906778.

Mitra, U. & Poor, H. V. (1994). Neural network techniques for adaptive multiuser demodulation, *IEEE Journal Selected Areas on Communications*, Vol. 12, pp. 1460 1470. ISSN 07338716.

Murillo-Fuentes, J. J. & Pérez-Cruz, F. (2009). Gaussian process regressors for multiuser detection in DS-CDMA systems. *IEEE Transactions on communications*. Vol 47, No 7.

O'Hagan, A. & Kingman, J. F. (1978). Curve fitting and optimal design for prediction, *Journal of the Royal Statistical Society. Series B*, Vol. 40, No. 1. ISSN 1369-7412.

Pérez-Cruz, F., Navia-Vázquez, A., Alarcón-Diana, P. & Artés-Rodríguez, A. (2001). SVC based equalizer for burst TDMA transmissions, *Signal Processing*, Vol. 81, No. 8, pp. 1681–1693. ISSN 01651684.

Pérez-Cruz, F. & Bousquet, O. (2004). Kernel methods and their potential use in signal processing, *IEEE Signal Processing Magazine*, Vol. 21, No. 3, pp. 57–65. ISSN 10535888.

Pérez-Cruz, F., Martínez-Olmos, P. & Murillo-Fuentes, J.J. (2007). Accurate posterior probability estimates for channel equalization using Gaussian processes for classification, *Proceedings of the IEEE 8th Workshop on Signal Processing Advances in Wireless Communications (SPAWC'07)*, pp. 1-5, Helsinki, Finland, June.

Pérez-Cruz, F. & Murillo-Fuentes, J. J. (2008). Digital communication receivers using Gaussian processes for machine learning, *EURASIP Journal on Advances in Signal Processing*, Vol. 2008. ISSN 16876172.

Pérez-Cruz, F., Murillo-Fuentes, J. J. & Caro, S. (2008). Nonlinear channel equalization with Gaussian processes for regression, *IEEE Transactions on Signal Processing*, Vol. 56, No. 10, pp. 5283-5286, October. ISSN 1053587X.

Pham, D.S., Zoubir, A.M., Brcic, R.F. & Yee Hong Leung. (2007). A nonlinear *M*-estimation approach to robust asynchronous multiuser detection in non-Gaussian noise, *IEEE Transactions on Signal Processing*, Vol. 55, No. 5., pp. 1624-1633. ISSN 1053587X.

Platt, J.C. (2000). Probabilities for SV machines, In: *Advances in Large Margin Classifiers*, M.I.T. Press.. ISBN 0262194481.

Proakis, J.G. & Salehi, M. (2002), *Communication Systems Engineering*, 2nd ed., New York: Prentice Hall. ISBN 0130617938.

Quiñonero-Candela, J. & Rasmussen, C. E. (2005). A unifying view of sparse approximate Gaussian process regression, *The Journal of Machine Learning Research*, Vol. 6, No. 2, pp. 1939–1960. ISSN 1532-4435.

Sánchez-Fernández, M., Prado-Cumplido, M., Arenas-García, J. & Pérez-Cruz, F. (2004). SVM multiregression for nonlinear channel estimation in multiple-input multiple-output systems, *IEEE Transactions on Signal Processing*, Vol. 52, No. 8, pp. 2298-2307. ISSN 1053587X.

Scharf, L. L (1990). *Statistical Signal Processing: Detection, Estimation, and Time Series Analysis*, Addison-Wesley, New York, NY, USA. ISBN 0201190389.

Schölkopf, B. & Smola, A. (2001). *Learning with Kernels*, MIT Press, Cambridge, Mass, USA. ISBN 0262194759.

Tanner, R. & Cruickshank, D. (1997). Volterra based receivers for DS-CDMA, *Proceedings of the 8th IEEE International Symposium on Personal, Indoor and Mobile Radio Communications (PIMRC'97)*, Vol. 3, pp. 1166–1170, Helsinki, Finland, September.

Vapnik, V. (1998). *Statistical Learning Theory*, John Wiley & Sons, New York, NY, USA. ISBN 0471030031.

Verdú, S. (1998). *Multiuser detection*. Cambrigde University Press. ISBN 0521593735.

Williams, C. K. & Rasmussen, C. E. (1996). Gaussian processes for regression, In: *Advances in Neural Information Processing Systems*, pp. 514–520, MIT Press, Cambridge, ISBN 9780262201070.

Williams, C. K. & Barber, D. (1998). Bayesian classification with Gaussian processes, *IEEE Transactions on Pattern Analysis and Machine Intelligence*, Vol. 20, No. 12, pp. 1342-1351. ISSN 01628828.

Williams, C. K. (1999). Prediction with Gaussian process: from linear regression to linear prediction and beyond, In: *Learning in Graphical Models*, pp. 599–621, MIT Press, Cambridge, Mass, USA. ISBN 026260032-3.

Williams, C. K. & Rasmussen, C. E. (2006). *Gaussian processes for Machine Learning*, MIT Press, Cambridge, ISBN 026218253X.

Adaptive Weighted Morphology Detection Algorithm of Plane Object in Docking Guidance System

Guo Yan-Ying1, Yang Guo-Qing1 and Jiang Li-Hui 2
1 Nanjing University of Aeronautics and Astronautics
2 Tianjin key lab for advanced signal processing Civil Aviation University of China
China

1. Introduction

Aerodrome docking auto-guidance system is no-manual work guidance plane from taxiway to gate position and nicety anchor process. Aerodrome docking auto-guidance system can ensure plane safe nice anchor, and make corridor bridge meet plane. At present there are no departments of docking auto-guidance system in China. Based on vision detect method of aerodrome docking auto-guidance system refer to literatures a flat lot. In the paper, importantly study image pretreatment algorithm based on vision detection of aerodrome docking auto-guidance system, process and so on. Docking system chart is figure 1.

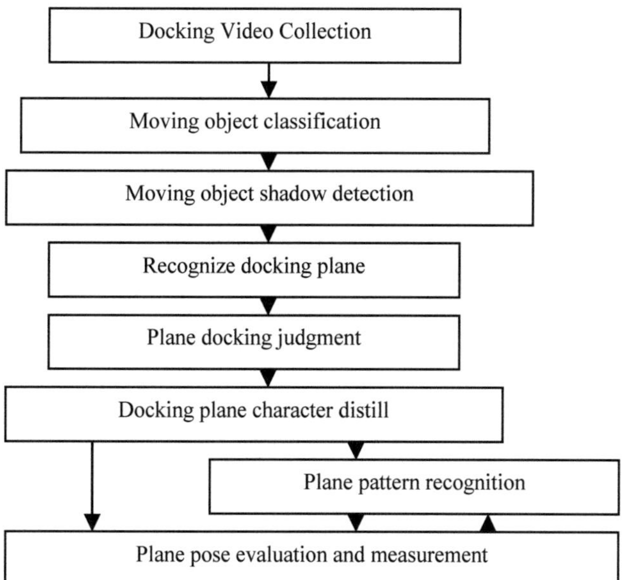

Fig. 1. System overview of visual docking guidance system

The edge of image embodies a great deal of information, is the important attribute to obtain image features during image identification. Edge detection could draw the outline of target object to reach object identification. Essentially, image edge is the discontinuous reflection of part of image; it indicates one ending of one field and starting of another field. Effect of edge detection influenced directly accomplishment of after work (Lima, P.; Bonarini, A. & Mataric, M. (2004)). Edges can also be defined as where gradient of image intensity function reaches its local maximum. In other words, edge points are points in the image where pixel brightness changes drastically. Typically, edge points are associated with the boundaries of objects in the image and edge detection can also be used for region segmentation and feature extraction. Edge detection methods can be classified into directional and non-directional or gradient-based operators (M. Pesaresi and J. A. Benediktsson2001, Heath M., Sarkar S., Sanocki T., and Bowyer K 1998, Ziou D. and Tabbone S 1997). Directional operators use two masks and two convolutions. While non-directional use single mask and convolution but they are sensitive to noise due to gradient nature of the operators. In near year, classical popular gradient-based edge detection algorithms were experimented on the binary images There is many methods of edge detection, traditional method adopt edge detection operator to solve two dimensional real function, then selecting proper threshold to extract edge, these classical edge detection operator solution mainly is Roberts, Prewitt, Sobel and Canny operator, etc. When image is in the condition without noise interruption, these operators could provide perfect edge (M. K. Kundu, B. B. Chaudhuri and D. Dutta Majumder, 1991). But, actually noise existed and presented abrupt change between noise and edge, and high frequency information in frequency field. So it is difficult for edge detection. Under such circumstance, classical operator couldn't extract edge well, firstly filter the noise, and then detect edge. This could not only bring extra calculation amount, but wipe off the faint edge (W. K. Pratt, 1991). Mathematical morphology (MM) base on group algorithm, characteristic of non-linearity, and it not only presents image group features to well detect image edge, but also satisfies real-time request. What's more? Based on edge detection, through changing the shape and size of structure element extract image edge, in order to overcome the influence of noise (SONG J, DELPE J 1990,(50)). MM has achieved the status of a powerful tool in the design of edge detection and nonlinear filters for signal/image processing (Lima, P.; Bonarini, A. & Mataric, M. 2004, M. Pesaresi and J. A. Benediktsson2001, Heath M., Sarkar S., Sanocki T., and Bowyer K 1998) .

In this paper, we present a new edge detection algorithm based on adaptive weighted morphological operations. The primary objective of the adaptive weighted morphological grads operations in the proposed algorithm is to generate the high connectively edge features of the image. Then apply edge to select structure element, If the edge direction exists, a big weight factor is put; if doesn't exist, a small weight factor is put. Thus we can achieve an intensified edge detector.

This paper is organized as follows: Section 2 introduces the weighted morphological operations. And proposes adaptive weighted morphological edge detection used in the proposed algorithm. Section3 presents comprehensive comparison results between the proposed algorithms with other existing methods. The conclusions and discussions are provided in the last section.

2. Adaptive Weighted Morphological Algorithm

2.1 Basic Theory of Mathematical Morphology and Conventional Edge Conventional Edge Detection Operators

Mathematical Morphology is a framework based exclusively on set theory, which has found great success and applicability in digital image processing. The mathematical foundation of mathematical morphology comes from Minkowsy's set operations, through which its two basic operators are defined: dilation and erosion. Dilation can be stated in a simplified, intuitionist manner, as adding pixels to an image, or enlarging it. On the other hand, erosion can be stated in a similar manner as taking pixels away from an image, or shrinking it. The combination and interaction of these two operators, dilation and erosion, give rise to other two operations of singular importance in mathematical morphology: opening and closing. On one hand, opening consists of applying an erosion followed by a dilation to a set, with the same structuring element. As a result, small holes are enlarged. On the other hand, closing consists on applying a dilation followed by an erosion to a set, with the same structuring element. As a result, small holes are closed.

The objective of the present paper is to state mathematical morphology basic operations in terms of cellular automata, with the goal of enlightening the framework of mathematical morphology with the theory of cellular automata. Mathematical Morphology (MM) is a new science based on strict math theory basis , taking set theory as basis ,analyzing and understanding the digital image, which is also a good tool of geometry morphologic analysis and description; having be a new theory and method under digital image management area, producing great influence on digital image management theory and technology. In digital image, edge contains a great deal of valuable information, and it can reflect character of object, so it has an important intention about image analysis and image filtering. Math Morphology is the tool for analyzing the image based on structure element. Basic ideas are to measure and extract corresponding shape using structure element which have specific figuration to reach the image of analyzing and identification.

There are 4 basic algorithms in MM: dilation, erosion, opening and closing algorithm, they are of own characteristic in binary image and grey-scale image. These basic algorithms also induce and combine various math morphological algorithms (SONG J, DELPE J 1990).

A. Dilation and Erosion

Dilation and erosion operations are fundamental to morphological processing. In fact, many of the morphological algorithms are based on these two primitive operations.

1) Dilation

With A and B as sets in Z^2, the dilation of A by B, denoted $A \oplus B$, is defined as

$$A \oplus B = \left\{ z \mid \left(\hat{B} \right)_z \bigcap A \neq \varnothing \right\} \tag{1}$$

Equation (1) is based on obtaining the reflection of B about its origin and shifting this reflection by z, such that $\hat{B}$ and A overlap by at least one element. Based on this interpretation, equation (1) may be rewritten as

$$A \oplus B = \left\{ z \mid \left[\left(\hat{B} \right)_z \bigcap A \right] \subseteq A \right\} \tag{2}$$

Set B is commonly referred to as the structuring element in dilation, as well as below morphological operations.
2) Erosion

For sets A and B in the Z^2 , the erosion of A by B, denoted $A \otimes B$, is defined as

$$A \otimes B = \left\{ z \mid \left(B \right)_z \subseteq A \right\} \tag{3}$$

In a word, the equation (3) indicates that the erosion of A by B is the set of all points z such that B, translated by z , is contained in A.
Dilation and erosion are duals of each other with respect to set complementation and reflection. That is,

$$\left(A \otimes B \right)^c = A^c \oplus \hat{B} \tag{4}$$

B. Opening and Closing
As can be seen from the equation (1) and (3), dilation expands an image and erosion shrinks it. Two other important morphological operations are introduced below: opening and closing. Opening generally smoothes the contour of an object, breaks narrow isthmuses, and eliminates thin protrusion. Closing also tends to smooth sections of contours but, as opposed to opening, it generally fuses narrow breaks and long thin gulfs, eliminates small holes, and fills gaps in the contour.

The opening of the set A by structuring element B, denoted $A \circ B$, is defined as

$$A \circ B = \left(A \otimes B \right) \oplus B \tag{5}$$

Thus, the opening by B is the erosion of A by B, followed by dilation of the result by B.
Similarly, the closing of set A by structuring element B, denoted $A \bullet B$, is defined as

$$A \bullet B = \left(A \oplus B \right) \otimes B \tag{6}$$

Which, in words, says that the closing of by B is simply the dilation of A by B, followed by the erosion of the result by B.
Use the basic operations of dilation, erosion, opening and closing to develop several basic gray-scale morphological algorithms, especially, for edge extraction via the morphological operations. Throughout the discussions that follow, digital image functions of the form $f(x, y)$ and $b(x, y)$ are dealt with, where $f(x, y)$ is the input image and $b(x, y)$ is a

structuring element, itself a sub-image function. The assumption is that these functions that assign a gray-level value which is a real number from the set of real numbers.

A. Gray-Scale Dilation

Gray-scale dilation of f by b, denoted $f \oplus b$, is defined as

$$(f \oplus b)(s,t) = \max\left\{f(s-x,t-y)+b(x,y) \mid (s-x),(t-y) \in D_f;(x,y) \in D_b\right\} \quad (7)$$

Where D_f and D_b are the domains of f and b, respectively. f and b are functions rather than sets.

The condition that $(s-x)$ and $(t-y)$ have to be in the domain of f, and x and y have to be in the domain of b, is analogous to the condition in the binary definition of dilation, where the two sets have to overlap by at least one element.

B. Gray-scale Erosion

Gray-scale erosion, denoted $f \otimes b$, is defined as

$$(f \otimes b)(s,t) = \min\left\{f(s+x,t+y)-b(x,y) \mid (s+x),(t+y) \in D_f;(x,y) \in D_b\right\} \quad (8)$$

Where D_f and D_b are the domains of f and b, respectively. The condition that $(s+x)$ and $(t+y)$ have to be in the domain of f, and x and y have to be in the domain of b, is analogous to the condition in the binary definition of erosion, where the structuring element has to be completely contained by the set being eroded.

C. Gray-scale Opening and Closing

The expressions for opening closing of gray-scale images have the same form as their binary counterparts. The opening of image f by sub-image (structuring element) b, denoted $f \circ b$, is

$$f \circ b = (f \otimes b) \oplus b \quad (9)$$

Opening is the erosion of f by b, followed by a dilation of the result by b.

Similarly, the closing of f by b, denoted $f \bullet b$, is

$$f \bullet b = (f \oplus b) \otimes b \quad (10)$$

The opening and closing for gray-scale images are duals with respect to complementation and reflection. That is,

$$\left(f \bullet b\right)^c = f^c \circ \hat{b} \tag{11}$$

Because $f^c = -f\left(x, y\right)$, equation (11) can be written also as

$$-\left(f \cdot b\right)^c = \left(-f \circ \hat{b}\right) \tag{12}$$

Opening and closing of images have a simple geometric interpretation. Suppose that we view an image function $f(x, y)$ in 3-D perspective, with x and y axes being the usual spatial coordinates and the third axis being gray-level values. In this representation, the image appears as a discrete surface whose value at any point (x, y) is the value of f at those coordinates. Suppose that we open f by a spherical structuring element b, viewing this element as a "rolling ball". Then the mechanics of opening f by b may be interpreted geometrically as the process of pushing the ball against the underside of the surface, while at the same time rolling it so that the entire underside of the surface of the highest points reached by any part of the sphere as it slides over the entire undersurface of f.

C. Conventional Edge Detection Operators in Edge Detection

1) Robert Operator

Robert operator is an easy edge detection operator using local difference operator to detect edge. It is an effective operator for the image with steep low noise. Robert operator can be expressed as the form of two as shown in Fig. 2. Two masks are used to calculate $\nabla_x f$ and $\nabla_y f$ respectively.

1	0
0	-1

0	1
-1	0

Fig.2. Two masks of Robert operator in x and y direction.

2) Sobel Operator

Sobel operator is used to detect edge in the form of filter operator. Sobel operator can be expressed as the form of two masks as shown in Fig. 3. They are used to calculate the convolution of each pixel. The first mask has strong effect on vertical edge. The second mask has strong effect on horizontal edge. The max values of two convolutions are regarded as the output points. The result is an edge magnitude image.

-1	0	1		1	2	1
-2	0	2		0	0	0
-1	0	1		-1	-2	-1

Fig.3. Two masks of Sobel operator in x and y direction.

3) Prewitt Operator

The same as Sobel operator each pixel in the image is calculated the convolution by using two masks shown in Fig. 4 and gain the max values in different directions. The result is also an edge magnitude image.

-1	0	1		1	1	1
-1	0	1		0	0	0
-1	0	1		-1	-1	-1

Fig.4. Two masks of Prewitt operator in x and y direction.

In the process of digital image management, difference gradient operator often combines with threshold technique for image edge detection. In the same condition of difference gradient operator, morphological gradient operator can also combine with threshold for using to complete edge detection. In the process of which, if gradient value of one place is large, then shows that change was rapid at this point of image, so edge is likely to pass through. These gradients can be give out as digital difference format. Three morphological gradient operators were defined.

2.2 Weighted Morphological Operators

We define weighted erosion (WER) and dilation (WDI) as (1) (2).

$$WER(k,l) = \min_{u,v}\{X(k+u,l+v)/B(u,v)\} \tag{13}$$

$$WER(k,l) = \min_{u,v}\{X(k+u,l+v)/B(u,v)\} \tag{14}$$

There is X original image, B structuring element. The other operators, such as weighted opening (WOP) and closing (WCL), are simply cascades of weighted erosion and dilation which can be described as $WOP(X) = WDI(WER(X))$ and $WCL(X) = WER(WDI(X))$, respectively. Weighted open-closing (WOPCL) and close-opening (WCLOP) are denoted as $WOPCL(X) = WCL(WOP(X))$ and $WCLOP(X) = WOP(WCL(X))$, respectively. The structuring element B has a normalized weight factor and its elements are calculated such that the edge directional point's weight is 1 and the farthest point's weight is assigned a weight factor $\omega > 1$, leading to an emphasis on the effect of the edge directional point and a reduction of the effect of the neighborhood points. The rest of the weights are calculated based on an increment $\Delta\omega = (\omega - 1)/d$, where d is the distance between the edge directional point and the farthest point from the edge directional point. In the vertical and horizontal directions, the weight decrease by $\Delta\omega$, each step starting from the edge directional point. For example, for an SE of size 3×3 with its edge direction at the horizontal direction, if $\omega_1 = 3$, the SE will look like B_1, where $\Delta\omega = 2$, and for $\omega_2 = 3$, for the same edge direction point (underlined) at the oblique 45 angle, it will change to B_2,where $\Delta\omega = 1$.

$$B_1 = \begin{bmatrix} -1 & -1 & -1 \\ \underline{1} & \underline{1} & \underline{1} \\ -1 & -1 & -1 \end{bmatrix} \qquad B_2 = \begin{bmatrix} \underline{1} & 0 & -1 \\ 0 & \underline{1} & 0 \\ -1 & 0 & \underline{1} \end{bmatrix}$$

2.3 Adaptive Weighted Morphological Edge Detection

In mathematical morphological operations, there are always two sets involved: The shape of an image is determined by the values that the signal takes on. The shape information of the image is extracted by using a structuring element to operate on the image. So morphological image processing lies on morphological operations combination and structuring elements. In case operations' mode is selected, relevant result is ascertained by structuring elements. Yet designing effective structuring elements is a difficult task. In this paper, a new algorithm based adaptive weighted morphological operations is proposed, adaptive select structuring element to extract edge. Morphological grads operator $(X \oplus B) - (X \Theta B)$ can reinforce comparatively speculate grey transition region in images. So the operator is applied to detect edge in the paper and simultaneity adaptive select structuring element to extract edge.

The weighted morphological operators emphasize the edge direction points of window effect. Therefore an adaptive weighted morphological transformation algorithm is proposed. If pixel in the edge of window is edge, a big weight factor is put; if it doesn't exist, a small weight factor is put. Thus the probability of the edge detection is improved by morphological operations. So the first step is looking for edge in this paper. Circumrotate cover edge search method is adopted. SE apply rectangle cover figure.1, let it circumrotation goes around the center edge of SE. Then ensure position of grey variance maximum in rectangle cover, so we may employ variance as domanial estimate. By way of preferably extract edge of image, apply figure formal cover mode.

The structuring element is confirmed, then adopt adaptive weighted matrix to detect image edge. The structuring element B has a normalized weight factor and its elements are calculated such that the edge directional point's weight is 1 and the farthest point's weight is assigned a weight factor $0 < \omega < 1$, leading to an emphasis on the effect of the edge directional point and a reduction of the effect of the neighborhood points. The rest of the weights are calculated based on an increment $\Delta\omega = (1-\omega)/d$, where d is the distance between the edge directional point and the farthest point from the edge directional point. In the vertical and horizontal directions, the weight decrease by $\Delta\omega$, each step starting from the edge directional point.

Finally, whether or not edge pixels exist is judged by selecting weight SE can let non-edge pixels give small weight factor, yet let edge pixels give big weight factor. When the structuring elements is toned or restrained, edge is given prominence by morphological swell operation; edge is given weaken by morphological erode operation. So edge is much more extruded. At the same time some of the small detail edges are more distinct.

3. Simulation Experiments and Results

In this paper, the Lena image and Docking plane image are used in this experiment to process edge detection. Several popular gradient-based edge detection algorithms were experimented on the images, including Sobel, Laplacian of Gaussian and so on. The original image, as shown in Fig.5, Laplacian of Gaussian Edge Detector image, as shown in Fig.6, Sobel edge detector image, as shown in Fig.7, and the proposed method image, as shown in Fig.8.Edge detect image of docking plane is shown in Fig.9.
As can be seen from the images, Sobel edge detector is highly subjected to detection of false edges. This is probably due to the high threshold value used to detect weak edges in the Sobel detector. The most common error that occurred in four detectors (Sobel and LoG) tested are missing true edges. This is especially obvious in Laplacian of Gaussian detector probably due to the smoothing operation prior to edge detection. Laplacian of Gaussian detector also produces a small degree of disconnected edges especially in complex shapes such as map in Lena. The proposed method can not only primely extract detail edge, but also superbly preserve integer effect.
The proposed method is based on whether or not edge pixels exist is judged by selecting weight SE can let non-edge pixels give small weight factor, yet let edge pixels give big weight factor. The method can generate the high connectively edge features by other method effectively. Image edges are clear and false edges almost not exist. At the same time some of the small details edges are more distinct. Therefore, the proposed method is advantage of their algorithm comparing with other algorithm.

Fig. 5. Original image

Fig. 6. LOG edge image

Fig. 7. Sobel edge detection image

Fig. 8. the proposed method image

Fig.9. (a)

Fig.9. (b)

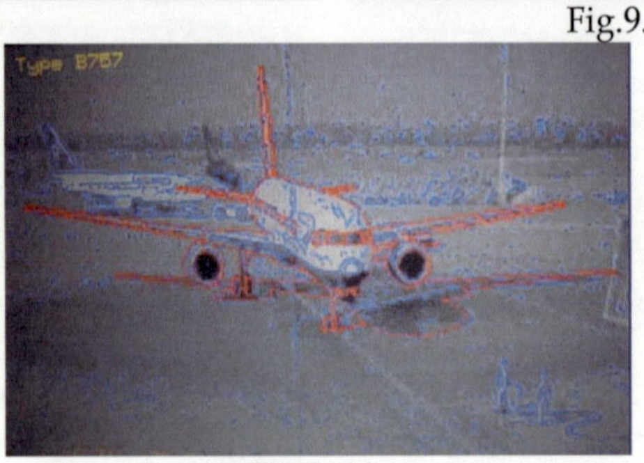

Fig.9. (c)

Fig. 9. (a) (b) (c) the proposed method images

4. Conclusion

In this paper, we presented an image segmentation algorithm based on adaptive weighted mathematical morphology edge detectors. The performance of the proposed algorithm has been demonstrated on the Lena image. The input of the proposed algorithm is a grey level image. The image was first processed by the mathematical morphological closing and dilation residue edge detector to enhance the edge features and sketch out the contour of the image, respectively. Then the adaptive weight SE operation was applied to the edge-extracted image to fuse edge gaps and hill up holds. Experimental results show it can not only primely extract detail edge, but also superbly preserve integer effect comparative to classical edge detection algorithm.

5. References

Lima, P.; Bonarini, A. & Mataric, M. (2004). *Name of Book in Italics,* Publisher, ISBN, Place of Publication.

M. K. Kundu, B. B. Chaudhuri and D. Dutta Majumder, A parallel Graytone thinning algorithm (PGTA), Pattern Recognition. 12, 491- 496 (1991).

W. K. Pratt, Digital Image Processing, 2nd edn. Wiley, New York (1991).

SONG J, DELPE J. The analysis of morphological filters with multiple structuring elements [J]. Comp V is Graphics 7& Image Proces, 1990,(50): 308~328.

Yao, Y. ACHARYA, R. and SRIHARI, S. "Image enhancement using mathematical morphology with adaptive structuring elements", nonlinear image processing, 1994, pp: 198-208(Vol. 2180 of SPIE Proceedings).

M. Pesaresi and J. A. Benediktsson, "A new approach for the morphological segmentation of high-resolution satellite imagery," IEEE Trans. Geosci. Remote Sensing, vol. 39, no. 2, pp. 309-320, 2001.

Heath M., Sarkar S., Sanocki T., and Bowyer K.: Comparison of Edge Detectors: A Methodology and Initial Study. Computer Vision and Image Understanding, 69(1): 38–54,1998.

Ziou D. and Tabbone S.: Edge Detection Techniques- An Overview, Technical report, No. 195, Dept Math & Informatique. Universit de Sherbrooke ,1997.

M. H. Sedaaghi and Q. H. Wu, "Weighted morphological filter," Electronics Letters Online No:198, 2002.

P. Soille and H. Talbot, "Directional morphological filtering," IEEE Trans.Pattern Anal. Machine Intell, vol. 23, no.11, pp. 1313-1329, 2001.

R.V. Babu, K.R. Ramakrishnan, and S.H. Srinivasan, "Video Object Segmentation: Compressed Domain Approach," IEEE Transactions on Circuits and Systems for Video Technology, vol. 14, no. 4, pp. 462-474 ,April, 2004.

13

Model-based Reinforcement Learning with Model Error and Its Application

Yoshiyuki Tajima and Takehisa Onisawa
University of Tsukuba,
Japan

1. Introduction

Many systems working with humans, e.g., humanoid robot, environmental intelligence, portable information assistant (Isozumi et al., 2003), have been studied in recent years. These systems need autonomous learning approaches for adaptation to various users' requests and environment changes. One of approaches to autonomous learning is Reinforcement Learning (RL) (S.Sutton et al., 1998). Study on shooting robot is an example of its early applications to practical problems (Asada et al., 1994). This study shows that RL can be used for autonomous systems. RL, however, cannot be applied easily to every practical problem since RL needs much time for learning. Therefore, other methods instead of RL are necessary for practical applications. One of the methods is Model-based RL, which has an inner model of environment and improves the learning efficiency by this model. That is, if an agent can get knowledge of a task and environment, then the agent uses it for learning. Model-based RL, however, has also some another problem when the inner model has some model error, because the agent learns some behavior by the inner model with the error. Although this problem is inevitable for Model-based RL, there are few studies on this problem.

This chapter gives careful consideration on the effects of the model error for Model-based RL and proposes a new approach, Model Error based Forward Planning Reinforcement Learning (ME-FPRL) (Tajima, et al., 2006) to solve the abovementioned problem. ME-FPRL controls learning based on errors of the inner model and can make the learning efficiency high. And ME-FPRL is applied to the pursuit of a target by a robot camera. The results of this application show that ME-FPRL learns more efficiently than usual RL and Model-based RL. Finally, conclusions and future work are shown.

2. Model-based reinforcement learning

This section introduces the framework of Model-based RL and describes one of Model-based RL algorithm as a preparation for ME-FRPL.

2.1 Framework of RL and model-based RL

Fig.1 shows the framework of RL. RL is based on Monte Carlo Methods and Dynamic Programming. An agent that learns with RL acquires some appropriate actions. In the RL method, it takes an action to environment. Environment changes by the action of the agent and gives reward to the agent according to the environment change. After the agent gets reward, the agent evaluates the action. Then, the agent observes the new state of environment and takes a new action to environment in order to get more reward. The agent learns the appropriate behavior by these interactions with environment and finally acquires the behavior giving maximum rewards.

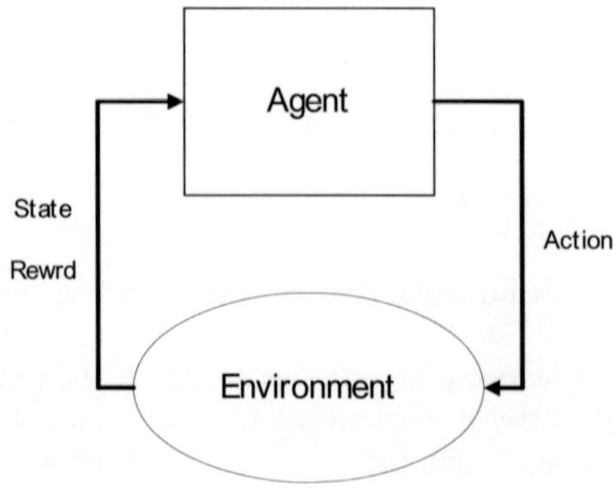

Fig.1. Framework of RL

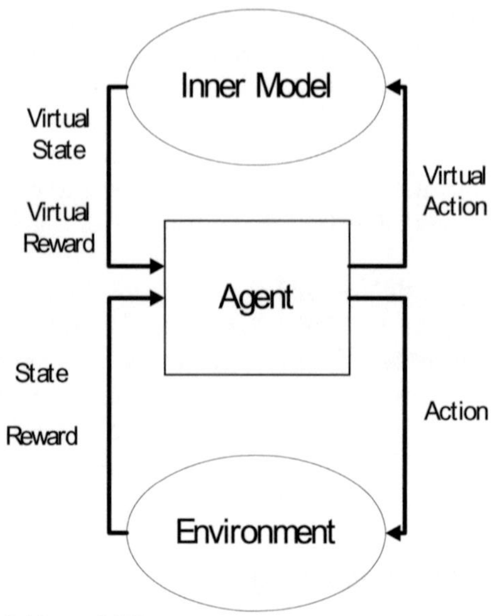

Fig. 2. Framework of Model-based RL

Fig.2 shows the framework of Model-based RL. An agent that uses the Model-based RL method has an inner model of environment and improves learning efficiency using the inner model. Model-based RL, however, has some problems about the error of the inner model.

The agent learns the behavior by both interactions with real environment and those with the inner model. The learning by the interaction with environment is called direct learning, and the learning by the interaction with the inner model is called indirect learning. If the agent's model is correct, that is, the same as environment, the agent can get a good performance by indirect learning because the model generates good experiences for the learning. On the other hand, if the inner model has some errors, or has some differences from real environment, the agent cannot learn the behavior correctly and the learning efficiency becomes low. It is found that Model-based RL has the problem on the error of the inner model.

2.2 Value function

In the RL algorithm, knowledge is expressed by a value function. The value function $V^{\pi}(s)$ is defined as Eq. (1), where $s \in S$ is the state of environment, $a \in A$ is the action taken by an agent, r is a reward given to an agent according to environment changes, t is the step of time, $\pi(s,a)$ is a policy and E_{π} is the expectation of a policy.

$$V^{\pi}(s) = E_{\pi}\{\sum_{k=0}^{\infty} \gamma^k r_{t+k+1} \mid s_t = s\} \tag{1}$$

An action-value function $Q^{\pi}(s,a)$ is defined as Eq. (2). The action-value function is often used for expressing knowledge because it is easy to find the best action on the current state. The best action a^* is obtained by Eq. (3). When $Q^{\pi}(s,a)$ is optimized and the agent continues taking a^* each state, the agent can reach goal efficiently.

$$Q^{\pi}(s,a) = E_{\pi}\{\sum_{k=0}^{\infty} \gamma^k r_{t+k+1} \mid s_t = s, a_t = a\} \tag{2}$$

$$a^* = \arg\max_{a} Q^{\pi}(s,a) \tag{3}$$

This action-value function is optimized by the interaction between the agent and environment with some RL algorithms, e.g., TD-learning, Q-learning, SARSA-learning (S.Sutton et al., 1998).

2.3 Model-based RL with trajectory sampling

To get the optimized value function efficiently, an agent can use an inner model with the Model-based RL algorithm. In the Model-based RL algorithm, it is important for the agent to generate some experiences using the inner model. These experiences using the inner model are called virtual experiences in this paper. One of the methods of generating the virtual experiences is the trajectory sampling method. In trajectory sampling, the virtual experiences are generated from the current state. In Model-based RL with trajectory sampling, at first, the agent chooses a next action virtually with the policy, e.g., $\varepsilon - greedy$, and it predicts a next state and a next reward from the current state and the chosen action using the inner model. Then, the agent updates the value function. Finally the agent sets the current state to the predicted state and sets current reward to predicted reward. The agent gets some experience by the continuation of this process. Fig.3 shows the concrete Model-based RL algorithm with trajectory sampling. In this algorithm $policy(s,Q)$ is the action on s and Q with some policy, $Model(s,a)$ is the inner model, N_p is the number of indirectory learning, N_l is the length of trajectory, $\alpha(0 \le \alpha \le 1)$ is a step size parameter, and $\gamma(0 \le \gamma \le 1)$ is a discount rate.

(0) Initialize all variables and $a \leftarrow policy(s,Q)$
Do forever:
(1) $s \leftarrow$ current state
(2) Execute action a, Observe resultant state s' and reward r
(3) $a' \leftarrow policy(s,Q)$
(4) $Q(s,a) \leftarrow Q(s,a) + \alpha[\hat{r} + \gamma Q(s',a') - Q(s,a)]$
(5) Update $Model(s,a)$
(6) Repeat N_p times:
(6-1) $\hat{s} \leftarrow s$, $\hat{a} \leftarrow a$
(6-2)Repeat N_l times:
(6-2-1) s', $r \leftarrow Model(s,a)$、 $\hat{s}' \leftarrow s'$, $\hat{r} \leftarrow r$
(6-2-2) $\hat{a}' \leftarrow policy(s,Q)$
(6-2-3) Push $(\hat{s},\hat{a},\hat{r},\hat{s}',\hat{a}')$ on stack
(6-2-4) $\hat{s} \leftarrow \hat{s}'$、 $\hat{a} \leftarrow \hat{a}'$
(6-3) while stack has some item:
(6-3-1) Pop $(\hat{s},\hat{a},\hat{r},\hat{s}',\hat{a}')$
(6-3-2) $Q(\hat{s},\hat{a}) \leftarrow Q(\hat{s},\hat{a}) + \alpha[\hat{r} + \gamma Q(\hat{s}',\hat{a}') - Q(\hat{s},\hat{a})]$
(7) $s \leftarrow s'$、 $a \leftarrow a'$
($\hat{s},\hat{a},\hat{r},\hat{s}',\hat{a}'$ are temporary variable)

Fig. 3. Algorithm of Model-based RL with Trajectory Sampling

3. Model error and MEFP-RL

This section describes the effect of some model error on Model-based RL, and introduces the ME-FRPL algorithm that can reduce its effect.

3.1 Effect of model error

An agent of Model-based RL can learn behavior efficiently when virtual experiences are equal to real experiences that are generated by environment. On the other hands, some virtual experiences different from real experiences give some bad effects to learning. These effects depend on the amount of the model error. Then, let us discuss the effect of the model on Model-based RL with trajectory sampling, where it is assumed that $N_p = 1$, $N_l = 1$.

The learning rate multiplied by TD-Error (S.Sutton et al., 1998) usually denotes the amount of learning with one update in RL. Then, the amount of learning with real experiences and that with virtual experiences are denoted as the amount of direct learning and as the amount of indirect learning, respectively in this paper. The amount of direct learning Δ_d is given by Eq. (4) and the amount of indirect learning Δ_i is given by Eq. (5), where α_d is a direct learning rate, α_i is an indirect learnign rate, and the sign of $\wedge$ shows the prediction by the inner model. Eq. (5) is rewritten to Eq. (6) because frist $\hat{s}$ is s and first $\hat{a}$ is a in Q (See (6-1) in Fig.3), and when $N_p = 1$ and $N_l = 1$. So, the amount of all learning $\Delta_d + \Delta_i$ is given by Eq.(7).

$$\Delta_d = \alpha_d[r + \gamma Q(s',a') - Q(s,a)] \tag{4}$$

$$\Delta_i = \alpha_i[r + \gamma Q(\hat{s}',\hat{a}') - Q(\hat{s},\hat{a})] \tag{5}$$

$$\Delta_i = \alpha_i[r + \gamma Q(\hat{s}',\hat{a}') - Q(s,a)] \tag{6}$$

$$\Delta_d + \Delta_i = \alpha_d[r + \gamma Q(s',a') - Q(s,a)] + \alpha_i[r + \gamma Q(\hat{s}',\hat{a}') - Q(s,a)] \tag{7}$$

Here, let the state dissimilarity $sds(s_a, s_b)$ between state s_a and state s_b be defined as the number of the necessary action for giving $s_a = s_b$. In this argument, if the agent can change s_a to s_b by K steps of actions, it is assumed that the agent can also change s_b to s_a with the same number (K step) of actions, though the former actions are usually different from the latter ones. Q is multiplied by γ each getting away from the goal when the agent does not gets some reward. If learning is almost convergent and the agent chooses only greedy action, $sds(s',\hat{s}')$ is constant. When s' is closer to a goal than $\hat{s}'$, then $Q(\hat{s}',\hat{a}') \geq Q(s',a')$. When $\hat{s}'$ is closer to a goal than s', then $Q(\hat{s}',\hat{a}') \leq Q(s',a')$. That is, $Q(\hat{s}',\hat{a}')$ is smaller than $\gamma^{-sds(s',\hat{s}')}Q(s',a')$ and $Q(\hat{s}',\hat{a}')$ is larger than $\gamma^{sds(s',\hat{s}')}Q(s',a')$. The relation between $Q(s',a')$ and $Q(\hat{s}',\hat{a}')$ is given by Eq. (8) using equilibrium parameter k.

$$Q(\hat{s}',\hat{a}') = \gamma^k Q(s',a') \quad (-sds(s',\hat{s}') \leq k \leq sds(s',\hat{s}')) \tag{8}$$

Now, applying Eq.(8) to Eq.(7), the amount of all learning $\Delta_d + \Delta_i$ is rewritten to Eq.(9).

$$\Delta_d + \Delta_i = (\alpha_d + \alpha_i)r - (\alpha_d + \alpha_i)Q(s,a) + (\alpha_d\gamma + \alpha_i\gamma^{k+1})Q(s',a') \tag{9}$$

When k becomes very small minus value, $\alpha_i\gamma^{k+1}$ becomes to very big value. If the learning is convergence , $\Delta_d > 0$, and $Q(s,a)$ is only effected by $Q(s',a')$, $\gamma Q(s',a') = Q(s,a)$. So $\Delta_d + \Delta_i$ is given by (10).

$$\Delta_d + \Delta_i = (\alpha_d + \alpha_i)r + \alpha_i Q(s,a)(\gamma^k - 1) \tag{10}$$

If the model does not have any error, $\Delta_d + \Delta_i = (\alpha_d + \alpha_i)r$. That is, some inner model error makes some effect exponentially with change of k.

3.2 Decreasing effect of model error

Let α_i be defined by $\alpha_d h\gamma^{|k|}$ $(0 \le h \le 1)$. Then, $\Delta_d + \Delta_i$ is given by (11). Let us discuss the effect of some inner model error.

$$\begin{aligned}\Delta_d + \Delta_i &= (\alpha_d + \alpha_d h\gamma^{|k|})r - (\alpha_d + \alpha_d h\gamma^{|k|})Q(s,a) + (\alpha_d\gamma + \alpha_d h\gamma^{|k|}\gamma^{k+1})Q(s',a') \\ &= \alpha_d\{(1+h\gamma^{|k|})r - (1+h\gamma^{|k|})Q(s,a) + (\gamma + h\gamma^{|k|}\gamma^{k+1})Q(s',a')\}\end{aligned} \tag{11}$$

1. When $k \ge 0$, $\Delta_d + \Delta_i$ is rewritten to Eq.(12).

$$\Delta_d + \Delta_i = \alpha_d\{(1+h\gamma^k)r - (1+h\gamma^k)Q(s,a) + (\gamma + h\gamma^k\gamma^{k+1})Q(s',a')\} \tag{12}$$

   In this case, if k becomes large, $\Delta_d + \Delta_i$ becomes Δ_d. That is, the effect of the learning is reduced.

2. When $k < 0$, $\Delta_d + \Delta_i$ is rewritten to Eq.(13).

$$\Delta_d + \Delta_i = \alpha_d\{(1+h\gamma^{-k})r - (1+h\gamma^{-k})Q(s,a) + (\gamma + h\gamma)Q(s',a')\} \tag{13}$$

   In this case, if k becomes small, $\Delta_d + \Delta_i$ becomes $\Delta_d + \alpha_d h\gamma Q(s',a')$. That is, the effect of the learning is $\alpha_d h\gamma Q(s',a')$.

From these results, the model error does not make effect exponentially when α_i is equal to $\alpha_d h\gamma^{|k|}$ because the effect of the learning is smaller than $\alpha_d h\gamma Q(s',a')$. However, k is an unknown value because the relation between $Q(s',a')$ and $Q(\hat{s}',\hat{a}')$ is changed every learning procedure and every update. On the other hand, $sds(s',\hat{s}')$ is estimated by the model error. Because the relation beteween k and $sds(s',\hat{s}')$ is given by Eq.(8)($|k| \le sds(s',\hat{s}')$), Eq.(14) is obatined.

$$h\gamma^{sds(s',\hat{s}')} \le h\gamma^{|k|} \tag{14}$$

Threfore, the model error does not make effect exponentially when α_i is $\alpha_d h\gamma^{sds(s',\hat{s}')}$ instead of $\alpha_d h\gamma^{|k|}$.

3.3 ME-FPRL

On the basis of these results discussed in 3.2, Model Error based Forward Planning Reinforcement Learning (ME-FPRL) algorithm is propsed. Fig.4 shows the algorithm of ME-FPRL, where $\alpha(0 \le \alpha \le 1)$ is a step size parameter, $\gamma(0 \le \gamma \le 1)$ is a discount rate and ρ is a tradeoff parameter. This algorithm is based on Model-Based RL with the Trajectory Sampling and controls the amount of indirect learning by estimating the current error. Therefore, the proposed learning algorithm has robustness against the error. *ModelAcy* is estimated at state dissimilarity that is obtained by the current state dissimilarity, where the current state dissimilarity is defined as the latest number of necessary actions. In this algorithm, when ρ is nearly equal to 1, the latest state dissimilarity $sds(s',\hat{s}')$ affects *ModelAcy* very well, and on the other hand when ρ is nearly equal to 0, the previous state dissimilarity affects *ModelAcy* very well. N_l, N_p and N_{plan} are parameter values of indirect learning. N_l is the length of the trajectory, N_p is the number of indirect learning, and h is the parameter to change ratio of indirect learning.

(0) Initialize all variable and $a \leftarrow policy(s,Q)$
Do forever:
(1) $s \leftarrow$ current state
(2) Execute action a, Observe resultant state s' and reward r
(3) $a' \leftarrow policy(s,Q)$
(4) $Q(s,a) \leftarrow Q(s,a) + \alpha[\hat{r} + \gamma Q(s',a') - Q(s,a)]$
(5) Update $Model(s,a)$
(6) $ModelAcy(s,a) \leftarrow (1-\rho)\cdot ModelAcy(s,a) + \rho\cdot\gamma^{sds(s',\hat{s}')}$
(7) Repeat N_p times
(7-1) $\hat{s} \leftarrow s$、 $\hat{a} \leftarrow a$、 $ComAcy \leftarrow 1$
(7-2)Repeat N_l times:
(7-2-1) s'、 $r \leftarrow Model(s,a)$、 $\hat{s}' \leftarrow s'$、 $\hat{r} \leftarrow r$
(7-2-2) $\hat{a}' \leftarrow policy(s,Q)$
(7-2-3) $ComAcy \leftarrow ComAcy \cdot ModelAcy(\hat{s},\hat{a})$
(7-2-3) Push $(\hat{s},\hat{a},\hat{r},\hat{s}',\hat{a}',ComAcy)$ on stack
(7-2-4) $\hat{s} \leftarrow \hat{s}'$、 $\hat{a} \leftarrow \hat{a}'$
(7-3) while stack has some item:
(7-3-1) Pop $(\hat{s},\hat{a},\hat{r},\hat{s}',\hat{a}',ComAcy)$
(7-3-2) $Q(\hat{s},\hat{a}) \leftarrow Q(\hat{s},\hat{a}) + ComAcy \cdot \alpha h / N_{plan}[\hat{r} + \gamma Q(\hat{s}',\hat{a}') - Q(\hat{s},\hat{a})]$
(8) $s \leftarrow s'$、 $a \leftarrow a'$
($\hat{s},\hat{a},\hat{r},\hat{s}',\hat{a}',ComAcy$ are temporary variable)

Fig. 4. Algorithm of ME-FPRL

4. Application to pursuing target task

In this section, at first, ME-FPRL is extended to a liner method for the continuous state space. Then, ME-FPRL is applied to pursuing target task and the efficiency of ME-FPRL is shown.

4.1 Continuous state spaces

In a real world, some tasks such as the control of robots are very complex because the state space is continuous and very large. Therefore, an agent needs much time to learn some behaviors on the continuous state space. This problem is known as *curse of dimensionality* (S.Sutton et al., 1998). To deal with this problem, there is a method to convert the original state space into the feature space with enough size to be able to solve the problem. This converting method is called *function approximation* (S.Sutton et al., 1998). One of function approximation methods is the liner method. In the liner method, the action-value function Q is defined by Eq. (15).

$$Q(s,a)=\sum_{i=1}^{I}\theta(i,a)\phi(i,s)\,, \tag{15}$$

where s is a state, $\theta(i,a)$ is a parameter, $\phi(i,s)$ $(0\le\phi(i,s)\le 1)$ is a feature vector, i is an index of a feature vector and I is a size of feature vector. $Q(s,a)$ is defined as summation of products of $\theta(i,a)$ and $\phi(i,s)$. That is, $Q(s,a)$ is a linear function of $\phi(i,s)$. The action-value function is optimized by the general gradient-descent update, and if a feature vector is given by the linear approximation method, the action-value function converges to a local optimum (S.Sutton et al., 1998). ME-FPRL is modified by the liner method in order to apply ME-FPRL to some practical tasks. Fig.5 shows the algorithm of ME-FPRL with the function approximation.

4.2 Pursuing target task

(0) Initialize all variable and $a\leftarrow policy(s,Q)$
Do forever:
(1) $s\leftarrow$ current state
(2) Execute action a, Observe resultant state s' and reward r
(3) $a'\leftarrow policy(s,Q)$
(4) $\delta\leftarrow r+\gamma\sum_{i=1}^{n}\theta(i,a')\phi(i,s')-\sum_{i=1}^{n}\theta(i,a)\phi(i,s)$
foreach i in I: $\theta(i,a)\leftarrow\theta(i,a)+\alpha\cdot\phi(i,s)\cdot\delta$
(5) Update $Model(s,a)$
(6) $ModelAcy(s,a)\leftarrow(1-\rho)\cdot ModelAcy(s,a)+\rho\cdot\gamma^{sds(s',\hat{s}')}$
(7) Repeat N_p times
(7-1) $\hat{s}\leftarrow s$ 、 $\hat{a}\leftarrow a$ 、 $ComAcy\leftarrow 1$
(7-2)Repeat N_l times:
(7-2-1) s' 、 $r\leftarrow Model(s,a)$ 、 $\hat{s}'\leftarrow s'$ 、 $\hat{r}\leftarrow r$
(7-2-2) $\hat{a}'\leftarrow policy(s,Q)$
(7-2-3) $ComAcy\leftarrow ComAcy\cdot ModelAcy(\hat{s},\hat{a})$
(7-2-3) Push $(\hat{s},\hat{a},\hat{r},\hat{s}',\hat{a}',ComAcy)$ on stack
(7-2-4) $\hat{s}\leftarrow\hat{s}'$ 、 $\hat{a}\leftarrow\hat{a}'$
(7-3) while stack has some item:
(7-3-1) Pop $(\hat{s},\hat{a},\hat{r},\hat{s}',\hat{a}',ComAcy)$
(7-3-2) $\delta\leftarrow\hat{r}+\gamma\sum_{i=1}^{n}\theta(i,\hat{a}')\phi(i,\hat{s}')-\sum_{i=1}^{n}\theta(i,\hat{a})\phi(i,\hat{s})$
foreach i in I: $\theta(\hat{s},\hat{a})\leftarrow\theta(\hat{s},\hat{a})+ComAcy\cdot\alpha h/N_{plan}\cdot\delta$
(8) $s\leftarrow s'$ 、 $a\leftarrow a'$
($\hat{s},\hat{a},\hat{r},\hat{s}',\hat{a}',ComAcy,\delta$ are temporary variable)

Fig.5. Algorithm of ME-FPRL with function approximation

The pursuing target task is a basic problem in the control of a robot system and many control methods are proposed for this problem. However, a control policy adjusted to a robot cannot be applied to another robot system because of different dynamics of each robot system. That is, adjustment of control policy that adapts dynamics is important for each robot system, and machine learning is one of the solutions to control it. In this study, ME-FPRL is applied to the pursuing target task. A four-legged robot shown in Fig.6 (SONY AIBO ERS-7M3) acquires the control policy to pursue a target shown in Fig.7 by learning. This robot has a CCD camera moving pan/tilt directions. Fig. 6 also shows the default position. The robot can recognize the target using simple image processing. And, the agent can sense the direction of the camera. The target is moved like a pendulum by the servomotor. In this section, this robot is called an agent simply.

4.3 Action and reward

In this task, the purpose of the agent is that it learns behavior that can continue catching the target in the center of the camera. In order to catch the target, the agent chooses one of five kinds of actions: *Turn to top*, *Turn to bottom*, *Turn to right*, *Turn to left*, and *Stop*. When the agent chooses *Turn to top* or *Turn to bottom*, the tilt direction of the camera is changed. When the agent chooses *Turn to right* or *Turn to left*, the pan direction of the camera is changed. These changes are for every five degrees. When the agent chooses *Stop*, the direction of the camera is not changed. The state space is expressed by the target position with axes of pan and tilt, and the agent changes its state by these 5 kinds of actions.
The agent gets one of the following three kinds of rewards: 10 points; catching a target at near the center of the camera, -10 points; catching a target out of the center of the camera, -20 points; missing a target. The agent gets best policy based on these rewards.

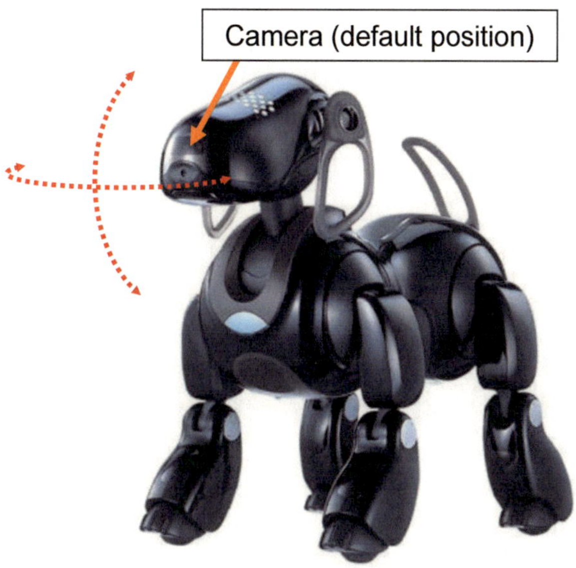

Fig. 6. A Four-legged Robot

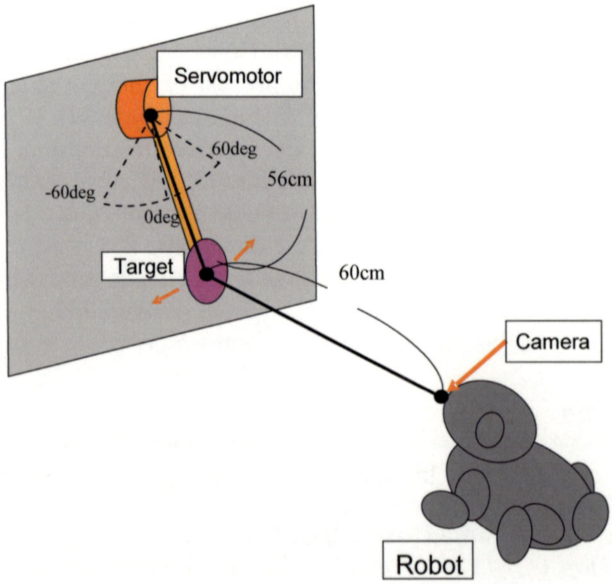

Fig. 7. Relation between robot and target

4.4 Learning agents

In order to confirm the validity of ME-FPRL, the learning efficiencies of the control policy with RL, model-based RL and ME-FPRL are compared with each other.
An agents' action is chosen by Gibbs (or Boltzmann) Sampler (S.Sutton et al., 1998) based on Eq.(16) showing Gibbs distribution, where τ is a time constant. The agent using Gibbus Sampler chooses one of the actions like $\varepsilon - greedy$ when τ is equal to 0, and chooses one of the actions with equal probability when τ is equal to 1.

$$Gibbs(s,Q,a) = \frac{\exp(Q(s,a)/\tau)}{\sum_{b\in A}\exp(Q(s,b)/\tau)} \tag{16}$$

The agent approximates state spaces by the CMAC (S.Sutton et al., 1998), that is a liner approximation method. In the CMAC, state spaces are expressed by some tiles. The number of tiles is defined as $Tiling$. In this application, parameter values are set as follows: $Tiling = 50$, $\alpha = 0.2/Tiling$, $\gamma = 0.8$, $\rho = 0.3$, $N_p = 8$, $N_l = 3$, $N_{plan} = N_p/3$, $h = 0.9$, $\tau = 0.4$. θ and the initial value of $ModelAcy$ are 0.

4.5 Inner model and its learning

The agent with the model-based method has an inner model. In this application, dynamics of the target are constructed by multi-layered artificial neural networks (Nakano, et al., 2006). Fig.8 shows the inner model of the target having two networks (Net1, Net2). These networks are switched over by the direction of target's movement. That is, Net1 deals with the prediction of a right-handed rotation and Net2 deals with the prediction of a left-handed rotation. These networks are obtained by using the error back propagation methods for the learning (Nakano, et al, 2006). Each network is constructed by an input layer with 18 nodes, a hidden layer with 20 nodes and an output layer with 18 nodes. Although the state space for RL is expressed in the relative coordinate value about target position, the state space for this model is expressed in absolute coordinate value about target position without depending on the direction of the camera in this model. Therefore, all predictions by this model do not

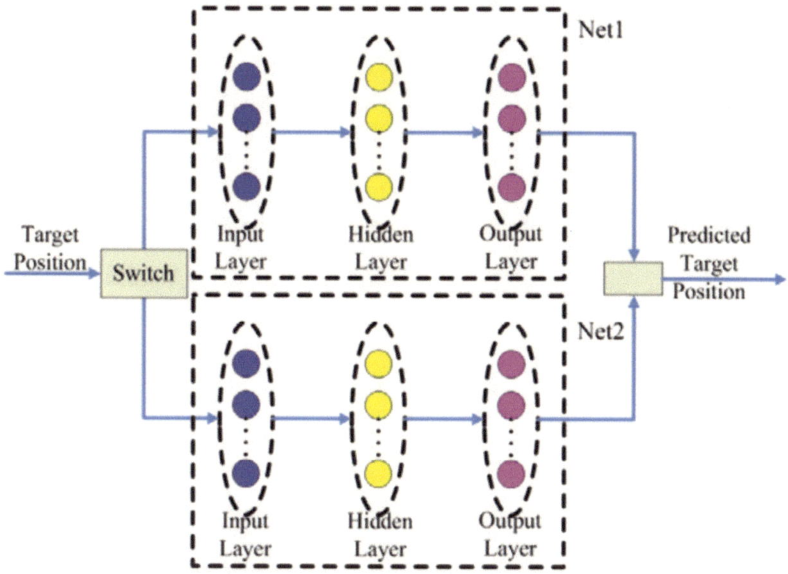

Fig. 8. Inner Model with Two Neural Networks

depend on camera direction. Before performing the task, the agent learns a trace of the target with this model. The target has a pendulum swing between 0 deg and 60 deg with constant speed. The agent memories 1000 times target positions that change momentarily. After the observation, the agent learns the trace by the memorized target positions.

4.6 Experiment and its result

In this experiment, the task is composed of 100 episodes, one episode ends when the robot catches a target in the center of a camera for 40 steps or when the robot loses the target completely. In the first half, 50 episodes, the target has a pendulum swing between 0 deg and 60 deg. In the latter half, 50 episodes, the target has a pendulum swing between 60 deg and -60 deg. That is, the trace of the target is changed at the 50th episodes. Therefore, the agent learns behavior against the unknown trace of a target. Fig.9 shows experimental results with RL, Fig.10 shows those with ME-FPRL and Fig.11 shows those with model-based RL. In these figures, a horizontal axis means the number of episodes, and a vertical axis means the number of steps that the agent catches the target. Table 1 shows the number of episode times that the agent catches the 40 steps target. The agent with Model-based RL catches the target st the 2nd episode, the most quickly among three three methods. The agent with ME-FPRL catches the target at the 8th episode, the second best. However, the agent with Model-based RL often misses the target even in the latter half. On the other hand the agent with ME-FPRL can continue catching the target competely after the 8th episode. Althoufh the number of episode times that the agent with RL misses the target in the latter half is small comparing with the agent with Model-based RL, it takes the longest times to catches the target for the first time. Therefore, it is found that ME-FPRL is the most efficient in the early stage and the most robust aginst the disturbance among the three methods.

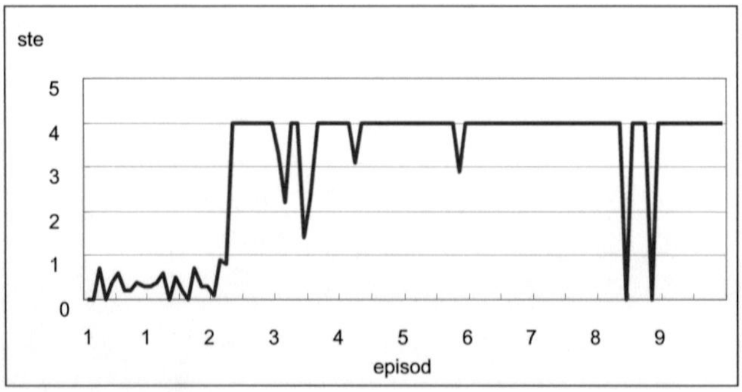

Fig. 9. Experimental Results of RL

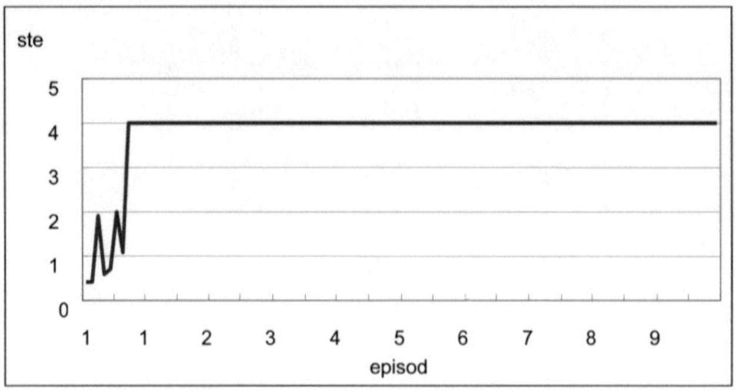

Fig. 10. Experimental Results of ME-FPRL

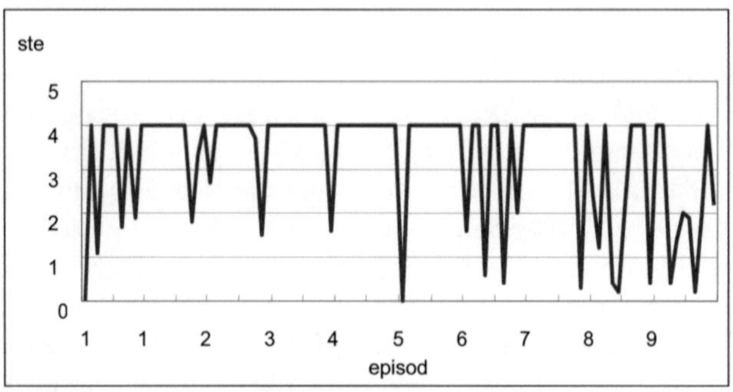

Fig. 11. Experimental Results of Model-based RL

Learning Methods	1st-50th episode	51st - 100th episode	Total (1st - 100th episode)
RL	22	47	69
ME-FPRL	43	50	93
Model-based RL	39	31	70

Table 1. The number of Episode Times that Agent Catches 40 Steps Target

5. Conclusions

In this chapter, the learning algorithm ME-FPRL is discussed. And it applied to the pursuit target task. Application results show that the ME-FPRL is more efficient than a RL or Model-based RL. As a result, ME-FPRL is found to be able to apply to practical tasks. Our future work is constructing more an efficient learning system by using some advice and communication.

6. References

Takakatsu Isozumi:Development of Humanoid Robot,Kawata Giho,Vol. 22, 2003

Shintaro Anzui, Satoshi Hukuda, Masahiro Hamasaki, Ikki Ohmukai, Hideaki Takeda, and Takahira Yamaguti. (2005). A Recommendation System for Personal Digital Assistance with Ontologies, *The 19th Annual Conference of the Japanese Society for Artificial Intelligence*

Richard S.Sutton and Andrew G.Garto (1998). *Reinforcement learning: an introduction.* The MIT Press

M. Asada, S. Noda, S. Tawaratsumida, and K. Hosoda (1994). Vision-Based Behavior Acquisition for a Shooting Robot by Using A Reinforcement Learning. *Proc. of IAPR/IEEE Workshop on Visual Behaviors-1994,* pp.112-118

Yoshiyuki Tajima, Takehisa Onisawa (2006). Model-based Reinforcement Learning with Model Error. *International Symposium on Computational Intelligence and Industrial Applications(ISCIIA),* pp127-134, Guangzhou, China

David Muse, Kevin Burn, Stefan Wermter (2006). Reinforcement Learning for Platform-Independent Visual Robot Control. *IEEE World Congress on Computational Intelligence,*pp.4766-4773

Ryohey Nakano (2005). *Basic Theory of Neural Network Information Processing.* Surikogakusya

14

Objective-based Reinforcement Learning System for Cooperative Behavior Acquisition

Kunikazu Kobayashi, Koji Nakano, Takashi Kuremoto and Masanao Obayashi
Yamaguchi University
Japan

1. Introduction

This chapter discusses the emergence of cooperative behavior in multiagent system and presents an objective-based reinforcement learning system in order to acquire cooperative behavior.
Reinforcement learning is a method that agents will acquire the optimum behavior by trial and error by being given rewards in an environment as a compensation for its behavior (Kaelbling et al., 1996; Sutton & Barto, 1998; Weber et al. 2008). Most of studies on reinforcement learning have been conducted for single agent learning in a static environment. The Q-learning which is a typical learning method is proved that it converges to an optimum solution for Markov decision process (MDP) (Watkins & Dayan, 1992). However, in a multiagent environment, as plural agents' behavior may affect the state transition, the environment is generally considered as non Markov decision process (non-MDP), and we must face critical problems whether it is possible to solve (Stone & Veloso, 2000).
On the above problems in a multiagent environment, Arai et al. have compared Q-learning with profit sharing (PS) (Grefenstette, 1988) using the pursuit problem in a grid environment (Arai et al., 1997). As a result, Q-learning has instability for learning because it uses Q values of the transited state in an updating equation. However, PS can absorb the uncertainty of the state transition because of cumulative discounted reward. Therefore, they concluded that PS is more suitable than Q-learning in the multiagent environment (Arai et al., 1997; Miyazaki & Kobayashi, 1998). Uchibe et al. have presented the capability of learning in a multiagent environment since relation between actions of a learner and the others is estimated as a local prediction model (Uchibe et al., 2002). However, PS has a problem of inadequate convergence because PS reinforces all the pairs of a state and an action irrespective of the achievement of a purpose (Nakano et al., 2005).
This chapter presents an objective-based reinforcement learning system for multiple autonomous mobile robots to solve the above problem and to emerge cooperative behavior (Kobayashi et al, 2007). The proposed system basically employs PS as a learning method but a PS table, which is used for PS learning, is divided into two kinds of PS tables to solve the above problem. One is to learn cooperative behavior using information on other agents' positions and the other is to learn how to control basic movements. Through computer

simulation and real robot experiment using a garbage collecting problem, the performance of the proposed system is evaluated. As a result, it is verified that agents select the most available garbage for cooperative behavior using visual information in an unknown environment and move to the target avoiding obstacles.

This chapter is organized as follows. At first, an outline of reinforcement learning is described. Next, an objective-based reinforcement learning system for multiple autonomous mobile robots is presented. After that, the performance of the proposed system is evaluated through both computer simulation and real robot experiment. Finally, this chapter is concluded with a discussion and future work.

2. Reinforcement learning

Reinforcement learning is a method that agents will acquire the optimum behavior by trial and error by being given rewards in an environment as a compensation for its behavior (Kaelbling et al., 1996; Sutton & Barto, 1998; Weber et al. 2008). It is a kind of unsupervised learning, which does not require direct teacher signals. It is originally modeled by conditional response of animals, where they tend to cause a specific action by giving reward, i.e. food or water, when and only when they cause a specific action for a cue.

Reinforcement learning can be classified into two categories, i.e. exploration oriented and exploitation oriented learning (Yamamura et al., 1995). In the exploration oriented learning, it will evaluate the action at each state as estimating an environment. On the other hand, in the exploitation oriented learning, it will propagate the evaluation obtained at a state into all the states and actions to reach the state. The representatives of exploration oriented and exploitation oriented learning are Q-learning (Watkins & Dayan, 1992) and PS (Grefenstette, 1988), respectively.

2.1 Q-learning

The Q-learning is guaranteed that every state will converge to the optimal solution by appropriately adjusting a learning rate in the MDP environment (Watkins & Dayan, 1992). The state-action value function is denoted by $Q(s,a)$ and updated so as to take the optimal action by exploring it in a learning space. The following is the algorithm of Q-learning.

<Algorithm: Q-learning>

Step 1. Initialize $Q(s,a)$ for any state $s \in S$ and action $a \in A$, where S means the set of all the states and A is the set of all the possible actions.

Step 2. Initialize s.

Step 3. Choose action a based on a policy, such as greedy policy, Boltzmann policy and so on.

Step 4. Take action a, obtain reward r and then transit the next state s'.

Step 5. Update $Q(s,a)$ by equation (1).

$$Q(s,a) \leftarrow Q(s,a) + \alpha\{r + \gamma \max_{a' \in A} Q(s',a') - Q(s,a)\}, \tag{1}$$

where α denotes a learning rate, $0 < \alpha \leq 1$ and γ is a discount rate.

Step 6. Repeat from Step 2 to 5 until s reaches a terminal.

2.2 Profit sharing (PS)

The PS defines a rule as a pair of state and action, and reinforces a series of rules when it gets reward (Grefenstette, 1988). Then, it distributes reward into a weight of rule, $w(s,a)$. As described above, the PS empirically conducts learning through updating $w(s,a)$. The PS is guaranteed that it could obtain a rational policy (Miyazaki et al., 1994). A geometrically decreasing function is known as one of the most simple reinforcement function which satisfies the rationality theorem. The PS reinforces all the rules at the end of an episode, which is defined by trails from an initial state to the goal state. Therefore, it could reinforce many rules using only one reward. The following is the algorithm of PS.

<Algorithm: Profit sharing>

Step 1. Initialize $w(s,a)$ for any state $s \in S$ and action $a \in A$, where S means the set of all the states and A is the set of all the possible actions.

Step 2. Initialize s.

Step 3. Choose action a based on a policy, such as greedy policy, Boltzmann policy and so on.

Step 4. Take action a, obtain reward r, then reserve rule $\{s,a\}$ and reward r, and then transit the next state s'.

Step 5. If $r \neq 0$, then $w(s,a)$ is updated by equation (2).

$$W(s_t,a_t) \leftarrow W(s_t,a_t) + f(t,r), \tag{2}$$

where $f(t,r)$ denotes a reinforcement function and t is time, $t = 0,1,\cdots,T_G$, T_G means time at the goal state.

Step 6. Repeat from Step 2 to 5 until s reaches a terminal.

3. Objective-based reinforcement learning system

3.1 Architecture

This chapter presents an objective-based reinforcement learning system as illustrated in Fig. 1. The proposed system is composed of three parts; an action controller, a learning controller and an evaluator. The feature of the system is to divide behavior of an agent into cooperative and basic behavior to learn separately. The learning of cooperative behavior is using information of the other agents' positions and the present state. The learning of basic behavior is to learn how to control own basic behavior such as *go forward* or *turn right*.

In a general learning method, when an agent acquires a reward it can hardly estimates own action whether it can cooperate or not. To solve this problem, the proposed system divides behavior into two kinds of behavior and each one is evaluated using different criteria. Dividing behavior into the above two kinds of behavior results in the following two merits.

- It could prevent degrading learning efficiency due to mutual interference between both learning.
- It could promote fast convergence due to clarification of both learning.

For action control and evaluation, the proposed method employs individual groups of action and evaluation corresponding to cooperative and basic behavior, respectively.

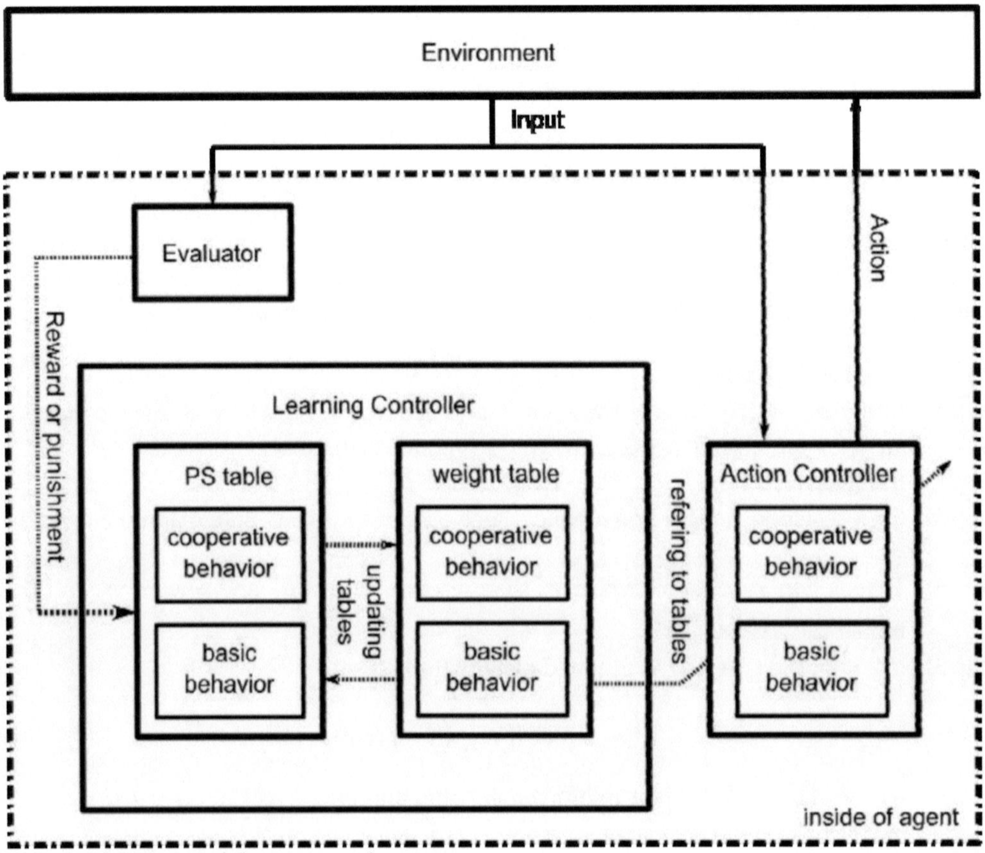

Fig. 1. Architecture of the proposed system.

3.2 Action controller

In the proposed system, an action is selected by the weight of rules, which is produced by inputs from an environment and groups of action. The action selection is conducted by the Boltzmann distribution. It is described by the weight $w(s,a)$ of rules created by the pairs of a state s and an action a and defined as equation (3).

$$B(a \mid s) = \frac{e^{w(s,a)/T}}{\sum_{b \in A} e^{w(s,b)/T}}, \tag{3}$$

where $B(a \mid s)$ is a probability selecting action a at state s, T is a positive temperature constant and A is a set of available actions.

The Boltzmann method is one of soft-max action selection methods and makes the probability of action change so as to preferentially select the action with large weight (Sutton & Barto, 1998). If T becomes large, all the possible actions tend to occur equally. On the other hand, If T becomes small, the action with the largest weight value tend to be selected because the difference of selection probability is enhanced. Then, if the extreme case $T \to 0$, the action selection becomes greedy.

3.3 Learning controller

The PS is employed as a learning method for an agent. The weight $w(s,a)$ of rules is updated by

$$w(s,a) = w(s,a) + f(t,r), \tag{4}$$

where t is a time, r is a reward and $f(\cdot,\cdot)$ is a reinforcement function. In this chapter, the following function is used as function f.

$$f(t,r) = r\gamma^{t_G - t}, \tag{5}$$

where γ is a decay rate and t_G is a time in the goal state. Equation (5) satisfies the rationality theorem of PS which guarantees successful convergence (Miyazaki et al., 1994).
In the proposed system, two PS tables are prepared to cooperative and basic behavior learning. These two tables are separated and the weights are updated independently.

3.4 Evaluator

The different criteria are prepared for cooperative and basic behavior. This is because one can judge whether success and failure of agent's behavior come from cooperative behavior or basic behavior.

4. Experiment

The proposed system was applied to a garbage collecting problem which is one of the standard multiagent tasks (Ishiguro et al, 1997). The two kinds of experiments, i.e. computer simulation and real robot experiment, were conducted to evaluate the performance of the proposed system.
In computer simulation, it is confirmed whether cooperative behavior could be emerged using the garbage collecting problem with two agents. After that, it is evaluated that the values of parameters obtained in computer simulation could apply to real robot experiment. Finally, it is shown that the proposed system could be improved its performance through further learning in real robot experiment.

4.1 Experimental setting

In the experiment, Khepera robot as shown in Fig. 2 is used for an agent. The Khepera robot is a small-size robot, developed by K-Team[1] at the Microprocessor Systems Laboratory, Swiss Federal Institute of Technology and widely used for research development. It equips two wheels drived by two DC motors, a color CCD camera DCC-2010N and a gripper.
The robot identifies garbage and other robots by using an image captured by the color CCD camera. Then, the images are processed by an image processing board IP7000BD developed by Hitachi Information & Control Solutions, Ltd.

---

[1] URL http://www.k-team.com.

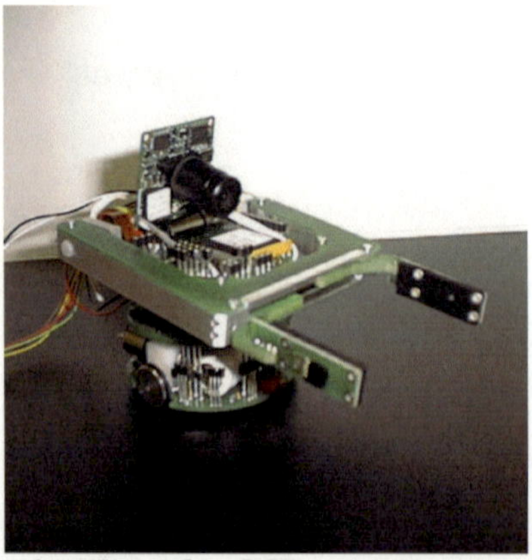

Fig. 2. Khepera robot equipped with a color CCD camera and a gripper.

4.2 Problem setting

In an experimental field, there are two agents, some garbage and one garbage can, and then agents must collect all the garbage and take it to the garbage can.
As shown in Fig. 3, an input for the agent is classified into nine sub-states, combinations of three sorts of orientations (left, front or right) and three sorts of distances (near, middle or far). In computer simulation, an agent can perceive the front sector as shown in Fig. 3(a). In real robot experiment, an image captured by the color CCD camera is divided into nine areas as shown in Fig. 3(b). In Fig. 3(b), the far-front area is large because the robot tends to go forward, and the near-front area is small because the robot can grip the garbage.

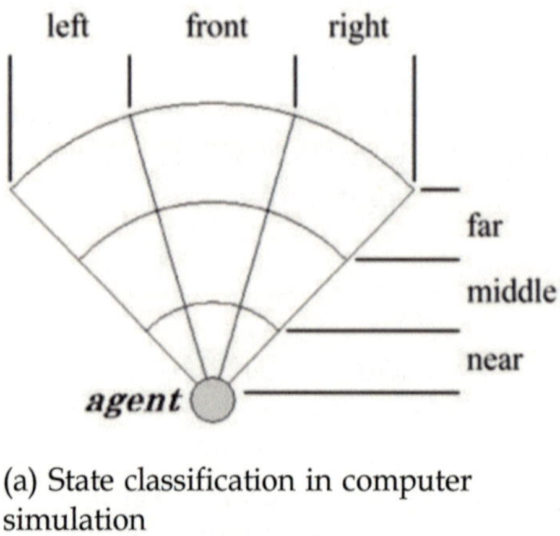

(a) State classification in computer simulation

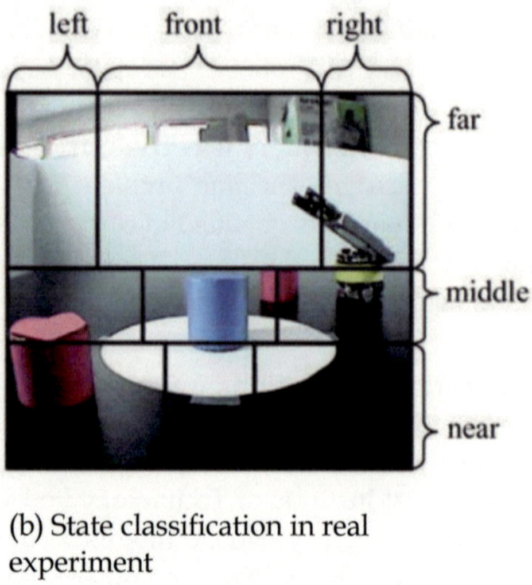

(b) State classification in real experiment

Fig. 3. State classification in computer simulation and in real experiment.

For cooperative behavior learning, an agent gets the relative coordinate of the other agent from visual information and selects the target garbage. For basic behavior learning, an agent gets the relative coordinate of the target garbage and information on obstacles and determines the direction of movement. Here, the obstacles refer to all the things except for

own agent and the target garbage, such as the other agent, non-target garbage, etc. To reduce the number of states for obstacles, it is focused only on the nearest obstacle.
For cooperative behavior learning, the number of states for the other agent including non-observable state is 10 and the number of pairs of rules is 9. Therefore, the total number of rules is 90. For basic behavior learning, the number of states is 9 for the relative coordinate of the target garbage and 8 for information on obstacles. So, the total number of rules is 216.
The reward and the decay rate for PS are defined as follows: $r = 2.0$ and $\gamma = 0.8$ for success and $r = -0.8$ and $\gamma = 0.6$ for failure.

The action of agents is evaluated using four kinds of criterion as shown in Table 1. In this table, the symbol 'o' means reward or punishment is considered and the symbol `x' is not considered.

Condition	Cooperative action	Basic action
Reward: an agent arrives at the target garbage or the garbage can.	o	o
Punishment: an agent decides the same garbage with other agents.	o	x
Punishment: an agent bumps obstacles.	x	o
Punishment: an agent loses the target.	x	o

Table 1. Definition of reward and punishment.

4.3 Computer simulation

A simulation field is a 21x21 grid world and there are ten garbage, two agents and one garbage can in the field as shown in Fig. 4.

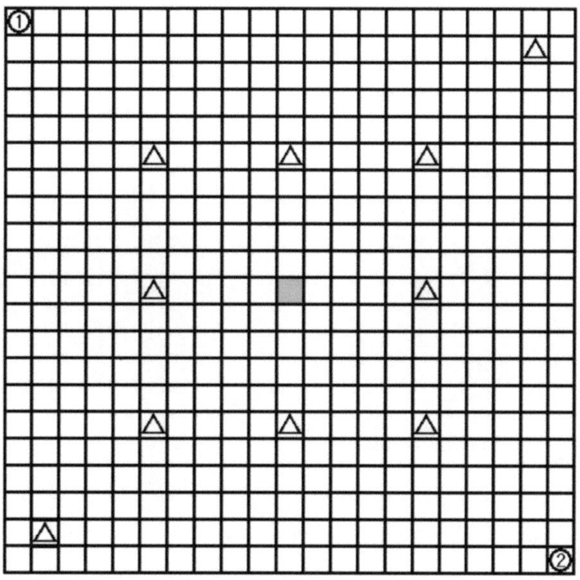

Fig. 4. Initial position of two agents denoted by circle, ten garbage by triangle and one garbage can by shaded square.

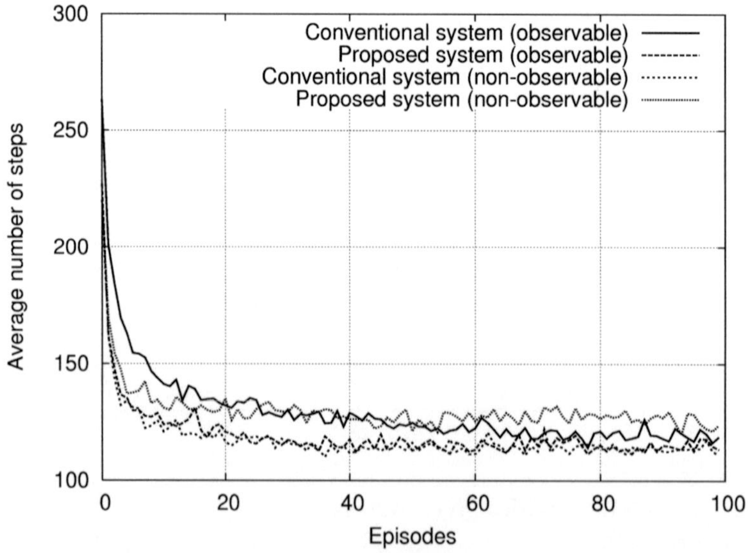

Fig. 5. Performance comparison of the proposed and conventional systems.

	Observable	Non-observable
Conventional method	118.7	111.1
Proposed method	113.3	123.8

Table 2. The average number of steps in the final trial.

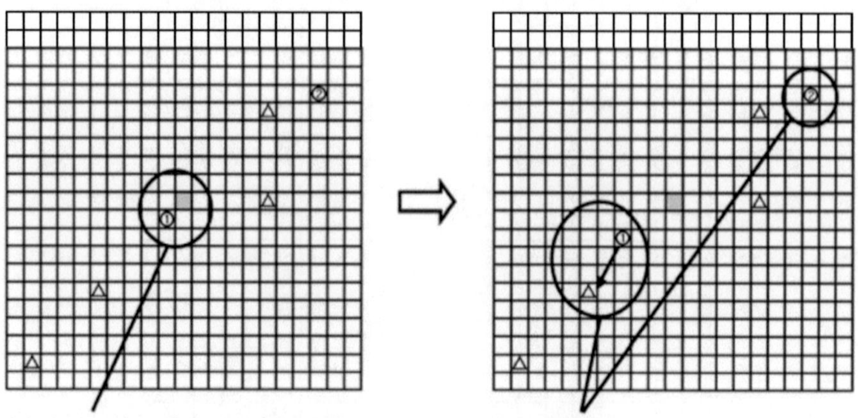

(a) Agent 1 arrives at the trash can.

(b) Agent 1 moves to the garbage opposite to agent 2.

Fig. 6. An example of cooperative behavior acquired in the proposed system with observing the other agent.

One trial is defined as until all the garbage is collected, and 100 trials are considered as one episode. The number of average steps is calculated after repeating 100 episodes. At this time, $w(s,a)$ are initialized for each episode. To verify the effectiveness of the proposed system, it is compared with the standard PS system (conventional system).

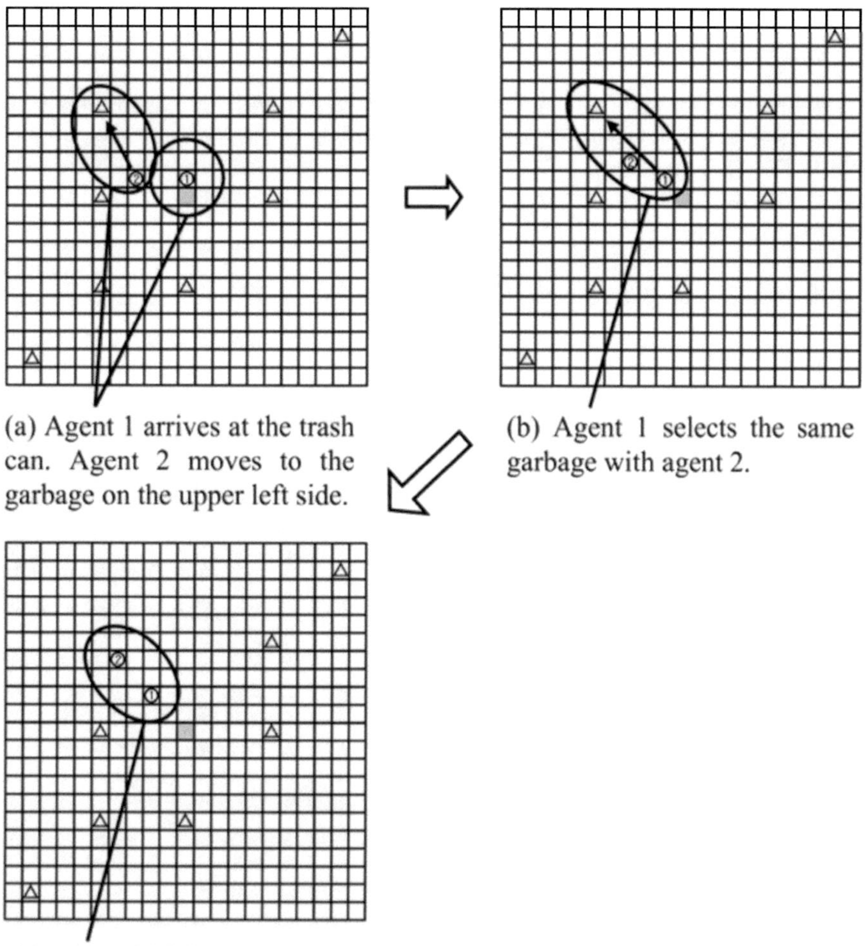

(a) Agent 1 arrives at the trash can. Agent 2 moves to the garbage on the upper left side.

(b) Agent 1 selects the same garbage with agent 2.

(c) Agent 2 picks up the target garbage. Agent 1 increases the number of steps because of a waste of time-steps.

Fig. 7. An example of cooperative behavior acquired in the proposed system without observing the other agent.

Figure 5 and Table 2 show the result of the computer simulation. In the case that one agent can observe the other, the agent using the proposed system learns faster than the agent

using the conventional system. From this result, it is shown that the proposed system realizes cooperative behavior. However, when the agent is compared with the agent which is using the conventional system and do not observe the other agent, the performance of the proposed agent is similar to that of the conventional agent.
Figure 6 illustrates cooperative behavior observed in the experiment in which agent observes the other one. After agent 1 took the garbage to the garbage can (Fig. 6(a)), it does not select the garbage near agent 2 as the object, but another one opposite to agent 2 (Fig. 6(b)). Such behavior often occurred after learning with observing the other agents. On the other hand, Fig. 7 depicts cooperative behavior without observing the other agent. After agent 1 reached the garbage can (Fig. 7(a)), as it selected the garbage which are also targeted by agent 2 (Fig. 7(b)), it is clear that the number of steps is increased because of a waste of time-steps (Fig. 7(c)).

4.4 Real robot experiment

Two Khepera robots, an image processing board IP7000BD, a color CCD camera DCC-2010N and a robot control PC are used in the experiment. An experiment field is a 1[m]x1[m] square surrounded by white walls and there are five garbage, two robots and one garbage can as shown in Fig. 8.

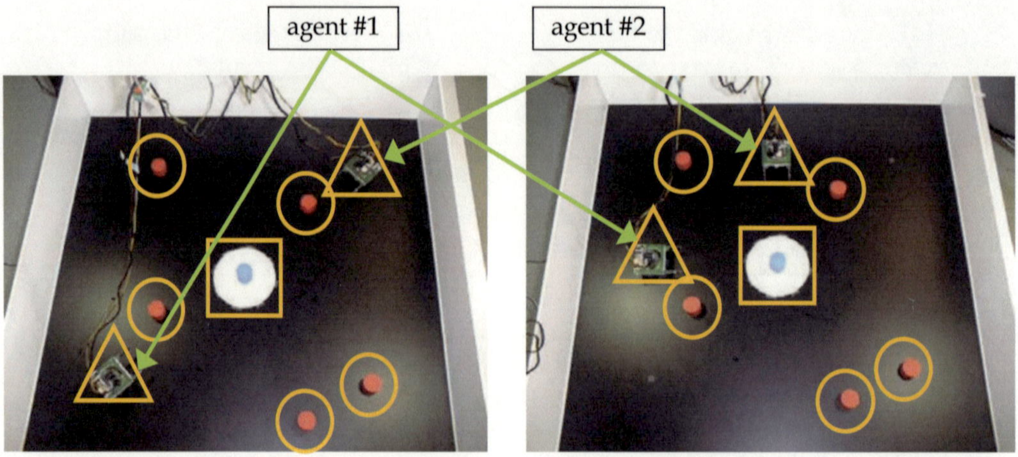

(a) Arrangement #1 (b) Arrangement #2

Fig. 8. Initial position of two agents denoted by circle, five garbage by triangle and one garbage can by square.

The following three kinds of the experiments were conducted to evaluate the learning ability of the proposed system.

Exp. 1. The robots are controlled using the learned weights in the simulation, which are not updated during Exp. 1.

Exp. 2. The robots are controlled using the learned weights in the simulation, which are updated during Exp. 2.

Exp. 3. The robots are controlled using the learned weights in Exp. 2 after the initial position of robots is changed.

Table 3 shows that the number of average steps in Exp. 2 is decreased compared with that in Exp. 1. Thus, the learned weights in the simulation are available for the real robot environment, and furthermore, the proposed system can learn flexibly in real environment. On the other hand, the number of average steps in Exp. 3 is not increased compared with Exp. 2. Therefore, the weights learned in real environment are applicable to different environments, and this shows that the proposed system is robust.

	Average number of steps
Exp. 1	201.9
Exp. 2	178.2
Exp. 3	161.1

Table 3. The average number of steps in Exp. 1 to 3.

5. Conclusion

This chapter has proposed the objective-based reinforcement learning system for multiple autonomous mobile robots to acquire cooperative behavior. In the proposed system, robots select the most available target garbage for cooperative behavior using visual information in an unknown environment, and move to the target avoiding obstacles. The proposed system employs profit sharing (PS) and a characteristic of the system is using two kinds of PS tables. One is to learn cooperative behavior using information on other robot's positions, the other is to learn how to control basic movements. Through computer simulation and real robot experiment using a garbage collecting problem, it was verified that the proposed system is effective compared with the conventional system.

The future problem is to solve a trade-off between reducing the number of inputs and recognizing the external environment.

6. References

Arai, S.; Miyazaki, K. & Kobayashi, S. (1997). Generating Cooperative Behavior by Multi-Agent Reinforcement Learning, *Proceedings of the 6th European Workshop on Learning Robots (EWLR-6)*, pp.143-157.

Grefenstette, J. J. (1988). Credit Assignment in Rule Discovery Systems Based on Genetic Algorithms, *Machine Learning*, Vol.3, pp.225-245, ISSN: 0885-6125.

Ishiguro, A.; Watanabe, Y.; Kondo, T.; Shirai, Y. & Uchikawa, Y. (1997). Robot with a Decentralized Consensus-making Mechanism Based on the Immune System, *Proceedings of the International Symposium on Autonomous Decentralized Systems (ISADS'97)*, pp.231-237.

Kaelbling, L. P.; Littman, M. L. & Moore, A. P. (1996). Reinforcement Learning: A Survey, *Journal of Artificial Intelligence Research*, Vol.4, pp.237-285, ISSN: 11076-9757.

Kobayashi, K.; Nakano, K.; Kuremoto, T. & Obayashi, M., (2007). Cooperative Behavior Acquisition of Multiple Autonomous Mobile Robots by an Objective-based Reinforcement Learning System, *Proceedings of International Conference on Control, Automation and Systems (ICCAS2007)*, pp.777-780.

Miyazaki, K.; Yamamura, M. & Kobayashi, S. (1994). On the Rationality of Profit Sharing in Reinforcement Learning, *Proceedings of the 3rd International Conference on Fuzzy Logic, Neural Nets and Soft Computing (Iizuka'94)*, pp.285-288.

Miyazaki, K. & Kobayashi, S. (1998). Learning Deterministic Policies in Partially Observable Markov Decision Processes, *Proceedings of International Conference on Intelligent Autonomous System (IAS-5)*, pp.250-257.

Nakano, K.; Obayashi, M.; Kobayashi, K. & Kuremoto, T., (2005). Cooperative Behavior Acquisition for Multiple Autonomous Mobile Robots, *Proceedings of the Tenth International Symposium on Artificial Life and Robotics (AROB2005)*, CD-ROM.

Stone, P. & Veloso, M. (2000). Multiagent systems: A Survey From a Machine Learning Perspective, *Autonomous Robots*, Vol.8, No.3, pp.345-383, ISSN: 0929-5593.

Sutton, R. S. & Barto, A. G. (1998). *Reinforcement Learning: An Introduction*, MIT Press, ISBN: 978-0-262-19398-6, Cambridge, UK.

Uchibe, E.; Asada, M. & Hosoda, K. (2002). State Space Construction for Cooperative Behavior Acquisition in the Environments Including Multiple Learning Robots, *Journal of the Robotics Society of Japan*, Vol.20, No.3, pp.281-289, ISSN: 0289-1824 (in Japanese).

Yamamura, M.; Miyazaki, K. & Kobayashi, S. (1995). A survey on learning for agents, *Journal of Japanese Society for Artificial Intelligence*, Vol.10, No.5, pp.683-689, ISSN: 1346-0714 (in Japanese).

Watkins, C. J. C. H. & Dayan, P. (1992). Q-learning, *Machine Learning*, Vol.8, pp.279-292, ISSN: 0885-6125.

Weber, C.; Elshaw, M. & Mayer, N. M. (2008). *Reinforcement Learning, Theory and Application*, I-Tech Education and Publishing, ISBN: 978-3-902613-14-1, Vienna, Austria.

15

Heuristic Dynamic Programming Nonlinear Optimal Controller

Asma Al-tamimi[1], Murad Abu-Khalaf[2] and Frank Lewis[3]
[1]*The Hashemite University,* [2]*Math work,* [3]*The University of Texas at Arlington*
[1]*Jordan,* [2,3] *USA*

1. Introduction

This chapter is concerned with the application of approximate dynamic programming techniques (ADP) to solve for the value function, and hence the optimal control policy, in discrete-time nonlinear optimal control problems having continuous state and action spaces. ADP is a reinforcement learning approach (Sutton & Barto,1998) based on adaptive critics (Barto et al.,1983), (Widrow et al.,1973) to solve dynamic programming problems utilizing function approximation for the value function. ADP techniques can be based on value iterations or policy iterations. In contrast with value iterations, policy iterations require an initial stabilizing control action, (Sutton & Barto, 1998). (Howard,1960) proved convergence of policy iteration for Markov Decision Processes with discrete state and action spaces. Lookup tables are used to store the value function iterations at each state. (Watkins,1989) developed Q-learning for discrete state and action MDPs, where a 'Q function' is stored for each state/action pair, and model dynamics are not needed to compute the control action.

ADP was proposed by (Werbos, 1990,1991,1992) for discrete-time dynamical systems having continuous state and action spaces as a way to solve optimal control problems, (Lewis & Syrmos, 1995), forward in time. (Bertsekas & Tsitsiklis, 1996) provide a treatment of Neurodynamic programming, where neural networks (NN) are used to approximate the value function. (Cao, 2002) presents a general theory for learning and optimization.

(Werbos, 1992) classified approximate dynamic programming approaches into four main schemes: Heuristic Dynamic Programming (HDP), Dual Heuristic Dynamic Programming (DHP), Action Dependent Heuristic Dynamic Programming (ADHDP), (a continuous-state-space generalization of Q-learning (Watkins, 1989)), and Action Dependent Dual Heuristic Dynamic Programming (ADDHP). Neural networks are used to approximate the value function (the critic NN) and the control (the action NN), and backpropagation is used to tune the weights until convergence at each iteration of the ADP algorithm. An overview of ADP is given in (Si et al. , 2004) (e.g. (Ferrari & Stengel, 2004), and also (Prokhorov & Wunsch, 1997), who deployed new ADP schemes known as Globalized-DHP (GDHP) and ADGDHP.

ADP for linear systems has received ample attention. An off-line policy iteration scheme for discrete-time systems with known dynamics was given in (Hewer, 1971) to solve the discrete-time Riccati equation. In (Bradtke et al, 1994). implemented an (online) Q-learning policy iteration method for discrete-time linear quadratic regulator (LQR) optimal control problems. A convergence proof was given. (Hagen, 1998) discussed, for the LQR case, the relation between the Q-learning method and model-based adaptive control with system identification. (Landelius, 1997) applied HDP, DHP, ADHDP and ADDHP value iteration techniques, called greedy policy iterations therein, to the discrete-time LQR problem and verified their convergence. It was shown that these iterations are in fact equivalent to iterative solution of an underlying algebraic Riccati equation, which is known to converge (Lancaster & Rodman, 1995). (Lu & Balakrishnan, 2000) showed convergence of DHP for the LQR case.

(Morimoto et al, 2003) developed differential dynamic programming, a Q-learning method, to solve optimal zero-sum game problems for nonlinear systems by taking the second-order approximation to the Q function. This effectively provides an exact Q-learning formulation for linear systems with minimax value functions. In our previous work (Al-tamimi at el,2007), we studied ADP value iteration techniques to solve the zero-sum game problem for linear discrete-time dynamical systems using quadratic minimax cost. HDP, DHP, ADHDP and ADDHP formulations were developed for zero-sum games, and convergence was proven by showing the equivalence of these ADP methods to iterative solution of an underlying Game Algebraic Riccati Equation, which is known to converge. Applications were made to H-infinity control.

For nonlinear systems with continuous state and action spaces, solution methods for the dynamic programming problem are more sparse. Policy iteration methods for optimal control for continuous-time systems with continuous state space and action spaces were given in (Abu-khalaf & Lewis, 2005) (Abu-Khalaf at el, 2004), but complete knowledge of the plant dynamics is required. The discrete-time nonlinear optimal control solution relies on solving the discrete-time (DT) Hamilton-Jacobi-Bellman (HJB) equation (Lewis & Syrmos, 1995), exact solution of which is generally impossible for nonlinear systems. Solutions to the DT HJB equation with known dynamics and continuous state space and action space were given in(Huang, 1999), where the coefficients of the Taylor series expansion of the value function are systematically computed. In (Chen & Jagannathan, 2005), the authors show that under certain conditions a second-order approximation of the discrete-time (DT) Hamilton-Jacobi-Bellman (HJB) equation can be considered; under those conditions discussed in that paper, the authors solve for the value function that satisfies the second order expansion of the DT HJB instead of solving for the original DT HJB. The authors apply a policy iteration scheme on this second order DT HJB and require an initially stable policy to start the iterations scheme. The authors also used a single (critic) neural network to approximate the value function of the second order DT HJB. These are all off-line methods for solving the HJB equations that require full knowledge of the system dynamics.

Convergence proofs for the on-line value-iteration based ADP techniques for nonlinear discrete-time systems are even more limited. (Prokhorov & Wunsch, 1997) use NN to approximate both the value (e.g. a critic NN) and the control action. Least mean squares is used to tune the critic NN weights and the action NN weights. Stochastic approximation is used to show that, at each iteration of the ADP algorithm, the critic weights converge. Likewise, at each iteration the action NN weights converge, but overall convergence of the ADP algorithm to the optimal solution is not demonstrated. A similar approach was used in (Si et al., 2004).

In (He & Jagannathan, 2005), a generalized or asynchronous version of ADP (in the sense of (Sutton & Barto, 1998) was used whereby the updates of the critic NN and action NN are interleaved, each NN being updated at each time step. Tuning was performed online. A Lyapunov approach was used to show that the method yields uniform ultimate bounded stability and that the weight estimation errors are bounded, though convergence to the exact optimal value and control was not shown. The input coupling function must be positive definite.

In this chapter, we provide a full, rigorous proof of convergence of the online value-iteration based HDP algorithm, to solve the DT HJB equation of the optimal control problem for general nonlinear discrete-time systems. It is assumed that at each iteration, the value update and policy update equations can be exactly solved. Note that this is true in the specific case of the LQR, where the action is linear and the value quadratic in the states. For implementation, two NN are used- the critic NN to approximate the value and the action NN to approximate the control. Full knowledge of the system dynamics is not needed to implement the HDP algorithm; in fact, the internal dynamics information is not needed. As a value iteration based algorithm, of course, an initial stabilizing policy is not needed for HDP.

The point is stressed that these results also hold for the special LQR case of linear systems $\dot{x} = Ax + Bu$ and quadratic utility. In the general folklore of HDP for the LQR case, only a single NN is used, namely a critic NN, and the action is updated using a standard matrix equation derived from the stationarity condition(Lewis & Syrmos1995). In the DT case, this equation requires the use of both the plant matrix A, e.g. the internal dynamics, and the control input coupling matrix B. However, by using a second action NN, the knowledge of the A matrix is not needed. This important issue is clarified herein.

Section two of the chapter starts by introducing the nonlinear discrete-time optimal control problem. Section three demonstrates how to setup the HDP algorithm to solve for the nonlinear discrete-time optimal control problem. In Section four, we prove the convergence of HDP value iterations to the solution of the DT HJB equation. In Section five , we introduce two neural network parametric structures to approximate the optimal value function and policy. As is known, this provides a procedure for implementing the HDP algorithm. We also discuss in that section how we implement the algorithm without having to know the plant internal dynamics. Finally, Section six presents two examples that show the practical effectiveness of the ADP technique. The first example in fact is a LQR example which uses HDP with two NNs to solve the Riccati equation online without knowing the A matrix. The second example considers a nonlinear system and the results are compared to solutions based on State Dependent Riccati Equations (SDRE).

2. The Discrete-Time HJB Equation

Consider an affine in input nonlinear dynamical-system of the form

$$x_{k+1} = f(x_k) + g(x_k)u(x_k). \tag{1}$$

where $x \in \mathbb{R}^n$, $f(x) \in \mathbb{R}^n$, $g(x) \in \mathbb{R}^{n \times m}$ and the input $u \in \mathbb{R}^m$. Suppose the system is drift-free and, without loss of generality, that $x = 0$ is an equilibrium state, e.g. $f(0) = 0$, $g(0) = 0$. Assume that the system (1) is stabilizable on a prescribed compact set $\Omega \in \mathbb{R}^n$.

Definition 1. Stabilizable system: A nonlinear dynamical system is defined to be stabilizable on a compact set $\Omega \in \mathbb{R}^n$ if there exists a control input $u \in \mathbb{R}^m$ such that, for all initial conditions $x_0 \in \Omega$ the state $x_k \to 0$ as $k \to \infty$.

It is desired to find the control action $u(x_k)$ which minimizes the infinite-horizon cost function given as

$$V(x_k) = \sum_{n=k}^{\infty} Q(x_n) + u^T(x_n) R u(x_n) \tag{2}$$

for all x_k, where $Q(x) > 0$ and $R > 0 \in \mathbb{R}^{m \times m}$. The class of controllers needs to be stable and also guarantee that (2) is finite, *i.e.* the control must be admissible (Abu-Khalaf & Lewis, 2005).

Definition 2 Admissible Control: A control $u(x_k)$ is defined to be admissible with respect to (2) on Ω if $u(x_k)$ is continuous on a compact set $\Omega \in \mathbb{R}^n$, $u(0) = 0$, u stabilizes (1) on Ω, and $\forall x_0 \in \Omega$, $V(x_0)$ is finite.

Equation (2) can be written as

$$\begin{aligned} V(x_k) &= x_k^T Q x_k + u_k^T R u_k + \sum_{n=k+1}^{\infty} x_n^T Q x_n + u_n^T R u_n \\ &= x_k^T Q x_k + u_k^T R u_k + V(x_{k+1}) \end{aligned} \tag{3}$$

where we require the boundary condition $V(x = 0) = 0$ so that $V(x_k)$ serves as a Lyapunov function. From Bellman's optimality principle 0, it is known that for the infinite-horizon optimization case, the value function $V^*(x_k)$ is time-invariant and satisfies the discrete-time Hamilton-Jacobi-Bellman (HJB) equation

$$V^*(x_k) = \min_{u_k}(x_k^T Q x_k + u_k^T R u_k + V^*(x_{k+1})) \tag{4}$$

Note that the discrete-time HJB equation develops backward-in time.

The optimal control u^* satisfies the first order necessary condition, given by the gradient of the right hand side of (4) with respect to u as

$$\frac{\partial(x_k^T Q x_k + u_k^T R u_k)}{\partial u_k} + \frac{\partial x_{k+1}}{\partial u_k}^T \frac{\partial V^*(x_{k+1})}{\partial x_{k+1}} = 0 \tag{5}$$

and therefore

$$u^*(x_k) = \frac{1}{2} R^{-1} g(x_k)^T \frac{\partial V^*(x_{k+1})}{\partial x_{k+1}} \tag{6}$$

Substituting (6) in (4), one may write the discrete-time HJB as

$$V^*(x_k) = x_k^T Q x_k + \frac{1}{4}\frac{\partial V^{*T}(x_{k+1})}{\partial x_{k+1}} g(x_k) R^{-1} g(x_k)^T \frac{\partial V^*(x_{k+1})}{\partial x_{k+1}} + V^*(x_{k+1}) \tag{7}$$

where $V^*(x_k)$ is the value function corresponding to the optimal control policy $u^*(x_k)$ .. This equation reduces to the Riccati equation in the linear quadratic regulator (LQR) case, which can be efficiently solved. In the general nonlinear case, the HJB cannot be solved exactly.

In the next sections we apply the HDP algorithm to solve for the value function V^* of the HJB equation (7) and present a convergence proof.

3. The HDP Algorithm

The HDP value iteration algorithm (Werbos, 1990) is a method to solve the DT HJB online. In this section, the HDP algorithm in the general nonlinear discrete-time setting is presented.

3.1 The HDP algorithm

In the HDP algorithm, one starts with an initial value, e.g. $V_0(x) = 0$ and then solves for u_0 as follows

$$u_o(x_k) = \arg\min_u (x_k^T Q x_k + u^T R u + V_0(x_{k+1})) \tag{8}$$

Once the policy u_0 is determined, iteration on the value is performed by computing

$$\begin{aligned} V_1(x_k) &= x_k^T Q x_k + u_0^T(x_k) R u_0(x_k) + V_0(f(x_k) + g(x_k) u_0(x_k)) \\ &= x_k^T Q x_k + u_0^T(x_k) R u_0(x_k) + V_0(x_{k+1}) \end{aligned} \tag{9}$$

The HDP value iteration scheme therefore is a form of incremental optimization that requires iterating between a sequence of action policies $u_i(x)$ determined by the greedy Update

$$\begin{aligned} u_i(x_k) &= \arg\min_u (x_k^T Q x_k + u^T R u + V_i(x_{k+1})) \\ &= \arg\min_u (x_k^T Q x_k + u^T R u + V_i(f(x_k) + g(x_k) u)) \\ &= \frac{1}{2} R^{-1} g(x_k)^T \frac{\partial V_i(x_{k+1})}{\partial x_{k+1}} \end{aligned} \tag{10}$$

and a sequence $V_i(x) \ge 0$ where

$$\begin{aligned} V_{i+1}(x_k) &= \min_u (x_k^T Q x_k + u^T R u + V_i(x_{k+1})) \\ &= x_k^T Q x_k + u_i^T(x_k) R u_i(x_k) + V_i(f(x_k) + g(x_k) u_i(x_k)) \end{aligned} \tag{11}$$

with initial condition $V_0(x_k) = 0$.

Note that, as a value-iteration algorithm, HDP does not require an initial stabilizing gain. This is important as stabilizing gains are difficult to find for general nonlinear systems.

Note that i is the value iterations index, while k is the time index. The HDP algorithm results in an incremental optimization that is implemented forward in time and online. Note that unlike the case for policy iterations in (Hewer, 1971), the sequence $V_i(x_k)$ is not a sequence of cost functions and are therefore not Lyapunov functions for the corresponding policies $u_i(x_k)$ which are in turn not necessarily stabilizing. In Section four it is shown that $V_i(x_k)$ and $u_i(x_k)$ converges to the value function of the optimal control problem and to the corresponding optimal control policy respectively.

3.2 The Special Case of Linear Systems

Note that for the special case of linear systems, it can be shown that the HDP algorithm is one way to solve the Discrete-Time Algebraic Riccati Equation (DARE) (Landelius, 1997)). Particularly, for the discrete-time linear system

$$x_{k+1} = A x_k + B u_k \tag{12}$$

the DT HJB equation (7) becomes the DARE

$$P = A^T P A + Q - A^T P B (R + B^T P B)^{-1} B^T P A \tag{13}$$

with $V^*(x_k) = x_k^T P x_k$.

In the linear case, the policy update (10) is

$$u_i(x_k) = -(R + B^T P_i B)^{-1} B^T P_i A x_k \tag{14}$$

Substituting this into (11), one sees that the HDP algorithm (10), (11) is equivalent to

$$\begin{aligned} P_{i+1} &= A^T P_i A + Q - A^T P_i B (R + B^T P_i B)^{-1} B^T P_i A \\ P_0 &= 0 \end{aligned} \tag{15}$$

It should be noted that the HDP algorithm (15) solves the DARE forward in time, whereas the dynamic programming recursion appearing in finite-horizon optimal control 0 develops backward in time

$$\begin{aligned} P_k &= A^T P_{k+1} A + Q - A^T P_{k+1} B (R + B^T P_{k+1} B)^{-1} B^T P_{k+1} A \\ P_N &= 0 \end{aligned} \tag{16}$$

where N represents the terminal time. Both equations (15) and (16) will produce the same sequence of P_i and P_k respectively. It has been shown in 0 and (Lancaster, 1995) that this sequence converges to the solution of the DARE after enough iterations.
It is very important to point out the difference between equations (14) and (15) resulting from HDP value iterations with

$$u_i(x_k) = \underbrace{-(R + B^T P_i B)^{-1} B^T P_i A}_{K_i} x_k \tag{17}$$

$$\begin{aligned} &(A + BK_i)^T P_{i+1}(A + BK_i) - P_{i+1} = -Q - K_i^T R K_i \\ &(P_0, u_0): \text{ Initial stable control policy with corresponding Lyapunov function} \end{aligned} \tag{18}$$

resulting from policy iterations, those in(Hewer, 1971). Unlike P_i in (15), the sequence P_i in (18) is a sequence of Lyapunov functions. Similarly the sequence of control policies in (17) is stabilizing unlike the sequence in (14).

4. Convergence of the HDP Algorithm

In this section, we present a proof of convergence for nonlinear HDP. That is, we prove convergence of the iteration (10) and (11) to the optimal value, *i.e.* $V_i \to V^*$ and $u_i \to u^*$ as $i \to \infty$. The linear quadratic case has been proven by (Lancaster, 1995) for the case of known system dynamics.
Lemma 1. Let μ_i be any arbitrary sequence of control policies and Λ_i be defined by

$$\Lambda_{i+1}(x_k) = Q(x_k) + \mu_i^T R \mu_i + \Lambda_i(\underbrace{f(x_k) + g(x_k)\mu_i(x_k)}_{x_{k+1}}). \tag{19}$$

Let u_i and V_i be the sequences defined by (10) and (11). If $V_0(x_k) = \Lambda_0(x_k) = 0$, then $V_i(x_k) \le \Lambda_i(x_k)\ \forall i$.
Proof: Since $u_i(x_k)$ minimizes the right hand side of equation (11) with respect to the control u, and since $V_0(x_k) = \Lambda_0(x_k) = 0$, then by induction it follows that $V_i(x_k) \le \Lambda_i(x_k)\ \forall i$. ■
Lemma 2. Let the sequence V_i be defined as in (11). If the system is controllable, then: There exists an upper bound $Y(x_k)$ such that $0 \le V_i(x_k) \le Y(x_k)\ \forall i$.

If the optimal control problem (4) is solvable, there exists a least upper bound $V^*(x_k) \le Y(x_k)$ where $V^*(x_k)$ solves (7), and that $\forall i: 0 \le V_i(x_k) \le V^*(x_k) \le Y(x_k)$.

Proof: Let $\eta(x_k)$ be any stabilizing and admissible control policy, and Let $V_0(x_k) = Z_0(x_k) = 0$ where Z_i is updated as

$$\begin{aligned} Z_{i+1}(x_k) &= Q(x_k) + \eta^T(x_k) R \eta(x_k) + Z_i(x_{k+1}) \\ x_{k+1} &= f(x_k) + g(x_k)\eta(x_k) \end{aligned}. \tag{20}$$

It follows that the difference

$$
\begin{aligned}
Z_{i+1}(x_k) - Z_i(x_k) &= Z_i(x_{k+1}) - Z_{i-1}(x_{k+1}) \\
&= Z_{i-1}(x_{k+2}) - Z_{i-2}(x_{k+2}) \\
&= Z_{i-2}(x_{k+3}) - Z_{i-3}(x_{k+3}) \\
&\;\;. \\
&\;\;. \\
&\;\;. \\
&= Z_1(x_{k+i}) - Z_0(x_{k+i})
\end{aligned}
\tag{21}
$$

Since $Z_0(x_k) = 0$, it then follows that

$$
\begin{aligned}
Z_{i+1}(x_k) &= Z_1(x_{k+i}) + Z_i(x_k) \\
&= Z_1(x_{k+i}) + Z_1(x_{k+i-1}) + Z_{i-1}(x_k) \\
&= Z_1(x_{k+i}) + Z_1(x_{k+i-1}) + Z_1(x_{k+i-1}) + Z_{i-2}(x_k) \\
&= Z_1(x_{k+i}) + Z_1(x_{k+i-1}) + Z_1(x_{k+i-2}) + \ldots\ldots + Z_1(x_k)
\end{aligned}
\tag{22}
$$

and equation (22) can be written as

$$
\begin{aligned}
Z_{i+1}(x_k) &= \sum_{n=0}^{i} Z_1(x_{k+n}) \\
&= \sum_{n=0}^{i} (Q(x_{k+n}) + \eta^T(x_{k+n}) R \eta(x_{k+n})) \\
&\le \sum_{n=0}^{\infty} (Q(x_{k+n}) + \eta^T(x_{k+n}) R \eta(x_{k+n}))
\end{aligned}
\tag{23}
$$

Since $\eta(x_k)$ is an admissible stabilizing controller, $x_{k+n} \to 0$ as $n \to \infty$ and

$$\forall i: \;\; Z_{i+1}(x_k) \le \sum_{i=0}^{\infty} Z_1(x_{k+i}) = Y(x_k)$$

Using Lemma 1 with $\mu_i(x_k) = \eta(x_k)$ and $\Lambda_i(x_k) = Z_i(x_k)$, it follows that

$$\forall i: \;\; V_i(x_k) \le Z_i(x_k) \le Y(x_k)$$

which proves part a). Moreover if $\eta(x_k) = u^*(x_k)$, then

$$\underbrace{\sum_{n=0}^{\infty} (Q(x_{k+n}) + u^{*T}(x_{k+n}) R u^*(x_{k+n}))}_{V^*(x_k)} \le \underbrace{\sum_{n=0}^{\infty} (Q(x_{k+n}) + \eta^T(x_{k+n}) R \eta(x_{k+n}))}_{Y(x_k)}$$

and hence $V^*(x_k) \le Y(x_k)$ which proves part b) and shows that $\forall i: 0 \le V_i(x_k) \le V^*(x_k) \le Y(x_k)$ for any $Y(x_k)$ determined by an admissible stabilizing policy $\eta(x_k)$. ∎

Theorem 1. Consider the sequence V_i and u_i defined by (11) and (10) respectively. If $V_0(x_k)=0$, then it follows that V_i is a non-decreasing sequence

$$\forall i: V_{i+1}(x_k) \geq V_i(x_k)$$

and as $i \to \infty$

$$V_i \to V^*,\ u_i \to u^*$$

that is the sequence V_i converges to the solution of the DT HJB (7).

Proof: From Lemma 1, let μ_i be any arbitrary sequence of control policies and Λ_i be defined by

$$\Lambda_{i+1}(x_k) = Q(x_k) + \mu_i^T R \mu_i + \Lambda_i(\underbrace{f(x_k) + g(x_k)\mu_i(x_k)}_{x_{k+1}})$$

If $V_0(x_k) = \Lambda_0(x_k) = 0$, it follows that $V_i(x_k) \leq \Lambda_i(x_k) \quad \forall i$. Now assume that $\mu_i(x_k) = u_{i+1}(x_k)$ such that

$$\begin{aligned}\Lambda_{i+1}(x_k) &= Q(x_k) + \mu_i^T R \mu_i + \Lambda_i(f(x_k) + g(x_k)\mu_i(x_k)) \\ &= Q(x_k) + u_{i+1}^T R u_{i+1} + \Lambda_i(f(x_k) + g(x_k)u_{i+1}(x_k))\end{aligned} \tag{24}$$

and consider

$$V_{i+1}(x_k) = Q(x_k) + u_i^T R u_i + V_i(f(x_k) + g(x_k)u_i(x_k)) \tag{25}$$

It will next be proven by induction that if $V_0(x_k) = \Lambda_0(x_k) = 0$, then $\Lambda_i(x_k) \leq V_{i+1}(x_k)$. Induction is initialized by letting $V_0(x_k) = \Lambda_0(x_k) = 0$ and hence

$$\begin{aligned}V_1(x_k) - \Lambda_0(x_k) &= Q(x_k) \\ &\geq 0 \\ V_1(x_k) &\geq \Lambda_0(x_k)\end{aligned}$$

Now assume that $V_i(x_k) \geq \Lambda_{i-1}(x_k)$, then subtracting (24) from (25) it follows that

$$V_{i+1}(x_k) - \Lambda_i(x_k) = V_i(x_{k+1}) - \Lambda_{i-1}(x_{k+1}) \geq 0$$

and this completes the proof that $\Lambda_i(x_k) \leq V_{i+1}(x_k)$.

From $\Lambda_i(x_k) \leq V_{i+1}(x_k)$ and $V_i(x_k) \leq \Lambda_i(x_k)$, it then follows that

$$\forall i: V_i(x_k) \leq V_{i+1}(x_k).$$

From part a) in Lemma 2 and the fact that V_i is a non-decreasing sequence, it follows that $V_i \to V_\infty$ as $i \to \infty$. From part b) of Lemma 2, it also follows that $V_\infty(x_k) \le V^*(x_k)$.
It now remains to show that in fact V_∞ is V^*. To see this, note that from (11) it follows that

$$V_\infty(x_k) = x_k^T Q x_k + u_\infty^T(x_k) R u_\infty(x_k) + V_\infty(f(x_k) + g(x_k) u_\infty(x_k))$$

and hence

$$V_\infty(f(x_k) + g(x_k) u_\infty(x_k)) - V_\infty(x_k) = -x_k^T Q x_k - u_\infty^T(x_k) R u_\infty(x_k)$$

and therefore $V_\infty(x_k)$ is a Lyapunov function for a stabilizing and admissible policy $u_\infty(x_k) = \eta(x_k)$. Using part b) of Lemma 2 it follows that $V_\infty(x_k) = Y(x_k) \ge V^*(x_k)$. This implies that $V^*(x_k) \le V_\infty(x_k) \le V^*(x_k)$ and hence $V_\infty(x_k) = V^*(x_k)$, $u_\infty(x_k) = u^*(x_k)$. ■

5. Neural network approximation for Value and Action

We have just proven that the nonlinear HDP algorithm converges to the value function of the DT HJB equation that appears in the nonlinear discrete-time optimal control. It was assumed that the action and value update equations (10), (11) can be exactly solved at each iteration. In fact, these equations are difficult to solve for general nonlinear systems. Therefore, for implementation purposes, one needs to approximate u_i, V_i at each iteration. This allows approximate solution of (10), (11).
In this section, we review how to implement the HDP value iterations algorithm with two parametric structures such as neural networks (Werbos, 1990) and (Lewis & Jaganathan, 1999). The important point is stressed that the use of two NN, a critic for value function approximation and an action NN for the control, allows the implementation of HDP in the LQR case *without knowing* the system internal dynamics matrix A. This point is not generally appreciated in the folklore of ADP.

5.1 NN Approximation for Implementation of HDP Algorithm for Nonlinear Systems

It is well known that neural networks can be used to approximate smooth functions on prescribed compact sets (Hornik & Stinchcombe, 1990). Therefore, to solve (11) and (10), $V_i(x)$ is approximated at each step by a critic NN

$$\hat{V}_i(x) = \sum_{j=1}^{L} w_{vi}^j \phi_j(x) = W_{Vi}^T \boldsymbol{\phi}(x) \tag{26}$$

and $u_i(x)$ by an action NN

$$\hat{u}_i(x) = \sum_{j=1}^{M} w_{ui}^j \sigma_j(x) = W_{ui}^T \boldsymbol{\sigma}(x) \tag{27}$$

where the activation functions are respectively $\phi_j(x), \sigma_j(x) \in C^1(\Omega)$. Since it is required that $V_i(x=0)=0$ and $u_i(x=0)=0$, we select activation functions with $\phi_j(0)=0, \sigma_j(0)=0$. Moreover, since it is known that V^* is a Lyapunov function, and Lyapunov proofs are convenient if the Lyapunov function is symmetric and positive definite, it is convenient to also require that the activation functions for the critic NN be symmetric, i.e. $\phi_j(x)=\phi_j(-x)$. The neural network weights in the critic NN (26) are w_{vi}^j. L is the number of hidden-layer neurons. The vector $\boldsymbol{\phi}(x) \equiv [\phi_1(x)\, \phi_2(x) \cdots \phi_L(x)]^T$ is the vector activation function and $W_{Vi} \equiv \left[w_{vi}^1\, w_{vi}^2 \cdots w_{vi}^L\right]^T$ is the weight vector at iteration i. Similarly, the weights of the neural network in (27) are w_{ui}^j. M is the number of hidden-layer neurons. $\boldsymbol{\sigma}(x) \equiv [\sigma_1(x)\, \sigma_2(x) \cdots \sigma_L(x)]^T$ is the vector activation function, and $W_{ui} \equiv \left[w_{ui}^1\, w_{ui}^2 \cdots w_{ui}^L\right]^T$ is the vector weight.

According to (11), the critic weights are tuned at each iteration of HDP to minimize the residual error between $\hat{V}_{i+1}(x_k)$ and the target function defined in equation (28) in a least-squares sense for a set of states x_k sampled from a compact set $\Omega \subset \mathbb{R}^n$.

$$\begin{aligned} d(x_k, x_{k+1}, W_{Vi}, W_{ui}) &= x_k^T Q x_k + \hat{u}_i^T(x_k) R \hat{u}_i(x_k) + \hat{V}_i(x_{k+1}) \\ &= x_k^T Q x_k + \hat{u}_i^T(x_k) R \hat{u}_i(x_k) + W_{Vi}^T \boldsymbol{\phi}(x_{k+1}) \end{aligned} \tag{28}$$

The residual error (c.f. temporal difference error) becomes

$$\left(W_{Vi+1}^T \boldsymbol{\phi}(x_k) - d(x_k, x_{k+1}, W_{Vi}, W_{ui})\right) = e_L(x). \tag{29}$$

Note that the residual error in (29) is explicit, in fact linear, in the tuning parameters W_{Vi+1}. Therefore, to find the least-squares solution, the method of weighted residuals may be used 0. The weights W_{Vi+1} are determined by projecting the residual error onto $de_L(x)/dW_{Vi+1}$ and setting the result to zero $\forall x \in \Omega$ using the inner product, *i.e.*

$$\left\langle \frac{de_L(x)}{dW_{Vi+1}}, e_L(x) \right\rangle = 0, \tag{30}$$

where $\langle f,g \rangle = \int_\Omega f g^T dx$ is a Lebesgue integral. One has

$$0 = \int_\Omega \phi(x_k)\left(\phi^T(x_k) W_{Vi+1} - d^T(x_k, x_{k+1}, W_{Vi}, W_{ui})\right) dx_k \tag{31}$$

Therefore a unique solution for W_{Vi+1} exists and is computed as

$$W_{Vi+1} = \left(\int_{\Omega} \phi(x_k)\phi(x_k)^T dx \right)^{-1} \int_{\Omega} \phi(x_k) d^T(\phi(x_k), W_{Vi}, W_{ui}) dx \tag{32}$$

To use this solution, it is required that the outer product integral be positive definite. This is known as a persistence of excitation condition in system theory. The next assumption is standard in selecting the NN activation functions as a basis set.

Assumption 1. The selected activation functions $\{\phi_j(x)\}^L$ are linearly independent on the compact set $\Omega \subset \mathbb{R}^n$.

Assumption 1 guarantees that excitation condition is satisfied and hence $\int_{\Omega} \phi(x_k)\phi(x_k)^T dx$ is of full rank and invertible and a unique solution for (32) exists.

The action NN weights are tuned to solve (10) at each iteration. The use of $\hat{u}_i(x_k, W_{ui})$ from (27) allows the rewriting of equation (10) as

$$W_{ui} = \arg\min_{w} \left(x_k^T Q x_k + \hat{u}_i^T(x_k, w) R \hat{u}_i(x_k, w) + \hat{V}_i(x_{k+1}^i) \right)\Big|_{\Omega} \tag{33}$$

where $x_{k+1}^i = f(x_k) + g(x_k)\hat{u}_i(x_k, w)$ and the notation means minimization for a set of points x_k selected from the compact set $\Omega \in \mathbb{R}^n$.

Note that the control weights W_{ui} appear in (33) in an implicit fashion, *i.e.* it is difficult to solve explicitly for the weights since the current control weights determine x_{k+1}. Therefore, one can use an LMS algorithm on a training set constructed from Ω. The weight update is therefore

$$W_{ui}\big|_{m+1} = W_{ui}\big|_m - \alpha \left. \frac{\partial (x_k^T Q x_k + \hat{u}_i^T(x_k, W_{ui}|_m) R \hat{u}_i(x_k, W_{ui}|_m) + \hat{V}_i(x_{k+1}))}{\partial W_{ui}} \right|_{W_{ui}|_m}$$
$$W_{ui}\big|_{m+1} = W_{ui}\big|_m - \alpha\sigma(x_k) \left(2R\hat{u}_i(x_k, W_{ui}|_m) + g(x_k)^T \frac{\partial \phi(x_{k+1})}{\partial x_{k+1}} W_{Vi} \right)^T \tag{34}$$

where α is a positive step size and m is the iteration number for the LMS algorithm. By a stochastic approximation type argument, the weights $W_{ui}|_m \Rightarrow W_{ui}$ as $m \Rightarrow \infty$, and satisfy (33). Note that one can use alternative tuning methods such as Newton's method and Levenberg-Marquardt in order to solve (33).

In Figure 1, the flow chart of the HDP iteration is shown. Note that because of the neural network used to approximate the control policy the internal dynamics, *i.e.* $f(x_k)$ is not needed. That is, the internal dynamics can be unknown.

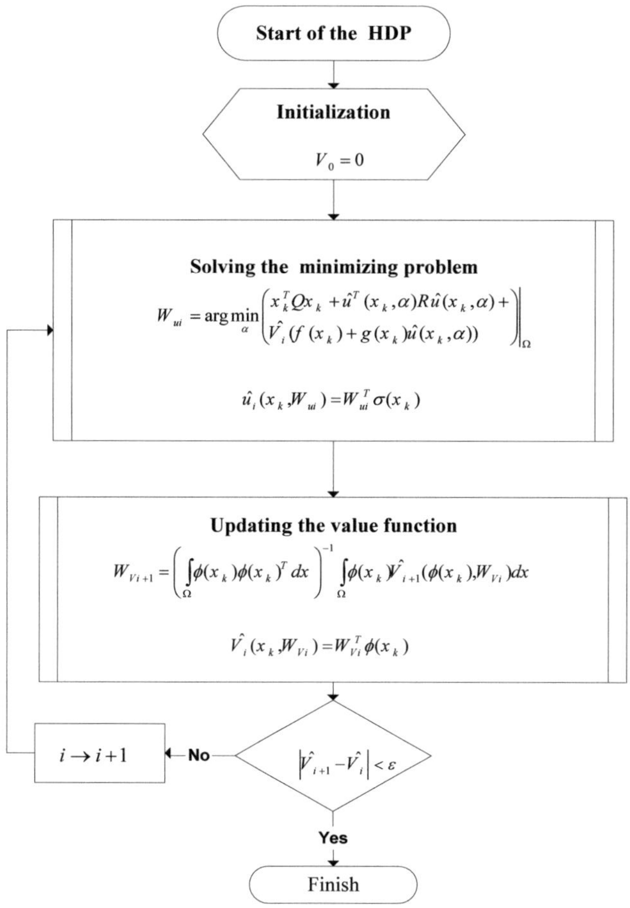

Fig. 1. Flow chart shows the proposed algorithm

Remark. Neither $f(x)$ nor $g(x)$ is needed to update the critic neural network weights using (32). Only the input coupling term $g(x)$ is needed to update the action neural network weights using (34). Therefore the proposed algorithm works for system with partially unknown dynamics- no knowledge of the internal feedback structure $f(x)$ is needed.

5.2 HDP for Linear Systems Without Knowledge of Internal Dynamics

The general practice in the HDP folklore for linear quadratic systems is to use a critic NN to approximate the value, and update the critic weights using a method such as the batch update (32), or a recursive update method such as LMS. In fact, the critic weights are nothing but the elements of the Riccati matrix and the activation functions are quadratic polynomials in terms of the states. Then, the policy is updated using

$$u_i(x_k) = -(R + B^T P_i B)^{-1} B^T P_i A x_k \tag{35}$$

Note that this equation requires the full knowledge of both the internal dynamics matrix A and the control weighting matrix B . However, we have just seen (see remark above) that the knowledge of the A matrix can be avoided by using, instead of the action update (35), a second NN for the action

$$\hat{u}_i(x) = W_{ui}^T \sigma(x)$$

In fact the action NN approximates the effects of A and B given in (35), and so effectively learns the A matrix.
That is, using two NN even in the LQR case avoids the need to know the internal dynamics A. In fact, in the next section we give a LQR example, and only the input coupling matrix B is needed for the HDP algorithm. Nevertheless, the HDP converges to the correct LQR Riccati solution matrix P.

6. Simulation Examples

In this section, two examples are provided to demonstrate the solution of the DT HJB equation. The first example will be a linear quadratic regulator, which is a special case of the nonlinear system. It is shown that using two NN allows one to compute the optimal value and control (i.e. the Riccati equation solution) online *without knowing the system matrix* A . The second example is for a DT nonlinear system. MATLAB is used in the simulations to implement some of the functions discussed in the chapter.

6.1 Unstable multi-input linear system example

In this example we show the power of the proposed method by using an unstable multi-input linear system. We also emphasize that the method does not require knowledge of the system A matrix, since two neural networks are used, one to provide the action. This is in contrast to normal methods of HDP for linear quadratic control used in the literature, where the A matrix is needed to update the control policy.
Consider the linear system

$$x_{k+1} = Ax_k + Bu_k \, . \tag{36}$$

It is known that the solution of the optimal control problem for the linear system is quadratic in the state and given as

$$V^*(x_k) = x_k^T P x_k$$

where P is the solution of the ARE. This example is taken from (Stevens & Lewis, 2003), a linearized model of the short-period dynamics of an advanced (CCV-type) fighter aircraft. The state vector is

$$x = [\alpha \quad q \quad \gamma \quad \delta_e \quad \delta_f]^T$$

where the state components are, respectively, angel of attack, pitch rate, flight-path, elevator deflection and flaperon deflection. The control input are the elevator and the flaperon and given as

$$u = [\delta_{ec} \quad \delta_{fc}]^T$$

The plant model is a discretized version of a continuous-time model given in (Bradtke & Ydestie, 0

$$A = \begin{bmatrix} 1.0722 & 0.0954 & 0 & -0.0541 & -0.0153 \\ 4.1534 & 1.1175 & 0 & -0.8000 & -0.1010 \\ 0.1359 & 0.0071 & 1.0 & 0.0039 & 0.0097 \\ 0 & 0 & 0 & 0.1353 & 0 \\ 0 & 0 & 0 & 0 & 0.1353 \end{bmatrix}$$

$$B = \begin{bmatrix} -0.0453 & -0.0175 \\ -1.0042 & -0.1131 \\ 0.0075 & 0.0134 \\ 0.8647 & 0 \\ 0 & 0.8647 \end{bmatrix}$$

Note that system is not stable and with two control inputs. The proposed algorithm does not require a stable initial control policy. The ARE solution for the given linear system is

$$P = \begin{bmatrix} 55.8348 & 7.6670 & 16.0470 & -4.6754 & -0.7265 \\ 7.6670 & 2.3168 & 1.4987 & -0.8309 & -0.1215 \\ 16.0470 & 1.4987 & 25.3586 & -0.6709 & 0.0464 \\ -4.6754 & -0.8309 & -0.6709 & 1.5394 & 0.0782 \\ -0.7265 & -0.1215 & 0.0464 & 0.0782 & 1.0240 \end{bmatrix} \tag{37}$$

and the optimal control $u_k^* = Lx_k$, where L is

$$L = \begin{bmatrix} -4.1136 & -0.7170 & -0.3847 & 0.5277 & 0.0707 \\ -0.6315 & -0.1003 & 0.1236 & 0.0653 & 0.0798 \end{bmatrix} \tag{38}$$

For the LQR case the value is quadratic and the control is linear. Therefore, we select linear activation functions for the action NN and quadratic polynomial activations for the critic NN. The control is approximated as follows

$$\hat{u}_i = W_{ui}^T \sigma(x_k) \tag{39}$$

where W_u is the weight vector, and the $\sigma(x_k)$ is the vector activation function and is given by

$$\sigma^T(x) = \begin{bmatrix} x_1 & x_2 & x_3 & x_4 & x_5 \end{bmatrix}$$

and the weights are

$$W_u^T = \begin{bmatrix} w_u^{1,1} & w_u^{1,2} & w_u^{1,3} & w_u^{1,4} & w_u^{1,5} \\ w_u^{2,1} & w_u^{2,2} & w_u^{2,3} & w_u^{2,4} & w_u^{2,5} \end{bmatrix}$$

The control weights should converge to

$$\begin{bmatrix} w_u^{1,1} & w_u^{1,2} & w_u^{1,3} & w_u^{1,4} & w_u^{1,5} \\ w_u^{2,1} & w_u^{2,2} & w_u^{2,3} & w_u^{2,4} & w_u^{2,5} \end{bmatrix} = -\begin{bmatrix} L_{11} & L_{12} & L_{13} & L_{14} & L_{15} \\ L_{21} & L_{22} & L_{23} & L_{24} & L_{25} \end{bmatrix}$$

The approximation of the value function is given as

$$\hat{V}_i(x_k, W_{Vi}) = W_{Vi}^T \phi(x_k)$$

where W_V is the weight vector of the neural network given by

$$W_V^T = \begin{bmatrix} w_v^1 & w_v^2 & w_v^3 & w_v^4 & w_v^5 & w_v^6 & w_v^7 & w_v^8 & w_v^9 & w_v^{10} & w_v^{11} & w_v^{12} & w_v^{13} & w_v^{14} & w_v^{15} \end{bmatrix}$$

and $\phi(x_k)$ is the vector activation function given by

$$\phi^T(x) =$$
$$\begin{bmatrix} x_1^2 & x_1x_2 & x_1x_3 & x_1x_4 & x_1x_5 & x_2^2 & x_2x_3 & x_4x_2 & x_2x_5 & x_3^2 & x_3x_4 & x_3x_5 & x_4^2 & x_4x_5 & x_5^2 \end{bmatrix}$$

In the simulation the weights of the value function are related to the P matrix given in (37) as follows

$$\begin{bmatrix} P_{11} & P_{12} & P_{13} & P_{14} & P_{15} \\ P_{21} & P_{22} & P_{23} & P_{24} & P_{25} \\ P_{31} & P_{32} & P_{33} & P_{34} & P_{35} \\ P_{41} & P_{42} & P_{43} & P_{44} & P_{45} \\ P_{51} & P_{52} & P_{53} & P_{54} & P_{55} \end{bmatrix} = \begin{bmatrix} w_v^1 & 0.5w_v^2 & 0.5w_v^3 & 0.5w_v^4 & 0.5w_v^5 \\ 0.5w_v^2 & w_v^6 & 0.5w_v^7 & 0.5w_v^8 & 0.5w_v^9 \\ 0.5w_v^3 & 0.5w_v^7 & w_v^{10} & 0.5w_v^{11} & 0.5w_v^{12} \\ 0.5w_v^4 & 0.5w_v^8 & 0.5w_v^{11} & w_v^{13} & 0.5w_v^{14} \\ 0.5w_v^5 & 0.5w_v^9 & 0.5w_v^{12} & 0.5w_v^{14} & w_v^{15} \end{bmatrix}$$

The value function weights converge to

$$W_V^T = [55.5411 \quad 15.2789 \quad 31.3032 \quad -9.3255 \quad -1.4536 \quad 2.3142 \quad 2.9234 \quad -1.6594 \quad -0.2430$$

$$24.8262 \quad -1.3076 \quad 0.0920 \quad 1.5388 \quad 0.1564 \quad 1.0240]$$

The control weights converge to

$$W_u = \begin{bmatrix} 4.1068 & 0.7164 & 0.3756 & -0.5274 & -0.0707 \\ 0.6330 & 0.1005 & -0.1216 & -0.0653 & -0.0798 \end{bmatrix}$$

Note that the value function weights converge to the solution of the ARE (37), also the control weights converge to the optimal policy (38) as expected.

6.2 Nonlinear system example

Consider the following affine in input nonlinear system

$$x_{k+1} = f(x_k) + g(x_k)u_k \tag{40}$$

where

$$f(x_k) = \begin{bmatrix} 0.2x_k(1)\exp(x_k^2(2)) \\ .3x_k^3(2) \end{bmatrix} \quad g(x_k) = \begin{bmatrix} 0 \\ -.2 \end{bmatrix}$$

The approximation of the value function is given as

$$\hat{V}_{i+1}(x_k, W_{Vi+1}) = W_{Vi+1}^T \phi(x_k)$$

The vector activation function is selected as

$$\begin{aligned} \phi(x) = [&x_1^2 \quad x_1x_2 \quad x_2^2 \quad x_1^4 \quad x_1^3x_2 \\ &x_1^2x_2^2 \quad x_1x_2^3 \quad x_2^4 \quad x_1^6 \quad x_1^5x_2 \quad x_1^4x_2^2 \\ &x_1^3x_2^3 \quad x_1^2x_2^4 \quad x_1x_2^5 \quad x_2^6] \end{aligned}$$

and the weight vector is

$$W_V^T = \begin{bmatrix} w_v^1 & w_v^2 & w_v^3 & w_v^4 & \ldots\ldots & w_v^{15} \end{bmatrix}.$$

The control is approximated by

$$\hat{u}_i = W_{ui}^T \sigma(x_k)$$

where the vector activation function is

$$\begin{aligned} \sigma^T(x) = [&x_1 \quad x_2 \quad x_1^3 \quad x_1^2x_2 \quad x_1x_2^2 \\ &x_2^3 \quad x_1^5 \quad x_1^4x_2 \quad x_1^3x_2^2 \quad x_1^2x_2^3 \\ &x_1x_2^4 \quad x_2^5] \end{aligned}$$

and the weights are

$$W_u^T = \begin{bmatrix} w_u^1 & w_u^2 & w_u^3 & w_u^4 & \ldots & w_u^{12} \end{bmatrix}.$$

The control NN activation functions are selected as the derivatives of the critic activation functions, since the gradient of the critic activation functions appears in (34). The critic activations are selected as polynomials to satisfy $\hat{V}_i(x=0)=0$ at each step. Note that then automatically one has $\hat{u}_i(x=0)=0$ as required for admissibility. We decided on 6th order polynomials for VFA after a few simulations, where it came clear that 4th order polynomials are not good enough, yet going to 8th order does not improve the results.
The result of the algorithm is compared to the discrete-time State Dependent Riccati Equation (SDRE) proposed in (Cloutier, 1997).
The training sets is $x_1 \in [-2,2], x_2 \in [-1,1]$. The value function weights converged to the following

$$W_V^T = [1.0382 \;\; 0 \;\; 1.0826 \;\; .0028 \;\; \text{-}0 \;\; \text{-}.053 \;\; 0 \;\; \text{-}.2792 \;\; \text{-}.0004 \;\; 0 \;\; \text{-}.0013 \;\; 0 \;\; .1549 \;\; 0 \;\; .3034]$$

and the control weights converged to

$$W_u^T = [\, 0 \;\; \text{-}.0004 \;\; 0 \;\; 0 \;\; 0 \;\; .0651 \;\; 0 \;\; 0 \;\; 0 \;\; \text{-}.0003 \;\; 0 \;\; \text{-}.0046]$$

The result of the nonlinear optimal controller derived in this chapter is compared to the SDRE approach. Figure 2 and Figure 3 show the states trajectories for the system for both methods.

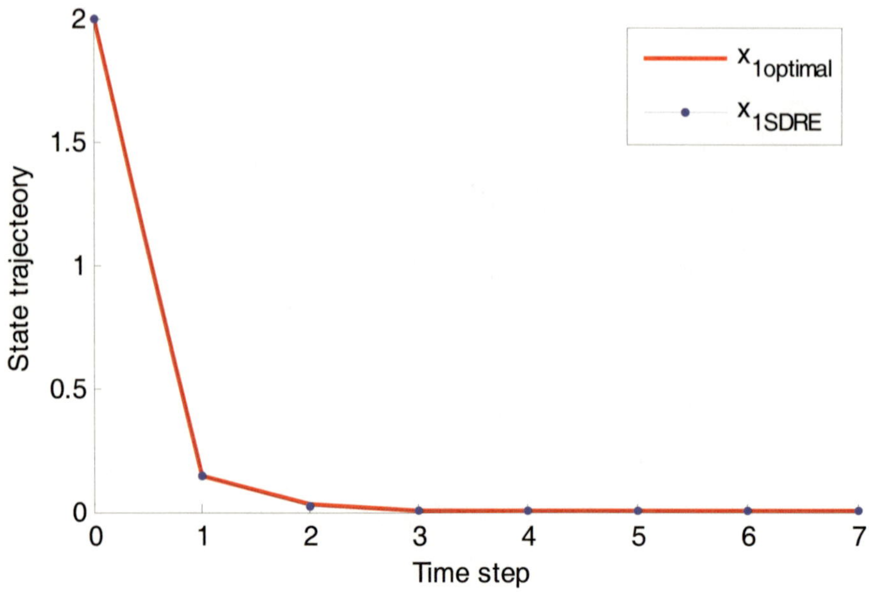

Fig. 2. The state trajectory for both methods

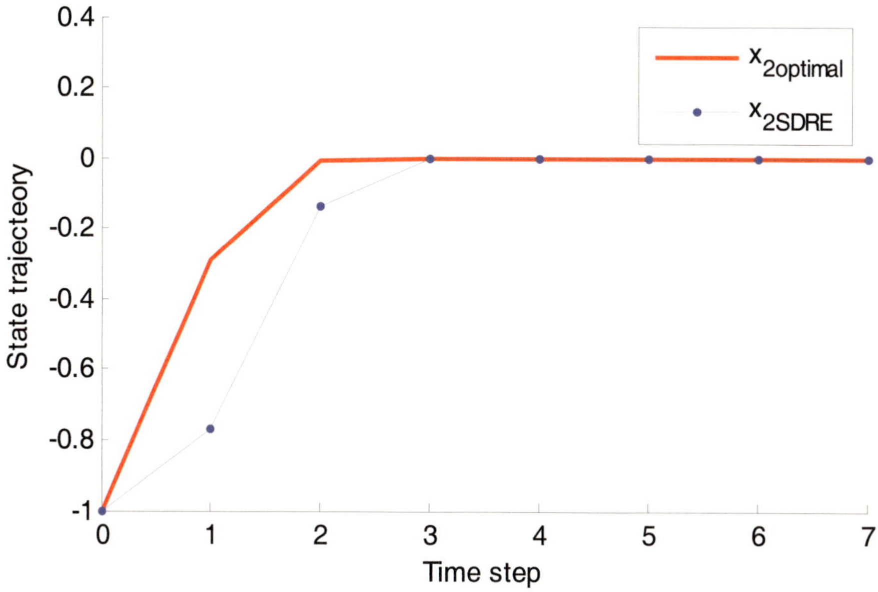

Fig. 3. The state trajectory for both methods

In Figure 4, the cost function of the SDRE solution and the cost function of the proposed algorithm in this chapter are compared. It is clear from the simulation that the cost function for the control policy derived from the HDP method is lower than that of the SDRE method. In Figure 5, the control signals for both methods are shown.

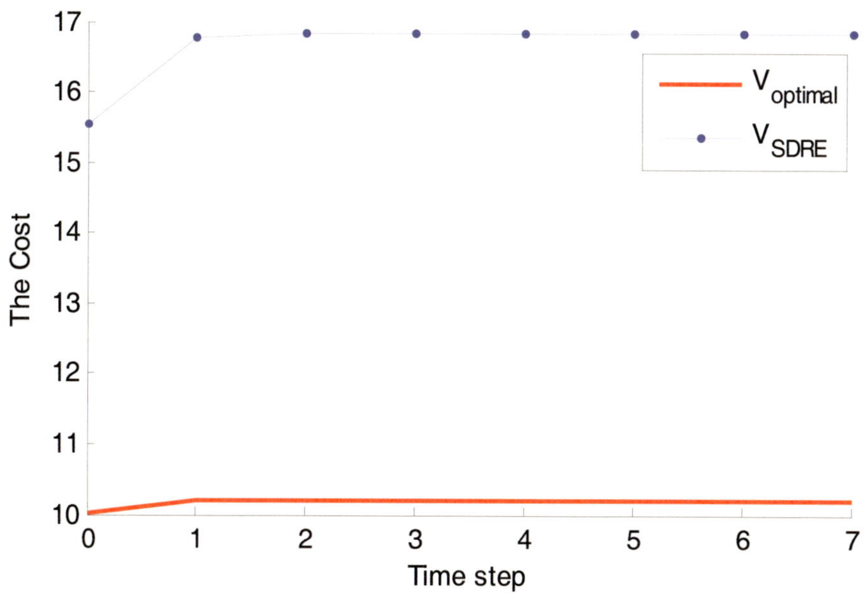

Fig. 4. The cost function for both methods

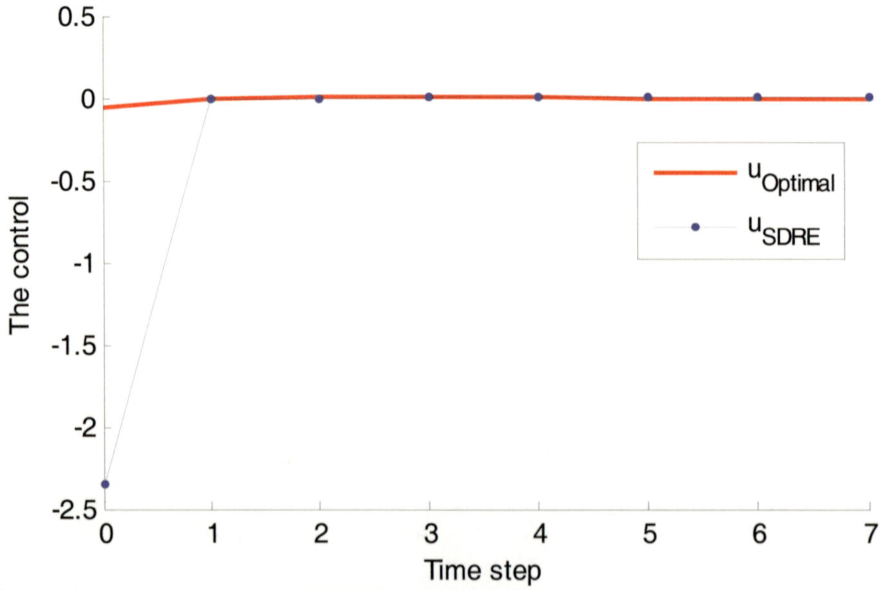

Figure 5. The control signal input for both methods

7. Conclusion

We have proven convergence of the HDP algorithm to the value function solution of Hamilton-Jacobi-Bellman equation for nonlinear dynamical systems, assuming exact solution of value update and the action update at each iteration.

Neural networks are used as parametric structures to approximate at each iteration the value (i.e. critic NN), and the control action. It is stressed that the use of the second neural network to approximate the control policy, the internal dynamics, *i.e.* $f(x_k)$, is not needed to implement HDP. This holds as well for the special LQR case, where use of two NN avoids the need to know the system internal dynamics matrix A. This is not generally appreciated in the folkloric literature of ADP for the LQR. In the simulation examples, it is shown that the linear system critic network converges to the solution of the ARE, and the actor network converges to the optimal policy, without knowing the system matrix A. In the nonlinear example, it is shown that the optimal controller derived from the HDP based value iteration method outperforms suboptimal control methods like those found through the SDRE method.

8. References

Abu-Khalaf, M., F. L. Lewis. (2005).Nearly Optimal Control Laws for Nonlinear Systems with Saturating Actuators Using a Neural Network HJB Approach. *Automatica*, vol. 41, pp. 779 - 791.

Abu-Khalaf, M., F. L. Lewis, and J. Huang.(2004).Hamilton-Jacobi-Isaacs formulation for constrained input nonlinear systems. *43rd IEEE Conference on Decision and Control,* 2004, pp. 5034 - 5040 Vol.5.

Al-Tamimi, A. , F. L. Lewis, M. Abu-Khalaf (2007). Model-Free Q-Learning Designs for Discrete-Time Zero-Sum Games with Application to H-Infinity Control. *Automatica,* volume 43, no. 3. pp 473-481.

Al-Tamimi, A., M. Abu-Khalaf, F. L. Lewis.(2007). Adaptive Critic Designs for Discrete-Time Zero-Sum Games with Application to H-Infinity Control. *IEEE Transactions on Systems, Man, Cybernetics-Part B, Cybernaetics,* Vol 37, No 1, pp 240-24.

Barto, A. G., R. S. Sutton, and C. W. Anderson.(1983). Neuronlike elements that can solve difficult learning control problems. *IEEE Trans. Syst., Man, Cybern.,* vol. SMC-13, pp. 835–846.

Bertsekas, D.P. and J. N. Tsitsiklis.(1996). Neuro-Dynamic Programming. *Athena Scientific,* MA.

Bradtke, S. J., B. E. Ydestie, A. G. Barto (1994).Adaptive linear quadratic control using policy iteration. *Proceedings of the American Control Conference* , pp. 3475-3476, Baltmore, Myrland..

Chen, Z., Jagannathan, S.(2005). Neural Network -based Nearly Optimal Hamilton-Jacobi-Bellman Solution for Affine Nonlinear Discrete-Time Systems. *IEEE CDC 05* ,pp 4123-4128.

Cloutier, J. R. (1997). State –Dependent Riccati equation Techniques: An overview. *Proceeding of the American control conference,* Albuquerque, NM, pp 932-936.

Ferrari, S., Stengel, R.(2004) Model-Based Adaptive Critic Designs. pp 64-94, Eds J. Si, A.
Barto, W. Powell, D. Wunsch *Handbook of Learning and Approximate Dynamic Programming,* Wiley.

Finlayson, B. A.(1972). The *Method of Weighted Residuals and Variational Principles.* Academic Press, New York.

Hagen, S. B Krose.(1998). Linear quadratic Regulation using Reinforcement Learning. *Belgian_Dutch Conference on Mechanical Learning,* pp. 39-46.

He, P. and S. Jagannathan.(2005).Reinforcement learning-basedoutput feedback control of nonlinear systems with input constraints. *IEEE Trans. Systems, Man, and Cybernetics -Part B:Cybernetics,* vol. 35, no.1, pp. 150-154.

Hewer, G.A.(1971). An iterative technique for the computation of the steady state gains for the discrete optimal regulator. *IEEE Trans. Automatic Control,* pp. 382-384.

Hornik, K., M. Stinchcombe, H. White.(1990) .Universal Approximation of an Unknown Mapping and Its Derivatives Using Multilayer Feedforward Networks. *Neural Networks,* vol. 3, pp. 551-560.

Howard, R.(1960). *Dynamic Programming and Markov Processes.,* MIT Press, Cambridge, MA.

Huang, J.(1999).An algorithm to solve the discrete HJI equation arising in the L_2-gain optimization problem. INT. J. Control, Vol 72, No 1, pp 49-57.

Kwon, W. H and S. Han. (2005). *Receding Horizon Control,* Springer-Verlag, London.

Lancaster, P. L. Rodman. (1995). *Algebraic Riccati Equations.* Oxford University Press, UK.

Landelius, T.(1997). *Reinforcement Learning and Distributed Local Model Synthesis.* PhD Dissertation, Linkoping University, Sweden.

Lewis, F. L., V. L. Syrmos.(1995) Optimal Control, 2nd ed., John Wiley.

Lewis, F. L., Jagannathan, S., & Yesildirek, A. (1999). *Neural Network Control of Robot Manipulators and Nonlinear Systems*. Taylor & Franci.

Lin W.,and C. I. Byrnes.(1996).H_{∞}Control of Discrete-Time Nonlinear System. *IEEE Trans. on Automat. Control* , vol 41, No 4, pp 494-510..

Lu, X., S.N. Balakrishnan.(2000). Convergence analysis of adaptive critic based optimal control. *Proc. Amer. Control Conf.*, pp. 1929-1933, Chicago.

Morimoto, J., G. Zeglin, and C.G. Atkeson. (2003). Minimax differential dynamic programming: application to a biped walking robot. *Proc. IEEE Int. Conf. Intel. Robots and Systems*, pp. 1927-1932, Las Vegas.

Murray J., C. J. Cox, G. G. Lendaris, and R. Saeks.(2002).Adaptive Dynamic Programming. *IEEE Trans. on Sys., Man. and Cyb.*, Vol. 32, No. 2, pp 140-153.

Narendra, K.S. and F.L. Lewis.(2001).Special Issue on Neural Network feedback Control. Automatica, vol. 37, no. 8.

Prokhorov, D., D. Wunsch.(1997). Adaptive critic designs. *IEEE Trans. on Neural Networks*, vol. 8, no. 5, pp 997-1007.

Prokhorov, D., D. Wunsch(1997).Convergence of Critic-Based Training. *Proc. IEEE Int. Conf. Syst., Man, Cybern.*, vol. 4, pp. 3057—3060.

Si, J. and Wang.(2001). On-Line learning by association and reinforcement. *IEEE Trans. Neural Networks*, vol. 12, pp.264-276.

Si, Ji. A. Barto, W. Powell, D. Wunsch.(2004). *Handbook of Learning and Approximate Dynamic Programming*. John Wiley, New Jersey.

Stevens B., F. L. Lewis.(2003). Aircraft Control and Simulation, 2nd edition, John Wiley, New Jersey.

Sutton, R.S., A.G. Barto.(19998). *Reinforcement Learning, MIT Press.* Cambridge, MA .

Watkins, C.(1989). *Learning from Delayed Rewards*. Ph.D. Thesis, Cambridge University, Cambridge, England.

Werbos, P.J.(1991). A menu of designs for reinforcement learning over time. , *Neural Networks for Control*, pp. 67-95, ed. W.T. Miller, R.S. Sutton, P.J. Werbos, Cambridge: MIT Press.

Werbos, P.J. (1992). *Approximate dynamic programming for real-time control and neural modeling*. Handbook of Intelligent Control, ed. D.A. White and D.A. Sofge, New York: Van Nostrand Reinhold,.

Werbos, P.J. (1990). Neural networks for control and system identification. *Heuristics,* Vol. 3, No. 1, pp. 18-27.

Widrow, B., N. Gupta, and S. Maitra.(1973). Punish/reward: Learning with a critic in adaptive threshold systems. *IEEE Trans. Syst., Man, Cybern.*, vol. SMC-3, pp. 455–465.

Xi-Ren Cao. (2001). Learning and Optimization—From a Systems Theoretic Perspective. *Proc. of IEEE Conference on Decision and Control*, pp. 3367-3371.

16

Multi-Scale Modeling and Analysis of Left Ventricular Remodeling Post Myocardial Infarction: Integration of Experimental and Computational Approaches

Yufang Jin, Ph.D.[1] and Merry L. Lindsey, Ph.D.[2]
[1]*Department of Electrical and Computer Engineering, The University of Texas at San Antonio*
[2]*Division of Cardiology, Department of Medicine, The University of Texas Health Science Center at San Antonio*

Abstract

Progressive remodeling of the left ventricle (LV) following myocardial infarction (MI) involves spatiotemporal interactions among multiple cell types and the extracellular matrix environment. Despite the extensive experimental studies designed to elucidate the regulatory mechanisms, there is a growing recognition that the complexity of LV remodeling precludes the efficient identification of early diagnostic indicators after myocardial infarction. Currently, systemic approaches are needed to reduce this complexity. Previous studies in other systems demonstrate that establishing a multi-scale analytical model of LV remodeling response to MI will likely help in the development of prognostic therapies. In this review, we discuss the current approaches used for mathematical modeling of the LV, advantages and disadvantages of the approaches, and methods used to validate these models.

Keywords: mathematical model, left ventricular remodeling, extracellular matrix, inflammation, outcome prediction, model validation

1. Introduction

A myocardial infarction (MI) occurs when a coronary artery becomes totally closed off, resulting in the loss of oxygen to the downstream myocardium (a process termed ischemia). Following MI, the left ventricle (LV) undergoes a spectrum of responses at the gene and protein levels that are represented clinically as changes in LV size, shape, and function [1]. LV remodeling encompasses many alterations, including LV wall thinning, LV dilation, and infarct expansion; inflammation and necrotic myocyte resorption; fibroblast accumulation and scar formation; and endothelial cell activation and neovascularization [2, 3]. LV remodeling is also influenced by variations in leukocyte response (neutrophil and macrophage influx), blood pressure and volume, molecular changes (neurohormonal activation and cytokine production), and extracellular matrix responses (fibrosis and activation of proteases, particularly the matrix metalloproteinases (MMPs) and serine proteases) [4]. In addition, pre-existing conditions such as increased age, diabetes, or the use of drugs such as angiotensin converting enzyme inhibitors and β adrenergic receptor inhibitors can influence remodeling outcomes. Basically, LV remodeling after MI is a complex wound healing response that involves the dynamic spatiotemporal interactions between the various cell types and the acellular components.

2. Rationale for Mathematical Modeling of LV Remodeling

While research over the past 30 years has accumulated vast amounts of experimental data and has greatly improved our understanding of LV remodeling post-MI, this knowledge has not been translated to the effective identification of early diagnostic indicators that can accurately predict the post-MI patient who is at high risk to develop heart failure. This is evidenced by the fact that long-term heart failure survival post-MI has not been improved, and a five year mortality rate of 50% persists [5]. MI is the number one cause of heart failure, accounting for 70% of all heart failure cases [6]. Therefore, using mathematical modeling approaches to understand how the LV progresses during the post-MI response may provide mechanistic insight into LV remodeling that can be used to develop novel therapeutic strategies.

The complexity of LV remodeling and the inability of one experiment to all-inclusively examine all parameters (or even examine only the most critical parameters) make it impossible to experimentally study this problem at the whole systems level. What is needed is to separate the system into its constituent parts and recombine these parts together to understand the whole system.

This superposition approach is successful if the system is linear and the tested variables are independent from each other. LV remodeling, however, involves many components with coupled feedback loops and nonlinear saturating kinetic responses. The remodeling process exhibits "emergent behavior", which means that remodeling displays system dynamics that are not attributable to any specific component but rather to the whole system. Therefore, analyzing individual components in isolation is not likely to reveal the full spectrum of system behavior. Indeed, there is growing recognition that complex biological progression should be examined based on spatiotemporal interactions [7-14]. Spatiotemporal interactions can be characterized in terms of mathematical relations built on the mechanism of the system and validated by experimental data. In particular, the availability of high-throughput quantitative data and improved computing power have recently made mathematical modeling of LV remodeling more feasible.

In this review, we will focus on the temporal profiles of biochemical components in the LV post-MI in mice, current mathematical modeling methods that can be used to develop models, and methods to validate the mathematical model with experimental data.

3. Temporal Profiles of LV remodeling

MI occurs when there is a sustained interruption of the blood supply to the heart, leading to rapid death of the myocytes in the affected part of the cardiac wall. Since cardiac myocytes are post-mitotic cells, the necrotic myocytes cannot be replaced with cells with similar characteristics, as occurs in other wound healing systems such as the skin and liver. Instead, the infarct area is repaired with granulation tissue that matures into a scar. Progressive LV remodeling post-MI can be divided into four phases: the necrotic phase immediately after MI, the acute inflammatory response phase from day 1-7, the formation of granulation tissue phase (1-3 weeks), and the remodeling phase (> 3 weeks) [15, 16].

3.1 Cellular changes

In normal mouse myocardium, the Baudino laboratory has shown that myocytes, fibroblasts, vascular smooth muscle cells, and endothelial cells accounts for 56%, 27%, 10%, and 7% of total cell numbers, respectively [17]. Post MI, myocytes die and the major cell types are (myo)fibroblasts, endothelial cells, and inflammatory cells (including neutrophils, macrophages, and lymphocytes).

Necrotic phase: myocytes

As early as six hours post-MI, myocyte death is apparent. Apoptosis is believed to be responsible for the early myocyte death in the first 6 hrs to 8 hrs post-MI, whereas necrosis is more of a secondary event that occur 12 hrs to 4 days after myocardial infarction [18]. This secondary event may be caused by the fact that the majority of apoptotic cells cannot be consumed or phagocytosed by neighboring cells. In reaction to this, an inflammatory response is initiated within the infarct region. The influx of leukocytes is the hallmark of the inflammatory response phase.

Inflammatory response phase: neutrophils, macrophages, and lymphocytes

The early inflammatory response after myocardial infarction takes place within 12 - 16 hours after the onset of ischemia (in the absence of reperfusion). Neutrophils are the first immune response cells to arrive at a site of infection. Neutrophils produce enzymes such as elastase and matrix metalloproteinase (MMPs) that allow inflammatory cells to migrate into the infarct tissue to remove the necrotic myocytes. The number of neutrophils migrated to the infarct region peaks at 1-3 days after MI and is significantly declined by day 5 post-MI [19]. After releasing storage granule components, neutrophils undergo apoptosis and are subsequently removed by macrophages.

Macrophages follow the neutrophils influx and have a strong phagocytic function to remove necrotic myocytes and apoptotic neutrophils. Activated macrophages are differentiated from peripheral blood monocytes [21]. Macrophage proliferation is not a significant component, since previous studies have shown that <5% of macrophages undergo mitotic division [20, 21]. Macrophages infiltrate into the infarct from days 2-7 and peak at day 4 , indicating that the acute inflammatory response occurs within 4 days and is marked by the removal of necrotic tissue and repair. Macrophage infiltration gradually decreases after day 14, even though macrophage densities are still higher than control at day 28 post-MI [19]. Macrophages do not die locally in the scar tissue but emigrate to the lymph node system for disposal [22]. Macrophages play a pivotal role in the transition between inflammation response and fibrotic phase stimulated by macrophage secretory product, transforming growth factor β (TGF-β).

Lymphocyte infiltration peaks at 1 week post-MI and gradually decreases, suggesting that the transformation from an acute to chronic inflammation begins within 1 week. Of these three leukocyte cell types, the lymphocyte is the least understood in terms of post-MI responses.

Formation of granulation tissue phase: fibroblasts
Two to 3 days post-MI, the granulation tissue begins to form around the border of the infarct region. This tissue is rich in inflammatory cells, fibroblasts, and blood vessels.[16] During this phase, fibroblasts start ECM deposition, which increases the myocardial tensile strength. Myofibroblasts first appear in the infarct at day 3 and remain at high levels through day 28 post-MI. The major source of fibroblasts is the resident cell [23] and the circulating fibrocyte is a minor source. Previous study has shown that proliferation rate of fibroblasts in C57BL/6J mice was 15.4±1.1% 4 days post-MI, declined to 4.1±0.6% by 1 week, progressively slowed to 0.2±0.6% after 2 weeks, and 0.03±0.1% after 4 weeks [24]. Our lab also demonstrated that fibroblast proliferation rates decrease by day 28 post-MI, indicating that fibroblast densities may reach a saturation point. It has also been shown that myofibroblasts replicated at the border of the infarct zone migratE inward at day 4, more centrally at one week, sporadically at 2 weeks, and ceased by 4 weeks [24, 25]. In addition, our previous studies have shown that fibroblast growth rate, secretion rate, and migration are modulated by TGF-β.

Remodeling phase: myofibroblasts
Approaching 3 weeks post-MI, the cell number in the granulation tissue starts to decrease. This is the first hallmark of the remodeling phase of infarct wound healing. Apoptosis plays an important role in the decreasing cell numbers. However, a unique feature of the cardiac scar, compared with skin scars, is the persistent presence of fibroblasts. Fibroblasts have been visualized in human post-MI scars as late as 17 years after the MI. This implies that fibroblasts in the cardiac scar are crucial mediators of remodeling and may be less prone to apoptosis than in other types of scars.

Angiogenesis: endothelial cells
Angiogenesis is the process of generating new capillary blood vessels, which restores blood supply to the heart. The angiogenesis phase overlaps with the inflammatory and granulation tissue phases, and improves cell survival during these phases. Activation and proliferation of endothelial cells are essential steps in angiogenesis. It has been shown that continuous endothelial cell activation increases angiogenesis [26]. Virag and colleagues have shown that proliferation rates of endothelial cell in C57BL/6J mice are 2.9±0.5% at 4 days post-MI, decline to 0.7±0.1% by 1 week, and remain at low levels of 0.2±0.1% after 2 weeks and 0.4±0.3% after 4 weeks [24]. Endothelial cells, therefore, are important contributors to post-MI remodeling.

3.2 Cytokine and Growth Factor changes post-MI

Multiple cytokines have been measured at the gene and protein levels. IL-1β levels increase within 3 hours, remain high at 6-12 hours, and decrease by 24 hours post-MI in C57/BL6J mice [27]. TNF-α levels are elevated on days 1 and 2, significantly decline by day 7, and gradually decrease to baseline levels by day 28. IL-6 shares a similar temporal profile with TNF-α [28]. IL-10 is elevated on day 1, peaks on day 2 and shows sustained increases at day

7, and declines significantly on day 28. TGF-β1 mRNA expression significantly increases at day 3 and gradually decreases from days 7 to 28, even though their expression levels are still higher than controls [29]. In addition, Schnoor and colleagues have recently demonstrated that macrophages contain mRNAs for a large number of collagens (particularly collagen VI) and fibronectin [30].

3.3 ECM changes

The cardiac extracellular matrix (ECM) provides the environment for cell migration, proliferation, adhesion, and cell-to-cell signaling. Cardiac ECM includes collagens (types I, III, IV, V, and VI); matricellular proteins (tenascins, thrombospondins, and secreted protein acidic and rich in cysteine); proteoglycans (lumican, versican, and biglycan); glycosaminoglycans (hyaluronic acid and dermatan sulfate); and glycoproteins (fibronectin, laminins, periostin, fibromodulin, and vitronectin) [31]. Extracellular proteases include serine proteases and MMPs that are present either bound to the ECM, in various cell types, or in circulating blood. In addition, the development of LV remodeling has been linked to the discontinuity and disruption of the supporting collagen network within in the ECM [32]. Therefore, cardiac ECM is a vital component of LV remodeling.

Collagen III levels are elevated 3 days post-MI in rat. The increase in collagen III is followed by an increase in collagen I production to increase the tensile strength of the infarct tissue [33].

The major source of collagen in the heart is the fibroblast. In addition, post-MI fibroblasts expressing collagen mRNA are always co-localized with lymphocytes and macrophages in rats [34, 35], implicating inflammation as a necessary component of the fibrotic response. Fibroblasts in the post-MI LV are primarily myofibroblasts that have differentiated from resident fibroblasts or from infiltrating fibrocytes. Whether the source (resident or infiltrating) yields myofibroblasts with different characteristics has not been examined.

Multiple MMPs and tissue inhibitors of metalloproteinases (TIMPs) have been shown to be altered post-MI in both human and animal studies. MMPs -1, -2, -3, -7, -8, -9, -12, -13, -14 and TIMPs -1 and -2 levels increase, while TIMP-3 and TIMP-4 levels decrease post-MI [36-38]. Specifically, MMP-9 levels are elevated from days 1-3, decrease after day 3 while still holding high levels at day 7 [39-41]. MMP-3 is one of the key factors related to MMP-9 activation. MMP-3 expression is up-regulated 2 days post-MI, reaches the maximum at 4 days and remains up regulated throughout the 14-day [42].

Developing a Multi-scale Mathematical Model of LV Remodeling

Temporal profiles of cellular function and ECM changes reveal that dynamic interactions during LV remodeling process involve cardiac function, cellular function, protein expression, and gene expression. Accordingly, a full spectrum of the LV remodeling may only be obtained by integrative knowledge on genes, protease, cells, tissue and the whole organ.

A pyramid modeling structure is shown in Figure 1 to illustrate the possible layers of a complete model of the heart. The top layer includes LV changes in structure, function, and geometry, which can be regulated by the 2nd layer components including mechanical, electrical, chemical signals, and surgery/wound exercise. Components in the 2nd layer can be further related with tissue components and cellular functions regulated by biochemical molecules and genes in the 3rd layer. Mathematical modeling focusing on the upper layer of the pyramid are simplified composite models to characterize the system features, while the under lying modular models are complicate, but capable of providing more detailed predictions. However, there is always a tradeoff between model simplicity and adaptability of the mathematical model.

Most of the current models for the heart are structural models or cellular models, due to the richness of related experimental data. Previous studies have reported structural model focusing on mechanical properties [43, 44] and cellular model focusing on electrophysiology [45-49]. Our team has recently developed the first model for scar formation post-MI, which demonstrated the interactions among macrophage, fibroblasts, MMP-9, TGF-β_1 and collagen.

For a cellular model built on properties of proteins, it is possible for the model to reach down to genetic level by reconstructing the effects of particular mutations. Examples using Markov models of cardiac sodium channel have been studied by Rudy and colleagues [50]. In addition, the cellular model can also reach up to a whole organ model including both the electrical and mechanical behaviors of heart [51, 52]. We predict that incorporation of molecular/genetic models, cellular models and structural/functional models will be one of the most exciting prospects of computational biology in the coming years.

4. Modeling Methodology

Various modeling techniques, such as nonlinear dynamics, physical chemistry, and stoichiometric network analysis have been applied to describe the underlying framework of biological systems [53]. Dependent on the attempting problem, different modeling methods can be taken to describe the system.

Ordinary differential equations (ODE) methods have been used to represent continuous, deterministic systems for temporal mechanics. ODE modeling takes a population view of a system rather than modeling the stochastic behavior of individual proteins or molecules. The variables of the ODEs generally represent average concentrations of the components. Partial differential equations (PDEs) are the spatial counterpart of ODE and have been widely used to model spatially restricted reactions in a system, taking into account diffusion processes in the chemical reactions.

ODE and PDE models have strength on elucidating the quantitative spatial and temporal interactions in the system. ODE/PDE models also integrate nonlinearity terms easily, matching with the embedded nonlinearity of the biological system. In addition, control design, stability and sensitivity analysis techniques of ODE based model have been well developed, which make the ODE based model an excellent tool to analyze and predict the effects of interventions beyond the range of available data. Our team and other researchers have analyzed stability of ODE based model [54, 55]. Parameter sensitivity analysis has been presented by Marino and colleagues [56]. Given a system dynamics $F(\theta_i,\ x_j), i=1,2,\cdots n,\ and\ j=1,2,\cdots,m$ with parameters θ_i and variables x_j, Sensitivity of parameter θ_i is defined as $S_{\theta_i}^F = \frac{\partial F}{\partial \theta_i}\frac{\theta_i}{F}$. A negative $S_{\theta_i}^F$ means increasing parameter θ_i will decrease the value of function F at this specific point; a positive means increasing parameter θ_i will increasing the value of function F. The maximum absolute value of the sensitivity function tells us which parameter affects the system dynamics most.

However, ODE methods require exact knowledge of reaction rate and concentrations of the biochemical factors, which is hard to acquire in some biological systems. In case of the non-precise measurement of the parameters, parameter sensitivity analysis is generally desired for system performance and validation of the parameters calls for parameter search in a given space to optimize the fitting between computational predictions and experimental data.

Non-ODE methods have also been widely applied to model biological systems where the actions of individual elements of a system, rather than the population behavior, is of interest [57]. Stochastic methods have been applied to model the individual behavior of molecules and represent variability in the overall behavior of a system [58]. Stochastic method has the advantages on handling imprecise data, where concentrations of molecules are represented by relative levels rather than exact values in ODE methods.

Agent-based modeling method has also been developed based on the rules and mechanisms of behavior of individual component of a system [59]. Agents represent the system components which share the same mechanism identified by experimental results. The mechanisms are expressed as a series of conditional (if-then) statements and computer programs are written to describe the rules of behavior. Agent-based methods provide an easy way to translate basic Scientific data to model. However, it requires extensive computational power to simulate large numbers of agents of a real system. In addition, agent-based model is very difficult to validate and calibrate with experimental data.

There are also other model methods, such as Petri nets, process algebra (PEPA) and SBML-based graphical model, but ODE/PDE model, stochastic model, and agent-based model are the most commonly applied techniques. The strength and weakness of the aforementioned modeling methods are summarized in Table 1.

5. Mathematical Modeling Procedure

A well established mathematical model is easy to understand, reproduce, and test. A modeling standard for reproducibility has been presented by Dr. Bassingwaite [60]. A recommended modeling procedure is summarized as following steps.

1) Identify the functionality of the model. A modeler has to determine the scope of the model and make realistic assumptions to develop the model at this step.

2) Determine the structure and content of the model. A modeler will identify variables of the ODE/stochastic model (concentrations, mass, etc) or agents for the agent-based model, units of the variables, parameters of the model (reaction rate, growth rate), inputs/outputs (ODE model), or nodes/edges (stochastic model).

3) Quantify the mathematical relation based on physical chemistry laws, mass balance, charge balance, energy balance for ODE model, evolutionary probability for stochastic model, and behavior rules for agent-based model. For example, the mass balance equation for a compartmental modeling can be written as

Mass change = Sources - Sinks.

4) Verify the mathematical relation based on unitary balance of equations, variables and parameters.

5) Develop software to compute the mathematical model and compare the numerical solution with available analytical solution.

6) Validate the mathematical model.

5.1 Validation of the Mathematical model

The crucial component of a model is the ability of the model to accurately reflect the real-world process being modeled. Validation of the model, therefore, is a necessary step to evaluate the similarity. Validation of mathematical model focuses on two aspects: 1) assumptions made during the model development, and 2) behavior of the model. Validation of an assumption can be addressed by explicit statement of conditions and rules to implement the model. All models represent some degree of abstraction of the system, assumptions of the model determines the degree of abstraction. Therefore, clarity of the assumptions is the key for model validation.

Behavior of the model can be validated by comparing the behavior of the model with real-world experimental data. When the behavior of the model matches with the experimental data, the model is validated for the particular case. Mismatch of the model behavior and experimental data requires further investigation on either model structure or parameters calibration.

Practically, validation of the mathematical model includes the following aspects. 1) Confirm that defined initial and boundary conditions (generally based on the assumptions) are appropriate to the physiology and physical chemistry data. 2) Compare computational and experimental results to see if the two sets of values are compatible. This comparison is made by determining the fitting error between the computational and experimental results. 3) Optimize and document parameters with respect to the fitting errors. 4) Test predictions of the model with new experiments.

A good model will satisfy a desired fitting of experimental results. If the lack of fitting is caused by structural defects, a more extensive literature search is needed to find the missing regulatory mechanisms. To minimize the fitting error caused by parameter calibration, parameter optimization is needed to minimize the fitting error. The most commonly applied technique is least squared based optimization which minimize the value of $\sum_{i=1}^{N} e_i^2$, where e_i is the fitting error at ith fitting point and N denotes the total fitting points. Thus, a desirable parameter setting of the model will be obtained with respect to a given fitting error.

6. Conclusion

In summary, progressive LV remodeling following MI involves spatiotemporal profiles of cellular, protein, and genetic components. Although this review focuses on the modeling of LV remodeling post-MI, it is worth mentioning that modeling techniques have been widely applied to other gene regulatory networks, metabolic pathways, cells, and organs [49, 61-66]. However, integration of multi-scale mathematical models into the whole organ model still needs intensive investigation. It is anticipated that integrated computational and experimental approaches will greatly facilitate researchers in their everyday experimental work and shed insight on regulatory mechanisms of LV remodeling as well as other disease processes.

7. Acknowledgements

We acknowledge funding to MLL from NIH (R01 HL075360), the American Heart Association (GIA 0855119F), and the Morrison Trust, and funding to YJ from NSF (EEC-0649172), NIH (1SC2HL101430), and AT&T foundation.

8. References

[1] Cohn JN, Ferrari R, Sharpe N. Cardiac Remodeling- Concepts and Clinical Implications: A Consensus Paper From an International Forum on Cardiac Remodeling. J Am Coll Cardiol. 2000; 35(3): 569-82.

[2] Pfeffer MA, Braunwald E. Ventricular Remodeling After Myocardial Infarction. Experimental observations and clinical implications. Circulation. 1990; 81: 1161-72.

[3] Cohn JN, Ferrari R, Sharpe N. Cardiac remodeling--concepts and clinical implications: a consensus paper from an international forum on cardiac remodeling. Journal of the American College of Cardiology. 2000; 35(3): 569-82.

[4] Lindsey ML. MMP induction and inhibition in myocardial infarction. Heart Fail Rev. 2004 Jan; 9(1): 7-19.

[5] Sutton MSJ, Pfeffer MA, Moye L, Plappert T, Rouleau JL, Lamas G, et al. Cardiovascular Death and Left Ventricular Remodeling Two Years After Myocardial Infarction : Baseline Predictors and Impact of Long-term Use of Captopril: Information From the Survival and Ventricular Enlargement (SAVE) Trial. Circulation. 1997 November 18, 1997; 96(10): 3294-9.

[6] Horwich TB, Patel J, MacLellan WR, Fonarow GC. Cardiac troponin I is associated with impaired hemodynamics, progressive left ventricular dysfunction, and increased mortality rates in advanced heart failure. Circulation. 2003 Aug 19; 108(7): 833-8.

[7] Callard R, George AJ, Stark J. Cytokines, chaos, and complexity. Immunity. 1999; 11(5): 507-13.

[8] Godin PJ, Buchman TG. Uncoupling of biological oscillators: A complementary hypothesis concerning the pathogenesis of multiple organ dysfunction syndrome. Critical Care Medicine. 1996; 24(7): 1107-16.

[9] Seely AJE, Christou NV. Multiple organ dysfunction syndrome: Exploring the paradigm of complex nonlinear systems. Critical Care Medicine. 2000; 28(7): 2193-200.

[10] Kitano H. Systems Biology: A Brief Overview. Science. 2002 March 1, 2002; 295(5560): 1662-4.

[11] Noble D. Modeling the Heart--from Genes to Cells to the Whole Organ. Science. 2002 March 1, 2002; 295(5560): 1678-82.

[12] Csete ME, Doyle JC. Reverse Engineering of Biological Complexity. Science. 2002 March 1, 2002; 295(5560): 1664-9.

[13] Davidson EH, Rast JP, Oliveri P, Ransick A, Calestani C, Yuh C-H, et al. A Genomic Regulatory Network for Development. Science. 2002 March 1, 2002; 295(5560): 1669-78.

[14] Hunter PJ, Pullan AJ, Smaill BH. Modleign Total Heart Function. Annual Review of Biomedical Engineering. 2003; 5(1): 147-77.

[15] Bonvini RF, Hendiri T, Camenzind E. Inflammatory response post-myocardial infarction and reperfusion: a new therapeutic target? Eur Heart J Suppl. 2005 October 1, 2005; 7(suppl_I): I27-36.

[16] W. M. Blankesteijn, E. Creemers, E. Lutgens, J. P. M. Cleutjens, M. J. A. P. Daemen, J. F. M. Smits. Dynamics of cardiac wound healing following myocardial infarction: observations in genetically altered mice. Acta Physiologica Scandinavica. 2001; 173(1): 75-82.

[17] Banerjee I, Fuseler JW, Price RL, Borg TK, Baudino TA. Determination of cell types and numbers during cardiac development in the neonatal and adult rat and mouse. Am J Physiol Heart Circ Physiol. 2007 Sep; 293(3): H1883-91.

[18] Haunstetter A, Izumo S. Apoptosis : Basic Mechanisms and Implications for Cardiovascular Disease. Circ Res. 1998 June 15, 1998; 82(11): 1111-29.

[19] Yang F, Liu YH, Yang XP, Xu J, Kapke A, Carretero OA. Myocardial infarction and cardiac remodelling in mice. Exp Physiol. 2002 September 1, 2002; 87(5): 547-55.

[20] Burke B LC. The Macrophage. 2nd ed. Oxford: Oxford University Press; 2002.

[21] Krause SW, Rehli M, Kreutz M, Schwarzfischer L, Paulauskis JD, Andreesen R. Differential screening identifies genetic markers of monocyte to macrophage maturation. J Leuko Biol. 1996; 60: 510-45.

[22] Bellingan GJ, Caldwell H, Howie SE, Dransfield I, Haslett C. In vivo fate of the inflammatory macrophage during the resolution of inflammation: inflammatory macrophages do not die locally, but emigrate to the draining lymph nodes. J Immunol. 1996 September 15, 1996; 157(6): 2577-85.

[23] Quan TE, Cowper S, Wu S-P, Bockenstedt LK, Bucala R. Circulating fibrocytes: collagen-secreting cells of the peripheral blood. The International Journal of Biochemistry & Cell Biology. 2004; 36(4): 598-606.

[24] Virag JI, Murry CE. Myofibroblast and Endothelial Cell Proliferation during Murine Myocardial Infarct Repair. Am J Pathol. 2003 December 1, 2003; 163(6): 2433-40.

[25] Gabbiani G. Evolution and clinical implications of the myofibroblast concept. Cardiovasc Res. 1998 June 1, 1998; 38(3): 545-8.

[26] Rajashekhar G, Willuweit A, Patterson CE, Sun P, Hilbig A, Breier G, et al. Continuous Endothelial Cell Activation Increases Angiogenesis: Evidence for the Direct Role of Endothelium Linking Angiogenesis and Inflammation. J Vasc Res. 2006; 43(2): 193-204.

[27] Hwang M-W, Matsumori A, Furukawa Y, Ono K, Okada M, Iwasaki A, et al. Neutralization of interleukin-1[beta] in the acute phase of myocardial infarction promotes the progression of left ventricular remodeling. Journal of the American College of Cardiology. 2001; 38(5): 1546-53.

[28] Vandervelde S, van Luyn MJA, Rozenbaum MH, Petersen AH, Tio RA, Harmsen MC. Stem cell-related cardiac gene expression early after murine myocardial infarction. Cardiovasc Res. 2007 March 1, 2007; 73(4): 783-93.

[29] Sun Y, Zhang JQ, Zhang J, Lamparter S. Cardiac remodeling by fibrous tissue after infarction in rats. Journal of Laboratory and Clinical Medicine. 2000; 135(4): 316-23.

[30] Schnoor M, Cullen P, Lorkowski J, Stolle K, Robenek H, Troyer D, et al. Production of Type VI Collagen by Human Macrophages: A New Dimension in Macrophage Functional Heterogeneity. J Immunol. 2008 April 15, 2008; 180(8): 5707-19.

[31] Banerjee I, Yekkala K, Borg TK, Baudino TA. Dynamic interactions between myocytes, fibroblasts, and extracellular matrix. Annals of the New York Academy of Sciences. 2006 Oct; 1080: 76-84.

[32] Greenberg B. Cardiac Remodeling: Mechanism and Treatment. New York: Taylor and Francis; 2006.
[33] Cleutjens J, Verluyten M, Smiths J, Daemen M. Collagen remodeling after myocardial infarction in the rat heart. Am J Pathol. 1995 August 1, 1995; 147(2): 325-38.
[34] Hinglais N, Huedes D, Nicoletti A, Mandet C, Maryvonne L, J B, et al. Colocalization of myocardial fibrosis and inflammatory cells in rats. Laboratory Investigation. 1994; 70(2): 286-94.
[35] Lacey D, Sampey A, Mitchell R, Bucala R, Santos L, Leech M, et al. Control of fibroblast-like synoviocyte proliferation by macrophage migration inhibitory factor. Arthritis Rheum. 2003 Jan; 48(1): 103-9.
[36] Lindsey ML, Escobar GP, Mukherjee R, Goshorn DK, Sheats NJ, Bruce JA, et al. Matrix Metalloproteinase-7 Affects Connexin-43 Levels, Electrical Conduction, and Survival After Myocardial Infarction. Circulation. 2006 June 27, 2006; 113(25): 2919-28.
[37] Peterson JT, Li H, Dillon L, Bryant JW. Evolution of matrix metalloprotease and tissue inhibitor expression during heart failure progression in the infarcted rat. Cardiovascular Research. 2000; 46: 307-15.
[38] Krishnamurthy P, Peterson J, Subramanian V, Singh M, Singh K. Inhibition of matrix metalloproteinases improves left ventricular function in mice lacking osteopontin after myocardial infarction. Molecular and Cellular Biochemistry. 2009; 322(1): 53-62.
[39] Webb CS, Bonnema DD, Ahmed SH, Leonardi AH, McClure CD, Clark LL, et al. Specific Temporal Profile of Matrix Metalloproteinase Release Occurs in Patients After Myocardial Infarction: Relation to Left Ventricular Remodeling. Circulation. 2006 September 5, 2006; 114(10): 1020-7.
[40] Vanhoutte D, Schellings M, Pinto Y, Heymans S. Relevance of matrix metalloproteinases and their inhibitors after myocardial infarction: A temporal and spatial window. Cardiovasc Res. 2006 February 15, 2006; 69(3): 604-13.
[41] Sun M, Dawood F, Wen W-H, Chen M, Dixon I, Kirshenbaum LA, et al. Excessive Tumor Necrosis Factor Activation After Infarction Contributes to Susceptibility of Myocardial Rupture and Left Ventricular Dysfunction. Circulation. 2004 November 16, 2004; 110(20): 3221-8.
[42] Mukherjee R, Bruce JA, McClister JDM, Allen CM, Sweterlitsch SE, Saul JP. Time-dependent changes in myocardial structure following discrete injury in mice deficient of matrix metalloproteinase-3. Journal of Molecular and Cellular Cardiology. 2005; 39(2): 259-68.
[43] McCulloch A, Bassingthwaighte J, Hunter P, Noble D. Computational biology of the heart: from structure to function. Prog Biophys Mol Biol. 1998; 69(2-3): 153-5.
[44] McCulloch AD, Hunter PJ, Smaill BH. Mechanical effects of coronary perfusion in the passive canine left ventricle. Am J Physiol. 1992 Feb; 262(2 Pt 2): H523-30.
[45] Antzelevitch C, Nesterenko VV, Muzikant AL, Rice JJ, Chen G, Colatsky T. Influence of transmural repolarization gradients on the electrophysiology and pharmacology of ventricular myocardium. Cellular basis for the Brugada and longâ€"QT syndromes. Philosophical Transactions of the Royal Society of London Series A: Mathematical, Physical and Engineering Sciences. 2001 June 15, 2001; 359(1783): 1201-16.

[46] Boyett MR, Zhang H, Garny A, Holden AV. Control of the pacemaker activity of the sinoatrial node by intracellular Ca2+. Experiments and modelling. Philosophical Transactions of the Royal Society of London Series A: Mathematical, Physical and Engineering Sciences. 2001 June 15, 2001; 359(1783): 1091-110.

[47] Nygren A, Leon LJ, Giles WR. Simulations of the human atrial action potential. Philosophical Transactions of the Royal Society of London Series A: Mathematical, Physical and Engineering Sciences. 2001 June 15, 2001; 359(1783): 1111-25.

[48] Peirce SM, Van Gieson EJ, Skalak TC. Multicellular simulation predicts microvascular patterning and in silico tissue assembly. Faseb J. 2004 Apr; 18(6): 731-3.

[49] Luo CH, Rudy Y. A dynamic model of the cardiac ventricular action potential. I. Simulations of ionic currents and concentration changes. Circ Res. 1994 Jun; 74(6): 1071-96.

[50] Clancy CE, Rudy Y. Linking a genetic defect to its cellular phenotype in a cardiac arrhythmia. Nature. 1999; 400(6744): 566-9.

[51] Winslow RL, Scollan DF, Holmes A, Yung CK, Zhang J, Jafri MS. Electrophysiological modeling of cardiac ventricular function: from cell to organ. Annu Rev Biomed Eng. 2000; 2: 119-55.

[52] Nickerson DP, Smith NP, Hunter PJ. A model of cardiac cellular electromechanics. Philosophical Transactions of the Royal Society of London Series A: Mathematical, Physical and Engineering Sciences. 2001 June 15, 2001; 359(1783): 1159-72.

[53] van Riel NAW. Dynamic modelling and analysis of biochemical networks: mechanism-based models and model-based experiments. Brief Bioinform. 2006 December 1, 2006; 7(4): 364-74.

[54] Jin Y, Lindsey M. Stability analysis of genetic regulatory network with additive noises. BMC Genomics. 2008; 9 Suppl 1: S21.

[55] Waugh H, Sherratt J. Macrophage Dynamics in Diabetic Wound Dealing. Bulletin of Mathematical Biology. 2006; 68(1): 197-207.

[56] Marino S, Hogue IB, Ray CJ, Kirschner DE. A methodology for performing global uncertainty and sensitivity analysis in systems biology. Journal of Theoretical Biology. 2008; 254(1): 178-96.

[57] Cassman MC, Arkin A, Doyle F, Katagiri F, Lauffenburger D, Stokes C. International Research and Development in Systems Biology; 2005.

[58] Phillips A, Cardelli L. A Graphical Representation for the Stochastic Pi-calculus. Concurrent models in molecular biology; 2005; 2005.

[59] Mi Q, Riviere B, Clermont G, Steed D, Vodovotz Y. Agent-based model of inflammation and wound healing: insights into diabetic foot ulcer pathology and the role of transforming growth factor-β1. Wound Repair and Regeneration. 2007(15): 671-82.

[60] Bassingwaite J. Standards for modeling, unit balancing, modular code, green salads, oatmeal, fiver, exercise, and robustness in complex multiscale systems 2008 [cited; Available from: www.physiome.org

[61] Lin J, Lopez EF, Jin Y, Van Remmen H, Bauch T, Han HC, et al. Age-related cardiac muscle sarcopenia: Combining experimental and mathematical modeling to identify mechanisms. Exp Gerontol. 2008 Apr; 43(4): 296-306.

[62] Vempati P, Karagiannis ED, Popel AS. A Biochemical Model of Matrix Metalloproteinase 9 Activation and Inhibition. J Biol Chem. 2007 December 28, 2007; 282(52): 37585-96.

[63] Han HC. A biomechanical model of artery buckling. Journal of biomechanics. 2007; 40(16): 3672-8.
[64] Dallon JC, Sherratt JA. A mathematical model for fibroblast and collagen orientation. Bull Math Biol. 1998 Jan; 60(1): 101-29.
[65] Stelling J, Gilles ED. Mathematical modeling of complex regulatory networks. IEEE Trans Nanobioscience. 2004 Sep; 3(3): 172-9.
[66] Vodovotz Y, Clermont G, Chow C, An G. Mathematical models of the acute inflammatory response. Current Opinion in Immunology. 2004(10): 383-90.

Figure Legends

Figure 1. Pyramid structure of LV remodeling post-MI. Progressive LV remodeling includes tissue components, cell functions, protein interactions and gene regulation. A multi-scale mathematical model should weave the components into a model for the whole system.

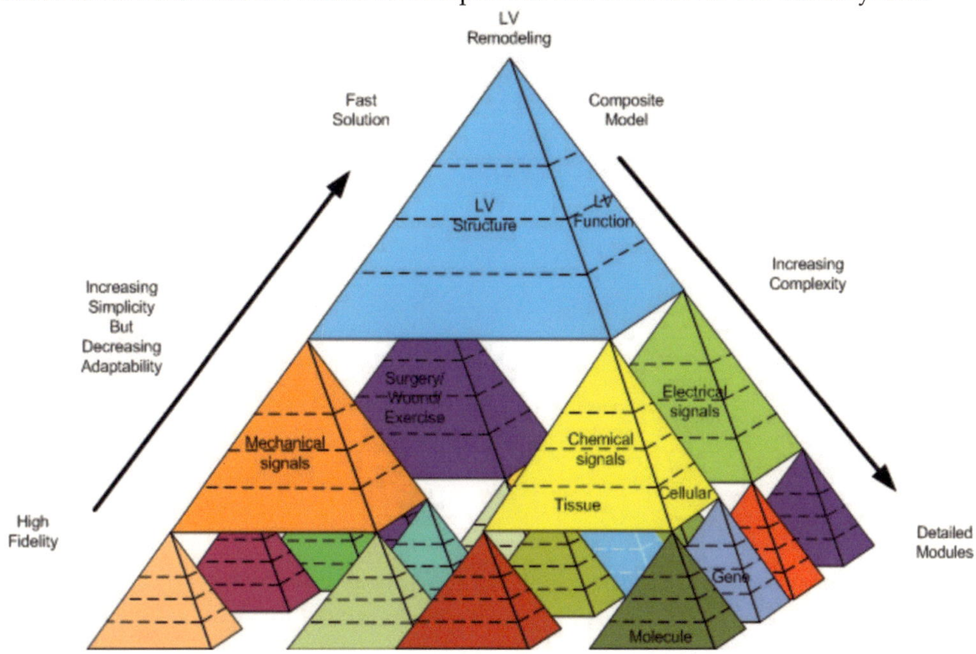

Table Legends

Modeling Technique	Strengths	Weaknesses
Ordinary/partial differential equation model	Continuous and deterministic model for exact values with biophysical meaning Characterizes temporal and spatial interactions Well developed stability analysis techniques Provides good prediction on unmeasured data	Requires exact knowledge of the system and precise measurement of the parameters
Stochastic model	Probability based model Robust to imprecise parameters	Provides relative levels instead of exact values
Agent-based model	Easy to translate from experimental knowledge to system behavior	High requirement on computational power Hard to validate the model and calibrate parameters

Table 1. Summary of the strengths and weaknesses of different mathematical methods.